THE POETICAL WORKS

OF

ROBERT BROWNING

General Editor: IAN JACK

THE POETICAL WORKS
OF
ROBERT
BROWNING

Volume I

PAULINE
PARACELSUS

EDITED BY
IAN JACK
AND
MARGARET SMITH

CLARENDON PRESS · OXFORD
1983

Oxford University Press, Walton Street, Oxford OX2 6DP
London Glasgow New York Toronto
Delhi Bombay Calcutta Madras Karachi
Kuala Lumpur Singapore Hong Kong Tokyo
Nairobi Dar es Salaam Cape Town
Melbourne Auckland
and associates in
Beirut Berlin Ibadan Mexico City Nicosia

Oxford is a trade mark of Oxford University Press

Published in the United States by
Oxford University Press, New York

© Ian Jack and Margaret Smith 1983

British Library Cataloguing in Publication Data
Browning, Robert
The poetical works of Robert Browning.—
(Oxford English texts)
Vol. 1
I. Title   II. Jack, Ian
III. Smith, Margaret
821'.8   PR4201
ISBN 0–19–811893–7

Library of Congress Cataloging in Publication Data
Browning, Robert, 1812–1889.
The poetical works of Robert Browning.
(Oxford English texts)
Includes bibliographical references.
Contents: v. 1. Pauline; Paracelsus—v. 2. Strafford; Sordello.
I. Jack, Ian Robert James.   II. Smith, Margaret, Middleton.   III. Title
PR4203.J3 1982   821'.8   82–12603
ISBN 0–19–811893–7 (v. 1)

Typeset by Phoenix Photosetting, Chatham
and printed in Great Britain by
Thomson Litho Ltd, East Kilbride, Scotland

PREFACE AND ACKNOWLEDGEMENTS

THIS edition has been planned by Ian Jack, who is responsible for the principal part of the Introductions, the explanatory notes, and most of the Appendices. Margaret Smith is responsible for the text, the textual part of the Introductions, and Appendices B and D.

First we wish to thank the authorities of a number of libraries whose assistance has been indispensable. The librarian of the Forster Collection in the Victoria and Albert Museum has permitted us to print the holograph manuscript of *Paracelsus*, and to quote the notes in the 'Mill' copy of *Pauline*. We are grateful to the authorities of the Lowell Collection in the Houghton Library at Harvard for information about their copy of *Pauline*. We are indebted to the librarians of the Beinecke Library at Yale and the Turnbull Library in Wellington for microfilms of their annotated copies of *Paracelsus*. We have also been granted access to the annotated copy of that poem in the Sterling Library, while Dr Lola L. Szladits of the Berg Collection in New York Public Library has been most helpful. We are very much indebted to the authorities of Boston Public Library, and in particular to Mr James Lawton, for photographs of their proof copy of *Sordello*. Mr Mark F. Weimer and others at Syracuse University Library, New York, have gone out of their way to assist us. We have used the annotated copy of *Sordello* in the British Library, as well as their copy of *The Poetical Works* of 1888–9 annotated by Browning (the 'Dykes Campbell' copy). We have been greatly helped by the staff of Cambridge University Library, by Mr Vincent Quinn, Librarian of Balliol College, and by Mr Anthony Burton of the Victoria and Albert Museum Library. Professor Jack Herring of the Armstrong Library at Baylor has helped us with microfilms. Many other librarians have been kind enough to answer our enquiries.

Professor Richard L. Purdy, the authority on Thomas

Hardy, has permitted us to consult and quote from the unpublished Browning letters in his possession.

No one has helped us more than Mr Philip Kelley, whose knowledge of the whereabouts of Browning manuscripts is unrivalled. During the later stages of our work his *Checklist* of the Brownings' correspondence has proved a valuable tool. Mr Kevin Van Anglen and Professor Robert L. Blackmore have gone to great trouble to transcribe and check for us material in American libraries which we were unable to visit. Professor John Grube drew our attention to an important document relating to *Sordello* (Appendix D, Volume II).

Dr Daniel Waley has been astonishingly patient with a series of minute questions about the period of Italian history which he knows in such detail. Dr John Gilmour has been our learned consultant on botanical matters, while the leading authority on Paracelsus, Dr Walter Pagel, has most kindly answered a number of questions. In matters relating to the troubadours we have been fortunate in having Dr Leslie Topsfield to advise us, while Professor Walter Ullmann has also been generous with his knowledge.

Colleagues of the senior editor at Pembroke College, Cambridge, have answered questions on German literature, astronomy, mineralogy, lizards, and other matters. His particular thanks are due to Dr Malcolm Lyons for assistance with Greek, and Dr Richard McCabe for help with Latin. Other Cambridge scholars who have come to our assistance have been Professor Uberto Limentani, Dr John Beer, and the late Professor Geoffrey Lampe. Mr Edward G. Tasker was good enough to check the text of the 'Lines to the Memory of James Dow' inscribed on the tombstone in Barnsley.

Not our least debt is to Dr Leofranc Holford-Strevens, whose scrupulous learning has provided reassurance and support.

I.J.
M.S.

7 May 1980

CONTENTS

GENERAL INTRODUCTION

BROWNING has been so indifferently served by his editors that until now the best course for a serious reader has been to use the sixteen-volume *Poetical Works* of 1888—9, together with the further volume published in 1894, the *New Poems* of 1914, and DeVane's invaluable *Handbook* as revised in 1955. The present edition has been inspired by the conviction that a writer of such stature deserves the careful study habitually devoted to a major poet. It is our aim to provide a more accurate text than has hitherto been available (with full details of revisions), supplemented by all available information about the genesis and composition of each poem and by explanatory notes elucidating difficult passages and pointing out probable or possible echoes of earlier writers.

When I first approached the Delegates of the Clarendon Press, more than a quarter of a century ago, I received immediate encouragement. One of the principal reasons for the long delay has been the announcement and then the gradual appearance of the Ohio edition, of which four volumes have been published between 1969 and the time of writing. If it had proved a success I should have turned to other undertakings with a mixture of regret and relief, but in fact it has been, by common consent, the least satisfactory of all ambitious editions of our poets. It would be invidious to comment on its shortcomings here and is the less necessary because they have been pointed out by a number of reviewers, most notably by the late John Pettigrew, a Canadian scholar who died in 1977 at the age of 47.[1] I had written to Professor Pettigrew before I heard of his death, to seek his help and if possible his collabora-

---

[1] See, in particular, 'Back to his Book then' (*Essays in Criticism*, October 1972, pp. 436–41), 'The Ohio *Browning*' (ibid, October 1975, pp. 480–3), and 'For "Flute" read "Lute"; or, Notes on the "Notes" on *Sordello* in the Ohio Edition' (*The Library*, June 1978, pp. 162–9). One may also consult T. J. Collins in *Victorian Studies* for June 1970 and in the *Browning Newsletter* for Spring 1970, and Morse Peckham's 'Lessons to be learned from the Ohio Browning Edition' in *Studies in Browning and his Circle*, Fall 1973, in which a former member of the editorial board of the Ohio edition reported 'hundreds and hundreds of errors' in the 'text, emendations, variants, and explanatory notes' of the first two volumes.

tion. Before he died he had all but completed a Penguin edition of Browning which should be published shortly before the present volume.

It will be evident that an editor of Browning is in a situation very different from that of the editors of most of our principal poets. While he may consult useful editions of a number of the individual poems he cannot enjoy the reassuring sense that he is following a series of illustrious predecessors who have provided a sure foundation on which he may build. The story of the publication of one of the least important of Browning's poems may serve as an extreme instance of the muddle and inaccuracy which have too often characterized the study of his life and work. The lines printed on p. 540 below were first published in a periodical in 1914 as a 'Sonnet . . . addressed to the memory of his parents'. Later the same year Kenyon reprinted them in *New Poems*: he dropped the inappropriate word 'Sonnet', showed a modicum of caution by describing the lines as 'apparently' addressed to Browning's parents, but added the conjecture that 'They were probably written in 1866', the year in which the poet's father had died. There the matter rested until 1948, when a writer in *Notes and Queries* reported that 'this poem with six additional lines first appeared in 1832 on a gravestone in the additional burial ground belonging to St. Mary's Church, Barnsley, Yorkshire', and showed that the inscription on the tomb made it clear that they had nothing to do with Browning's parents but had been written in memory of Dr James Dow and members of his family—a fact which might have occurred to anyone reading the amusing account of W. A. Dow's importunity in Macready's *Diaries*, published in 1912 and of acknowledged importance in relation to *Strafford*. DeVane recorded this discovery in the revised edition of his *Handbook*, accepting the date 1832, failing to mention the obvious error 'Sanctuary-papers' for 'Sanctuary-tapers' in l.11, and giving 'E. J. Bradford' instead of E. G. Bayford as the name of the contributor to *Notes and Queries*.[1] It was left to Professor John Maynard to point out that the lines must have been written not in 1832 but in 1836 or

---

[1] Excellent as it is, DeVane's book contains numerous errors, not least in relation to *Sordello*. We have pointed these out, in the interests of accuracy, although mistakes in less reliable works have usually been passed over in silence.

1837. The 'Sonnet . . . addressed to the memory of [Browning's] parents', 'probably written in 1866', thus turns out to be a lapidary inscription of twenty lines of blank verse which Browning was induced to write in commemoration of four people whom he had never known. The whole thing is reminiscent of the party game in which a story or rumour is passed from one guest to another, to emerge at the end in a garbled and often unrecognizable form.

In one respect, however, an editor of Browning is in a fortunate situation. The poet was frequently asked questions about his work, and he was usually remarkably patient and good-humoured in his replies. Long before the foundation of the Browning Society he had more than once admitted that no one had ever 'brought the good news from Ghent to Aix', and in his later years he was constantly being interrogated about his poems. 'Browning kept clear of our Society', Furnivall was later to write,

and we kept it clear of him. But when we couldn't understand a passage or a poem, I either walkt over or wrote to him, and got his explanation of it. At first I didn't take the volume with me, and he amused me very much by saying: "'Pon my word I don't know what I *did* mean by the poem. I gave away my last copy six years ago, and haven't seen a line of it since. But I'll borrow a copy to-morrow and look at it again. If I don't write before Sunday, come to lunch and I'll tell you all about it".[1]

As we know from a letter to George Smith, Browning even thought of providing notes of his own for his final collected edition. On 12 November 1887 he wrote: 'I have changed my mind about the *notes* I thought of adding to the poems . . . I am so out of sympathy with all this "biographical matter" connected with works which ought to stand or fall by their own merits quite independently of the writer's life and habits, that I prefer leaving my poems to speak for themselves as they best can—and to end as I began long ago'.[2]

---

[1] 'Recollections of Robert Browning' in the *Pall Mall Gazette*, 14 December 1889, reprinted in *Browning's Trumpeter*, p. 195.
[2] Quoted in 'Browning's Final Revisions', by Philip Kelley and William S. Peterson: *Browning Institute Studies* (The Browning Institute, New York), vol. i (1973), p. 91. In fact it might be said that he 'began long ago' by providing notes in *Paracelsus*. Being human, Browning was inconsistent in this matter. In general he was unwilling to publish notes of his own, but helpful to readers who wrote for his assistance.

While such a decision is entirely understandable, particularly when it is taken by a man of seventy-five, we notice that it was 'biographical matter' to which Browning particularly objected, and one has only to read his letters to Furnivall and others to find that they contain (in effect) a rich collection of notes for the guidance of his readers: it is one of our aims to append each of these to the appropriate poem or passage. A reader who does not insist on working with a plain text is surely entitled to have Browning's own comment on Sordello's 'mood of mind' in Book I (lines 523 ff.) and his explanation of the name 'Elys' in the same letter.[1] There is little to be said for an annotated edition which does not quote his explanation that the 'sad dishevelled ghost' that approaches the poet in Venice is a figure 'wherein I put, comprize, typify and figure to myself Mankind, the whole poor-devildom one sees cuffed and huffed from morn to midnight, that, so typified, she may come at times and keep my pact in mind, prick up my republicanism and remind me of certain engagements I have entered into with myself about that same', and his statement that the appearance of this poor woman 'renewed me, gave me fresh spirit, and made me after finishing Book 3d commence Book 4th'.[2]

Information from Browning himself is also to be found in other places, usually in scraps but sometimes in richer deposits. In 1884, for example, Emily Hickey thanked him warmly 'for his explanation of three or four passages' in *Strafford*, which she had edited for the use of her pupils, adding that she was 'specially indebted to him for most of the note on v. 2, 40'.[3] Of the greatest general value, however, is the *Handbook* by Mrs Sutherland Orr first published in 1885 and subsequently revised, which Browning himself described as 'the best of helps to anyone in need of such when reading—or about to read—my works'.[4] While he must not be held responsible for each individual statement in this book he admitted to Furnivall that he had 'answered every now [and] then a question', and we know that he not only read the first and second editions in proof (so that gross errors, at least, are

[1] *Letters*, p. 92 (to Edward Dowden).
[2] *New Letters*, p. 18 (to Fanny Haworth), referring to Book III, l. 696.
[3] P. vii.
[4] Griffin and Minchin, p. 271 n. 1.

likely to have been eliminated) but also occasionally provided Mrs Orr with a prose summary of a poem or passage.[1] It follows that this work, by 'simply the dearest woman friend I can boast of in the world',[2] remains of exceptional importance.

Such assistance is particularly welcome with *Sordello*, which Mrs Orr described—in words which are still true almost a century later—as 'the one of Mr. Browning's works which still remains to be read'.[3] The extreme difficulty of this poem is one of the reasons for the absence of a satisfactory edition of Browning's work as a whole: an erudite admirer of his once suggested to me that it might be feasible to begin an edition of the Poetical Works 'after' *Sordello*, while the editor of an American edition which includes the whole of *The Ring and the Book* simply omits *Sordello* on the ground that it 'is considered by competent students of Browning's poetry "wholly unintelligible"'.[4] The bewilderment began with the printer or subeditor of the first edition, who wrote 'qy. connexion from p. *208*' at the top of p. 209, before line 877 of Book V, prompting an emphatic reply from Browning, in large handwriting heavily underlined, '*All right*'. The reviewer in the *Athenæum*, who seems to have worked hard on the poem, quoted a passage from Book III and commented: 'If the above specimen be within the compass of the reader's faculties, then he may refer to the volume, which abounds in such'.[5] It follows that the task of an annotator of *Sordello* is a formidable one. Robert Bridges described 'The Wreck of the Deutschland' as 'a great dragon folded in the gate to forbid all entrance', to the poetry of Gerard Manley Hopkins,[6] but *Sordello* is a monster which has proved much more formidable. In spite of the labours of David Duff, Arthur J. Whyte and others this remarkable poem, which is as important to those concerned with the early Victorian mind as to admirers of the poetry of Browning, 'still remains to be read'. Many of our friends, some of them specialists in Victorian literature, have confessed that they can

---

[1] *Trumpeter*, p. 124 n. 5.
[2] Ibid., p. 123.
[3] *Handbook* (1st edn.), p. 33.
[4] *Poems and Plays of Robert Browning*, edited by Saxe Commins (The Modern Library, New York 1934), p. xvii.
[5] No. 657 (30 May 1840), p. 432a, quoting ll. 799–861.
[6] *Poems of Gerard Manley Hopkins*, edited by Robert Bridges (1918), p. 106: previously quoted in this connection in *Browning's Major Poetry*, by Ian Jack (1973), p. 22.

make nothing of it. The author of one recent study of Browning apparently believes that it is written in blank verse.

A feature of this edition is the inclusion in the explanatory notes of comments by three early readers of the poems. It is because of the survival of the copy of *Pauline* with 'John Mill, the metaphysical head, *his* marginal note[s]'[1] and Browning's occasional rejoinders that we know for certain that the poem contains allusions to Æschylus and Sophocles and to the actor Edmund Kean. Whereas that copy has been known to many writers on Browning, so far as I am aware the copy of *Paracelsus* annotated by Alfred Domett and now in New Zealand has not been used before. I quote a number of his remarks, notably his references to Coleridge's *Aids to Reflection* and to Carlyle's essay on Novalis. There are also three particularly important copies of *Sordello*. The first is a proof which contains not only corrections and other markings made for and by the printer, but also marginal comments of considerable value in a hand as yet unidentified. The second contains notes by Domett and a few replies by Browning. Domett asterisks ll. 533–4 of Book I, for example, and comments: 'an eloquent but not overclear amplification of Byron's lines' (*Don Juan*, I. ccxiv. 7–8); while opposite the description of Palma at ll. 948 ff. of the same Book he poses a tantalizing question: 'is not this the attitude of the girl in a picture in the Louvre?' Opposite v. 576 ff. he remarks, even more interestingly: 'As you take from thought the need of expressing itself by (its own) *deeds*—i.e. *corporeal actions*. so take from mind the need of expressing itself by thoughts—i.e. *mental actions*—& you have God's naked wil[l]—So doing—the Germans get their pure Reason'. When Browning saw this copy, with its comments laudatory, plaintive, and perplexed, he scribbled in replies to one or two of the queries: opposite 'Him' in v. 977, for example, Domett had written 'Salinguerra (?)' in the margin, and Browning corrects him: '(no—Young Ecelin)'. In reply to a question about another passage Browning provides a prose summary: the fact that he did not disdain to do this, here and on other occasions, is a great encouragement to a modern editor.[2]

These annotations by readers close to Browning, with his occasional replies, are of value because they remind us of the

[1] Kintner, i. 28.   [2] For the third annotated copy, see Vol. II, Appendix B.

severity of the challenge which *Sordello* presented to even the best-qualified of his contemporaries. They take us some way (at least) towards reading the poem as he intended it to be read. But they have a further interest. As Domett commented in his *Diary*, Browning 'would always listen to friendly criticism of his work', and on occasion we can see him revising what he had written in response to such comments. It was in Domett's copy that he began writing the elucidatory headnotes which accompanied the first reprinting of the poem (in the *Poetical Works* of 1863) and which remained until the format of the 1888–9 edition led to their being jettisoned. It is remarkable that these invaluable notes, which serve as stepping-stones across turbulent water, were not reprinted again until 1970—a circumstance which has no doubt contributed to the continuing neglect of the poem.

While elucidation is the principal aim of the explanatory notes in this edition, another is to point out passages in earlier writers which Browning is or may be echoing. It is appropriate that the earliest piece in this volume, 'The First-Born of Egypt' (Appendix F), should have its source in Exodus, since the Bible is the greatest influence of all, throughout his writings. Echoes of Coleridge and Shelley are also to be found in this early poem. The great influence of Shelley on *Pauline*, so often pointed out by earlier scholars, is abundantly illustrated in the notes to that poem, which also includes references to Æschylus, Pindar, Shakespeare, Milton, Wordsworth, Byron, Keats, and Carlyle. In *Paracelsus* and *Sordello* the range of reference expands to include a great many other writers, notably 'revered and magisterial Donne'[1] and Francis Quarles, whose *Emblems* Browning later described as his 'childhood's pet book'.[2] It is hoped that such annotation, supplemented by that provided in our later volumes, will provide correlatives which will help to make it possible to plot more exactly the place of Browning in the tradition of English poetry, in which he is still too often regarded as a sort of 'sport'.

As Johnson pointed out, 'It is impossible for an expositor not to write too little for some, and too much for others'. Whatever he does he is bound to 'explain many lines which the

---

[1] *The Two Poets of Croisic*, line 912.   [2] Griffin and Minchin, p. 31.

learned will think impossible to be mistaken, and omit many for which the ignorant will want his help'.[1] I have decided that it is better that a captious reviewer should express astonishment at my supposing readers in need of some scrap of information which he himself happens to possess than that those seriously interested in Browning should be sent empty away. The notes rest silently at the foot of the page, plucking no one by the sleeve. Those who know some or all of the languages quoted will not (as I hope) be offended that I have provided translations for those who are less fortunate than themselves.

Throughout my co-editor and I have been supported by a fine remark of Browning's own, in a letter known only from an extract in a bookseller's catalogue: 'Purely disinterested scholarship [has] always seemed to me to have far more important bearings, moral and intellectual, than are commonly recognized'.[2]

I.J.

---

[1] *Preface to Shakespeare.*
[2] *The Brownings' Correspondence: A Checklist*, by Philip Kelley and Ronald Hudson: 67: 33.

TEXTUAL INTRODUCTION

DURING Browning's lifetime his poems and plays were published, some of them in many different editions, over a span of 56 years. The textual editor has the challenging task of presenting the gradual evolution of the poet's art in a way that will enable the reader to perceive clearly its direction and pattern. He must also attempt to evaluate each edition so that he can make an informed assessment of the accuracy of the author's last revised text, and if necessary suggest emendations. He will acknowledge Browning's concern for accuracy, but he will be aware of the possibility of errors in long and complex works transmitted through many editions, and finally corrected by the poet in the last year of his life.

The present editors, in the course of their work on the texts, have realised that they have the additional task of dispelling a number of myths. The standard bibliography of Browning's works, first published in 1953,[1] includes in its description of *Paracelsus* the statement 'Collation of the MS with the 1st ed. shows about 90 lines to have been added to the poem in press.' The tale improves in the telling. In 1955 DeVane helpfully increases the number of lines and defines their location: 'almost a hundred lines were added to the text while the poem was in the press. Almost fifty of the new lines were given to Part II, and the rest were scattered throughout.'[2] In fact the extra lines are phantoms: the first edition (1835) has the same number of lines as the MS, and, though the punctuation is extensively altered, there are only about a dozen insignificant changes in wording. Lines were indeed added in the edition of 1849, but many of the lines of the MS and *1835* were omitted or changed, so that the 'myth' is not even a straightforward error in specifying the edition.

A brief factual account of the publication of the works included in our first two volumes therefore seems desirable. *Pauline*

[1] *Robert Browning: A Bibliography, 1830–1950*, compiled by L. N. Broughton, C. S. Northup, and R. Pearsall (1953, new edition, 1970).
[2] W. C. DeVane, *A Browning Handbook*, p. 49.

was published anonymously in 1833. Browning, always on the defensive about the poem, was reluctant to let Elizabeth Barrett see it in 1846—'let me wait a few days,—to correct the misprints which affect the sense, and to write you the history of it'[1]—and he omitted it from his collected works until 1868. *Paracelsus* first appeared in 1835. Again Browning was displeased with the presentation—'(Errors of the press—past calculation!)'[2]—but the poem brought him recognition, and he republished it, much revised, in the 2-volume edition of his poems in 1849. *Strafford* was first published on the day of its first performance in 1837; *Sordello* appeared in 1840. A proof-copy of *Sordello* in the Boston Public Library contains some interesting revisions, and demonstrates Browning's concern for accuracy: 'Be particular with this word', he warns the printer, who had understandably set 'breeze' for 'breese' at ii. 773.

The 2-volume edition of the *Poems* in January 1849 was the first of Browning's works to be produced by Chapman. It includes *Paracelsus* and most of the pieces from *Bells and Pomegranates*, but not *Strafford* or *Sordello*. As Browning explains in his preface, 'The various Poems and Dramas have received the author's most careful revision.' Sarianna Browning's copy, now in the Armstrong Browning library, is dated 1848, and is probably a binding of the final revises: it contains a few minor variants from the 1849 copies.[3] Joseph Arnould had received an advance copy of the edition by 26 December 1848.[4] The 1849 text of *Paracelsus* is of great interest, many of its readings occurring in no other edition, as our notes show. We are able to trace the progress of the revisions Browning made for it in the annotated copy of the first edition now in the Berg Collection of the New York Public Library.

Chapman brought out a 3-volume edition of Browning's works in 1863. This sold well, for in November Browning wrote to Mrs Story that Chapman wanted to postpone publication of his new poems, *Dramatis Personæ*, in order to 'take advantage of the sort of success (for me) that the edition is

---

[1] Letter of 11 January 1846; Kintner, i. 380.
[2] Inscription by Browning in the Ashley Library copy of the first edition, in *B.L.*
[3] On this copy, first discovered and reported on by Ian Jack, see John Pettigrew, 'Baylor's 1848 *Poems*', *Browning Newsletter* No. 8, Spring 1972.
[4] Donald Smalley, 'Arnould and Browning', in *PMLA* 1965, p. 98.

getting'.[1] Although Browning told Moncure Conway on 17 September 1863 that there were 'no changes of importance in any of the poems', he had in fact made a thorough revision of *Paracelsus*, *Sordello* and *Strafford*, and of the poems from *Men and Women*, first published in 1855,[2] and he had carefully supervised the production of the edition. When a line was omitted from 'A Lovers' Quarrel' 'through a blunder of the printer's', the sheet was cancelled 'before many copies had been issued', and the correct text was printed.[3] Although Browning noticed other errors, *1863* is on the whole a reliable text, and is of special significance in the development of *Paracelsus* and *Strafford*.

In his letter of 26 November 1863 Browning had told Mrs Story that he 'did *not* send her' a copy of the 1863 collection 'because a prettier one is in prospect.' This was the fourth edition, dated 1865, and adorned with a photograph of the poet. Browning corrected the errors he had noticed in the third edition, and introduced some hundreds of revisions. (The Broughton, Northup and Pearsall bibliography is incorrect in describing it as a 'reprint'.) The revisions of *Sordello* and *Paracelsus* are useful but unobtrusive; those in *Strafford* and the poems of *Men and Women* are of more interest.[4] Unfortunately the fourth edition is less reliable than the third: it has a number of careless misprints (including the extraordinary 'blooming' for 'booming' in *Sordello*, i. 317) and it is likely that Browning gave it less than his usual attention. He had edited a selection of Elizabeth's poems for Chapman, and had been pre-occupied with his 'Roman murder story'—'16,000 lines, or over,— done in less than two years, Isa!', as he wrote to Miss Blagden on 19 May 1866.[5] We have therefore regarded with suspicion doubtful readings which first entered the text in 1865, and in the few instances where corruption seems certain, we have restored the readings of *1863*.

Dissatisfied on other grounds with Chapman as a publisher,

---

[1] 26 Nov. 1863. G. R. Hudson (ed.) *Browning to his American Friends*, p. 136.
[2] See A. C. Dooley, 'The Textual Significance of Robert Browning's 1865 *Poetical Works*', *Pub. Bibliographical Society of America*, 71, pp. 212–18.
[3] See N. J. Hart, 'A Browning Letter on "The Poetical Works" of 1863', in *Notes and Queries*, June 1974, pp. 213–15.
[4] Examples of revisions in *Men and Women* are given in A. C. Dooley, op. cit., pp. 216–17.
[5] McAleer (ed.), *Dearest Isa* (1951), p. 239.

Browning turned to George Smith of Smith, Elder & Co., who produced a new collected edition in 6 volumes in 1868. The copy-text for most of the poems (all but *Pauline* and *Dramatis Personæ*) was the edition of 1865, prepared by Browning, and including numerous revisions of punctuation and slight changes in wording, designed to improve clarity and style. *Pauline* was reprinted for the first time, in order to 'forestall' unauthorized transcripts. Browning revised its punctuation thoroughly, and made a very few verbal revisions—in spite of his disclaimer '(no syllable is changed)' in the preface. The copy of the 1833 *Pauline* in the Lowell Collection of the Houghton Library at Harvard contains the corrections Browning made for this edition; as we point out in our textual introduction to the poem, some of the apparent revisions of 1868 do not appear in the Lowell copy, and are probably errors. This seems the more likely because Browning himself, complaining of the two 'vile misprints' in the 1868 version of *Colombe's Birthday*, asserted that the edition was 'full of such. They come of the printer's laziness, who, if the type gets misplaced, prefers to replace it as he best can, without troubling the 'Reader' who may be at hand."[1] It is true that *1868* corrects several of the errors of *1865*, but others persisted, some of them surviving into later editions.

Nevertheless the 1868 edition sold well, and was frequently reprinted, in for example 1872, 1879, 1884 and 1886. Broughton, Northup and Pearsall assert that these stereotype reprints are 'without alterations in the text'; in fact a sample collation of two volumes of the 1879 reprint shows fairly numerous minor variants, mainly in punctuation; some look like deliberate corrections, others are probably caused by worn type. Some of the punctuation of the 1888–9 edition was first introduced into the text in one or other of these reprints—a fact that is relevant when one works out the stemma of *Strafford* editions: a reprint was used by Miss Hickey in preparing her editions of the play, which in turn contribute to the text produced by Browning in 1888.

Browning began to prepare a complete edition of his works

---

[1] Quoted by John Maynard in his review of Vol. IV of the Ohio *Works of Robert Browning, Studies in Browning and his Circle*, Vol. 2, no. 2, Fall 1974. Neither error is corrected in later editions within Browning's lifetime.

for Smith, Elder in 1887; he decided against supplying notes, explaining 'I am correcting them carefully, and *that* must suffice.'[1] In December 1887 he decided that he had 'gone over them [i.e. the texts of those poems previously collected in the 1868 *Poetical Works*] so often that I see little or nothing to amend in the poems, except in the punctuation.'[2] In the event, he made quite extensive changes in the text of *Pauline*, claiming permission to 'diminish' the faults of 'juvenile haste'. Because *Pauline* was so revised, after such a lapse of time, we have printed the 1833 and 1888 texts on facing pages, so that the reader may compare them. We have also given parallel texts of *Paracelsus* (a transcript of the original MS to be compared with the edition of 1888) because of the intrinsic interest of the MS version, the exceptionally large number of different editions, and the thorough recasting of the poem on two separate occasions (1849 and 1863).

Although Browning praised the 'scrupulous accuracy of the Printers'[3] in setting up the 1888–9 edition, he noticed a number of errors in the course of publication. Consisting of 16 volumes in all, the edition was issued at the rate of one volume a month between April 1888 and July 1889. From 10 April 1889 to 5 June 1889 Browning sent corrections for the volumes already published. The printer used up uncorrected sheets before resetting the type; thus as Philip Kelley and W. S. Peterson explain, errors are corrected in some copies and not in others.[4] 'Some of these corrected volumes—identical in appearance to those of the first "printing"—were issued during 1889 as part of the 1888–9 edition, so that thereafter any given set of the edition might contain one or more corrected volumes.'

Before his death in 1889 Browning provided additional lists of corrections for the first ten volumes: one set inserted as revisions in the copy formerly owned by James Dykes Campbell, now in the British Library, and another for Vols IV–X in the form of a list now in Brown University Library. Most, but

[1] Letter to George Smith, 12 Nov. 1887, quoted by Michael Hancher in 'Browning and the *Poetical Works* of 1888–1889', *Browning Newsletter*, Spring 1971, p. 25.
[2] Letter to George Smith, 31 Dec. 1887, ibid., p. 25.
[3] Letter to George Smith, 6 May 1888, ibid., p. 26.
[4] P. Kelley and W. S. Peterson, 'Browning's Final Revisions', in *Browning Institute Studies*, i (1973), 87–118. See also A. C. Dooley, 'Browning's *Poetical Works* of 1888–1889', *Studies in Browning and his Circle*, Vol. 7, no. 1, Spring 1979, pp. 43ff.

not all, of these corrections were incorporated in the corrected reprint published after Browning's death, of which all the volumes were dated 1889 (issued early in 1890).

We agree with Messrs Kelley and Peterson that the reprint of 1889 is not a satisfactory basis for an authoritative edition. It was not read in proof by Browning, it does not incorporate all the corrections he provided, its end-of-line punctuation is unreliable, and it contains some glaring misprints not present in the volumes published in 1888–July 1889. Our edition is therefore based on that of 1888–9, collated with extant MSS, with the principal editions of the poems before 1888, and with the 1889 reprint. Our emendations are based on Browning's own corrections, or, when the 1888–9 text is unquestionably faulty, on the readings of previous editions. All the poems in our first two volumes were issued in 1888; references to *1889* in our textual notes are to the posthumous reprint.

M.S.

General note on the recording of variants in this edition

Printed editions

We aim to record substantive variants, and variants in accidentals which significantly affect the meaning. Variants not recorded are, for example, apostrophes denoting omission of letters (shouldst/should'st, adored/ador'd); capitalization and spelling variants of no special importance (East/east—unless personification is involved; Thy/thy when unambiguously referring to God; ancles/ankles; recognise/recognize etc.); alternation between colons and semi-colons, with a few exceptions; hyphenation unless it indicates a different meaning; and commas with a minimal influence on meaning. A one-word lemma will normally be a punctuation variant. The words before and after substantive variants are given to aid identification, except where the variant begins or ends a line, when only one accompanying word or phrase is given. The date of the edition(s) in which variants occur is stated; the readings of editions not specified are normally the same as those in the basic text (in most cases, that of 1888). Reprints of *1868*, however, are assumed to be *substantially* the same as *1868*. Emendations are marked with an asterisk.

Manuscripts

Our recording varies according to the nature of the manuscript and its relation to the printed editions; selection criteria are explained in the textual introductions to individual poems. Angle brackets indicate deletions: ⟨ ⟩; square brackets additions or substitutions: [ ]; ogee brackets enclose comments by the editors: { }.

Primary texts and editions of Browning's works consulted for Volumes I and II.

Manuscript: Paracelsus. Forster Collection, Victoria and Albert Museum.

First editions: Pauline. March 1833. Saunders and Otley.
      Paracelsus. August 1835. Effingham Wilson.
      Strafford. May 1837. Longman.
      Sordello. March 1840. Moxon.

Collected Poetical Works and later editions.

1849. *Poems,* 2 vols. Chapman & Hall. Includes *Paracelsus.*

1863. *The Poetical Works,* 3 vols. Chapman & Hall. 'Third Edition'. Contains *Strafford* in vol. ii, *Paracelsus* and *Sordello* in vol. iii.

1865. *The Poetical Works,* 3 vols. Chapman & Hall. 'Fourth Edition.' (issued January 1866.) A revised reprint of the third edition.

1868. *The Poetical Works,* 6 vols. Smith, Elder & Co. Vol i contains *Pauline, Paracelsus,* and *Strafford*: Vol ii contains *Sordello.*

1879. *The Poetical Works,* 6 vols. Smith, Elder & Co. One of several reprints of the 1868 edition.

1882. *Strafford.* Printed for the use of the North London Collegiate School for Girls.

1884. *Strafford.* G. Bell & Sons. Edited by Emily H. Hickey.

1888–9. *The Poetical Works,* 16 vols. Smith, Elder & Co. Issued monthly from April 1888 to July 1889.
      Vol i (1888) contains *Pauline* and *Sordello.*
      Vol ii (1888) contains *Paracelsus* and *Strafford.*

1889. *The Poetical Works,* 16 vols. Smith Elder & Co. A corrected reprint of the 1888–9 edition. All volumes dated 1889; issued early 1890.

For secondary texts (manuscript fragments, annotated and proof copies), see the textual introductions to the individual poems.

REFERENCES AND ABBREVIATIONS

Note: the place of publication is given if it is not London or Oxford

Berdoe   *The Browning Cyclopædia*, by Edward Berdoe, 2nd edition, 1892.

Biographie Universelle   *Biographie Universelle, ancienne et moderne*, 52 vols., Paris, 1811–28.

Browning Collections   *The Browning Collections* (sale catalogue of Sotheby, Wilkinson and Hodge, 1913): reprinted in Volume 6 of *Sale Catalogues of Libraries of Eminent Persons* [General Editor, A. N. L. Munby], edited by J. Woolford, 1972.

Browning Newsletter   *The Browning Newsletter* (Armstrong Browning Library, Waco, Texas).

Browning Society Notes (The Browning Society, London).

Browning and Domett   *Robert Browning and Alfred Domett*, edited by Frederic G. Kenyon, 1906.

Browning and his Circle   *Studies in Browning and His Circle* (Armstrong Browning Library, Waco, Texas).

Chatterton   *Browning's Essay on Chatterton*, edited by Donald Smalley, Cambridge, Mass., 1948.

Checklist   *The Brownings' Correspondence: A Checklist*, compiled by Philip Kelley and Ronald Hudson (The Browning Institute and Wedgestone Press), 1978. Supplements in later volumes of *Browning Institute Studies*.

DeVane   *A Browning Handbook*, by William Clyde DeVane, 2nd edition, New York 1955 (1st ed., 1935).

Drew   *Robert Browning: A Collection of Critical Essays*, edited by Philip Drew, 1966.

Duff   *An Exposition of Browning's 'Sordello'* by David Duff, 1906.

Gosse   *Robert Browning: Personalia*, by Edmund Gosse, Boston and New York, 1890.

Griffin and Minchin   *The Life of Robert Browning*, by W. Hall Griffin, completed and edited by Harry Christopher Minchin, 3rd edition, revised and enlarged, 1938 (1st ed., 1910).

Handbook   *A Handbook to the Works of Robert Browning*, by Mrs Sutherland Orr, 7th edition, 1896 (1st ed., 1885).

Harrison   'Birds in the Poetry of Browning', by Thomas P. Harrison: *Review of English Studies*, NS, vol. vii, no. 28 (October 1956), pp. 393–405.

Holmes   'The Sources of Browning's *Sordello*', by Stewart W. Holmes: *Studies in Philology* 34 (1937), pp. 467–96.

Hood   'Browning's Ancient Classical Sources', by T. L. Hood: *Harvard Studies in Classical Philology*, xxxiii (1922), pp. 79–180.

Irvine and Honan   *The Book, the Ring, and the Poet*, by William Irvine and Park Honan, 1974.

Johnson   *A Dictionary of the English Language*, by Samuel Johnson, 9th ed., 2 vols., 1806.

Kintner   *The Letters of Robert Browning and Elizabeth Barrett Barrett 1845–1846*, edited by Elvan Kintner, 2 volumes, Cambridge, Mass., 1969.

Lemprière   *A Classical Dictionary*, by J. Lemprière, 5th edition, 1804.

Letters   *Letters of Robert Browning Collected by Thomas J. Wise*, edited by Thurman L. Hood, 1933.

Life   *Life and Letters of Robert Browning*, by Mrs. Sutherland Orr, new edition revised . . . by Frederic G. Kenyon, 1908 (1st ed., 1891).

Litzinger and Smalley   *Browning: The Critical Heritage*, edited by Boyd Litzinger and Donald Smalley, 1970.

Maynard   *Browning's Youth*, by John Maynard, 1977.

Miller   *Robert Browning: A Portrait*, by Betty Miller, 1952.

New Letters   *New Letters of Robert Browning*, edited by William Clyde DeVane and Kenneth Leslie Knickerbocker, New Haven, 1950.

NQ   *Notes and Queries.*

OED   *Oxford English Dictionary.*

Parleyings   *Browning's Parleyings: The Autobiography of a Mind*, by William Clyde DeVane, 1927.

Pettigrew   'For "Flute" read "Lute"; or, Notes on the "Notes" on *Sordello* in the Ohio Edition', by John Pettigrew: *The Library*, 5th series, vol. xxxiii, no. 2 (June 1978), pp. 162–9.

PMLA   *Publications of the Modern Language Association of America.*

Pottle   *Shelley and Browning: A Myth and Some Facts*, by Frederick A. Pottle, Chicago 1923 (reprinted by Archon Books, 1965).

Raymond   *The Infinite Moment and Other Essays in Robert Brown-ing*, by William O. Raymond, 2nd edition, enlarged, Toronto 1965.

RES   *Review of English Studies.*

Sharp   *Life of Robert Browning*, by William Sharp, 1890.

Smalley (see *Chatterton*).

Trumpeter   *Browning's Trumpeter: The Correspondence of Robert Browning and Frederick J. Furnivall 1872–1889*, edited by William S. Peterson (Washington, DC), 1979.

TLS   *Times Literary Supplement.*

Whyte   *Sordello by Robert Browning*, edited by Arthur J. Whyte, 1913.

Abbreviations and signs used in the textual notes

*	Emendation.
. . . .	Omission by the editors.[1]
>	Altered to produce a revised reading.
{ }	Comment by the editors.
[ ]	Addition or substitution.
⟨ ⟩	Deletion.
i.w.	Illegible word or words.
Berg	Annotated copy of *Paracelsus* (1835) in the Berg Collection, New York Public Library.
DC	British Library copy of Browning's *Poetical Works* (1888–89), formerly belonging to James Dykes Campbell, and corrected by Browning.
Domett	Copy of *Sordello* (1840), annotated by A. Domett, in the British Library.
Lowell	Annotated copy of *Pauline* (1833) in the Lowell Collection of the Houghton Library, Harvard.
Mill	Annotated copy of *Pauline* (1833) in the Forster Collection, Victoria and Albert Museum.
1840 proof	Proof copy of *Sordello* (1840) in Boston Public Library, USA.
SB	Annotated copy of *Sordello* (1840) at Syracuse University, NY.
Yale	Annotated copy of *Paracelsus* (1835) in Yale University Library.

[1] It should be noted that RB and EBB often used ' . . ' as a form of punctuation in their letters. The normal '. . .' is used in this edition to indicate an omission, except in the textual notes, where '. . . .' is used.

BROWNING'S DEDICATION OF *THE POETICAL WORKS*

I DEDICATE THESE VOLUMES TO MY OLD
FRIEND JOHN FORSTER, GLAD AND
GRATEFUL THAT HE WHO, FROM THE
FIRST PUBLICATION OF THE VARIOUS
POEMS THEY INCLUDE, HAS BEEN THEIR
PROMPTEST AND STAUNCHEST HELPER,
SHOULD SEEM EVEN NEARER TO ME
NOW THAN ALMOST THIRTY YEARS AGO.

R.B.

LONDON: *April* 21, 1863.

This dedication first appeared (but for the word 'ALMOST', added in 1868) in *The Poetical Works* of 1863. Forster had won Browning's undying gratitude by his reviews of *Paracelsus* in the *Examiner* and the *New Monthly Magazine* in 1835–6. 'During those forty years', he wrote in 1875, '. . . I have been constant in remembering—and, when occasion was, declaring—that as you stood forward my very first critic, so you remained, to my apprehension, the best . . . So long as my poems last they will continue to record that fact and its consequences—their fitting preface': *New Letters*, pp. 229–30.

INTRODUCTION TO 'PAULINE'

> The first communication, to even the family circle
> or the trusted associate, is sure to be 'the work of a
> friend'.[1]

The celebrated copy of *Pauline* now in the library of the
Victoria and Albert Museum is a review copy which was sent
to John Stuart Mill. He read the poem carefully, added numer-
ous marginal comments and a brief critique at the end, and
then (finding that he could not place a review) returned the
copy to W. J. Fox, from whom he had received it. Fox sent it
back to Browning, who added annotations of his own.[2] Mill's
comments and Browning's replies are all recorded in our
notes, and two of the latter provide vital information about the
genesis of the poem.

Mill objected to the subscription at the end, 'Richmond:
October 22, 1832': 'this transition from speaking to Pauline to
writing a letter to the public with *place & date*', he wrote, 'is
quite horrible'. Browning replies: 'Kean was acting there: I
saw him in Richard III that night, and conceived the childish
scheme already mentioned: there is an allusion to Kean, page
47.[3] I don't know whether I had not made up my mind to *act*, as
well as to make verses, music, and God knows what.—que de
châteaux en Espagne!'[4] DeVane states that 22 October 'was,
curiously, not the date of composition, but of the conception

---

[1] See pp. 7–8 below.

[2] Fox returned the book to Browning on 10 October: Browning wrote his own
name and 'October 30*th*' (possibly altered from 'October 20*th*') on the last blank leaf.
We agree with Michael A. Burr ('Browning's Note to Forster': *Victorian Poetry* xii
(1974), pp. 343 ff.) that Browning's comments were all written at the same time. Of
the numerous accounts of the marginalia in this copy the fullest is 'The J. S. Mill
Marginalia in . . . *Pauline*: A History and Transcription', by William S. Peterson and
Fred L. Standley (*Papers of the Bibliographical Society of America*, 66, New York 1972),
135 ff. Comparison with the copy itself, here used throughout, reveals one or two
errors even in this transcription. See also Appendix B, below.

[3] Lines 669 ff.

[4] Perhaps misled by a letter of Browning's own (*Letters*, p. 195), DeVane states that
this note is in pencil: in fact it is in ink. More seriously, DeVane implies that this
comment of Browning's is to be found in a different copy from that containing Mill's
marginalia. Mill used pencil.

of the poem', and that is consistent with what Browning wrote to his friend Ripert-Monclar on 9 August 1837[1]—and indeed with the date 'January 1833' at the end of the epigraph.

Sir Edmund Gosse, on the other hand, to whom Browning gave many details of his life, states that he 'finished' the poem on 22 October, while Sarianna, 'his only confidante while the work was in progress, recalled quite explicitly that it was while he was finishing the poem, not—as he implies—while he was conceiving it, that he was seeing Kean'.[2]

The 'childish scheme' is described in an earlier note of Browning's in the same copy:

The following Poem was written in pursuance of a foolish plan which occupied me mightily for a time, and which had for its object the enabling me to assume & realize I know not how many different characters;—meanwhile the world was never to guess that "Brown, Smith, Jones, & Robinson" (as the Spelling-books have it) the respective authors of this poem, the other novel, such an opera, such a speech &c &c were no other[3] than one and the same individual. The present abortion was the first work of the *Poet* of the batch, who would have been more legitimately *myself* than most of the others; but I surrounded him with all manner of (to my then notion) poetical accessories, and had planned quite a delightful life for him.

Only this crab remains of the shapely Tree of Life in this Fools Paradise of mine. RB

In a similar note in another copy, now lost, Browning remarks that he 'forget[s], or [has] no wish to remember' this 'foolish plan', mentions only 'such an opera, such a comedy, such a speech',[4] terms the Poet 'Mr. V. A.', and comments on the text: '(I cannot muster resolution to deal with the printers' blunders after the American fashion, and bid people "for 'jocularity' read 'synthesis'"' to the end of the chapter.)'

Browning had just been in time to see the elder Kean in the most celebrated of all his Shakespearian roles. 'Just returned

---

[1] Unpublished letter in the possession of Professor Richard L. Purdy.
[2] *Robert Browning: Personalia*, by Edmund Gosse (1890), p. 27; Maynard, p. 222.
[3] Written 'noother'.
[4] This copy belonged to R. H. Shepherd, and subsequently to the Turnbull Library in Wellington, New Zealand. Cf. Maynard, pp. 436–7, and *Trumpeter*, p. 26. While the omission of the words 'this poem, the other novel' is not significant, the addition of 'such a comedy' confirms Browning's dramatic ambitions. This inscription is dated 'Dec. 14, 1838': see Burr, loc. cit., p. 345 n. There is another statement, very similar to these, in an unpublished letter in the possession of Professor Purdy.

from seeing Kean in Richard', Byron had written eighteen years before, in a letter available to Browning in Moore's *Letters and Journals of Lord Byron*:[1] 'By Jove, he is a soul! Life—nature—truth without exaggeration or diminution. Kemble's Hamlet is perfect;—but Hamlet is not Nature. Richard is a man; and Kean is Richard'. For years Hazlitt and other less eloquent critics had celebrated Kean's rendering of the part. By 1832 Kean had deteriorated in every respect, as we know from the report of John Doran, who saw his Richard III at the Haymarket in that very year: 'Genius was not traceable in that bloated face; intellect was all but quenched in those once matchless eyes; and the power seemed gone, despite the will that would recall it. I noted in a diary that night the above facts, and in addition, that by bursts he was as grand as he had ever been.'[2] Five months later he was to collapse while playing Othello at Covent Garden. Browning would have been second to no one in his sense of the poignancy of great genius in decline, and we note that he attended Kean's funeral on 25 May 1833.

Pauline was published in March 1833. The expenses of publication were met by Browning's aunt, Mrs Silverthorne, who gave him £30, of which £26. 5s. od. went to the printers, Saunders and Otley,[3] while the remainder was spend on advertising. In a highly self-conscious letter to W. J. Fox, signed only with his initials but suggesting that he might 'recollect an oddish sort of boy, who had the honour of being introduced to you at Hackney some years back', Browning described the poem—in terms which could hardly be less appropriate—as 'a free and easy sort of thing which he wrote some months ago "on one leg"' and expressed the hope that Fox might review the enclosed copy in the *Westminster Review*.[4] Fox's response must have been encouraging, because Browning soon sent

[1] i. 358 in the ed. of 1833.

[2] Quoted in *The Life and Adventures of Edmund Kean*, by J. Fitzgerald Molloy (2 vols., 1888), ii. 266. Cf. *Edmund Kean*, by H. N. Hillebrand (New York 1933). According to Furnivall, Browning 'when young . . . sent his copy of the original edition of *The Cenci* to Kean, and askt him to put it on the stage': *Browning's Trumpeter*, p. 131.

[3] Browning was later to tell Elizabeth Barrett that the printer 'never knew my name even!': see below, p. 11.

[4] *Life*, p. 52. It was not quite honest of Browning to tell Ripert-Monclar that *Pauline* was conveyed to Fox 'anonymously' (letter of August 9, 1837: Purdy Collection).

him no fewer than a dozen copies, clearly for distribution to potential reviewers. Fox obviously did his work well, since the anonymous poem was reviewed or briefly noticed in half-a-dozen periodicals. While one or two periodicals were merely dismissive—the *Literary Gazette*, for example, was content to characterize the book as 'Somewhat mystical, somewhat poetical, somewhat sensual, and not a little unintelligible,— . . . a dreamy volume, without an object, and unfit for publication'[1]—there were two reviews which accorded the poem a high measure of praise. The reviewer in the *Athenæum* quoted some eighty lines, and praised 'the nature, and passion, and fancy of the poem', while Fox himself wrote enthusiastically in the *Monthly Repository*: 'In recognising a poet we cannot stand upon trifles . . . Archimedes in the bath had many particulars to settle . . . , but he first gave a glorious leap and shouted *Eureka!*'[2]

Fox also commented, however, that 'The author cannot expect such a poem as this to be popular, to make "a hit", to produce a "sensation"', and this proved to be a notable understatement. It appears that the favourable reviews had no effect whatever. 'I willingly repeat', Browning wrote to Thomas James Wise in 1886, 'that to the best of my belief no single copy of the original edition of *Pauline* found a buyer; the book was undoubtedly "stillborn,"—and that despite the kindly offices of many friends, who did their best to bring about a successful birth'.[3] It is not surprising that only 24 copies of the book are now known to exist.[4]

A poem with a woman's name as its title and the words 'A Fragment of a Confession' as its sub-title inevitably invites speculation, and a good deal of criticism has circled round the question to what extent the poem is autobiographical, and whether 'Pauline' is to be identified with a real woman.

---

[1] 23 March (p. 183): Litzinger and Smalley, p. 34.

[2] It is a pity that Browning did not know that the writer of the former review, 'which gratified me and my people far beyond what will ever be the fortune of criticism now', as he later commented (*Letters*, p. 172), was Allan Cunningham. To Fox, whom Browning came to regard as his literary godfather, he wrote that he would never 'write a line without thinking of the source of my first praise, be assured' (*Life*, p. 54). Extracts from the two reviews are to be found in Litzinger and Smalley, pp. 34–6.

[3] *Letters*, p. 251.

[4] We owe this figure (which includes the copy missing from the Turnbull Library) to Mr Philip Kelley.

Any notion of the poem's being directly autobiographical must immediately be dismissed. No one has suggested that Browning was contemplating a period of exile in Switzerland or elsewhere with a French-speaking lover, while his remark that he had 'surrounded [the *Poet*] with all manner of (to my then notion) poetical accessories, and had planned quite a delightful life for him' emphasizes the element of fiction in the whole conception. In an unpublished letter he refers to the 'very delicious and romantic life' for which the poet was destined and states explicitly that he had destroyed a second Part of the poem.[1]

On the other hand Browning's insistence that 'The thing was my earliest attempt at "poetry always dramatic in principle"'[2] can hardly persuade us that *Pauline* is a purely dramatic composition, as 'My Last Duchess' and 'The Bishop Orders his Tomb' are purely dramatic compositions. Browning acknowledged that 'the *Poet* . . . would have been more legitimately *myself* than most of the others', and we notice that he is the same age as Browning,[3] had been brought up in a house full of books, apostrophizes Browning's favourite Andromeda, and has marked temperamental similarities to his creator.

In fact there is no real difficulty, and a passage in Browning's essay on Chatterton provides admirable guidance:

Is it worth while to mention, that the very notion of obtaining a free way for impulses that can find vent in no other channel (and consequently of a liberty conceded to an individual, and denied to the world at large), is implied in all literary production? By this fact is explained, not only the popular reverence for, and interest in even the personal history of, the acknowledged and indisputable possessors of this power . . . but also the as popular jealousy of allowing this privilege to the first claimant. And so instinctively does the Young Poet feel that his desire for this kind of self-enfranchisement will be resisted as a matter of course, that we will venture to say, in nine cases out of ten his first assumption of the licence will be made in a borrowed name. The first communication, to even the family

---

[1] Letter in the possession of Professor Purdy.
[2] Prefatory note to the 1868 *Poetical Works*: cf. p. 515, below.
[3] The meaning of the somewhat cryptic '*V.A.XX.*' has been missed by critics who believe that 'the persona is past forty'. See Burr, loc. cit., p. 348 n.

circle or the trusted associate, is sure to be "the work of a friend."[1]

Analogous strategies in poems which influenced *Pauline* will be mentioned shortly: meanwhile we may notice that the note in French supposed to be written by Pauline recalls Byron's habit of undercutting his own more confessional or romantic passages by appending a satirical comment, often in the last couplet of an *ottava rima* stanza. We may well conclude that Browning 'doth protest too much' about the dramatic nature of the poem and suspect that in his pursuit of 'self-enfranchisement' he had (as he feared) revealed more of his own character and aspirations than he had intended.[2] It is possible (indeed) that he had originally begun to write a much more openly confessional poem than *Pauline* as we have it, and that the acting of Kean modified his plan and suggested that he should give his poem a new slant and present it as one of a number of heterogeneous compositions which were to come before the public as the work of a number of different men. Among other advantages, such a procedure would have made the problem of sincerity less troubling—the question how far the poem had succeeded in tracing the exact graph of his own emotional and religious development.

The identity of 'Pauline' is another matter. When, with reference to Eliza Flower, Mrs. Orr wrote: 'If, in spite of his denials, any woman inspired *Pauline*, it can be no other than she',[3] she beckoned critics of the poem towards a desert of idle speculation. The role of Eliza and her sister Sarah is a matter of legitimate interest to anyone concerned with Browning's youth, and it has recently been carefully examined by John Maynard:[4] the fact remains that Pauline is (in Mill's words) a

---

[1] *Browning's Essay on Chatterton*, ed. Donald Smalley (Cambridge, Mass., 1948), p. 116.

[2] As DeVane points out (p. 48), when in 1867 Browning unwillingly gave R. H. Shepherd permission to print 'a few extracts', he insisted that he should 'preface these with mention of the fact that the poem was purely dramatic and intended to head a series of "Men & Women" such as I have afterwards introduced to the world under somewhat better auspices', and actually stipulated that Shepherd must make '*not* a single remark upon them': see W. L. Phelps, 'Notes on Browning's *Pauline*': *Modern Language Notes* (May 1932), p. 295.

[3] *Life*, p. 35.

[4] *Browning's Youth*, pp. 179 ff. He emphasizes that Eliza Flower was intensely musical, a fact which supports the notion that she may have played some part in

'mere phantom', with few characteristics except beauty, long hair, the ability to write in French, and the gift of silence which is necessary in the *muta persona* to whom a dramatic mono-logue is addressed. Those who have a liking for such 'clues' may seize on the reference to 'a winter flower' in line 711: the rest of us may be content to acknowledge the possibility that the name of the girl may have been suggested by that of Pauline de Villenoix, the young woman who tends Louis Lambert in Balzac's novel of that name.[1] It is likely that Browning will have heard of Balzac's novel, and possible that he had read it; but the resemblances between the speaker in Pauline and Lambert are more likely to be due to the spirit of the age than to direct influence.

By a fortunate chance a letter from Sarah Flower to her mentor (and Browning's friend) W. J. Fox survives to throw important light on the background of the poem. On 23 November 1827 she had sent him 'a regular confession of faith, or rather the want of it', telling him that her mind had been

wandering a long time, and now . . . seems to have lost sight of . . . a firm belief in the genuineness of the Scriptures . . . I do believe in the existence of an All-wise and Omnipotent Being—and that, involv-ing as it does the conviction that everything is working together for good, brings with it comfort I would not resign for worlds. Still, I would fain go to my Bible as I used to—but I cannot. The cloud has come over me gradually, and I did not discover the darkness in which my soul was shrouded until, in seeking to give light to others, my own gloomy state became too settled to admit of doubt. It was in answering Robert Browning that my mind refused to bring forward argument, turned recreant, and sided with the enemy.[2]

Although Browning was only fifteen at this time, she

---

suggesting the nature of the 'phantom'. In his Appendix D Maynard describes markings in the copy of *Pauline* now in the Widener Collection at Harvard. He remarks that it 'can be tentatively identified either as that possessed by Sarah Flower Adams [Sarah's married name] or as a deliberate forgery': the latter hypothesis seems the more likely, and the markings are (in any case) of very slight interest.

[1] See Henri-Léon Hovelaque, *La Jeunesse de Robert Browning* (Paris, 1932), pp. 121–5. Maynard is rightly cautious about the suggestion (see his index, 'Balzac'). In 1839 Browning wrote to Fanny Haworth about the serialization of Balzac's *Beatrix* 'in the feuilleton of the *Siècle*, day by day', and added: 'I receive it from Paris two days old': *New Letters*, p. 16. All that would be necessary, for the degree of 'influence' that is possible, would have been a notice of *Louis Lambert* in some periodical.

[2] Moncure D. Conway, *Centenary History of the South Place Society* (1894), p. 46.

describes him as 'very interesting from his great power of conversation and thorough originality'.[1]

The references to *Pauline* in Browning's letters to Elizabeth Barrett are instructive above all because of their evasiveness. 'I know myself—surely', he wrote on 26 February 1845, '—and always have done so—for is there not somewhere the little book I first printed when a boy, with John Mill, the metaphysical head, *his* marginal note that "the writer possesses a deeper self-consciousness than I ever knew in a sane human being"—So I never deceived myself much, nor called my feelings for people other than they were'.[2] 'Of course you are *self-conscious*', she replied: '—How c^d you be a poet otherwise?', adding: 'And was the little book written with Mr. Mill pure metaphysics, or what?'

In January of the following year she came on a reference to the poem in the *New Quarterly Review*, where it was described as 'a little work called "Pauline", written and published still earlier [than *Paracelsus*], . . . full of the most wonderful writing'.[3] '*I shall have 'Pauline' in a day or two*—yes, I shall & must . . & *will* . .', she wrote immediately. 'Must you see "Pauline"?', he replied on the following day. 'A[t] least then let me wait a few days,—to correct the misprints which affect the sense, and to write you the history of it; what is necessary you should know before you see it'. Three days later she explained that when she had mentioned the poem she had been 'on the point of sending for the book to the booksellers—then suddenly I thought to myself that I should wait & hear whether you very, very much would dislike my reading it—See now! Many readers have done virtuously, but *I*, . . . surpassed them all!—And now, because I may, I *"must* read

---

[1] Maynard states that 'Browning seems . . . not to have been writing any poetry between the verses associated with the Flowers [Appendix F below] and the composition of *Pauline* . . ., a period of as long as six years' (p. 202), and it appears to be true that nothing survives from this period.

[2] Kintner, pp. 28, 31–2. In 'Mill and "Pauline": The Myth and Some Facts' (*Victorian Studies*, ix (1965), p. 156), Masao Miyoshi points out that ' "self-consciousness" . . . can be understood more accurately as "self-awareness" and appositely cites Mill's use of the word in his *Autobiography* (1873, pp. 133–4): 'In this frame of mind it occurred to me to put the question directly to my self: "Suppose that all your objects in life were realized . . . would this be a great joy and happiness to you?" And an irrepressible self-consciousness distinctly answered, "No!" '

[3] Quoted by Kintner, p. 367. The following quotations are from pp. 375, 380, 386, 389, 391, 404 and 408.

it"—: & as there are misprints to be corrected, will you do
what is necessary, or what you think is necessary, & bring me
the book on Monday?' He replied:

Will you, and must you have "Pauline"? If I could pray you to
revoke that decision! For it is altogether foolish and *not* boylike—and
I shall, I confess, hate the notion of running over it—yet commented
it must be; more than mere correction! I was unluckily *precocious*—
but I had rather you *saw* real infantine efforts . . (verses at six years
old, and drawings still earlier) than this ambiguous, feverish—
Why not wait? When you speak of the "Bookseller"— I smile, in
glorious security—having a whole bale of sheets at the house-top:
he never knew my name even![1]—and I withdrew these after a very
little time.

'May God bless you!', she replied: '—Did I ever say that I had
an objection to read the verses at six years old . . or see the
drawings either? . . .—Only, "Pauline" I must have *some
day*—why not without the emendations?—But if you insist on
them, I will agree to wait a little . . if you promise *at last* to let
me see the book which I will not show . . Some day, then!'
'"Pauline" is altogether of a different sort of precocity', he
wrote again four days later, referring lightheartedly to his
early attempts at writing French verse: '—you shall see it
when I can muster resolution to transcribe the explanation
which I know is on the fly-leaf of a copy here'. At last she took
the hint, replying: 'I am satisfied with the promise to see it
some day . . when we are in the isle of the sirens, or ready for
wandering in the Doges' galleries . . . I seem to understand
that you would really rather wish me not to see it now . . & as
long as I *do* see it.! So *that shall* be!—Am I not good now, & not
a teazer?'

It is time to quote the compressed critique by Mill which
occasioned 'the explanation' and is responsible for such know-
ledge as we have of the evolution of the poem:

With considerable poetic powers, this writer seems to me possessed
with a more intense and morbid self-consciousness than I ever knew

---

[1] This is reminiscent of the practice of Sir Walter Scott, and perhaps supports the
conjecture that the death of 'The Great Unknown', the author of famous poems who
then became the anonymous author of a series of even more famous romances in
prose, may have helped to prompt Browning's 'foolish plan': cf. Ian Jack, *Browning's
Major Poetry* (1973), p. 11.

in any sane human being—I should think it a *sincere confession*
though of a most unloveable state, if the 'Pauline' were not evidently
a mere phantom. All about her [probably underlined] is full of incon-
sistency—he neither loves her nor fancies he loves her, yet insists
upon *talking* love to her—if she *existed* and loved him, he treats her
most ungenerously and unfeelingly. All his aspirings and yearnings
and regrets point to other things, never to her—then, he *pays her off*
towards the end by a piece of flummery, amounting to the modest
request that she will love him and live with him and give herself up to
him *without* his *loving her, moyennant quoi* he will think her and call
her everything that is handsome and he promises her that she shall
find it mighty pleasant. Then he leaves off by saying he knows he
shall have changed his mind by tomorrow, & despise 'these intents
which seem so fair',[1] but that having been thus visited once no doubt
he will again—& is therefore 'in perfect joy' bad luck to him! as the
Irish say.

A cento of most beautiful passages might be made from this
poem—& the psychological history of himself is powerful and
truthful, *truth-like* certainly all but the last stage. *That* he evidently
has not yet got into. The self-seeking & self-worshipping state is
well described—beyond that, I should think the writer had made, as
yet, only the next step; viz. into despising his own state. I even
question whether part even of that self-disdain is not *assumed*. He is
evidently *dissatisfied*, and feels part of the badness of his state, but he
does not write as if it were purged out of him—if he once could
muster a hearty hatred of his selfishness, it would *go*—as it is he feels
only the *lack* of *good*, not the positive *evil*. He feels not remorse, but
only disappointment[;] A mind in that state can only be regenerated by
some new passion, and I know not what to wish for him but that he
may meet with a *real* Pauline—

Meanwhile he should not attempt to shew how a person may be
recovered from this morbid state—for *he* is hardly convalescent, and
'what should we speak of but that which we know?'[2]

Such are the observations which Mill considered 'On the
whole . . . not flattering to the author—perhaps too strong in
the *expression* to be shown to him',[3] but while his detailed
marginalia include complaints of obscurity they also include
such comments as 'beautiful' and '*most* beautiful', and it is
clear from Browning's desire that he should review *Paracelsus*[4]

---

[1] Ll. 992 and 994.
[2] The allusion at the end is to John 3:11.
[3] Quoted in F. A. Hayek's *John Stuart Mill and Harriet Taylor* (1951), p. 43.
[4] See below, p. 112.

and his later comments to Elizabeth Barrett and others that he was pleased to have attracted the attention of so powerful a mind. When he told Furnivall that he only remembered the 'good natured' notices of his poems he immediately referred to the notes on which Mill had 'meant to construct an article . . .—till he found he had been forestalled'.[1]

Like Browning's biographers, Mill was misled by the title of the poem; and while they have been obsessed by the identity of the lady, he was distressed by the moral aspects of the case. In fact, however, the important background of *Pauline* is a literary background, and any part that any young woman may have played in inspiring it is as nothing to the part played by the poetry of Shelley, and in particular by his *Epipsychidion*[2]. While *Pauline* contains a number of verbal echoes of *Alastor*, and could well be described (in Mary Shelley's words about that poem) as 'the outpouring of [the poet's] own emotions', it is of *Epipsychidion* that the reader is most likely to be reminded. In the 'Advertisement' to that poem Shelley states that it is the work of a young man who had died 'as he was preparing for a voyage to one of the wildest of the Sporades, which he had bought, and where he had fitted up the ruins of an old building, and where it was his hope to have realised a scheme of life, suited perhaps to that happier and better world of which he is now an inhabitant, but hardly practicable in this', a passage which probably helped to inspire the notion of the happy exile of the lovers no doubt described in the second Part of *Pauline*. Browning might well have said of *Pauline*, as Shelley said of *Epipsychidion*, that 'The present Poem, like the *Vita Nuova* of Dante, is sufficiently intelligible to a certain class of readers without a matter-of-fact history of the circumstances to which it relates; and to a certain other class it must ever remain incomprehensible, from a defect of a common organ of perception for the ideas of which it treats'—although in his case 'the circumstances to which it relates' were imaginary circumstances. Shelley's reference to 'my unfortunate friend' is echoed in Pauline's phrase 'mon pauvre ami' (line 811 n.).[3] A

[1] *Trumpeter*, p. 22.

[2] *Epipsychidion* must have been one of the poems which prompted Browning to write the sentences in his Essay on Chatterton quoted earlier.

[3] Many of the echoes of Shelley recorded in our notes have been pointed out by earlier scholars, notably by F. A. Pottle in his *Shelley and Browning: A Myth and Some*

major difference between the poems, however, is that while
Epipsychidion is about love, and was inspired by Shelley's
passion for Emilia Viviani, *Pauline* is about the development of
the poet's own state of mind. The role of Pauline is that of the
auditor in a dramatic monologue, and her most important
contribution to the poem is her reported injunction to the poet
to describe 'the stages of all life' (884), beginning with his own
'first stage'.[1]

When Browning felt obliged to reprint the poem in 1868 he
described it as a 'boyish work' requiring 'an exculpatory
word'. He might well have said of it what Keats had said of
Endymion only fifteen years before:

> The imagination of a boy is healthy, and the mature imagination
> of a man is healthy; but there is a space of life between, in which the
> soul is in a ferment, the character undecided, the way of life uncer-
> tain, the ambition thick-sighted: thence proceeds mawkishness, and
> all the thousand bitters which those men I speak of must necessarily
> taste in going over the following pages.[2]

Such, or nearly such, were some of the qualities which Mill
found and disliked in *Pauline*. Beside his comments we may set
Joseph Arnould's more sympathetic description of the poem
as 'a strange, wild (in parts singularly magnificent), poet-
biography: his own early life as it presented itself to his own
soul viewed poetically:[3] in fact, psychologically speaking, his
"Sartor Resartus": . . . written and published . . . when Shel-
ley was his God'.[4] A month after these words were written
Dante Gabriel Rossetti read the book in the British Museum
and was so struck by its power that, 'having failed in an
attempt to procure a copy at the publisher's', he transcribed
the whole and wrote to Browning to say that its resemblances
'in style and feeling to [his] first acknowledged work, *Paracel-
sus*' had led him to 'a suspicion' that it might be by him and to
enquire, as 'a most enthusiastic admirer', whether his conjec-

---

Facts (1923: repr. Archon Books, 1965). We have appended the name 'Pottle' to a few
of our notes, as a token of a general indebtedness, although we reject some of Pottle's
suggestions and make a great many of our own.

[1] Stages or states. The words 'my state' occur in lines 50, 267, 586, 587 (*1888* only),
and 1030.

[2] Preface.

[3] The words 'viewed poetically' must be stressed.

[4] *Robert Browning and Alfred Domett*, ed. Frederic G. Kenyon (1906), p. 141.

ture was correct.[1] Twenty years were to pass before, 'with extreme repugnance, indeed purely of necessity', Browning was induced to reprint the poem.

No manuscript has survived. The main editions are those of 1833, 1868, and 1888–9. The intermediate 'editions' between 1868 and 1888 are largely reprints of *1868*, though some have minor alterations, mainly of spelling and punctuation, which were carried over into *1888*.

Of the copies of the first edition which are of special interest, that annotated by John Stuart Mill has been described above. Most of Browning's alterations in this copy are of punctuation: typically, the replacement of commas and dashes by colons and semi-colons. The comma after 'so' in line 392 and the capitalization of 'imagination' in line 284 are due to Mill's comments. Browning also capitalized the key ideas of 'love' and 'reason' in lines 637–45. A complete list of these changes, few of which were incorporated in later editions, is given in Appendix B. The handful of substantive alterations, and one or two of the more radical changes in accidentals, are included in our textual notes. It is tempting to adopt some of them, especially the deletion of the comma in the phrase 'led by thee, / Thro' youth' in line 36, and the changed placing of inverted commas in line 467; but the Mill copy was not available for Browning's use in the preparation of later editions, and he allowed the original punctuation of these two passages to stand.[2]

Another special copy of *1833* is one altered by Browning in preparation for the 1868 edition. It is inscribed in the poet's hand on the title-page 'To Frederick Locker—with all regard from his friend Robert Browning. Apr. 13 '69.' 'Corrections made at London, 1867.' and is in the Lowell Collection of the Houghton Library at Harvard. Browning's preface to the 1868 edition, dated December 25, 1867, explains why he made the corrections: 'The first piece in the series, [*i.e. Pauline*] I acknowledge and retain with extreme repugnance, indeed purely of necessity; for not long ago I inspected one, and am certified of the existence of other transcripts, intended sooner or later to

---

[1] *Letters of Dante Gabriel Rossetti*, ed. Oswald Doughty and John Robert Wahl, (4 vols., 1965–7), i. 32–3.
[2] On the Mill copy see the articles cited in the notes to pp. 3, 8 and 10 above. An annotated copy in the Rylands library is described in Appendix B.

be published abroad: by forestalling these, I can at least correct some misprints (no syllable is changed) and introduce a boyish work by an exculpatory word.' In fact the poet did a good deal more than he implies here. He revised the punctuation thoroughly, evidently aiming at greater smoothness, since he deleted many commas and converted full-stops into colons, as well as linking together some of *1833*'s separate sections, and changing many of its innumerable dashes into more specific marks. The Lowell copy shows that a few 'syllables' *were* changed: there are some half-dozen slight verbal revisions (of the type 'Wert' to 'Wast') and two insertions, one being the line and a half needed to explain the fragmentary sentence beginning at line 405. Nevertheless, Browning clearly intended to produce a presentable rather than a strikingly new text. Thus, though some of the 1868 readings which are unsupported by the Lowell copy may be corrections in proof, others may be printers' errors. Two of these Browning corrected in 1888, when he restored the 1833 reading at l.141, and changed 'wild' (probably a misprint for 'wide') to 'vast' at l.612; but he seems to have missed the change of 'old' to 'own' at l.238, and 'wide' to 'wild' (again) at l.91. Both of these 1868 readings seem inferior, and we have restored those of 1833. The readings of the Lowell copy are recorded only where they differ from those of 1868.[1]

When Browning prepared *Pauline* for the 1888 collected edition, he at first thought, as he says in the preface to that edition, 'that the honest course would be to reprint, and leave mere literary errors unaltered.' But when he received the proofs, he suddenly decided to revise the poem. He wrote to his publisher, George Smith, on 27 February 1888, 'a sudden impulse came over me to take the opportunity of just correcting the most obvious faults of expression, versification and construction,—letting the *thoughts*—such as they are—remain exactly as at first: I have only treated the imperfect expression of these just as I have now and then done for an amateur friend, if he asked me and I liked him enough to do so. Not a line is displaced, none added, none taken away.' (Mrs Orr, *Life and Letters*, p. 380). Comparison of the 1888 edition with its pre-

---

[1] For a note on the annotated copy in the John Rylands Library, see Appendix B.

decessors shows how extensively Browning revised. Up to about l.300 there are only a few revisions—mainly rearrangements of words within lines; but thereafter substantive changes abound. Without altering the order of the lines or making any long insertions, Browning carefully polished, clarified and variously 'improved' the poem, introducing more striking metaphors and more meaningful verbs, and aiming to present a more attractive and comprehensible picture of his youthful self. *1888*, as far as one can tell, conveys the revised version without obvious misprints, apart from a few minor punctuation errors: 'loneliness' for 'loveliness' in l.194 is perhaps suspect, but the sense is just acceptable, and the alterations in subsequent lines are clearly deliberate.

Browning made only one correction to the poem in the Dykes Campbell copy of *1888*, adding a comma at the end of l.332. The 1889 edition is, therefore, presumably incorrect in printing a colon there. Some copies of *1889* also have the misprint 'gowing' for 'glowing' at l.781.

There is no doubt that an editor must take the revised *Pauline* of 1888 as his basic text. We have set out the 1888 poem, emended mainly by reference to the Lowell and Dykes Campbell copies, on the right hand page. Starred footnotes indicate our few departures from the copy-text. The text of 1833 is printed opposite for comparison; for the sake of easy reference its lines are numbered to correspond with those of 1888, and not as an independent sequence.[1] The textual notes include all substantive variants and the more significant variants in accidentals.

[1] The edition of *Pauline* by N. H. Wallis (London, 1931) provides a useful comparison of the later texts with that of 1833, but is not completely accurate; for example, ll. 91, 294, and 548 of the 1833 text are incorrectly printed, and several substantive variants are omitted.

PAULINE

PAULINE;

A FRAGMENT OF A CONFESSION.

———

Plus ne suis ce que j'ai été,
Et ne le sçaurois jamais être.—Marot.

Plus ne suis: 'I am no longer what I have been, and can never be': Clément Marot (1496–1544), 'Les Épigrammes', ccxix. As Maynard points out, the Horatian commonplace occurs twice in *Childe Harold's Pilgrimage*, at IV. clxxxv. 6–7 ('I am not now / That which I have been') and at III. cxi: *Browning's Youth*, p. 436.

PAULINE

Non dubito, quin titulus libri nostri raritate sua quamplurimos alliciat ad legendum: inter quos nonnulli obliquæ opinionis, mente languidi, multi etiam maligni, et in ingenium nostrum ingrati accedent, qui temeraria sua ignorantia, vix conspecto titulo clamabunt Nos vetita docere, hæresium semina jacere: piis auribus offendiculo, præclaris ingeniis scandalo esse: . . . . adeo conscientiæ suæ consulentes, ut nec Apollo, nec Musæ omnes, neque Angelus de cœlo me ab illorum execratione vindicare queant: quibus et ego nunc consulo, ne scripta nostra legant, nec intelligant, nec meminerint: nam noxia sunt, venenosa sunt: Acherontis ostium est in hoc libro, lapides loquitur, caveant, ne cerebrum illis excutiat. Vos autem, qui æqua mente ad legendum venitis, si tantam prudentiæ discretionem adhibueritis, quantam in melle legendo apes, jam securi legite. Puto namque vos et utilitatis haud parum et voluptatis plurimum accepturos. Quod si qua repereritis, quæ vobis non placeant, mittite illa, nec utimini. Nam et ego vobis illa non Probo, sed Narro. Cætera tamen propterea non respuite . . . . . Ideo, si quid liberius dictum sit, ignoscite adolescentiæ nostræ, qui minor quam adolescens hoc opus composui.—*Hen. Corn. Agrippa, De Occult. Philosoph. in Præfat.**
    London: *January* 1833.
    V. A. XX.

[This introduction would appear less absurdly pretentious did it apply, as was intended, to a completed structure of which the poem was meant for only a beginning and remains a fragment.]

---

* The text of the preliminary quotation is that of *1888*, substantially the same as *1833*. The words '*in Præfat.*' had been added in 1868.

'*Non dubito*: 'I have no doubt that the strikingly unusual title of my book may attract a great many readers, among whom some slow-witted, biased individuals, and even many of an ill-natured, ungrateful disposition, will attack my abilities, and in their rash ignorance complain aloud, upon scarcely having seen the title (itself), that I teach forbidden doctrines and sow the seeds of heresy: that the work is an offence to pious ears, and a scandal to distinguished minds . . . so scrupulously taking care for their own consciences that neither Apollo, nor all the Muses, nor an angel from heaven could defend me from their execrations. I take this opportunity of advising such people not to read, understand, nor remember my writings, for they are harmful, they are poisonous. Hell-mouth is in this book, it speaks hard words. Let them beware lest it destroy their brains. But you who approach the work in an impartial spirit may read it quite safely once you employ as much wise discrimination as do the bees in gathering honey. I think you will gain more than a little useful knowledge, and a great deal of pleasure. Yet if you should find matters which displease you, push them aside, make no use of them. FOR I DO NOT RECOMMEND THESE THINGS TO YOUR ACCEPTANCE, I MERELY TELL YOU OF THEM. Yet do not reject all the rest on this account . . . Therefore if anything is stated more boldly than is proper, pardon my youthfulness. I could scarcely even be called a youth when I wrote this work.' The *De Occulta Philosophia* of Cornelius Agrippa was first published in Antwerp in 1531. Browning knew it in a collection of treatises on magic in his father's library: Maynard, pp. 210, 434–5.

As Pottle points out (p. 85), Browning's extract comes from the beginning of the Preface, and provides no evidence of extensive reading. He rightly observes that Browning omits more from the passage than is indicated: for example the words 'de Occulta Philosophia, sive de Magia' after 'nostri', and the words 'Magiæ nomen in deteriorem partem accipientes' before 'vix conspecto'—so that the references to magic are eliminated.

4 *vix conspecto titulo*: 'why?', Mill asked, very reasonably: the words are relevant to the title of Cornelius Agrippa's book, *De Occulta Philosophia*, but not to that of Browning's.

21 *V. A. XX.*: Vixi annos viginti, 'I am twenty years old'. Browning once termed the Poet 'Mr. V. A.' (p. 7, n³, above).

[*This introduction*: no doubt added because of Mill's comment: 'too much pretension in this motto'.

PAULINE
[1833]

PAULINE, mine own, bend o'er me—thy soft
    breast
Shall pant to mine—bend o'er me—thy sweet
    eyes,
And loosened hair, and breathing lips, and arms
Drawing me to thee—these build up a screen
To shut me in with thee, and from all fear,   5
So that I might unlock the sleepless brood
Of fancies from my soul, their lurking place,
Nor doubt that each would pass, ne'er to return
To one so watched, so loved, and so secured.
But what can guard thee but thy naked love?   10
Ah, dearest! whoso sucks a poisoned wound
Envenoms his own veins,—thou art so good,
So calm—if thou should'st wear a brow less light
For some wild thought which, but for me, were
    kept
From out thy soul, as from a sacred star.   15
Yet till I have unlocked them it were vain
To hope to sing; some woe would light on me;
Nature would point at one, whose quivering lip
Was bathed in her enchantments—whose brow
    burned
Beneath the crown, to which her secrets knelt;   20
Who learned the spell which can call up the dead,
And then departed, smiling like a fiend
Who has deceived God. If such one should seek

---

5 *1868* fear;   11 *1868* Ah dearest,   12 *1868* veins! Thou   15
1868 soul as . . . . star!   19 *1868* enchantments,   20 *1868* crown to
. . . . knelt,   23 *1868* God,—if *Mill* God:—If

PAULINE
[1888]

PAULINE, mine own, bend o'er me—thy soft
   breast
Shall pant to mine—bend o'er me—thy sweet
   eyes,
And loosened hair and breathing lips, and arms
Drawing me to thee—these build up a screen
To shut me in with thee, and from all fear;   5
So that I might unlock the sleepless brood
Of fancies from my soul, their lurking-place,
Nor doubt that each would pass, ne'er to return
To one so watched, so loved and so secured.
But what can guard thee but thy naked love?   10
Ah dearest, whoso sucks a poisoned wound
Envenoms his own veins! Thou art so good,
So calm—if thou shouldst wear a brow less light
For some wild thought which, but for me, were
   kept
From out thy soul as from a sacred star!   15
Yet till I have unlocked them it were vain
To hope to sing; some woe would light on me;
Nature would point at one whose quivering lip
Was bathed in her enchantments, whose brow
   burned
Beneath the crown to which her secrets knelt,   20
Who learned the spell which can call up the dead,
And then departed smiling like a fiend
Who has deceived God,—if such one should seek

15 *a sacred star*: cf. Shelley, 'The Witch of Atlas', 192: 'Harmonious as the
sacred stars above'.
   18 *Nature would point at one*: 'not I think an appropriate image—and it throws
considerable obscurity over the meaning of the passage': Mill.
   whose quivering lip: cf. Shelley, *Alastor* 291: 'his quivering lips.'
   19 *her enchantments*: the speaker is acquainted with forbidden knowledge.
   21 *Who learned the spell*: Pottle compares *Alastor*, 23–9. Cf. *Sordello*, i. 7 ff.

Again her altars, and stand robed and crowned
Amid the faithful: sad confession first,   25
Remorse and pardon, and old claims renewed,
Ere I can be—as I shall be no more.

I had been spared this shame, if I had sate
By thee for ever, from the first, in place
Of my wild dreams of beauty and of good,   30
Or with them, as an earnest of their truth.
No thought nor hope, having been shut from
     thee,
No vague wish unexplained—no wandering aim
Sent back to bind on Fancy's wings, and seek
Some strange fair world, where it might be a law;   35
But doubting nothing, had been led by thee,
Thro' youth, and saved, as one at length awaked,
Who has slept thro' a peril. Ah! vain, vain!

Thou lovest me—the past is in its grave,
Tho' its ghost haunts us—still this much is ours,   40
To cast away restraint, lest a worse thing
Wait for us in the darkness. Thou lovest me,
And thou art to receive not love, but faith,
For which thou wilt be mine, and smile, and take
All shapes, and shames, and veil without a fear   45
That form which music follows like a slave;
And I look to thee, and I trust in thee,
As in a Northern night one looks alway
Unto the East for morn, and spring and joy.
Thou seest then my aimless, hopeless state,   50
And resting on some few old feelings, won
Back by thy beauty, would'st that I essay.

31 *1868* truth: 32 *1868* hope   33 *1868* unexplained,   34 *1868*
fancy's wings   36 *Mill* But, doubting . . . . thee   38 *1868* through
a peril. Ah vain,   {*1868* consistently expands "tho'" and "thro'"}
39 *1868* me; the . . . . grave   40 *1868* us;   42 *1868* me;   51 *1868*
And, resting . . . . feelings

Again her altars and stand robed and crowned
Amid the faithful! Sad confession first,   25
Remorse and pardon and old claims renewed,
Ere I can be—as I shall be no more.

I had been spared this shame if I had sat
By thee for ever from the first, in place
Of my wild dreams of beauty and of good,   30
Or with them, as an earnest of their truth:
No thought nor hope having been shut from
    thee,
No vague wish unexplained, no wandering aim
Sent back to bind on fancy's wings and seek
Some strange fair world where it might be a law; 35
But, doubting nothing, had been led by thee,
Thro' youth, and saved, as one at length awaked
Who has slept through a peril. Ah vain, vain!

Thou lovest me; the past is in its grave
Tho' its ghost haunts us; still this much is ours,   40
To cast away restraint, lest a worse thing
Wait for us in the dark. Thou lovest me;
And thou art to receive not love but faith,
For which thou wilt be mine, and smile and take
All shapes and shames, and veil without a fear   45
That form which music follows like a slave:
And I look to thee and I trust in thee,
As in a Northern night one looks alway
Unto the East for morn and spring and joy.
Thou seest then my aimless, hopeless state,   50
And, resting on some few old feelings won
Back by thy beauty, wouldst that I essay

---

27 *as I shall be no more*: cf. the epigraph. Mill: 'same remark' (as on 18).
36 *But, doubting nothing*: 'not even *poetically* grammatical': Mill.
39 *the past*: cf. Shelley, *Epipsychidion*, 520–2: 'high Spirits call . . . the past /
Out of its grave', and *The Revolt of Islam*, 1819–20: 'let the past / Be as a grave
which gives not up its dead' (Pottle).
42 *in the dark*: cf. *Strafford*, II. ii. 41, one of many passages leading up to the
nightmare of 'Childe Roland to the Dark Tower Came'.
45–6 *and veil . . . which music follows like a slave*: 'qu. meaning?': Mill. Cf. Shelley,
'With a Guitar, to Jane', 1–2: 'Ariel to Miranda:—Take / This slave of Music'.
Cf. pp. 8–9, on Eliza Flower.

The task, which was to me what now thou art:
And why should I conceal one weakness more?

Thou wilt remember one warm morn, when
    Winter   55
Crept aged from the earth, and Spring's first
    breath
Blew soft from the moist hills—the black-thorn
    boughs,
So dark in the bare wood; when glistening
In the sunshine were white with coming buds,
Like the bright side of a sorrow—and the banks   60
Had violets opening from sleep like eyes—
I walked with thee, who knew not a deep
    shame
Lurked beneath smiles and careless words, which
      sought
To hide it—till they wandered and were mute;
As we stood listening on a sunny mound   65
To the wind murmuring in the damp copse,
Like heavy breathings of some hidden thing
Betrayed by sleep—until the feeling rushed
That I was low indeed, yet not so low
As to endure the calmness of thine eyes;   70
And so I told thee all, while the cool breast
I leaned on altered not its quiet beating;
And long ere words, like a hurt bird's complaint,
Bade me look up and be what I had been,
I felt despair could never live by thee.   75
Thou wilt remember:—thou art not more dear
Than song was once to me; and I ne'er sung
But as one entering bright halls, where all
Will rise and shout for him. Sure I must own
That I am fallen—having chosen gifts   80

55 *Lowell* morn when Winter *1868* morn when winter   56 *Lowell*
Spring's *1868* spring's   57 *1868* hills;   58 *1868* wood,   60 *1868*
sorrow,   61 *1868* eyes.   64 *1868* it till . . . . mute,   68 *1868*
sleep;   72 *1868* beating,   75 *1868* thee: 76 *1868* remember.
Thou   78 *1868* halls   79 *1868* him: sure   80 *1868* fallen,

The task which was to me what now thou art:
And why should I conceal one weakness more?

Thou wilt remember one warm morn when
    winter   55
Crept aged from the earth, and spring's first
    breath
Blew soft from the moist hills; the black-thorn
    boughs,
So dark in the bare wood, when glistening
In the sunshine were white with coming buds,
Like the bright side of a sorrow, and the banks   60
Had violets opening from sleep like eyes.
I walked with thee who knew'st not a deep
    shame
Lurked beneath smiles and careless words which
    sought
To hide it till they wandered and were mute,
As we stood listening on a sunny mound   65
To the wind murmuring in the damp copse,
Like heavy breathings of some hidden thing
Betrayed by sleep; until the feeling rushed
That I was low indeed, yet not so low
As to endure the calmness of thine eyes.   70
And so I told thee all, while the cool breast
I leaned on altered not its quiet beating:
And long ere words like a hurt bird's complaint
Bade me look up and be what I had been,
I felt despair could never live by thee: 75
Thou wilt remember. Thou art not more dear
Than song was once to me; and I ne'er sung
But as one entering bright halls where all
Will rise and shout for him: sure I must own
That I am fallen, having chosen gifts   80

---

56 *spring's first breath*: Pottle compares *Queen Mab*. ix. 167 ('Spring's awaken-
ing breath'), as well as *The Revolt of Islam*, 2221–2 and *Alastor*, 11–12.
   60 *the bright side of a sorrow*: the 'silver lining', as in *Comus*, 221.
   69–70 *That I was low . . . eyes*: 'not *distinct* enough': Mill.
   70 *the calmness of thine eyes*: cf. the sonnet, 'Eyes, calm beside thee', published
in 1834: see Appendix E, below.

Distinct from theirs—that I am sad—and fain
Would give up all to be but where I was;
Not high as I had been, if faithful found—
But low and weak, yet full of hope, and sure
Of goodness as of life—that I would lose   85
All this gay mastery of mind, to sit
Once more with them, trusting in truth and love,
And with an aim—not being what I am.
Oh, Pauline! I am ruined! who believed
That tho' my soul had floated from its sphere   90
Of wide dominion into the dim orb
Of self—that it was strong and free as ever:—
It has conformed itself to that dim orb,
Reflecting all its shades and shapes, and now
Must stay where it alone can be adored.   95
I have felt this in dreams—in dreams in which
I seemed the fate from which I fled; I felt
A strange delight in causing my decay;
I was a fiend, in darkness chained for ever
Within some ocean-cave; and ages rolled,   100
Till thro' the cleft rock, like a moonbeam, came
A white swan to remain with me; and ages
Rolled, yet I tired not of my first joy
In gazing on the peace of its pure wings.
And then I said, "It is most fair to me,   105
"Yet its soft wings must sure have suffered
      change
"From the thick darkness—sure its eyes are dim—
"Its silver pinions must be cramped and numbed
"With sleeping ages here; it cannot leave me,

81 *1868* sad   82 *1868* was,   83 *1868* been if faithful found,   91
Lowell Of wide dominion   *1868* Of wild dominion   92 *1868* self—that it. . . .
ever! *Mill* that>yet   104 *1868* wings: 107 *1868* darkness, sure
. . . . dim,

Distinct from theirs—that I am sad and fain
Would give up all to be but where I was,
Not high as I had been if faithful found,
But low and weak yet full of hope, and sure
Of goodness as of life—that I would lose   85
All this gay mastery of mind, to sit
Once more with them, trusting in truth and love
And with an aim—not being what I am.

Oh Pauline, I am ruined who believed
That though my soul had floated from its sphere   90
Of wide dominion into the dim orb
Of self—that it was strong and free as ever!
It has conformed itself to that dim orb,
Reflecting all its shades and shapes, and now
Must stay where it alone can be adored.   95
I have felt this in dreams—in dreams in which
I seemed the fate from which I fled; I felt
A strange delight in causing my decay.
I was a fiend in darkness chained for ever
Within some ocean-cave; and ages rolled,   100
Till through the cleft rock, like a moonbeam, came
A white swan to remain with me; and ages
Rolled, yet I tired not of my first free joy
In gazing on the peace of its pure wings:
And then I said "It is most fair to me,   105
"Yet its soft wings must sure have suffered
     change
"From the thick darkness, sure its eyes are dim,
"Its silver pinions must be cramped and numbed
"With sleeping ages here; it cannot leave me,

*91 {Reading of *Lowell*} *1888, 89* Of wild dominion

81 *theirs*: referring to 'all' in l.78.
91 *wide dominion*: cf. *Prometheus Unbound*, I. 763 and 'Prince Athanase', 257.
93 *dim orb*: cf. *Prometheus Unbound*, III. ii. 2–3.
95 *where it alone can be adored*: 'the poet, having become self-centred, cannot worship anything beyond himself, but . . . he realises he is his own worst enemy': Wallis, p. 76.
99–100 *a fiend . . . Within some ocean-cave*: cf. *The Revolt of Islam*, 3535: 'Some said, I was a fiend from my weird cave'; and *Hellas*, 524: 'And ravening Famine left his ocean cave'. As Pottle remarks, 'This whole passage is very Shelleyan'.
102 *A white swan*: in classical mythology the swan is sacred to Apollo.

"For it would seem, in light, beside its kind,   110
"Withered—tho' here to me most beautiful."
And then I was a young witch, whose blue eyes,
As she stood naked by the river springs,
Drew down a god—I watched his radiant form
Growing less radiant—and it gladdened me;   115
Till one morn, as he sat in the sunshine
Upon my knees, singing to me of heaven,
He turned to look at me, ere I could lose
The grin with which I viewed his perishing.
And he shrieked and departed, and sat long   120
By his deserted throne—but sunk at last,
Murmuring, as I kissed his lips and curled
Around him, "I am still a god—to thee."
Still I can lay my soul bare in its fall,
For all the wandering and all the weakness   125
Will be a saddest comment on the song.
And if, that done, I can be young again,
I will give up all gained as willingly
As one gives up a charm which shuts him out
From hope, or part, or care, in human kind.   130
As life wanes, all its cares, and strife, and toil,
Seem strangely valueless, while the old trees
Which grew by our youth's home—the waving
        mass
Of climbing plants, heavy with bloom and
        dew—
The morning swallows with their songs like
        words,—   135
All these seem clear and only worth our
        thoughts.
So aught connected with my early life——
My rude songs or my wild imaginings,

110 *1868* light   112 *1868* "Withered,   114 *1868* god;   115 *1868*
radiant   119 *1868* perishing: 121 *Lowell* throne, but . . . . last,
1868 throne, but . . . .last   126 *1868* song: 130 *1868* hope or part
or care   131 *1868* cares and strife and toil   133 *1868* home,   134
1868 plants . . . . dew,   135 *1868* words,   136 *1868* thoughts:
137 *Lowell* So, aught . . . . life   *1868* So, aught . . . . life,

"For it would seem, in light beside its kind,   110
"Withered, tho' here to me most beautiful."
And then I was a young witch whose blue eyes,
As she stood naked by the river springs,
Drew down a god: I watched his radiant form
Growing less radiant, and it gladdened me;   115
Till one morn, as he sat in the sunshine
Upon my knees, singing to me of heaven,
He turned to look at me, ere I could lose
The grin with which I viewed his perishing:
And he shrieked and departed and sat long   120
By his deserted throne, but sunk at last
Murmuring, as I kissed his lips and curled
Around him, "I am still a god—to thee."

Still I can lay my soul bare in its fall,
Since all the wandering and all the weakness   125
Will be a saddest comment on the song:
And if, that done, I can be young again,
I will give up all gained, as willingly
As one gives up a charm which shuts him out
From hope or part or care in human kind.   130
As life wanes, all its care and strife and toil
Seem strangely valueless, while the old trees
Which grew by our youth's home, the waving
      mass
Of climbing plants heavy with bloom and
      dew,
The morning swallows with their songs like
      words,   135
All these seem clear and only worth our
      thoughts:
So, aught connected with my early life,
My rude songs or my wild imaginings,

114 *radiant form*: cf. *Prometheus Unbound* II. i. 64, III. iv. 155–6, and *Epipsychid-ion* 22.
    122 *Murmuring*: at the foot of p. 12, which ends with this line, Mill wrote: 'a curious idealization of self-worship, very fine, though'.
    132 *Seem strangely valueless*: cf. *Paracelsus*, III. 125.
    136 *clear*: underlined, no doubt by Mill, with a question-mark in the margin.

How I look on them—most distinct amid
The fever and the stir of after years!   140

I ne'er had ventured e'en to hope for this,
Had not the glow I felt at His award,
Assured me all was not extinct within.
Him whom all honor—whose renown springs up
Like sunlight which will visit all the world;   145
So that e'en they who sneered at him at first,
Come out to it, as some dark spider crawls
From his foul nets, which some lit torch invades,
Yet spinning still new films for his retreat.—
Thou didst smile, poet,—but, can *we* forgive?   150

Sun-treader—life and light be thine for ever;
Thou art gone from us—years go by—and spring
Gladdens, and the young earth is beautiful,
Yet thy songs come not—other bards arise,
But none like thee—they stand—thy majesties,   155
Like mighty works which tell some Spirit there
Hath sat regardless of neglect and scorn,
Till, its long task completed, it hath risen
And left us, never to return: and all
Rush in to peer and praise when all in vain.   160
The air seems bright with thy past presence yet,
But thou art still for me, as thou hast been

141 *Lowell* {as *1833*.}   *1868* ventured e'er to hope for this;   143 *1868*
within: 144 *1868* His whom all honor,   145 *1868* world,   149
1868 retreat.   150 *1868* poet, but can we forgive? {No paragraph
division.}   151 *1868* Sun-treader, life . . . . ever!   152 *1868* us; years
go by   154 *1868* not,   155 *1868* thee: they stand,   156 *1868*
spirit   159 *1868* return,

How I look on them—most distinct amid
The fever and the stir of after years!   140

I ne'er had ventured e'en to hope for this,
Had not the glow I felt at His award,
Assured me all was not extinct within:
His whom all honour, whose renown springs up
Like sunlight which will visit all the world,   145
So that e'en they who sneered at him at first,
Come out to it, as some dark spider crawls
From his foul nets which some lit torch invades,
Yet spinning still new films for his retreat.
Thou didst smile, poet, but can we forgive?   150

Sun-treader, life and light be thine for ever!
Thou art gone from us; years go by and spring
Gladdens and the young earth is beautiful,
Yet thy songs come not, other bards arise,
But none like thee: they stand, thy majesties,   155
Like mighty works which tell some spirit there
Hath sat regardless of neglect and scorn,
Till, its long task completed, it hath risen
And left us, never to return, and all
Rush in to peer and praise when all in vain.   160
The air seems bright with thy past presence yet,
But thou art still for me as thou hast been

140 *The fever and the stir*: cf. Wordsworth, 'Tintern Abbey', 52–3, and Keats, 'Ode to a Nightingale', 23.

142 His *award*: 'what does this mean? *His* opinion of yourself? only at the fourth reading of the poem I found out what this meant.' Mill. 'The award of fame to Him—The late acknowledgment of Shelley's genius': Browning. Cf. 419 ff., below. As Maynard points out (p. 209), Browning was probably thinking particularly of Medwin's 'Memoir of Shelley', serialized in the *Athenæum* in July and August 1832.

147 *as some dark spider*: 'bad simile the spider does not detest or scorn[?] the light': Mill.

151 *Sun-treader*: cf. Æschylus, *Prometheus Bound*, 791: πρὸς ἀντολὰς φλογῶπας ἡλιωτιβεῖς, 'toward the flaming dawn, sun-trodden'. Shelley thus becomes the dawn.

155 *majesties*: majestic achievements. Cf. *Sordello*, ii. 679, *Christmas-Eve* 723 ('the majesties of Art'), and *Parleyings*, *Avison* 52–3 ('the band / Of majesties familiar').

161 *The air seems bright*: cf. *Adonais* 494–5: 'The soul of Adonais, like a star, / Beacons from the abode where the Eternal are', and 'Hymn of Apollo', 10–11.

When I have stood with thee, as on a throne
With all thy dim creations gathered round
Like mountains,—and I felt of mould like them,   165
And creatures of my own were mixed with them,
Like things half-lived, catching and giving life.
But thou art still for me, who have adored,
Tho' single, panting but to hear thy name,
Which I believed a spell to me alone,   170
Scarce deeming thou wert as a star to men—
As one should worship long a sacred spring
Scarce worth a moth's flitting, which long grasses
    cross,
And one small tree embowers droopingly,
Joying to see some wandering insect won,   175
To live in its few rushes—or some locust
To pasture on its boughs—or some wild bird
Stoop for its freshness from the trackless air,
And then should find it but the fountain-head,
Long lost, of some great river—washing towns   180
And towers, and seeing old woods which will
    live
But by its banks, untrod of human foot,
Which, when the great sun sinks, lie quivering
In light as some thing lieth half of life
Before God's foot—waiting a wondrous change   185
—Then girt with rocks which seek to turn or stay
Its course in vain, for it does ever spread
Like a sea's arm as it goes rolling on,
Being the pulse of some great country—so
Wert thou to me—and art thou to the world.   190
And I, perchance, half feel a strange regret,

165 *1868* mountains, and   168 *1868* adored   171 *1868* Scarce deem-
ing thou wast as a star to men! *Mill* Scarce>Not men—>men:
176 *1868* rushes,   177 *1868* boughs,   178 *1868* air: 180 *1868*
river   182 *1868* banks   185 *1868* foot, waiting. . . .change;
186 *1868* Then   187 *Mill* course > course—   190 *1868* Wast thou to
me, and . . . . world!

When I have stood with thee as on a throne
With all thy dim creations gathered round
Like mountains, and I felt of mould like them,   165
And with them creatures of my own were mixed,
Like things half-lived, catching and giving life.
But thou art still for me who have adored
Tho' single, panting but to hear thy name
Which I believed a spell to me alone,   170
Scarce deeming thou wast as a star to men!
As one should worship long a sacred spring
Scarce worth a moth's flitting, which long grasses
    cross,
And one small tree embowers droopingly—
Joying to see some wandering insect won   175
To live in its few rushes, or some locust
To pasture on its boughs, or some wild bird
Stoop for its freshness from the trackless air:
And then should find it but the fountain-head,
Long lost, of some great river washing towns   180
And towers, and seeing old woods which will
    live
But by its banks untrod of human foot,
Which, when the great sun sinks, lie quivering
In light as some thing lieth half of life
Before God's foot, waiting a wondrous change;   185
Then girt with rocks which seek to turn or stay
Its course in vain, for it does ever spread
Like a sea's arm as it goes rolling on,
Being the pulse of some great country—so
Wast thou to me, and art thou to the world!   190
And I, perchance, half feel a strange regret

163–7 *When . . . life*: 'beautiful': Mill.
165 *of mould like them*: of similar nature to them.
167 *half-lived*: half endowed with life. Cf. l.184.
168 *But thou art still for me*: cf. l.162. The sentence is lost in a series of subordinate clauses: cf. ll.189–90.
169 *single*: alone in my adoration.
171 *a star to men!*: cf. l.161 n, above.
174 *embowers droopingly*: 'embowers' is a Miltonic word (*Paradise Lost*, ix. 1038) used by Shelley (in its various forms) in *Alastor* 404, 580, and elsewhere: 'drooping' occurs in lines 407, 501, and 601 of the same poem. Mill wrote '*most beautiful*' opposite lines 173–80.
178 *the trackless air*: as in *The Witch of Atlas*, 115.
184 *half of life*: half alive (cf. OED, 'life', IV.14.c): cf. 167.

That I am not what I have been to thee:
Like a girl one has loved long silently,
In her first loveliness, in some retreat,
When first emerged, all gaze and glow to view   195
Her fresh eyes, and soft hair, and lips which bleed
Like a mountain berry. Doubtless it is sweet
To see her thus adored—but there have been
Moments, when all the world was in his praise,
Sweeter than all the pride of after hours.   200
Yet, Sun-treader, all hail!—from my heart's heart
I bid thee hail!—e'en in my wildest dreams,
I am proud to feel I would have thrown up all
The wreathes of fame which seemed o'erhanging
    me,
To have seen thee, for a moment, as thou art.   205

And if thou livest—if thou lovest, spirit!
Remember me, who set this final seal
To wandering thought—that one so pure as thou
Could never die. Remember me, who flung
All honor from my soul—yet paused and said,   210
"There is one spark of love remaining yet,
"For I have nought in common with
    him—shapes
"Which followed him avoid me, and foul forms
"Seek me, which ne'er could fasten on his mind;

193 *1868* silently   194 *1868* loveliness   197 *1868* berry: doubt-
less   198 *1868* adored,   201 *1868* sun-treader, all hail!
From   202 *1868* I bid thee hail! E'en *Mill* bid > bid: 205 *1868* thee
for a moment {No paragraph division.}   206 *1868* livest,   210 *1868*
honor from my soul . . . . said,   212 *1868* him,

That I am not what I have been to thee:
Like a girl one has silently loved long
In her first loneliness in some retreat,
When, late emerged, all gaze and glow to view   195
Her fresh eyes and soft hair and lips which bloom
Like a mountain berry: doubtless it is sweet
To see her thus adored, but there have been
Moments when all the world was in our praise,
Sweeter than any pride of after hours.   200
Yet, sun-treader, all hail! From my heart's heart
I bid thee hail! E'en in my wildest dreams,
I proudly feel I would have thrown to dust
The wreaths of fame which seemed o'erhanging
    me,
To see thee for a moment as thou art.   205

And if thou livest, if thou lovest, spirit!
Remember me who set this final seal
To wandering thought—that one so pure as thou
Could never die. Remember me who flung
All honour from my soul, yet paused and said   210
"There is one spark of love remaining yet,
"For I have nought in common with him, shapes
"Which followed him avoid me, and foul forms
"Seek me, which ne'er could fasten on his mind;

199 *when all the world was in his praise* (*1833*): 'obscurely expressed': Mill. The word 'his' no doubt refers to 'one' in 193. It is delightful to feel that one is the only person to appreciate the beauty of a girl, so that one's praise represents that of the whole world.

201 *From my heart's heart*: cf. *Hamlet*, III. ii. 71: 'In my heart's core, ay, in my heart of heart'.

204 *The wreaths of fame*: cf. Keats, 'Sleep and Poetry', 35–6: 'To see the laurel wreath on high suspended / That is to crown our name when life is ended'. At the top of p. 18, which begins with this line, Mill wrote: 'The passages where the meaning is so imperfectly expressed as not to be easily understood, will be marked X'. Excluding those which are here accompanied by a note, these are ll. 207–8 ('set . . . thought' underlined), 338 ('I never doubted'), 373–4, 517–8, 557 ('I'd be sad to equal them'), 585–7, 599–600, 636 ('In their elements'), 670 ('Yet sunk by error to men's sympathy'), 672 ('As to call up their fears'), 676–7, and 921–2.

205 *To see thee*: cf. 'Memorabilia': 'Ah, did you once see Shelley plain . . .?'
207–8 *set . . . thought*: came to this final conclusion.

213–14 *Which followed him . . . his mind*: Mill comments: 'the obscurity of this is the greater fault as the meaning if I can *guess* it right is really poetical'.

"And tho' I feel how low I am to him,   215
"Yet I aim not even to catch a tone
"Of all the harmonies which he called up,
"So one gleam still remains, altho' the last."
Remember me—who praise thee e'en with tears,
For never more shall I walk calm with thee;   220
Thy sweet imaginings are as an air,
A melody, some wond'rous singer sings,
Which, though it haunt men oft in the still eve,
They dream not to essay; yet it no less,
But more is honored. I was thine in shame,   225
And now when all thy proud renown is out,
I am a watcher, whose eyes have grown dim
With looking for some star—which breaks on
     him,
Altered, and worn, and weak, and full of tears.

Autumn has come—like Spring returned to us,   230
Won from her girlishness—like one returned
A friend that was a lover—nor forgets
The first warm love, but full of sober thoughts
Of fading years; whose soft mouth quivers yet
With the old smile—but yet so changed and still!   235
And here am I the scoffer, who have probed
Life's vanity, won by a word again
Into my old life—for one little word
Of this sweet friend, who lives in loving me,
Lives strangely on my thoughts, and looks, and
     words,   240
As fathoms down some nameless ocean thing
Its silent course of quietness and joy.
O dearest, if, indeed, I tell the past,
May'st thou forget it as a sad sick dream;

217 *1868* up;   219 *1868* me   228 *1868* star which .... him
229 *1868* Altered and worn and weak   230 *Lowell* come like Spring
1868 come like spring   231 *1868* girlishness;   232 *1868* lover
235 *1868* smile   238 *Lowell* {as *1833*}   *1868* my own life—for
one   244 *1868* Mayst .... dream!

"And though I feel how low I am to him,   215
"Yet I aim not even to catch a tone
"Of harmonies he called profusely up;
"So, one gleam still remains, although the last."
Remember me who praise thee e'en with tears,
For never more shall I walk calm with thee;   220
Thy sweet imaginings are as an air,
A melody some wondrous singer sings,
Which, though it haunt men oft in the still eve,
They dream not to essay; yet it no less
But more is honoured. I was thine in shame,   225
And now when all thy proud renown is out,
I am a watcher whose eyes have grown dim
With looking for some star which breaks on
       him
Altered and worn and weak and full of tears.

Autumn has come like spring returned to us,   230
Won from her girlishness; like one returned
A friend that was a lover, nor forgets
The first warm love, but full of sober thoughts
Of fading years; whose soft mouth quivers yet
With the old smile, but yet so changed and still!   235
And here am I the scoffer, who have probed
Life's vanity, won by a word again
Into my old life—by one little word
Of this sweet friend who lives in loving me,
Lives strangely on my thoughts and looks and
       words,   240
As fathoms down some nameless ocean thing
Its silent course of quietness and joy.

O dearest, if indeed I tell the past,
May'st thou forget it as a sad sick dream!

---

*238 {Reading based on *Lowell*.}   *1888,89* my own life—by one

222–9 *A melody . . . full of tears*: 'beautiful': Mill.
225 *in shame*: when Shelley was unhonoured.
230–5 *Autumn . . . still!*: 'beautiful', Mill, who also underlined 'full of sober
thoughts/ Of fading years' and commented 'might be improved'.
230 *Autumn has come*: see Introduction on the probable date of composition.

Or if it linger—my lost soul too soon　　　245
Sinks to itself, and whispers, we shall be
But closer linked—two creatures whom the earth
Bears singly—with strange feelings, unrevealed
But to each other; or two lonely things
Created by some Power, whose reign is done,　　250
Having no part in God, or his bright world,
I am to sing; whilst ebbing day dies soft,
As a lean scholar dies, worn o'er his book,
And in the heaven stars steal out one by one,
As hunted men steal to their mountain watch.　　255
I must not think—lest this new impulse die
In which I trust. I have no confidence,
So I will sing on—fast as fancies come
Rudely—the verse being as the mood it paints.

I strip my mind bare—whose first elements　　260
I shall unveil—not as they struggled forth
In infancy, nor as they now exist,
That I am grown above them, and can rule them,
But in that middle stage, when they were full,
Yet ere I had disposed them to my will;　　265
And then I shall show how these elements
Produced my present state, and what it is.
I am made up of an intensest life,
Of a most clear idea of consciousness
Of self—distinct from all its qualities,　　270

247 *1868* linked,　　248 *1868* singly, with strange feelings　　250 *1868* power　　251 *1868* God or his bright world.　　252 *1868* sing　　256 *1868* think,　　257 *1868* trust; I . . . . confidence:　　258 *1868* So, I will sing on fast . . . . come;　　259 *1868* Rudely, the . . . . paints.　　260 *1868* bare,　　263 *1868* That I am grown above them and can rule—　270 *1868* self,

Or if it linger—my lost soul too soon   245
Sinks to itself and whispers we shall be
But closer linked, two creatures whom the earth
Bears singly, with strange feelings unrevealed
Save to each other; or two lonely things
Created by some power whose reign is done,   250
Having no part in God or his bright world.
I am to sing whilst ebbing day dies soft,
As a lean scholar dies worn o'er his book,
And in the heaven stars steal out one by one
As hunted men steal to their mountain watch.   255
I must not think, lest this new impulse die
In which I trust; I have no confidence:
So, I will sing on fast as fancies come;
Rudely, the verse being as the mood it paints.

I strip my mind bare, whose first elements   260
I shall unveil—not as they struggled forth
In infancy, nor as they now exist,
When I am grown above them and can rule—
But in that middle stage when they were full
Yet ere I had disposed them to my will;   265
And then I shall show how these elements
Produced my present state, and what it is.
I am made up of an intensest life,
Of a most clear idea of consciousness
Of self, distinct from all its qualities,   270

*259 {Reading of 1868} 1888,89 paints   *263 {Reading based on 1868}
1888,89 rule   {1888 has an imperfectly printed mark like a hyphen after
'rule'.}

   260 *I strip my mind bare*: probably a reminiscence of Descartes. 'Il se dépouille
de toute croyance, et réduit toute sa science à ce fait unique, à cette proposition,
la seule évidente pour lui, "Je pense, donc je suis"': *Biographie Universelle*, xi.
152. A vertical pencil line through 260–7 may be a deletion or simply a direc-
tion-sign to Mill's pencilled comment: 'this only says "you shall see what
you shall see" & is more prose than poetry'.
   261 *I shall unveil*: cf. Shelley, 'Scenes from the "Magico Prodigioso" of
Calderon', ii. 104–5: 'I will then unveil / Myself to thee'.
   269–70 *consciousness / Of self*: it is a central idealist doctrine that true know-
ledge must be regarded as a form of self-consciousness. Cf. Hegel, *The
Phenomenology of Mind*, trans. J. B. Baillie (2nd ed., 1949), pp. 217 ff. ('The truth
which conscious certainty of self realizes'). Browning stated explicitly, how-
ever, that he 'never read a line, original or translated, by Kant, Schelling, or
Hegel in my whole life' (*Trumpeter*, p. 51).

From all affections, passions, feelings, powers;
And thus far it exists, if tracked in all,
But linked in me, to self-supremacy,
Existing as a centre to all things,
Most potent to create, and rule, and call   275
Upon all things to minister to it;
And to a principle of restlessness
Which would be all, have, see, know, taste, feel,
    all—
This is myself; and I should thus have been,
Though gifted lower than the meanest soul.   280

And of my powers, one springs up to save
From utter death a soul with such desires
Confined to clay—which is the only one
Which marks me—an imagination which
Has been an angel to me—coming not   285
In fitful visions, but beside me ever,
And never failing me; so tho' my mind
Forgets not—not a shred of life forgets—
Yet I can take a secret pride in calling
The dark past up—to quell it regally.   290

A mind like this must dissipate itself,
But I have always had one lode-star; now,
As I look back, I see that I have wasted,
Or progressed as I looked toward that star—
A need, a trust, a yearning after God,   295
A feeling I have analysed but late,
But it existed, and was reconciled
With a neglect of all I deemed his laws,
Which yet, when seen in others, I abhorred.
I felt as one beloved, and so shut in   300

271 *1868* all: 273 *1868* linked,   282 *1868* such desire   284
Mill me—an imagination>me,—an Imagination   285 *1868* me, com-
ing   288 *1868* Forgets not, not . . . . forgets,   290 *1868* past
up   294 *1868* towards that   295 *1868* God:

From all affections, passions, feelings, powers;
And thus far it exists, if tracked, in all:
But linked, in me, to self-supremacy,
Existing as a centre to all things,
Most potent to create and rule and call   275
Upon all things to minister to it;
And to a principle of restlessness
Which would be all, have, see, know, taste, feel,
    all—
This is myself; and I should thus have been
Though gifted lower than the meanest soul.   280

And of my powers, one springs up to save
From utter death a soul with such desire
Confined to clay—of powers the only one
Which marks me—an imagination which
Has been a very angel, coming not   285
In fitful visions but beside me ever
And never failing me; so, though my mind
Forgets not, not a shred of life forgets,
Yet I can take a secret pride in calling
The dark past up to quell it regally.   290

A mind like this must dissipate itself,
But I have always had one lode-star; now,
As I look back, I see that I have halted
Or hastened as I looked towards that star—
A need, a trust, a yearning after God: 295
A feeling I have analysed but late,
But it existed, and was reconciled
With a neglect of all I deemed his laws,
Which yet, when seen in others, I abhorred.
I felt as one beloved, and so shut in   300

273 *self-supremacy*: the supremacy of self.
284 *imagination*: 'not imagination but *I*magination The absence of that capital
letter obscures the meaning.': Mill. Browning capitalized the letter as if for
revision, but the revision was not made.
285 *a very angel*: cf. Campbell, *Gertrude of Wyoming*, I. xix: 'Like angel-visits,
few and far between', anticipated by John Norris (in 'The Parting', st. iv) and
Robert Blair (in *The Grave*, 587–8).
289–90 *in calling | The dark past up*: cf. l.21, and *Sordello* i. 18–9. The word
'quell' is something of a favourite of Browning's.
300–1 *shut in | From fear*: cf. ll.4–5.

From fear—and thence I date my trust in signs
And omens—for I saw God every where;
And I can only lay it to the fruit
Of a sad after-time that I could doubt
Even his being—having always felt   305
His presence—never acting from myself,
Still trusting in a hand that leads me through
All danger; and this feeling still has fought
Against my weakest reason and resolves.

And I can love nothing—and this dull truth   310
Has come the last—but sense supplies a love
Encircling me and mingling with my life.

These make myself—for I have sought in vain
To trace how they were formed by circumstance,
For I still find them—turning my wild youth   315
Where they alone displayed themselves,
     converting
All objects to their use—now see their course!

They came to me in my first dawn of life,
Which passed alone with wisest ancient books,
All halo-girt with fancies of my own,   320
And I myself went with the tale—a god,
Wandering after beauty—or a giant,
Standing vast in the sunset—an old hunter,
Talking with gods—or a high-crested chief,
Sailing with troops of friends to Tenedos;—   325

301 *1868* fear: 302 *1868* omens, for . . . . everywhere;   306 *1868*
presence,   309 *1868* and resolve.   311 *1868* last: 313 *1868*
myself: *Mill* myself— > *myself*—   315 *1868* them turning   *Mill* For
I still find them— > And I still find them   317 *1868* use: now . . . .
course.   320 *1868* own;   322 *1868* beauty, or a giant   324 *1868*
gods, or . . . . chief,   325 *1868* Tenedos.

From fear: and thence I date my trust in signs
And omens, for I saw God everywhere;
And I can only lay it to the fruit
Of a sad after-time that I could doubt
Even his being—e'en the while I felt   305
His presence, never acted from myself,
Still trusted in a hand to lead me through
All danger; and this feeling ever fought
Against my weakest reason and resolve.

And I can love nothing—and this dull truth   310
Has come the last: but sense supplies a love
Encircling me and mingling with my life.

These make myself: I have long sought in vain
To trace how they were formed by circumstance,
Yet ever found them mould my wildest youth   315
Where they alone displayed themselves,
        converted
All objects to their use: now see their course!

They came to me in my first dawn of life
Which passed alone with wisest ancient books
All halo-girt with fancies of my own;   320
And I myself went with the tale—a god
Wandering after beauty, or a giant
Standing vast in the sunset—an old hunter
Talking with gods, or a high-crested chief
Sailing with troops of friends to Tenedos.   325

---

303 *lay it to the fruit*: consider it as the result of.
304 *a sad after-time*: cf. *Alastor*, 265–6: 'many a dream / Of after-times'.
311–12 *sense . . . my life*: 'explain better what this means': Mill.
321–2 *a god / Wandering after beauty*: perhaps Apollo pursuing Daphne. See Ovid, *Metamorphoses*, i. 452 ff., and cf. *Sordello*, i. 937–8.
322 *a giant*: perhaps Atlas: cf. *Metamorphoses*, iv. 627 ff.
323 *an old hunter*: probably Orion: cf. *Paracelsus* ii. 422–3.
324 *high-crested*: cf. Pindar, *Olympian Odes*, xiii. 111–12: ταί θ' ὑπ' Αἴτνας ὑψιλόφου καλλίπλουτοι, 'and the cities beautiful in wealth below high-crested Etna'.
325 *Tenedos*: 'It became famous during the Trojan war, as it was there that the Greeks concealed themselves the more effectually to make the Trojans believe that they were returning home, without finishing the siege. Apollo was particularly worshipped there': Lemprière.

I tell you, nought has ever been so clear
As the place, the time, the fashion of those lives.
I had not seen a work of lofty art,
Nor woman's beauty, nor sweet nature's face,
Yet, I say, never morn broke clear as those   330
On the dim clustered isles in the blue sea:
The deep groves, and white temples, and wet
    caves—
And nothing ever will surprise me now—
Who stood beside the naked Swift-footed,
Who bound my forehead with Proserpine's hair.   335

An' strange it is, that I who could so dream,
Should e'er have stooped to aim at aught
    beneath—
Aught low, or painful, but I never doubted;
So as I grew, I rudely shaped my life
To my immediate wants, yet strong beneath   340
Was a vague sense of powers folded up—
A sense that tho' those shadowy times were
    past,
Their spirit dwelt in me, and I should rule.

327 *1868* lives: 331 *1868* sea,   332 *1868, 1889* groves . . . . temples
. . . . caves: 335 *Mill* Proserpine's > Prosérpine's   336 *1868* And
strange it is . . . . dream   338 *1868* low, or painful; but . . . . doubted,
339 *1868* So,   340 *1868* wants;

I tell you, nought has ever been so clear
As the place, the time, the fashion of those lives:
I had not seen a work of lofty art,
Nor woman's beauty nor sweet nature's face,
Yet, I say, never morn broke clear as those   330
On the dim clustered isles in the blue sea,
The deep groves and white temples and wet
    caves,
And nothing ever will surprise me now—
Who stood beside the naked Swift-footed,
Who bound my forehead with Proserpine's hair. 335

And strange it is that I who could so dream
Should e'er have stooped to aim at aught
    beneath—
Aught low or painful; but I never doubted:
So, as I grew, I rudely shaped my life
To my immediate wants; yet strong beneath   340
Was a vague sense of power though folded up—
A sense that, though those shades and times
    were past,
Their spirit dwelt in me, with them should rule.

---

*332{Reading of *1888* as corrected in DC}   *1888* caves   *1889* caves:

326 *nought has ever been so clear*: the best commentary on this whole passage is
'Development', in *Asolando*, a poem which emphasizes that the narrator of
Pauline and Browning himself have a good deal in common.

334 *the naked Swift-footed*: Hermes, whom Zeus sent to fetch Proserpine from
the underworld.

335 *Proserpine's hair*: Browning added a mark of accentuation above the
second syllable. The reference to her hair is obscure. Lemprière states that
'Proserpine presided over the death of mankind, and . . . no one could die, if
the goddess herself, or Atropos her minister, did not cut off one of the hairs
from the head. From this superstitious belief, it was usual to cut off some of the
hair of the deceased, and to strew it at the door of the house, as an offering to
Proserpine'. She is associated with the story of the Golden Bough (*Aeneid* vi.
142 ff.): cf. l.527, below.

341 *a vague sense of power*: cf. *Sordello*, v. 517 ff.

342 *those shadowy times*: 'what times? your own imaginative time? or the
antique times themselves?': Mill.

343 *Their spirit dwelt in me*: cf. Romans 8:9: 'if so be that the Spirit of God
dwell in you'.

Then came a pause, and long restraint chained
  down
My soul, till it was changed. I lost myself,   345
And were it not that I so loathe that time,
I could recall how first I learned to turn
My mind against itself; and the effects,
In deeds for which remorse were vain, as for
The wanderings of delirious dream; yet thence   350
Came cunning, envy, falsehood, which so
  long
Have spotted me—at length I was restored,
Yet long the influence remained; and nought
But the still life I led, apart from all,
Which left my soul to seek its old delights,   355
Could e'er have brought me thus far back to
  peace.
As peace returned, I sought out some pursuit:
And song rose—no new impulse—but the one
With which all others best could be combined.
My life has not been that of those whose heaven 360
Was lampless, save where poesy shone out;
But as a clime, where glittering mountain-tops,
And glancing sea, and forests steeped in light,
Give back reflected the far-flashing sun;
For music, (which is earnest of a heaven,   365

349 *1868* vain   352 *1868* me: at length I was restored.   358 *1868*
rose, no new impulse   361 *1868* lampless *Mill* Was lampless, ...
shone > Is lampless, ... shines   365 *1868* music (which . . . .
heaven, *Mill* heaven, > Heaven,

Then came a pause, and long restraint chained
    down
My soul till it was changed. I lost myself,   345
And were it not that I so loathe that loss,
I could recall how first I learned to turn
My mind against itself; and the effects
In deeds for which remorse were vain as for
The wanderings of delirious dream; yet thence   350
Came cunning, envy, falsehood, all world's
    wrong
That spotted me: at length I cleansed my soul.
Yet long world's influence remained; and nought
But the still life I led, apart once more,
Which left me free to seek soul's old delights,   355
Could e'er have brought me thus far back to
    peace.

As peace returned, I sought out some pursuit;
And song rose, no new impulse but the one
With which all others best could be combined.
My life has not been that of those whose heaven   360
Was lampless save where poesy shone out;
But as a clime where glittering mountain-tops
And glancing sea and forests steeped in light
Give back reflected the far-flashing sun;
For music (which is earnest of a heaven,   365

344–5 *chained down* / *My soul*: cf. ll. 504–5, 593, 631 and perhaps 639. Pottle
points out the similarity to 'Julian and Maddalo', 181 ('How strong the chains
are which our spirit bind') and (less close) to the 'Ode to the West Wind', 55–6.
    354 *the still life I led*: an anticipation of Sordello's return to recuperate in
Goito.
    361 *lampless*: a favourite word of Shelley's, as in *Epipsychidion*, 26 and 503.
    364 *the far-flashing sun*: cf. *Hellas*, 331: 'the far flashing of their starry lances'.
    365 *For music*: Maynard gives a good account of Browning's early love of
music. He mentions that Browning once said to a friend: 'I was so fond of
music, even as a child, that when I was nine years old I should have been very
indignant if you had told me that I was going to be anything else than a
musician'; and that he told Ripert-Monclar 'that music, more than poetry, had
been his chief interest for many years of his life': p. 140. See l. 565 below.
    365 *earnest of a heaven*: 'The apostle *Paul* speaks of *the earnest of the Spirit*, 2
Cor. I. 22 [&c] phrases [which] signify the assurance which the Spirit of
adoption does give believers of their inheritance in heaven': Cruden s.v.
'earnest'.

Seeing we know emotions strange by it,
Not else to be revealed,) is as a voice,
A low voice calling Fancy, as a friend,
To the green woods in the gay summer time.
And she fills all the way with dancing shapes,   370
Which have made painters pale; and they go on
While stars look at them, and winds call to them,
As they leave life's path for the twilight world,
Where the dead gather. This was not at first,
For I scarce knew what I would do. I had   375
No wish to paint, no yearning—but I sang.

   And first I sang, as I in dream have seen,
Music wait on a lyrist for some thought,
Yet singing to herself until it came.
I turned to those old times and scenes, where all   380
That's beautiful had birth for me, and made
Rude verses on them all; and then I paused—
I had done nothing, so I sought to know
What mind had yet achieved. No fear was mine
As I gazed on the works of mighty bards,   385
In the first joy at finding my own thoughts
Recorded, and my powers exemplified,
And feeling their aspirings were my own.
And then I first explored passion and mind;
And I began afresh; I rather sought   390
To rival what I wondered at, than form

Seeing we know emotions strange by it,
Not else to be revealed,) is like a voice,
A low voice calling fancy, as a friend,
To the green woods in the gay summer time:
And she fills all the way with dancing shapes   370
Which have made painters pale, and they go on
Till stars look at them and winds call to them
As they leave life's path for the twilight world
Where the dead gather. This was not at first,
For I scarce knew what I would do. I had   375
An impulse but no yearning—only sang.

And first I sang as I in dream have seen
Music wait on a lyrist for some thought,
Yet singing to herself until it came.
I turned to those old times and scenes where all   380
That's beautiful had birth for me, and made
Rude verses on them all; and then I paused—
I had done nothing, so I sought to know
What other minds achieved. No fear outbroke
As on the works of mighty bards I gazed,   385
In the first joy at finding my own thoughts
Recorded, my own fancies justified,
And their aspirings but my very own.
With them I first explored passion and mind,—
All to begin afresh! I rather sought   390
To rival what I wondered at than form

366–7 *Seeing we know . . . to be revealed*: Mill has a cross opposite these lines, with the query: 'do you mean is *to you* as a voice &c.?'
370 *she*: underlined by Mill: 'who? Fancy or Music?' No doubt Fancy: cf. ll. 510–16.
371 *pale*: with envy.
376 *No wish to paint* (*1833*): note revision.
378 *Music wait on a lyrist*: probably suggested by the 'Æolian harp', 'a stringed instrument adapted to produce musical sounds on exposure to a current of air': OED.

Creations of my own; so much was light
Lent back by others, yet much was my own.

I paused again—a change was coming on,
I was no more a boy—the past was breaking   395
Before the coming, and like fever worked.
I first thought on myself—and here my powers
Burst out. I dreamed not of restraint, but gazed
On all things: schemes and systems went and
        came,
And I was proud (being vainest of the weak),   400
In wandering o'er them, to seek out some
        one
To be my own; as one should wander o'er
The white way for a star.

                *   *   *   *

On one, whom praise of mine would not offend,   405
Who was as calm as beauty—being such
Unto mankind as thou to me, Pauline,
Believing in them, and devoting all

392 *1868* so, much   394 *1868* again,   395 *1868* boy,   397 *1868*
myself,   398 *1868* out: I . . . . restraint   401 *1868* them   402
1868 own,   403, 404 *1868* star. | And my choice fell | Not so much on a
system as a man—   405 *Mill* one, whom . . . . offend, > One, whom
. . . . offend;   406 *1868* beauty,   407 *1868* Pauline,—

Creations of my own; if much was light
Lent by the others, much was yet my own.

I paused again: a change was coming—came:
I was no more a boy, the past was breaking   395
Before the future and like fever worked.
I thought on my new self, and all my powers
Burst out. I dreamed not of restraint, but gazed
On all things: schemes and systems went and
    came,
And I was proud (being vainest of the weak)   400
In wandering o'er thought's world to seek some
    one
To be my prize, as if you wandered o'er
The White Way for a star.

                              And my choice fell
Not so much on a system as a man—
On one, whom praise of mine shall not offend,   405
Who was as calm as beauty, being such
Unto mankind as thou to me, Pauline,—
Believing in them and devoting all

---

392 *so much was light* (*1833*): at the foot of p. 29 Mill wrote: 'this writer seems
to use "*so*", according to the colloquial vulgarism, in the sense of "therefore"
or "accordingly"—from which occasionally comes great obscurity &
ambiguity—as here'. Browning replies: 'The *recurrence* of "*so*" thus employed
is as vulgar as you please: but the usage itself of "*so* in the sense of accordingly" is
perfectly authorized,—take an instance or two, from Milton. So farewel Hope,
& with Hope farewel Fear! P.L.4.108 So on he fares, and to the border comes
Of Eden, do. 132. So down they sat and to their viands fell. 5.433. So both
ascend In the visions of God 11.376. So death becomes his final remedy 11.60.
So in his seed all nations shall be blest 12.450. So law appears imperfect 12.300.
So all shall turn degenerate 11.806. So violence proceeded, and oppression
11.671 So send them forth, tho sorrowing yet in peace 11.117.' In *1868*
Browning added a comma, to guard against ambiguity: in *1888* 'if' is substi-
tuted for 'so'.
395 *the past was breaking*: frost is said to 'break' or dissolve. Mill underlined
the words 'past' to 'coming', with a cross.
396 *the coming* (*1833*): the future, described by OED as rare, its only example
being later. Eliminated on revision.
396 *worked*: fermented. Cf. Scott, *Kenilworth*, xxxiv: 'Men's brains are
working like yeast'.
403 *The White Way*: the Milky Way.
404 *a man*: Shelley.
405 *one*: the suggested revision to 'One' in *Mill* is comparable to 'To look on
One' in *Childe Harold's Pilgrimage*, III. lxxvi. 4 (referring to Rousseau).

His soul's strength to their winning back to
    peace;
Who sent forth hopes and longings for their sake,   410
Clothed in all passion's melodies, which first
Caught me, and set me, as to a sweet task,
To gather every breathing of his songs.
And woven with them there were words, which
    seemed
A key to a new world; the muttering   415
Of angels, of some thing unguessed by man.
How my heart beat, as I went on, and found
Much there! I felt my own mind had conceived,
But there living and burning; soon the whole
Of his conceptions dawned on me; their praise   420
Is in the tongues of men; men's brows are
    high
When his name means a triumph and a pride;
So my weak hands may well forbear to dim
What then seemed my bright fate: I threw myself
To meet it. I was vowed to liberty,   425
Men were to be as gods, and earth as heaven.
And I—ah! what a life was mine to be,
My whole soul rose to meet it. Now, Pauline,
I shall go mad, if I recall that time.

        *   *   *   *

   O let me look back, e'er I leave for ever   430
The time, which was an hour, that one waits
For a fair girl, that comes a withered hag.
And I was lonely,—far from woods and fields,
And amid dullest sights, who should be loose
As a stag—yet I was full of joy—who lived   435
With Plato—and who had the key to life.

413 *1868* songs: 415 *1868* world,   418 *1868* there,   419 *1868*
burning! Soon   421   *1868* men,   422 *Lowell* pride.   *1868*
pride,   423 *1868* So,   425 *Lowell* it: I was   *1868* it, I was   426
1868 gods and . . . . heaven,   427 *1868* ah, what . . . . to be!   *Mill* be, >
be.   429 *1868* time!   431 *1868* time which . . . . hour that
one   432 *1868* girl that . . . . hag!   433 *1868* lonely,   435 *1868*
stag; yet . . . . joy,   436 *1868* Plato and . . . . life;

His soul's strength to their winning back to
    peace;
Who sent forth hopes and longings for their sake, 410
Clothed in all passion's melodies: such first
Caught me and set me, slave of a sweet task,
To disentangle, gather sense from song:
Since, song-inwoven, lurked there words which
    seemed
A key to a new world, the muttering   415
Of angels, something yet unguessed by man.
How my heart leapt as still I sought and found
Much there, I felt my own soul had conceived,
But there living and burning! Soon the orb
Of his conceptions dawned on me; its praise   420
Lives in the tongues of men, men's brows are
    high
When his name means a triumph and a pride,
So, my weak voice may well forbear to shame
What seemed decreed my fate: I threw myself
To meet it, I was vowed to liberty,   425
Men were to be as gods and earth as heaven,
And I—ah, what a life was mine to prove!
My whole soul rose to meet it. Now, Pauline,
I shall go mad, if I recall that time!

Oh let me look back ere I leave for ever   430
The time which was an hour one fondly waits
For a fair girl that comes a withered hag!
And I was lonely, far from woods and fields,
And amid dullest sights, who should be loose
As a stag; yet I was full of bliss, who lived   435
With Plato and who had the key to life;

---

409 *their winning*: winning them.
    414 *song-inwoven*: probably a new compound, though Shelley uses 'inwoven' on several occasions.
    419–20 *the orb / Of his conceptions*: the whole (great) scope of his ideas.
    430–1 *O let me look back . . . time*: 'fine': Mill.
    431 *hour*: dissyllabic in *1833*, as occasionally in Keats ('Full many a dreary hour have I past'): in 1888 it becomes monosyllabic.
    432 *For a fair girl that comes a withered hag*: cf. l.946: a common theme in mythology and folklore. Cf. *Lamia*, ii. 271 ff.

And I had dimly shaped my first attempt,
And many a thought did I build up on thought,
As the wild bee hangs cell to cell—in vain;
For I must still go on: my mind rests not.   440

'Twas in my plan to look on real life,
Which was all new to me; my theories
Were firm, so I left them, to look upon
Men, and their cares, and hopes, and fears, and
     joys;
And, as I pondered on them all, I sought   445
How best life's end might be attained—an end
Comprising every joy. I deeply mused.

And suddenly, without heart-wreck, I awoke
As from a dream—I said, 'twas beautiful,
Yet but a dream; and so adieu to it.   450
As some world-wanderer sees in a far meadow
Strange towers, and walled gardens, thick with
     trees,
Where singing goes on, and delicious mirth,
And laughing fairy creatures peeping over,
And on the morrow, when he comes to live   455
For ever by those springs, and trees, fruit-flushed
And fairy bowers—all his search is vain.
Well I remember   *   *   *   *
First went my hopes of perfecting mankind,
And faith in them—then freedom in itself,
And virtue in itself—and then my motives' ends,   460
And powers and loves; and human love went last.
I felt this no decay, because new powers
Rose as old feelings left—wit, mockery,

439 *1868* cell to cell; in vain,   440 *1868* on,   444–5 *1868* Men and
their cares and hopes and fears and joys; | And as . . . . on them all   449,
450 *1868* dream: I said "'Twas beautiful | "Yet but a dream, and . . . .
it!"   452 *1868* towers and walled gardens   457, 458 *1868* bowers, all
his search is vain. | First went   459 *1868* them, then . . . . itself   460
1868 itself, and then my motives, ends   461 *1868* loves,

And I had dimly shaped my first attempt,
And many a thought did I build up on thought,
As the wild bee hangs cell to cell; in vain,
For I must still advance, no rest for mind.   440

'Twas in my plan to look on real life,
The life all new to me; my theories
Were firm, so them I left, to look and learn
Mankind, its cares, hopes, fears, its woes and
         joys;
And, as I pondered on their ways, I sought   445
How best life's end might be attained—an end
Comprising every joy. I deeply mused.

And suddenly without heart-wreck I awoke
As from a dream: I said "'Twas beautiful,
"Yet but a dream, and so adieu to it!"   450
As some world-wanderer sees in a far meadow
Strange towers and high-walled gardens thick
         with trees,
Where song takes shelter and delicious mirth
From laughing fairy creatures peeping over,
And on the morrow when he comes to lie   455
For ever 'neath those garden-trees fruit-flushed
Sung round by fairies, all his search is vain.
First went my hopes of perfecting mankind,
Next—faith in them, and then in freedom's self
And virtue's self, then my own motives, ends   460
And aims and loves, and human love went last.
I felt this no decay, because new powers
Rose as old feelings left—wit, mockery,

---

439 *As the wild bee*: cf. note to *Sordello*, vi. 621.
   448 *And suddenly*: 'This, to page 36 [ll. 490–506], is finely painted & evidently
from experience.': Mill.
   451 *world-wanderer*: cf. *Prometheus Unbound*, I. 325: ''Tis Jove's world-
wandering herald, Mercury'.

And happiness; for I had oft been sad,
Mistrusting my resolves: but now I cast   465
Hope joyously away—I laughed and said,
"No more of this"—I must not think; at length
I look'd again to see how all went on.

My powers were greater—as some temple
      seemed
My soul, where nought is changed, and incense
      rolls   470
Around the altar—only God is gone,
And some dark spirit sitteth in his seat!
So I passed through the temple; and to me
Knelt troops of shadows; and they cried, "Hail,
      king!
"We serve thee now, and thou shalt serve no
      more!   475
"Call on us, prove us, let us worship thee!"
And I said, "Are ye strong—let fancy bear me
"Far from the past."—And I was borne away
As Arab birds float sleeping in the wind,
O'er deserts, towers, and forests, I being calm;   480
And I said, "I have nursed up energies,
"They will prey on me." And a band knelt low,
And cried, "Lord, we are here, and we will make
"A way for thee—in thine appointed life
"O look on us!" And I said, "Ye will worship   485
"Me; but my heart must worship too." They
      shouted,
"Thyself—thou art our king!" So I stood there
Smiling   *   *   *   *   *   *

---

465 *1868* resolves,   466 *1868* away: I . . . . said   467 *1868* this!" I
must not think: *Mill* this(")—I must not think;["]   469 *1868* grea-
ter: 471 *1868* altar, only . . . . gone   472 *1868* seat.   473 *1868*
So, I . . . . temple   474 *1868* shadows, and they cried   477 *1868* said
"Are ye strong? Let   478 *1868* past!" And . . . . away,   484 *1868* thee
. . . . life!   487 *Lowell*—"Thyself, thou . . . . So   *1868* "Thyself, thou
. . . . So,

Light-heartedness; for I had oft been sad,
Mistrusting my resolves, but now I cast   465
Hope joyously away: I laughed and said
"No more of this!" I must not think: at length
I looked again to see if all went well.

My powers were greater: as some temple
    seemed
My soul, where nought is changed and incense
    rolls   470
Around the altar, only God is gone
And some dark spirit sitteth in his seat.
So, I passed through the temple and to me
Knelt troops of shadows, and they cried "Hail,
    king!
"We serve thee now and thou shalt serve no
    more!   475
"Call on us, prove us, let us worship thee!"
And I said "Are ye strong? Let fancy bear me
"Far from the past!" And I was borne away,
As Arab birds float sleeping in the wind,
O'er deserts, towers and forests, I being calm.   480
And I said "I have nursed up energies,
"They will prey on me." And a band knelt low
And cried "Lord, we are here and we will make
"Safe way for thee in thine appointed life!
"But look on us!" And I said "Ye will worship   485
"Me; should my heart not worship too?" They
    shouted
"Thyself, thou art our king!" So, I stood there
Smiling—oh, vanity of vanities!

---

472 *sitteth in his seat*: cf. *Prometheus Unbound*, II. iv. 2–3: 'I see a mighty darkness / Filling the seat of power'.
474 *Hail, king!*: perhaps a reminiscence of the temptation of Christ: Luke 4.
479 *As Arab birds*: 'As both legs and wings of birds of paradise were removed prior to their shipment from the East to Europe, these birds were believed never to alight and to feed only on the dews of heaven, supported in the air by their long plumes': Harrison, pp. 400–1 n.
488 *vanity of vanities*: Ecclesiastes 1: 2.

And buoyant and rejoicing was the spirit
With which I looked out how to end my days;   490
I felt once more myself—my powers were mine;
I found that youth or health so lifted me,
That, spite of all life's vanity, no grief
Came nigh me—I must ever be light-hearted;
And that this feeling was the only veil   495
Betwixt me and despair: so if age came,
I should be as a wreck linked to a soul
Yet fluttering, or mind-broken, and aware
Of my decay. So a long summer morn
Found me; and e'er noon came, I had resolved   500
No age should come on me, ere youth's hopes
      went,
For I would wear myself out—like that morn
Which wasted not a sunbeam—every joy
I would make mine, and die; and thus I sought
To chain my spirit down, which I had fed   505
With thoughts of fame. I said, the troubled life
Of genius seen so bright when working forth
Some trusted end, seems sad, when all in
      vain—
Most sad, when men have parted with all
      joy
For their wild fancy's sake, which waited first,   510
As an obedient spirit, when delight
Came not with her alone, but alters soon,
Coming darkened, seldom, hasting to depart,
Leaving a heavy darkness and warm tears.

But I shall never lose her; she will live   515

491 *1868* myself,   496 *1868* so,   497 *Mill* be ⟨as⟩ a [mere] wreck
498 *1868* mind-broken   501 *1868* me ere youth's hope went,   502
1868 out,   503 *1868* sunbeam;   504 *1868* die. And   506 *1868*
fame: I said "The   507–559 {*1868* has inverted commas as in *1888*}
512 *1868* alone;   513 *Lowell* "Comes darkened, seldom, hasting   *1868*
"Comes darkened, seldom, hastening   514, 515 {No paragraph division
in *1868*.}

For buoyant and rejoicing was the spirit
With which I looked out how to end my course;   490
I felt once more myself, my powers—all mine;
I knew while youth and health so lifted me
That, spite of all life's nothingness, no grief
Came nigh me, I must ever be light-hearted;
And that this knowledge was the only veil   495
Betwixt joy and despair: so, if age came,
I should be left—a wreck linked to a soul
Yet fluttering, or mind-broken and aware
Of my decay. So a long summer morn
Found me; and ere noon came, I had resolved   500
No age should come on me ere youth was
     spent,
For I would wear myself out, like that morn
Which wasted not a sunbeam; every hour
I would make mine, and die.

                         And thus I sought
To chain my spirit down which erst I freed   505
For flights to fame: I said "The troubled life
"Of genius, seen so gay when working forth
"Some trusted end, grows sad when all proves
     vain—
"How sad when men have parted with truth's
     peace
"For falsest fancy's sake, which waited first   510
"As an obedient spirit when delight
"Came without fancy's call: but alters soon,
"Comes darkened, seldom, hastens to depart,
"Leaving a heavy darkness and warm tears.
"But I shall never lose her; she will live   515

497–8 *a soul / Yet fluttering*: cf. Sidney, *Astrophil and Stella*, cviii. 6: 'And my yong soule flutters to thee his nest'. Gk. ψυχή, 'soul', also means 'butterfly'.
    498 *mind-broken*: not in OED. Cf. Coverdale's *Treatise on Death*, III. vii. para. 7: 'with an unbroken mind': *Remains of Myles Coverdale*, ed. G. Pearson (2 vols., Cambridge 1844, 1846), ii. 125.
    505 *To chain my spirit down*: cf. *The Witch of Atlas*, 419–20: 'The lady-witch in visions could not chain / Her spirit'.
    514 *a heavy darkness*: cf. Shelley, 'Hymn to Mercury translated from the Greek of Homer', 650: 'Chasing the heavy shadows of dismay'.

Brighter for such seclusion—I but catch
A hue, a glance of what I sing, so pain
Is linked with pleasure, for I ne'er may tell
The radiant sights which dazzle me; but now
They shall be all my own, and let them fade   520
Untold—others shall rise as fair, as fast.
And when all's done, the few dim gleams
      transferred,—
(For a new thought sprung up—that it were well
To leave all shadowy hopes, and weave such lays
As would encircle me with praise and love;   525
So I should not die utterly—I should bring
One branch from the gold forest, like the knight
Of old tales, witnessing I had been there,)—
And when all's done, how vain seems e'en
      success,
And all the influence poets have o'er men!   530
'Tis a fine thing that one, weak as myself,
Should sit in his lone room, knowing the words
He utters in his solitude shall move
Men like a swift wind—that tho' he be
      forgotten,
Fair eyes shall glisten when his beauteous
      dreams   535
Of love come true in happier frames than his.
Ay, the still night brought thoughts like these, but
      morn
Came, and the mockery again laughed out
At hollow praises, and smiles, almost sneers;
And my soul's idol seemed to whisper me   540

516 *1868* seclusion.   517 *1868* so,   520 *1868* own;   521 *1868*
fast!   522 *Lowell* transferred."—   *1868* transferred,"—   523 *1868*
up that   524 *1868* hope, and   525 *1868* love,   526 *1868* So, I
. . . . utterly,   529 *Lowell* —"And . . . . success   *1868* "And . . . . suc-
cess   531 *1868* one weak as myself   538 *1868* Came   539 *1868*
smiles

"Dearer for such seclusion. I but catch
"A hue, a glance of what I sing: so, pain
"Is linked with pleasure, for I ne'er may tell
"Half the bright sights which dazzle me; but now
"Mine shall be all the radiance: let them fade   520
"Untold—others shall rise as fair, as fast!
"And when all's done, the few dim gleams
        transferred,"—
(For a new thought sprang up how well it were,
Discarding shadowy hope, to weave such lays
As straight encircle men with praise and love,   525
So, I should not die utterly,—should bring
One branch from the gold forest, like the knight
Of old tales, witnessing I had been there)—
"And when all's done, how vain seems e'en
        success—
"The vaunted influence poets have o'er men!   530
"'T is a fine thing that one weak as myself
"Should sit in his lone room, knowing the words
"He utters in his solitude shall move
"Men like a swift wind—that tho' dead and
        gone,
"New eyes shall glisten when his beauteous
        dreams   535
"Of love come true in happier frames than his.
"Ay, the still night brings thoughts like these,
        but morn
"Comes and the mockery again laughs out
"At hollow praises, smiles allied to sneers;
"And my soul's idol ever whispers me   540

521 *others shall rise as fair*: cf. Shelley, Sonnet to Byron, 6: 'Your creations rise as fast and fair'.
526 *I should not die utterly*: cf. *Endymion*, iii. 695 ff., and Horace, *Odes*, iii. 30. 6.
527 *One branch from the gold forest*: see *Aeneid*, vi. 136 ff.
530 *The vaunted influence*: the most celebrated formulation of this is the last sentence of Shelley's 'A Defence of Poetry' ('Poets are the unacknowledged legislators of the world'), published in 1840, in vol. i of Mary Shelley's ed. of his *Essays, Letters from Abroad, Translations and Fragments*.
532–4 *the words . . . like a swift wind*: cf. 'Ode to the West Wind' 66–7: 'Scatter, as from an unextinguished hearth / Ashes and sparks, my words among mankind!'
535 *New eyes shall glisten*: cf. *Sordello*, i. 39.

To dwell with him and his unhonoured name—
And I well knew my spirit, that would be
First in the struggle, and again would make
All bow to it; and I would sink again.

*   *   *   *   *

And then know that this curse will come on us,   545
To see our idols perish—we may wither,
Nor marvel—we are clay; but our low fate
Should not extend them, whom trustingly
We sent before into Time's yawning gulf,
To face what e'er may lurk in darkness there—   550
To see the painters' glory pass, and feel
Sweet music move us not as once, or worst,
To see decaying wits ere the frail body
Decays. Nought makes me trust in love so
     really,
As the delight of the contented lowness   555
With which I gaze on souls I'd keep for ever
In beauty—I'd be sad to equal them;
I'd feed their fame e'en from my heart's best
     blood,
Withering unseen, that they might flourish still.

*   *   *   *

Pauline, my sweet friend, thou dost not forget   560
How this mood swayed me, when thou first wert
     mine,
When I had set myself to live this life,
Defying all opinion. Ere thou camest
I was most happy, sweet, for old delights
Had come like birds again; music, my life,   565

541 *1868* name: 544 *1868* it, and I should sink   *Mill* would >
should   546 *1868* perish;   547 *1868* "Nor marvel, we are
clay,   548 *Lowell* extend them,   *1868* extend to them,   *Mill* extend
[to] them,   549 *1868* time's yawning gulf   550 *1868* whate'er might
lurk . . . . there.   554 *1868* "Decays!   557 *1868* beauty;   559
1868 "Withering unseen that . . . . still." {Paragraph division but no aster-
isks.}   561 *1868* me when thou first wast mine,

"To dwell with him and his unhonoured song:
"And I foreknow my spirit, that would press
"First in the struggle, fail again to make
"All bow enslaved, and I again should sink.

"And then know that this curse will come on us, 545
"To see our idols perish; we may wither,
"No marvel, we are clay, but our low fate
"Should not extend to those whom trustingly
"We sent before into time's yawning gulf
"To face what dread may lurk in darkness there. 550
"To find the painter's glory pass, and feel
"Music can move us not as once, or, worst,
"To weep decaying wits ere the frail body
"Decays! Nought makes me trust some love is
      true,
"But the delight of the contented lowness   555
"With which I gaze on him I keep for ever
"Above me; I to rise and rival him?
"Feed his fame rather from my heart's best
      blood,
"Wither unseen that he may flourish still."

Pauline, my soul's friend, thou dost pity yet   560
How this mood swayed me when that soul
      found thine,
When I had set myself to live this life,
Defying all past glory. Ere thou camest
I seemed defiant, sweet, for old delights
Had flocked like birds again; music, my life,   565

---

541 *his unhonoured song*: but cf. ll. 170 ff., above.
    542 *And I foreknow*: revision has created an anacoluthon: 'fail' must mean
'would fail'. Cf. *The Revolt of Islam*, 2676: 'For they foreknew the storm'.
    545 *this curse*: Maynard (pp. 157, 425 n. 86) cf. *Childe Harold's Pilgrimage*, IV.
cxxiii. 1–3: '. . . 'tis youth's frenzy—but the cure / Is bitterer still, as charm by
charm unwinds / Which robed our idols'.
    548 *extend them* (1833): 'to' obviously omitted in error: cf. textual notes.
    551 *the painter's glory pass*: i.e. our sense of the painter's glory.
    558 *Feed his fame*: in the *Essay on Shelley* Browning wrote of 'The signal
service it was the dream of my boyhood to render to his fame and memory'.

I nourished more than ever, and old lore
Loved for itself, and all it shows—the king
Treading the purple calmly to his death,
—While round him, like the clouds of eve, all
    dusk,
The giant shades of fate, silently flitting,   570
Pile the dim outline of the coming doom,
—And him sitting alone in blood, while friends
Are hunting far in the sunshine; and the boy,
With his white breast and brow and clustering
    curls
Streaked with his mother's blood, and striving
    hard   575
To tell his story ere his reason goes.
And when I loved thee, as I've loved so oft,
Thou lovedst me, and I wondered, and looked in
My heart to find some feeling like such love,
Believing I was still what I had been;   580
And soon I found all faith had gone from me,
And the late glow of life—changing like clouds,
'Twas not the morn-blush widening into day,
But evening, coloured by the dying sun
While darkness is quick hastening:—I will tell   585

567 1868 itself   Mill king > King   569 1868 While   571 1868
doom;   572 1868 And . . . . blood   Mill him > Him   573 1868
boy   Mill boy, > Boy,   582 1868 life,   585 1868 hastening.

Nourished me more than ever; then the lore
Loved for itself and all it shows—that king
Treading the purple calmly to his death,
While round him, like the clouds of eve, all
   dusk,
The giant shades of fate, silently flitting,   570
Pile the dim outline of the coming doom;
And him sitting alone in blood while friends
Are hunting far in the sunshine; and the boy
With his white breast and brow and clustering
   curls
Streaked with his mother's blood, but striving
   hard   575
To tell his story ere his reason goes.
And when I loved thee as love seemed so oft,
Thou lovedst me indeed: I wondering searched
My heart to find some feeling like such love,
Believing I was still much I had been.   580
Too soon I found all faith had gone from me,
And the late glow of life, like change on clouds,
Proved not the morn-blush widening into day,
But eve faint-coloured by the dying sun
While darkness hastens quickly. I will tell   585

567 (1833) the king: in the Mill copy Browning capitalized 'king' and wrote
ll. 956–7 of the Agamemnon of Æschylus, in Greek, with the reference. In
The Agamemnon of Æschylus transcribed by Robert Browning we have this version:
'So,—since to hear thee, I am brought about thus,— / I go into the palace—
purples treading'.

572 And him sitting alone: 'him' is altered to 'Him' in the Mill copy, where
Browning quotes ll.323–5 and 342–3 of the Ajax of Sophocles, with the
reference. 'But now, confounded in his abject woe, / Refusing food or drink,
he sits there still, / Just where he fell amid the carcases / Of the slain sheep and
cattle . . . Ho Teucer! where is Teucer? Will his raid / End never? And the while
I am undone!' (Loeb trans., by F. Storr, 1913). Mill wrote 'striking' opposite
the passage.

573 and the boy: altered to 'Boy' in the Mill copy, and annotated with
ll.1021–3 (first word) and 1026–7 of The Libation-Bearers of Æschylus, in
Greek, with the appropriate reference. (The text varies slightly). 'But—since I
would have you know—for I know not how 'twill end—methinks I am a
charioteer driving my team far outside the course . . . But while I still keep my
senses, I proclaim to those who hold me dear and declare that not without
justice did I slay my mother . . .' (Loeb trans., by H. Weir Smyth, 1926). The
speaker is Orestes, son of Agamemnon and Clytemnestra, who returns by the
strict order of Apollo and forces himself to kill his mother, who has murdered
his father. As a result he is haunted by the Furies.

583 the morn-blush: cf. Paradise Lost, xi. 184: 'short blush of morn'.

My state as though 'twere none of mine—
   despair
Cannot come near me—thus it is with me.

Souls alter not, and mine must progress still;
And this I knew not when I flung away
My youth's chief aims. I ne'er supposed the
   loss   590
Of what few I retained; for no resource
Awaits me—now behold the change of all.
I cannot chain my soul, it will not rest
In its clay prison; this most narrow sphere—
It has strange powers, and feelings, and desires,   595
Which I cannot account for, nor explain,
But which I stifle not, being bound to trust
All feelings equally—to hear all sides:
Yet I cannot indulge them, and they live,
Referring to some state or life unknown. . . .   600

My selfishness is satiated not,
It wears me like a flame; my hunger for
All pleasure, howsoe'er minute, is pain;
I envy—how I envy him whose mind
Turns with its energies to some one end!   605
To elevate a sect, or a pursuit,
However mean—so my still baffled hopes
Seek out abstractions; I would have but one
Delight on earth, so it were wholly mine;
One rapture all my soul could fill—and this   610
Wild feeling places me in dream afar,
In some wide country, where the eye can see
No end to the far hills and dales bestrewn
With shining towers and dwellings. I grow mad
Well-nigh, to know not one abode but holds   615

591 *1868* retained,   592 *1868* me: 594 *1868* prison, this most narrow
sphere: 595 *1868* powers and feelings   598 *1868* equally,   600
1868 unknown.   605 *1868* end,   606, 607 *1868* sect or a pursuit |
However mean! So,   609 *1868* mine,   610 *1868* fill: 612 *Lowell*
some wide country   *1868* some wild country   614 *1868* dwellings:

My state as though 'twere none of mine—
    despair
Cannot come near us—this it is, my state.

Souls alter not, and mine must still advance;
Strange that I knew not, when I flung away
My youth's chief aims, their loss might lead to
    loss   590
Of what few I retained, and no resource
Be left me: for behold how changed is all!
I cannot chain my soul: it will not rest
In its clay prison, this most narrow sphere:
It has strange impulse, tendency, desire,   595
Which nowise I account for nor explain,
But cannot stifle, being bound to trust
All feelings equally, to hear all sides:
How can my life indulge them? yet they live,
Referring to some state of life unknown.   600

My selfishness is satiated not,
It wears me like a flame; my hunger for
All pleasure, howsoe'er minute, grows pain;
I envy—how I envy him whose soul
Turns its whole energies to some one end,   605
To elevate an aim, pursue success
However mean! So, my still baffled hope
Seeks out abstractions; I would have one joy,
But one in life, so it were wholly mine,
One rapture all my soul could fill: and this   610
Wild feeling places me in dream afar
In some vast country where the eye can see
No end to the far hills and dales bestrewn
With shining towers and towns, till I grow mad
Well-nigh, to know not one abode but holds   615

594 *this most narrow sphere*: cf. *Paracelsus*, i. 797.
610 *all my soul could fill*: which could fill all my soul.
614 *towers and towns*: cf. ll. 180–1.

Some pleasure—for my soul could grasp them
     all,
But must remain with this vile form. I look
With hope to age at last, which quenching much,
May let me concentrate the sparks it spares.

This restlessness of passion meets in me   620
A craving after knowledge: the sole proof
Of a commanding will is in that power
Repressed; for I beheld it in its dawn,
That sleepless harpy, with its budding wings,
And I considered whether I should yield   625
All hopes and fears, to live alone with it,
Finding a recompence in its wild eyes;
And when I found that I should perish so,
I bade its wild eyes close from me for ever;—
And I am left alone with my delights,—   630
So it lies in me a chained thing—still ready
To serve me, if I loose its slightest bond—
I cannot but be proud of my bright slave.

And thus I know this earth is not my
     sphere,
For I cannot so narrow me, but that   635
I still exceed it; in their elements
My love would pass my reason—but since here
Love must receive its objects from this earth,
While reason will be chainless, the few truths

616 *1868* pleasure, for .... all   629 *1868* ever,   630 *1868*
delights;   631 *1868* So, it .... thing,   632 *1868* me if ....
bond: 635 *1868* me   637 *1868* reason; {*Mill* copy alters "love" to
"Love" and "reason" to "Reason" in lines 637, 639, 641, 645.}

Some pleasure, while my soul could grasp the
   world,
But must remain this vile form's slave. I look
With hope to age at last, which quenching much,
May let me concentrate what sparks it spares.

This restlessness of passion meets in me   620
A craving after knowledge: the sole proof
Of yet commanding will is in that power
Repressed; for I beheld it in its dawn,
The sleepless harpy with just-budding wings,
And I considered whether to forego   625
All happy ignorant hopes and fears, to live,
Finding a recompense in its wild eyes.
And when I found that I should perish so,
I bade its wild eyes close from me for ever,
And I am left alone with old delights;   630
See! it lies in me a chained thing, still prompt
To serve me if I loose its slightest bond:
I cannot but be proud of my bright slave.

How should this earth's life prove my only
   sphere?
Can I so narrow sense but that in life   635
Soul still exceeds it? In their elements
My love outsoars my reason; but since love
Perforce receives its object from this earth
While reason wanders chainless, the few truths

622 *that power*: underlined by Mill, with the comment: 'you should make
clearer *what* power'.
  629 *wild eyes*: cf. 'La Belle Dame Sans Merci', 16, 31.
  634 *How should this earth's life prove my only sphere?*: cf. 594, and *Queen Mab*,
iv. 16–7. See also *Sordello*, e.g. i. 563–4.
  635 *Can I so narrow sense*: the revision from 'me' to 'sense' makes the passage
more perplexing. The general argument is the idealist one that there must be
another world because the soul requires it. The poet states that, essentially, his
love is greater than his reason; but that, since in this existence we can only love
what we find in the world, while reason is not subject to such limitation, the
discoveries of his reason 'have sufficed to quell' such love as is available to him.
How wonderful love would be if it were set free (and therefore allowed to
surpass reason) and provided with a suitable object!
  637–43 *My love . . . seraphim*: 'self-flattery': Mill.
  637 *outsoars*: as in *The Revolt of Islam*, 3560, and *Adonais*, 352.
  639 *reasons wanders chainless*: cf. Byron, 'Sonnet on Chillon': 'Eternal Spirit of
the chainless Mind!'

Caught from its wanderings have sufficed to
    quell   640
All love below;—then what must be that
    love
Which, with the object it demands, would quell
Reason, tho' it soared with the seraphim?
No—what I feel may pass all human love,
Yet fall far short of what my love should be;   645
And yet I seem more warped in this than aught,
For here myself stands out more hideously.
I can forget myself in friendship, fame,
Or liberty, or love of mighty souls.

        *   *   *   *

But I begin to know what thing hate is—   650
To sicken, and to quiver, and grow white,
And I myself have furnished its first prey.
All my sad weaknesses, this wavering will,
This selfishness, this still decaying frame . . .
But I must never grieve while I can pass   655
Far from such thoughts—as now—Andromeda!
And she is with me—years roll, I shall change,
But change can touch her not—so beautiful
With her dark eyes, earnest and still, and hair
Lifted and spread by the salt-sweeping breeze;   660
And one red-beam, all the storm leaves in heaven,
Resting upon her eyes and face and hair,

641 *1868* below; then   644 *1868* No, what . . . . love   645 *1868*
should be.   647 *1868* hideously: 649 *1868* souls; {No paragraph
division.}   651 *1868* To sicken and to quiver and grow white—   652
Mill prey. > prey—   656 *1868* now,   657 *1868* me: 660 *1868*
breeze,   661 *1868* red beam,

Caught from its wanderings have sufficed to
    quell   640
Love chained below; then what were love, set
    free,
Which, with the object it demands, would pass
Reason companioning the seraphim?
No, what I feel may pass all human love
Yet fall far short of what my love should be.   645
And yet I seem more warped in this than aught,
Myself stands out more hideously: of old
I could forget myself in friendship, fame,
Liberty, nay, in love of mightier souls;
But I begin to know what thing hate is—   650
To sicken and to quiver and grow white—
And I myself have furnished its first prey.
Hate of the weak and ever-wavering will,
The selfishness, the still-decaying frame . . .
But I must never grieve whom wing can waft   655
Far from such thoughts—as now. Andromeda!
And she is with me: years roll, I shall change,
But change can touch her not—so beautiful
With her fixed eyes, earnest and still, and hair
Lifted and spread by the salt-sweeping breeze,   660
And one red beam, all the storm leaves in heaven,
Resting upon her eyes and hair, such hair,

647–8 *of old* / *I could forget myself*: an attempt to meet Mill's objection that in
1833 ll.648–9 are 'inconsistent with what precedes'.
656 *Andromeda!*: 'that of Polidoro di Caravaggio, of which Mr. Browning
possesses an engraving, which was always before his eyes as he wrote his
earlier poems': Mrs Orr, p. 21 n. Maynard reproduces the fine engraving by
Giovanni Volpato, considering this 'Almost certainly' the print which Brown-
ing possessed. Cf. Browning to Elizabeth Barrett: 'how some people use their
pictures . . . is a mystery to me . . .—prints put together in portfolios . . my
Polidoro's perfect Andromeda along with "Boors Carousing," by
Ostade,—where I found her,—my own father's doing': Kintner, i. 27. The
way in which the narrator of the poem suddenly thinks of a favourite painting
is strikingly reminiscent of Keats. In another letter Browning revealingly
brings together Shelley, Beethoven and 'my noble Polidoro': Kintner, ii. 704.
The obvious classical source for the myth of Perseus and Andromeda is Ovid,
Metamorphoses, iv. 663 ff. Browning recurs to the story in *Sordello* (ii. 211), and
elsewhere, as DeVane points out in 'The Virgin and the Dragon' (Drew, pp. 96
ff.).

As she awaits the snake on the wet beach,
By the dark rock, and the white wave just
     breaking
At her feet; quite naked and alone,—a thing   665
You doubt not, nor fear for, secure that God
Will come in thunder from the stars to save her.
Let it pass—I will call another change.
I will be gifted with a wond'rous soul,
Yet sunk by error to men's sympathy,   670
And in the wane of life; yet only so
As to call up their fears, and there shall come
A time requiring youth's best energies;
And strait I fling age, sorrow, sickness off,
And I rise triumphing over my decay.   675

*   *   *   *

And thus it is that I supply the chasm
'Twixt what I am and all that I would be.
But then to know nothing—to hope for
     nothing—
To seize on life's dull joys from a strange fear,
Lest, losing them, all's lost, and nought remains.   680

*   *   *   *

There's some vile juggle with my reason here—
I feel I but explain to my own loss
These impulses—they live no less the same.
Liberty! what though I despair—my blood
Rose not at a slave's name proudlier than now,   685

665 *1868* alone;   668 *1868* pass!   671 *1868* life,   672 *1868* fears;
674 *Lowell* And strait   *1868* And straight   675 *1868* {No asterisks.}
677 *1868* be: 678 *1868* nothing, to . . . . nothing,   679 *1868* fear
680 *1868* lost and nought remains! {No asterisks.}   681 *1868* here;
683 *1868* impulses;   684 *1868* despair?

As she awaits the snake on the wet beach
By the dark rock and the white wave just
    breaking
At her feet; quite naked and alone; a thing   665
I doubt not, nor fear for, secure some god
To save will come in thunder from the stars.
Let it pass! Soul requires another change.
I will be gifted with a wondrous mind,
Yet sunk by error to men's sympathy,   670
And in the wane of life, yet only so
As to call up their fears; and there shall come
A time requiring youth's best energies;
And lo, I fling age, sorrow, sickness off,
And rise triumphant, triumph through decay.   675

And thus it is that I supply the chasm
'Twixt what I am and all I fain would be:
But then to know nothing, to hope for
    nothing,
To seize on life's dull joys from a strange fear
Lest, losing them, all's lost and nought remains!   680

There's some vile juggle with my reason here;
I feel I but explain to my own loss
These impulses: they live no less the same.
Liberty! what though I despair? my blood
Rose never at a slave's name proud as now.   685

663 *the snake*: the serpent or dragon.
669 *I will be gifted*: 'an allusion to Kean': see p. 3 above.
670 *Yet sunk . . . to men's sympathy*: yet brought down by weakness to a level
at which I elicit the sympathy of mankind.
678–80 *But then . . . remains*: 'deeply true': Mill.
681 *juggle*: a favourite word, used in *Paracelsus* at ii. 9, ii. 178, and v. 194.
685 *Rose never at a slave's name*: Mill underlined l.686 and put a cross (indica-
ting obscurity) opposite it. Browning revised slightly, but the passage remains
obscure. The narrator is no doubt defending himself from any charge of
indifference and selfishness. His sympathies really 'live' (683) just as truly as
they did when he could lose himself in thoughts of 'liberty' (649). The words
'at a slave's name' probably mean 'the very thought of slavery existing' and not
'the idea of my being called a slave'.

And sympathy obscured by sophistries.
Why have not I sought refuge in myself,
But for the woes I saw and could not stay—
And love!—do I not love thee, my Pauline?

*   *   *   *

I cherish prejudice, lest I be left   690
Utterly loveless—witness this belief
In poets, tho' sad change has come there too·
No more I leave myself to follow them:
Unconsciously I measure me by them.
Let me forget it; and I cherish most   695
My love of England—how her name—a word
Of her's in a strange tongue makes my heart
   beat!. .

*   *   *   *

Pauline, I could do any thing—not now—
All's fever—but when calm shall come again—
I am prepared—I have made life my own—   700
I would not be content with all the change
One frame should feel—but I have gone in
   thought
Thro' all conjuncture—I have lived all life
When it is most alive—where strangest fate
New shapes it past surmise—the tales of men   705
Bit by some curse—or in the grasps of doom
Half-visible and still increasing round,
Or crowning their wide being's general aim. . . .

*   *   *   *

These are wild fancies, but I feel, sweet friend,
As one breathing his weakness to the ear   710

686 *1868* And sympathy, obscured by sophistries! {This line is deleted in
Mill.}   688 *1868* stay?   689 *1868* love! do {No paragraph divi-
sion.}   692 *1868* too;   693 *1868* follow them—   694 *1868* by
them—   696 *1868* name,   697 *1868* beat! {No asterisks.}   699
1868 again,   700 *1868* prepared: I . . . . own.   702 *1868* feel,
703 *1868* conjuncture,   704 *1868* alive,   706 *1868* curse   708
1868 aim. {No asterisks.}

Oh sympathies, obscured by sophistries!—
Why else have I sought refuge in myself,
But from the woes I saw and could not stay?
Love! is not this to love thee, my Pauline?
I cherish prejudice, lest I be left   690
Utterly loveless? witness my belief
In poets, though sad change has come there too;
No more I leave myself to follow them—
Unconsciously I measure me by them—
Let me forget it: and I cherish most   695
My love of England—how her name, a word
Of hers in a strange tongue makes my heart
    beat!

Pauline, could I but break the spell! Not now—
All's fever—but when calm shall come again,
I am prepared: I have made life my own.   700
I would not be content with all the change
One frame should feel, but I have gone in
    thought
Thro' all conjuncture, I have lived all life
When it is most alive, where strangest fate
New-shapes it past surmise—the throes of men   705
Bit by some curse or in the grasps of doom
Half-visible and still-increasing round,
Or crowning their wide being's general aim.

These are wild fancies, but I feel, sweet friend,
As one breathing his weakness to the ear   710

698–708 *Pauline . . . aim*: a vertical pencil line deletes these lines in the Mill copy.
702 *One frame*: i.e. he yearns to have every experience.
705–6 *men / Bit by some curse*: see l. 566 ff.
708 *Or crowning their wide being's general aim*: the punctuation of *1833*, indicating an aposiopesis, seems to make better sense than that of *1888*.

Of pitying angel—dear as a winter flower;
A slight flower growing alone, and offering
Its frail cup of three leaves to the cold sun,
Yet joyous and confiding, like the triumph
Of a child—and why am I not worthy thee?   715

*   *   *   *

I can live all the life of plants, and gaze
Drowsily on the bees that flit and play,
Or bare my breast for sunbeams which will kill,
Or open in the night of sounds, to look
For the dim stars; I can mount with the bird,   720
Leaping airily his pyramid of leaves
And twisted boughs of some tall mountain tree,
Or rise cheerfully springing to the heavens—
Or like a fish breathe in the morning air
In the misty sun-warm water—or with flowers   725
And trees can smile in light at the sinking sun,
Just as the storm comes—as a girl would look
On a departing lover—most serene.

Pauline, come with me—see how I could build
A home for us, out of the world; in thought—   730
I am inspired—come with me, Pauline!

Night, and one single ridge of narrow path
Between the sullen river and the woods
Waving and muttering—for the moonless night
Has shaped them into images of life,   735
Like the upraising of the giant-ghosts,
Looking on earth to know how their sons fare.
Thou art so close by me, the roughest swell

711 *1868* flower,   715 *1868* child: {No paragraph division.}   723
1868 heavens;   724 *1868* breathe-in the   725 *1868* water; or with
flowers   727 *1868* comes,   729 *1868* me,   730 *1868* world, in
thought!   731 *1868* inspired: 734 *1868* muttering,   737 *1868*
fare:

Of pitying angel—dear as a winter flower,
A slight flower growing alone, and offering
Its frail cup of three leaves to the cold sun,
Yet joyous and confiding like the triumph
Of a child: and why am I not worthy thee?   715
I can live all the life of plants, and gaze
Drowsily on the bees that flit and play,
Or bare my breast for sunbeams which will kill,
Or open in the night of sounds, to look
For the dim stars; I can mount with the bird   720
Leaping airily his pyramid of leaves
And twisted boughs of some tall mountain tree,
Or rise cheerfully springing to the heavens;
Or like a fish breathe deep the morning air
In the misty sun-warm water; or with flower   725
And tree can smile in light at the sinking sun
Just as the storm comes, as a girl would look
On a departing lover—most serene.

Pauline, come with me, see how I could build
A home for us, out of the world, in thought!   730
I am uplifted: fly with me, Pauline!

Night, and one single ridge of narrow path
Between the sullen river and the woods
Waving and muttering, for the moonless night
Has shaped them into images of life,   735
Like the uprising of the giant-ghosts,
Looking on earth to know how their sons fare:
Thou art so close by me, the roughest swell

713 *Its frail cup of three leaves*: cf. *Sordello* ii. 290.
719 *the night of sounds*: the night which is full of sounds.
721 *his pyramid of leaves*: cf. *Alastor*, 53–4: 'a pyramid / Of mouldering leaves'.
731 *fly with me*: cf. *Epipsychidion* 388: 'The day is come, and thou wilt fly with me'.
735 *images of life*: perhaps suggested by *Alastor*, 382–4: 'the gnarlèd roots / Of mighty trees, that stretched their giant arms / In darkness over it'.
736 *the giant-ghosts*: a reference to myths of a giant race at some unspecified time in antiquity: 'The existence of giants has been supported by all the writers of antiquity, and received as an undeniable truth': Lemprière.

Of wind in the tree-tops hides not the panting
Of thy soft breasts; no—we will pass to
   morning—   740
Morning—the rocks, and vallies, and old woods.
How the sun brightens in the mist, and here,—
Half in the air, like creatures of the place,
Trusting the element—living on high boughs
That swing in the wind—look at the golden
   spray.   745
Flung from the foam-sheet of the cataract,
Amid the broken rocks—shall we stay here
With the wild hawks?—no, ere the hot noon
   come
Dive we down—safe;—see this our new retreat
Walled in with a sloped mound of matted shrubs,   750
Dark, tangled, old and green—still sloping down
To a small pool whose waters lie asleep
Amid the trailing boughs turned water-plants
And tall trees over-arch to keep us in,
Breaking the sunbeams into emerald shafts,   755
And in the dreamy water one small group
Of two or three strange trees are got together,
Wondering at all around—as strange beasts herd
Together far from their own land—all
   wildness—
No turf nor moss, for boughs and plants pave all,   760
And tongues of bank go shelving in the waters,
Where the pale-throated snake reclines his head,
And old grey stones lie making eddies there;
The wild mice cross them dry-shod—deeper
   in—

740 *1868* breasts. No,   741 *1868* Morning, the rocks and valleys
742 *1868* here,   744 *1868* element,   745 *1868* spray   *Mill* spray,
746 *1868* cataract   747 *1868* rocks! Shall   748 *1868* hawks? No,
. . . . come,   749 *1868* safe! See   751 *1868* green,   753 *1868*
water-plants: 758 *1868* around,   759 *1868* land: all wildness,
763 *1868* there,   764 *1868* dry-shod: deeper in!

Of wind in the tree-tops hides not the panting
Of thy soft breasts. No, we will pass to
   morning—   740
Morning, the rocks and valleys and old woods.
How the sun brightens in the mist, and here,
Half in the air, like creatures of the place,
Trusting the element, living on high boughs
That swing in the wind—look at the silver
   spray   745
Flung from the foam-sheet of the cataract
Amid the broken rocks! Shall we stay here
With the wild hawks? No, ere the hot noon
   come,
Dive we down—safe! See this our new retreat
Walled in with a sloped mound of matted shrubs, 750
Dark, tangled, old and green, still sloping down
To a small pool whose waters lie asleep
Amid the trailing boughs turned water-plants:
And tall trees overarch to keep us in,
Breaking the sunbeams into emerald shafts,   755
And in the dreamy water one small group
Of two or three strange trees are got together
Wondering at all around, as strange beasts herd
Together far from their own land: all
   wildness,
No turf nor moss, for boughs and plants pave all, 760
And tongues of bank go shelving in the lymph,
Where the pale-throated snake reclines his head,
And old grey stones lie making eddies there,
The wild-mice cross them dry-shod. Deeper in!

---

748 Some copies of *1889* have 'come.'

746 *Flung from the foam-sheet of the cataract*: cf. *Alastor*, 345–6: 'fled, like foam /
Down the steep cataract of a wintry river'.
754 *overarch*: cf. *Alastor*, 434: 'the tall cedar overarching', and *Paradise Lost*, i.
303–4.
756 *the dreamy water*: Tennyson has 'the dreamy house' in 'Mariana', 61 (in
Poems, Chiefly Lyrical, 1830).
761 *go shelving*: cf. Shelley, 'The Question', 5: 'Along a shelving bank of
turf'.
764 *Deeper in!*: this sort of imperative stage-direction occurs in *Sordello*, e.g.
at i. 505.

Shut thy soft eyes—now look—still deeper in: 765
This is the very heart of the woods—all round,
Mountain-like, heaped above us; yet even here
One pond of water gleams—far off the river
Sweeps like a sea, barred out from land; but
    one—
One thin clear sheet has over-leaped and wound   770
Into this silent depth, which gained, it lies
Still, as but let by sufferance; the trees bend
O'er it as wild men watch a sleeping girl,
And thro' their roots long creeping plants stretch
    out
Their twined hair, steeped and sparkling; farther
    on,   775
Tall rushes and thick flag-knots have combined
To narrow it; so, at length, a silver thread
It winds, all noiselessly, thro' the deep wood,
Till thro' a cleft way, thro' the moss and stone,
It joins its parent-river with a shout.   780
Up for the glowing day—leave the old woods:
See, they part, like a ruined arch, the sky!
Nothing but sky appears, so close the root
And grass of the hill-top level with the air—
Blue sunny air, where a great cloud floats, laden   785
With light, like a dead whale that white birds
    pick,
Floating away in the sun in some north sea.
Air, air—fresh life-blood—thin and searching
    air—
The clear, dear breath of God, that loveth us:

765 *1868* still deeper in!   766 *1868* woods all round   768 *1868*
gleams;   778 *1868* winds, all noiselessly through . . . . wood   781
1868 day, leave . . . . woods!   782 *1868* arch: 783 *Lowell, Mill* root
> roots   *1868* roots   788 *1868* Air, air, fresh life-blood, thin and search-
ing air,   789 *1868* God that loveth us,

Shut thy soft eyes—now look—still deeper in! 765
This is the very heart of the woods all round
Mountain-like heaped above us; yet even here
One pond of water gleams; far off the river
Sweeps like a sea, barred out from land; but
    one—
One thin clear sheet has overleaped and wound 770
Into this silent depth, which gained, it lies
Still, as but let by sufferance; the trees bend
O'er it as wild men watch a sleeping girl,
And through their roots long creeping plants
    out-stretch
Their twined hair, steeped and sparkling; farther
    on,   775
Tall rushes and thick flag-knots have combined
To narrow it; so, at length, a silver thread,
It winds all noiselessly through the deep wood
Till thro' a cleft-way, thro' the moss and stone,
It joins its parent-river with a shout.   780

Up for the glowing day, leave the old woods!
See, they part, like a ruined arch: the sky!
Nothing but sky appears, so close the roots
And grass of the hill-top level with the air—
Blue sunny air, where a great cloud floats laden 785
With light, like a dead whale that white birds
    pick,
Floating away in the sun in some north sea.
Air, air, fresh life-blood, thin and searching
    air,
The clear, dear breath of God that loveth us,

---

*778 {Reading of Lowell copy} *1888,1889* winds, all   781 {Some copies of
1889} gowing day,   782 {Some copies of *1889*} part

768–77 *One pond . . . To narrow it*: 'good descriptive writing': Mill.
773 *as wild men watch*: a common subject for painters, the 'wild men' often
being satyrs.
776 *flag-knots*: cf. Shelley, 'The Question', 25–6: 'And nearer to the river's
trembling edge / There grew broad flag-flowers.'
781 *leave the old woods!*: cf. l.764 n., above.
789 *God that loveth us*: cf. Coleridge, 'The Rime of the Ancient Mariner',
616: 'For the dear God who loveth us'.

Where small birds reel and winds take their
    delight.   790
Water is beatiful, but not like air.
See, where the solid azure waters lie,
Made as of thickened air, and down below,
The fern-ranks, like a forest spread themselves,
As tho' each pore could feel the element;   795
Where the quick glancing serpent winds his
    way—
Float with me there, Pauline, but not like air.
Down the hill—stop—a clump of trees, see, set
On a heap of rocks, which look o'er the far plains,
And envious climbing shrubs would mount to
    rest,   800
And peer from their spread boughs. There they
    wave, looking
At the muleteers, who whistle as they go
To the merry chime of their morning bells, and all
The little smoking cots, and fields, and banks,
And copses, bright in the sun; my spirit wanders.   805
Hedge-rows for me—still, living, hedge-rows,
    where
The bushes close, and clasp above, and keep
Thought in—I am concentrated—I feel;—
But my soul saddens when it looks beyond;
I cannot be immortal, nor taste all.   810

790 *1868* delight!   791 *1833* beatiful, {misprint} *1868* beautiful, but not
like air: 796 *1868* way,   797 *1868* Pauline!—   798 *1868* hill!
Stop—   801 *1868* boughs; there   802 *1868* muleteers who   804,
805 *1868* cots and fields and banks | And copses bright in the sun. My spirit
wanders: 808 *1868* feel;

Where small birds reel and winds take their
    delight!   790
Water is beautiful, but not like air:
See, where the solid azure waters lie
Made as of thickened air, and down below,
The fern-ranks like a forest spread themselves
As though each pore could feel the element;   795
Where the quick glancing serpent winds his
    way,
Float with me there, Pauline!—but not like air.

Down the hill! Stop—a clump of trees, see, set
On a heap of rock, which look o'er the far plain:
So, envious climbing shrubs would mount to
    rest   800
And peer from their spread boughs; wide they wave,
    looking
At the muleteers who whistle on their way,
To the merry chime of morning bells, past all
The little smoking cots, mid fields and banks
And copses bright in the sun. My spirit wanders: 805
Hedgerows for me—those living hedgerows
    where
The bushes close and clasp above and keep
Thought in—I am concentrated—I feel;
But my soul saddens when it looks beyond:
I cannot be immortal, taste all joy.   810

---

  793 *thickened air*: cf. Prior, *Solomon*, i. 355–6: 'Water stop'd gives Birth / To
Grass and Plants, and thickens into Earth'.
  806 *Hedgerows for me*: this emphasizes the suggestion of 'muleteers' that the
speaker is in Switzerland, or elsewhere abroad. Lines 951 ff. strongly suggest
Switzerland, but also that the lovers have not yet begun their period of exile
there. Cf. 'Home-Thoughts, from Abroad' and 'De Gustibus', i.
  808 *concentrated*: stressed on the second syllable, as in Johnson.

O God! where does this tend—these struggling
aims!*

* Je crains bien que mon pauvre ami ne soit pas toujours parfaite-
ment compris dans ce qui reste à lire de cet étrange fragment—mais il
est moins propre que tout autre à éclaircir ce qui de sa nature ne peut
jamais être que songe et confusion. D'ailleurs je ne sais trop si en
cherchant à mieux co-ordonner certaines parties l'on ne courrait pas
le risque de nuire an seul mérite auquel une production si singuliere
peut prétendre—celui de donner une idée assez précise du genre
qu'elle n'a fait qu'ébaucher.—Ce début sans prétention, ce remue-
ment des passions qui va d'abord en accroissant et puis s'appaise par
degrés, ces élans de l'ame, ce retour soudain sur soi-même.—Et par
dessus tout, la tournure d'esprit toute parliculière de mon ami ren-
dent les changemens presque impossibles. Les raisons qu'il fait valoir
ailleurs, et d'autres encore plus puissantes, ont fait trouver grâce à
mes yeux pour cet écrit qu' autrement je lui eusse conseillé de jeter au
feu—Je n'en crois pas moins au grand principe dè toute composi-
tion—à ce principe de Shakspeare, de Raffaelle, de Beethoven, d'où il
suit que la concentration des idées est dûe bien plus à leur conception,
qu'à leur mise en execution . . . j'ai tout lieu de craindre que la
première de ces qualités ne soit encore étrangère à mon ami—et je
doute fort qu'un redoublement de travail lui fasse acquérir la sec-
onde. Le mieux serait de bruler ceci; mais que faire?
Je crois que dans ce qui suit il fait allusion à un certain examen qu'il
fit autrefois de l'âme ou plutot de son âme, pour découvrir la suité des
objets auxquels il lui serait possible d'attèndre, et dont chacun une
fois obtenu devait former une espèce de plateau d'où l'on pouvait
apercevoir d'autres buts, d'autres projets, d'autres jouissances qui, à
leur tour, devaient être surmontés. Il en résultait que l'oubli et le
sommeil devaient tout terminer. Cette idée que je ne saisis pas
parfaitement lui est peutêtre aussi intelligible qu'à moi.

PAULINE.

811 *1868* O God, where . . . . aims?*   Footnote: *1868* { substantially as *1888*
except "d'attendre" for "d'atteindre".}

O God, where do they tend—these struggling aims?*

* Je crains bien que mon pauvre ami ne soit pas toujours parfaitement compris dans ce qui reste à lire de cet étrange fragment, mais il est moins propre que tout autre à éclaircir ce qui de sa nature ne peut jamais être que songe et confusion. D'ailleurs je ne sais trop si en cherchant à mieux co-ordonner certaines parties l'on ne courrait pas le risque de nuire au seul mérite auquel une production si singulière peut prétendre, celui de donner une idée assez précise du genre qu'elle n'a fait qu'ébaucher. Ce début sans prétention, ce remuement des passions qui va d'abord en accroissant et puis s'apaise par degrés, ces élans de l'âme, ce retour soudain sur soi-même, et par-dessus tout, la tournure d'esprit tout particulière de mon ami, rendent les changemens presque impossibles. Les raisons qu'il fait valoir ailleurs, et d'autres encore plus puissantes, ont fait trouver grâce à mes yeux pour cet écrit qu'autrement je lui eusse conseillé de jeter au feu. Je n'en crois pas moins au grand principe de toute composition—à ce principe de Shakespeare, de Rafaelle, de Beethoven, d'où il suit que la concentration des idées est due bien plus à leur conception qu'à leur mise en exécution: j'ai tout lieu de craindre que la première de ces qualités ne soit encore étrangère à mon ami, et je doute fort qu'un redoublement de travail lui fasse acquérir la seconde. Le mieux serait de brûler ceci; mais que faire?

Je crois que dans ce qui suit il fait allusion à un certain examen qu'il fit autrefois de l'âme, ou plutôt de son âme, pour découvrir la suite des objets auxquels il lui serait possible d'atteindre, et dont chacun une fois obtenu devait former une espèce de plateau d'où l'on pouvait apercevoir d'autres buts, d'autres projets, d'autres jouissances qui, à leur tour, devaient être surmontés. Il en résultait que l'oubli et le sommeil devaient tout terminer. Cette idée, que je ne saisis pas parfaitement, lui est peut-être aussi inintelligible qu'à moi.

PAULINE.

811 *'I am very much afraid that my poor friend will not always be perfectly understood in what remains to be read of this strange fragment, but he is less fitted than anyone else to make clear what from its very nature must always remain a confused dream. Besides, I am not at all sure that in attempting better to co-ordinate certain parts one would not run the risk of damaging the only merit to which so singular a production can lay claim, that of giving a pretty exact idea of the type which has merely been sketched. This unpretentious opening, this stirring of the passions which increases at first and then is gradually allayed—these impulses of the soul, this sudden return upon himself, and above all the altogether exceptional cast of mind of my friend make alterations almost impossible. The reasons that he puts forward elsewhere, and others still more powerful, have led me to look with favour on this piece of writing, which I would otherwise have advised him to throw into the fire. This

What would I have? what is this "sleep," which
   seems
To bound all? can there be a "waking" point
Of crowning life? The soul would never rule—
It would be first in all things—it would have   815
Its utmost pleasure filled,—but that complete
Commanding for commanding sickens it.
The last point that I can trace is, rest beneath
Some better essence than itself—in weakness;
This is "myself"—not what I think should be,   820
And what is that I hunger for but God?
My God, my God! let me for once look on thee
As tho' nought else existed: we alone.
And as creation crumbles, my soul's spark
Expands till I can say, "Even from myself   825
"I need thee, and I feel thee, and I love thee;
"I do not plead my rapture in thy works
"For love of thee—or that I feel as one
"Who cannot die—but there is that in me
"Which turns to thee, which loves, or which
   should love."   830

---

814 *1868* rule;   815 *1868* things,   816 *1868* filled, but, that com-
plete,   817 *1868* Commanding, for commanding,   818 *Lowell, Mill*
{delete "that"}   *1868*   point I can trace is, rest,   819 *1868*
itself,   820 *1868* "myself," not . . . . be: 822 *1868* My God, my
God,   823 *1868* though. . . .existed, we alone!   825 *1868*
say,—Even   826 *1868* I need thee and I feel thee and I love
thee: 827f. *1868* {No inverted commas.}   828 *1868* thee,
nor   829 *1868* die: 830 *1868* loves or which should love. {No para-
graph division.}

What would I have? What is this "sleep" which
   seems
To bound all? can there be a "waking" point
Of crowning life? The soul would never rule;
It would be first in all things, it would have   815
Its utmost pleasure filled, but, that complete,
Commanding, for commanding, sickens it.
The last point I can trace is—rest beneath
Some better essence than itself, in weakness;
This is "myself," not what I think should be: 820
And what is that I hunger for but God?

My God, my God, let me for once look on thee
As though nought else existed, we alone!
And as creation crumbles, my soul's spark
Expands till I can say,—Even from myself   825
I need thee and I feel thee and I love thee.
I do not plead my rapture in thy works
For love of thee, nor that I feel as one
Who cannot die: but there is that in me
Which turns to thee, which loves or which
   should love.   830

---

does not mean that I do not believe in the great principle of all composi-
tion—that principle of Shakespeare, of Raphael, of Beethoven, from which it
follows that the concentration of ideas is due much more to their conception
than to their execution. I have good reason for fearing that the first of these
qualities is still unfamiliar to my friend, and I very much doubt whether a
redoubling of his effort would lead him to acquire the second. The best thing
would be to burn this; but what can one do?

I believe that in what follows he alludes to a certain examination of the soul,
or rather of his own soul, which he carried out formerly, in order to discover
the sequence of objectives which it would be possible for him to attain, and of
which each one (once attained) should form a sort of plateau from which one
could discern other aims, other projects, other pleasures which (in their turn)
should be surmounted. The conclusion was that oblivion and sleep should
bring an end to everything. This idea, which I do not altogether understand, is
perhaps equally incomprehensible to him.' Cf. the 'Advertisement' to *Epip-
sychidion*, and its reference to 'my unfortunate friend'. The conception of ascent
from one level to another is central in Browning, and memorably used in 'A
Grammarian's Funeral'.

812 *this "sleep"*: a reference to *Hamlet*, III. i. 60 ff.: 'to die, to sleep—No more;
and by a sleep to say we end . . .'

814 *Of crowning life?*: i.e. a life in another world. Browning is remembering
the Latin proverb, 'Finis coronat opus'. Cf. 708, above.

Why have I girt myself with this hell-dress?
Why have I laboured to put out my life?
Is it not in my nature to adore,
And e'en for all my reason do I not
Feel him, and thank him, and pray to
    him?—*Now*.   835
Can I forego the trust that he loves me?
Do I not feel a love which only ONE . . . . .
O thou pale form, so dimly seen, deep-eyed,
I have denied thee calmly—do I not
Pant when I read of thy consummate deeds,   840
And burn to see thy calm, pure truths out-flash
The brightest gleams of earth's philosophy?
Do I not shake to hear aught question thee? . . . .

If I am erring save me, madden me,
Take from me powers, and pleasures—let me die 845
Ages, so I see thee: I am knit round
As with a charm, by sin and lust and pride,
Yet tho' my wandering dreams have seen all
    shapes
Of strange delight, oft have I stood by thee—
Have I been keeping lonely watch with thee,   850
In the damp night by weeping Olivet,
Or leaning on thy bosom, proudly less—
Or dying with thee on the lonely cross—
Or witnessing thy bursting from the tomb!

A mortal, sin's familiar friend doth here   855
Avow that he will give all earth's reward,
But to believe and humbly teach the faith,

835 *Lowell* him—*now?* *1868* him—now?   838 *Lowell* deep-eyed,
1868 deep-eyed!   843 *1868* thee? {No paragraph division.}   845
1868 powers and pleasures,   846 *1868* thee!   852 *1868* less,   853
1868 cross,

Why have I girt myself with this hell-dress?
Why have I laboured to put out my life?
Is it not in my nature to adore,
And e'en for all my reason do I not
Feel him, and thank him, and pray to him—
    now?   835
Can I forego the trust that he loves me?
Do I not feel a love which only ONE . . .
O thou pale form, so dimly seen, deep-eyed!
I have denied thee calmly—do I not
Pant when I read of thy consummate power,   840
And burn to see thy calm pure truths out-flash
The brightest gleams of earth's philosophy?
Do I not shake to hear aught question thee?
If I am erring save me, madden me,
Take from me powers and pleasures, let me die   845
Ages, so I see thee! I am knit round
As with a charm by sin and lust and pride,
Yet though my wandering dreams have seen all
    shapes
Of strange delight, oft have I stood by thee—
Have I been keeping lonely watch with thee   850
In the damp night by weeping Olivet,
Or leaning on thy bosom, proudly less,
Or dying with thee on the lonely cross,
Or witnessing thine outburst from the tomb.

A mortal, sin's familiar friend, doth here   855
Avow that he will give all earth's reward,
But to believe and humbly teach the faith,

831–7 *Why have I . . . ONE . . .*: 'why should this follow the description of scenery?' Mill.

832 *to put out*: extinguish, annihilate my spiritual existence.

841 *out-flash*: the first occurrence of this verb in OED is in Carlyle's *Sartor Resartus* (1833–4), III. i: 'Such first outflashing of man's Freewill, to lighten, more and more into Day'.

851 *by weeping Olivet*: the mount of Olives, associated with Christ's agony in the garden (of Gethsemane): see Mark 14:26–42.

855 *sin's familiar friend*: cf. *Measure for Measure*, I. iv. 31: 'my familiar sin'.

In suffering, and poverty, and shame,
Only believing he is not unloved . . . .

And now, my Pauline, I am thine for ever!   860
I feel the spirit which has buoyed me up
Deserting me: and old shades gathering on;
Yet while its last light waits, I would say much,
And chiefly, I am glad that I have said
That love which I have ever felt for thee,   865
But seldom told; our hearts so beat together,
That speech is mockery, but when dark hours
      come;
And I feel sad; and thou, sweet, deem'st it strange;
A sorrow moves me, thou canst not remove.
Look on this lay I dedicate to thee,   870
Which thro' thee I began, and which I end,
Collecting the last gleams to strive to tell
That I am thine, and more than ever now—
That I am sinking fast—yet tho' I sink,
No less I feel that thou hast brought me
      bliss,   875
And that I still may hope to win it back.
Thou know'st, dear friend, I could not think all
      calm,
For wild dreams followed me, and bore me off,
And all was indistinct. Ere one was caught
Another glanced: so dazzled by my wealth,   880
Knowing not which to leave nor which to choose,
For all my thoughts so floated, nought was
      fixed—

859 *1868* unloved.   862 *1868* me,   867 *Lowell* mockery: but . . . .
come,   *1868*   mockery;   but   . . . .   come,   868   *1868*   sad,
and. . . .strange   869 *1868* remove,   873 *1868* now   874 *1868*
fast: yet though   877 *1868* knowest,   879 *1868* indistinct; ere   *Mill*
indistinct: ere   880 *1868* glanced; so,   882 *1868* fixed.

In suffering and poverty and shame,
Only believing he is not unloved.

And now, my Pauline, I am thine for ever!   860
I feel the spirit which has buoyed me up
Desert me, and old shades are gathering fast;
Yet while the last light waits, I would say much,
This chiefly, it is gain that I have said
Somewhat of love I ever felt for thee   865
But seldom told; our hearts so beat together
That speech seemed mockery: but when dark
      hours come,
And joy departs, and thou, sweet, deem'st it strange
A sorrow moves me, thou canst not remove,
Look on this lay I dedicate to thee,   870
Which through thee I began, which thus I end,
Collecting the last gleams to strive to tell
How I am thine, and more than ever now
That I sink fast: yet though I deeplier sink,
No less song proves one word has brought me
      bliss,   875
Another still may win bliss surely back.
Thou knowest, dear, I could not think all
      calm,
For fancies followed thought and bore me off,
And left all indistinct; ere one was caught
Another glanced; so, dazzled by my wealth,   880
I knew not which to leave nor which to choose,
For all so floated, nought was fixed and
      firm.

859 *not unloved*: between this and the following line Mill writes: 'strange transition'.

870 *I dedicate to thee*: cf. Shelley, 'Hymn to Intellectual Beauty', 61–2: 'I vowed that I would dedicate my powers / To thee and thine'.

875 *No less*: nonetheless.

877 *all calm*: in complete calm: cf. Keats, 'Hyperion', ii. 204: 'And to envisage circumstance, all calm'.

And then thou said'st a perfect bard was one
Who shadowed out the stages of all life,
And so thou badest me tell this my first stage;—   885
'Tis done: and even now I feel all dim the shift
Of thought. These are my last thoughts; I discern
Faintly immortal life, and truth, and good.
And why thou must be mine is, that e'en now,
In the dim hush of night—that I have done—   890
With fears and sad forebodings: I look
     thro'
And say, "E'en at the last I have her still,
"With her delicious eyes as clear as heaven,
"When rain in a quick shower has beat down
     mist,
"And clouds float white in the sun like broods of
     swans."   895
How the blood lies upon her cheek, all spread
As thinned by kisses; only in her lips
It wells and pulses like a living thing,
And her neck looks, like marble misted o'er
With love-breath, a dear thing to kiss and
     love,   900
Standing beneath me—looking out to me,
As I might kill her and be loved for it.

Love me—love me, Pauline, love nought but me;
Leave me not. All these words are wild and weak,
Believe them not, Pauline. I stooped so low   905
But to behold thee purer by my side,
To show thou art my breath—my life—a last

885 *Lowell* badest. . . .first stage.   *1868* bad'st. . . .first stage.   *Mill* badest. . . .First Stage;—   886 *1868* done,   887 *1868* thought; these   890 *1868* night, that I have done,   891 *1868* forebodings, I look through   892 *1868* And say,—E'en   895 *1868* And . . . . swans.   897 *1868* kisses!   899 *1868* looks   900 *1868* love-breath,—   901 *1868* beneath me,   903 *1868* but me,   904 *1868* not!   905 *1868* Pauline!   907 *1868* breath, my life,

And then thou said'st a perfect bard was one
Who chronicled the stages of all life,
And so thou bad'st me shadow this first stage.   885
'T is done, and even now I recognize
The shift, the change from last to past—discern
Faintly how life is truth and truth is good.
And why thou must be mine is, that e'en now
In the dim hush of night, that I have done,   890
Despite the sad forebodings, love looks
    through—
Whispers,—E'en at the last I have her still,
With her delicious eyes as clear as heaven
When rain in a quick shower has beat down
    mist,
And clouds float white above like broods of
    swans.   895
How the blood lies upon her cheek, outspread
As thinned by kisses! only in her lips
It wells and pulses like a living thing,
And her neck looks like marble misted o'er
With love-breath,—a Pauline from heights
    above,   900
Stooping beneath me, looking up—one look
As I might kill her and be loved the more.

So, love me—me, Pauline, and nought but me,
Never leave loving! Words are wild and weak,
Believe them not, Pauline! I stained myself   905
But to behold thee purer by my side,
To show thou art my breath, my life, a last

884 *Who chronicled*: quoting the original and revised versions of ll. 883–4,
DeVane comments: 'The difference implied in the single word ['chronicled'
instead of 'shadowed out'] is great: the earlier version reveals the autobio-
graphical and confessional poet of 1833; the later shows the "dramatic" poet
which he strove to become'; but as J. C. Maxwell pointed out the word
'shadow' remains in 1888, in l. 885, while 'chronicled' has the same essential
meaning as 'tell' (1833): 'Browning's Concept of the Poet: A Revision in
Pauline', *Victorian Poetry* (Morgantown, Virginia), i (1963), 237–8.
    885 *shadow*: paint, depict.
    890 *the dim hush of night*: cf. *Childe Harold's Pilgrimage*, III. lxxxvi: 'It is the
hush of night'.
    902 *As I might kill her*: cf. 'Porphyria's Lover', published in the *Monthly
Repository*, January 1836 (repr. in *Bells and Pomegranates*, III, 'Dramatic Lyrics'),
but perhaps written in 1834 (Griffin and Minchin, 73).

Resource—an extreme want: never believe
Aught better could so look to thee, nor seek
Again the world of good thoughts left for me.   910
There were bright troops of undiscovered suns,
Each equal in their radiant course. There were
Clusters of far fair isles, which ocean kept
For his own joy, and his waves broke on them
Without a choice. And there was a dim crowd   915
Of visions, each a part of the dim whole.
And a star left his peers and came with peace
Upon a storm, and all eyes pined for him.
And one isle harboured a sea-beaten ship,
And the crew wandered in its bowers, and
    plucked   920
Its fruits, and gave up all their hopes for home.
And one dream came to a pale poet's sleep,
And he said, "I am singled out by God,
"No sin must touch me." I am very
    weak,
But what I would express is,—Leave me not,   925
Still sit by me—with beating breast, and hair
Loosened—watching earnest by my side,
Turning my books, or kissing me when I
Look up—like summer wind. Be still to me
A key to music's mystery, when mind fails,   930
A reason, a solution and a clue.
You see I have thrown off my prescribed rules:
I hope in myself—and hope, and pant, and love—
You'll find me better—know me more than
    when

908 1868 Resource,   909 1868 thee;   910 1868 for me!   Mill me. >
me: 912 1868 course; there   915 1868 choice; and   916 1868
whole: 917 1868 And one star   918 1868 him;   921 1868 fruits
and . . . . home;   926 1868 me with . . . . breast   927 1868 Loosened,
be watching   929 1868 wind!   930 1868 mystery   931 1868
clue!   933 1868 hope and pant and love.   934 1868 better,

Resource, an extreme want: never believe
Aught better could so look on thee; nor seek
Again the world of good thoughts left for mine!   910
There were bright troops of undiscovered suns,
Each equal in their radiant course; there were
Clusters of far fair isles which ocean kept
For his own joy, and his waves broke on them
Without a choice; and there was a dim crowd   915
Of visions, each a part of some grand whole:
And one star left his peers and came with peace
Upon a storm, and all eyes pined for him;
And one isle harboured a sea-beaten ship,
And the crew wandered in its bowers and
      plucked   920
Its fruits and gave up all their hopes of home;
And one dream came to a pale poet's sleep,
And he said, "I am singled out by God,
"No sin must touch me." Words are wild and
      weak,
But what they would express is,—Leave me not,   925
Still sit by me with beating breast and hair
Loosened, be watching earnest by my side,
Turning my books or kissing me when I
Look up—like summer wind! Be still to me
A help to music's mystery which mind fails   930
To fathom, its solution, no mere clue!
O reason's pedantry, life's rule prescribed!
I hopeless, I the loveless, hope and love.
Wiser and better, know me now, not
      when

908 *an extreme want*: 'He here apparently accents éxtreme', Pottle comments
(p. 53), 'which seems to have been Shelley's invariable scansion, and moreover
he uses the word in the sense oftenest employed by Shelley; last, or final: cf.
"extreme unction"'.
915–6 *a dim crowd / Of visions*: cf. 'The Triumph of Life', 482–3: 'the air / Was
peopled with dim forms'. and *Prometheus Unbound*, III. iii. 49: 'And lovely
apparitions,—dim at first'.
926–7 *and hair / Loosened*: as in l. 3.
930 *music's mystery*: cf. *Prometheus Unbound*, II. i. 66: 'Like music which makes
giddy the dim brain'.
932 *You see (1833)*: Mill commented 'poor', and then he or someone else
crossed the word out.

You loved me as I was. Smile not; I have   935
Much yet to gladden you—to dawn on you.

No more of the past—I'll look within no more—
I have too trusted to my own wild wants—
Too trusted to myself—to intuition,
Draining the wine alone in the still night,   940
And seeing how—as gathering films arose,
As by an inspiration life seemed bare
And grinning in its vanity, and ends
Hard to be dreamed of, stared at me as fixed,
And others suddenly became all foul,   945
As a fair witch turned an old hag at night.
No more of this—we will go hand in hand,
I will go with thee, even as a child,
Looking no further than thy sweet commands.

And thou hast chosen where this life shall be—   950
The land which gave me thee shall be our home,
Where nature lies all wild amid her lakes
And snow-swathed mountains, and vast pines all
    girt
With ropes of snow—where nature lies all bare,
Suffering none to view her but a race   955
Most stinted and deformed—like the mute
    dwarfs
Which wait upon a naked Indian queen.
And there (the time being when the heavens are
    thick
With storms) I'll sit with thee while thou dost
    sing
Thy native songs, gay as a desert bird   960

935 *1868* not!   936 *1868* gladden you,   {No paragraph division.}
937 *1868* past! I'll . . . . more.   938 *1868* wants,   *939 to myself—to
intuition, {apparently 'intuition.' in *1833*, almost certainly a broken comma}
1868 to myself, to intuition—   941 *1868* how,   945 *1868* foul
947 *1868* this! We   949 *Lowell* farther . . . . commands.   *1868* farther
. . . . commands, {No paragraph division.}   950 *1868* shall be.   953
1868 mountains   956 *1868* deformed,

You loved me as I was. Smile not! I have   935
Much yet to dawn on you, to gladden you.

No more of the past! I'll look within no more.
I have too trusted my own lawless wants,
Too trusted my vain self, vague intuition—
Draining soul's wine alone in the still night,   940
And seeing how, as gathering films arose,
As by an inspiration life seemed bare
And grinning in its vanity, while ends
Foul to be dreamed of, smiled at me as fixed
And fair, while others changed from fair to foul   945
As a young witch turns an old hag at night.
No more of this! We will go hand in hand,
I with thee, even as a child—love's slave,
Looking no farther than his liege commands.

And thou hast chosen where this life shall be: 950
The land which gave me thee shall be our home,
Where nature lies all wild amid her lakes
And snow-swathed mountains and vast pines
    begirt
With ropes of snow—where nature lies all bare,
Suffering none to view her but a race   955
Or stinted or deformed, like the mute
    dwarfs
Which wait upon a naked Indian queen.
And there (the time being when the heavens are
    thick
With storm) I'll sit with thee while thou dost
    sing
Thy native songs, gay as a desert bird   960

938 *I have too trusted*: the only examples of 'too' for 'too much' to qualify a verb given in OED after 1509 are this and *Red Cotton Night-Cap Country*, iii. 790 (*Poetical Works*, xii, 1889, pp. 124–5): 'Would too distract . . . / Inquirer'.
    945 *from fair to foul*: cf. *Macbeth*, I. i. 10.
    946 *a young witch*: cf. l.432, above.
    951 *The land*: cf. 806 and note, and the French note to 811. Switzerland is now strongly suggested, although the lovers are not in that country at this point.
    956 *stinted*: for 'stunted', as in 'James Lee's Wife' 323–4 ('with stinted soul / And stunted body').

Who crieth as he flies for perfect joy,
Or telling me old stories of dead knights.
Or I will read old lays to thee—how she,
The fair pale sister, went to her chill grave
With power to love, and to be loved, and live.   965
Or we will go together, like twin gods
Of the infernal world, with scented lamp
Over the dead—to call and to awake—
Over the unshaped images which lie
Within my mind's cave—only leaving all   970
That tells of the past doubts. So when spring
     comes,
And sunshine comes again like an old smile,
And the fresh waters, and awakened birds,
And budding woods await us—I shall be
Prepared, and we will go and think again,   975
And all old loves shall come to us—but changed
As some sweet thought which harsh words veiled
     before;
Feeling God loves us, and that all that errs,
Is a strange dream which death will dissipate;
And then when I am firm we'll seek again   980
My own land, and again I will approach
My old designs, and calmly look on all
The works of my past weakness, as one views
Some scene where danger met him long before.
Ah! that such pleasant life should be but dreamed!   985

962 *1868* knights;   963 *Mill* she, > She,   964 *Mill* sister, > Sis-
ter   965 *1868* love and to be loved and live: 968 *1868* dead, to . . . .
awake,   970 *Lowell* cave: only leaving all   *1868* cave: only leaving
all,   971 *1868* So,   974 *1868* us,   976 *1868* us,   979 *1868*
dissipate.   980 *Lowell* firm   *1868* firm,   985 *1868* Ah that

Which crieth as it flies for perfect joy,
Or telling me old stories of dead knights;
Or I will read great lays to thee—how she,
The fair pale sister, went to her chill grave
With power to love and to be loved and live: 965
Or we will go together, like twin gods
Of the infernal world, with scented lamp
Over the dead, to call and to awake,
Over the unshaped images which lie
Within my mind's cave: only leaving all   970
That tells of the past doubt. So, when spring
    comes
With sunshine back again like an old smile,
And the fresh waters and awakened birds
And budding woods await us, I shall be
Prepared, and we will question life once more,   975
Till its old sense shall come renewed by change,
Like some clear thought which harsh words
    veiled before;
Feeling God loves us, and that all which errs
Is but a dream which death will dissipate.
And then what need of longer exile? Seek   980
My England, and, again there, calm approach
All I once fled from, calmly look on those
The works of my past weakness, as one views
Some scene where danger met him long before.
Ah that such pleasant life should be but dreamed!   985

---

*970 {Reading of *Lowell*}   *1888, 1889* all,

963 *how she*: altered to 'She' in Mill copy, by Browning, who adds line
523 and lines 916–20 (omitting four words) of the *Antigone* of Sophocles,
in Greek: 'My nature is for mutual love, not hate . . . And now he drags
me . . ., A bride unwed, amerced of marriage-song / And marriage-bed and
joys of motherhood, / By friends deserted to a living grave' (Loeb trans, by
F. Storr, 1912).

970 *my mind's cave*: Pottle (p. 55) cites analogous passages in Shelley, notably
The Cenci, II. ii. 89: 'the inmost cave of our own mind'.

974–5 *I shall be / Prepared*: underlined by Mill, with the comment: 'he is
always talking of being *prepared*—what for?' Browning replies: 'Why, "that's
tellings," as schoolboys say'. He used the phrase again in a letter in 1863:
Browning to his American Friends, ed. G. R. Hudson (1965), p. 132.

But whate'er come of it—and tho' it fade,
And tho' ere the cold morning all be gone
As it will be;—tho' music wait for me,
And fair eyes and bright wine, laughing like
    sin,
Which steals back softly on a soul half saved;   990
And I be first to deny all, and despise
This verse, and these intents which seem so fair;
Still this is all my own, this moment's pride,
No less I make an end in perfect joy.
E'en in my brightest time, a lurking fear   995
Possessed me. I well knew my weak resolves,
I felt the witchery that makes mind sleep
Over its treasures—as one half afraid
To make his riches definite—but now
These feelings shall not utterly be lost,   1000
I shall not know again that nameless care,
Lest leaving all undone in youth, some new
And undreamed end reveal itself too late:
For this song shall remain to tell for ever,
That when I lost all hope of such a change,   1005
Suddenly Beauty rose on me again.
No less I make an end in perfect joy,
For I, having thus again been visited,
Shall doubt not many another bliss awaits,
And tho' this weak soul sink, and darkness
    come,   1010
Some little word shall light it up again,
And I shall see all clearer and love better;
I shall again go o'er the tracts of thought,
As one who has a right; and I shall live
With poets—calmer—purer still each time,   1015
And beauteous shapes will come to me again,

986 *1868* it, and though   987 *Lowell* though . . . . gone   *1868* though
. . . . gone,   989 *1868* wine laughing like sin   990 *1868*
saved,   992 *1868* fair,—   996 *1868* me: 998 *1868* treas-
ure,   999 *1868* definite: 1000 *Mill* lost, > lost;   1006 *1868*
beauty   1007 *Mill* joy, > joy;   1012 *1868* better,   1014 *1868*
right,

But whate'er come of it, and though it fade,
And though ere the cold morning all be gone,
As it may be;—tho' music wait to wile,
And strange eyes and bright wine lure, laugh like
    sin
Which steals back softly on a soul half saved,   990
And I the first deny, decry, despise,
With this avowal, these intents so fair,—
Still be it all my own, this moment's pride!
No less I make an end in perfect joy.
E'en in my brightest time, a lurking fear   995
Possessed me: I well knew my weak resolves,
I felt the witchery that makes mind sleep
Over its treasure, as one half afraid
To make his riches definite: but now
These feelings shall not utterly be lost,   1000
I shall not know again that nameless care
Lest, leaving all undone in youth, some new
And undreamed end reveal itself too late:
For this song shall remain to tell for ever
That when I lost all hope of such a change,   1005
Suddenly beauty rose on me again.
No less I make an end in perfect joy,
For I, who thus again was visited,
Shall doubt not many another bliss awaits,
And, though this weak soul sink and darkness
    whelm,   1010
Some little word shall light it, raise aloft,
To where I clearlier see and better love,
As I again go o'er the tracts of thought
Like one who has a right, and I shall live
With poets, calmer, purer still each time,   1015
And beauteous shapes will come for me to seize,

988 *to wile*: OED has no example of this intransitive use of the verb. Cf.
'beguile'.
  991 *And I the first*: oddly expressed, but explained by *1833*.
  994 *I make an end*: of this poem or meditation, not of his life, as some critics
have supposed. Cf. 1009.
  1006 *beauty rose on me*: cf. *Childe Harold*, III. lxxviii. 6, 'the dead who rise
upon our dreams'.
  1013 *tracts of thought*: cf. *Œdipus Tyrannus*, 67.
  1016 *beauteous shapes*: cf. *Prometheus Unbound*, I. 202.

And unknown secrets will be trusted me,
Which were not mine when wavering—but now
I shall be priest and lover, as of old.

Sun-treader, I believe in God, and truth,   1020
And love; and as one just escaped from death
Would bind himself in bands of friends to feel
He lives indeed—so, I would lean on thee;
Thou must be ever with me—most in gloom
When such shall come—but chiefly when I die,   1025
For I seem dying, as one going in the dark
To fight a giant—and live thou for ever,
And be to all what thou hast been to me—
All in whom this wakes pleasant thoughts of me,
Know my last state is happy—free from doubt,   1030
Or touch of fear. Love me and wish me well!

RICHMOND,
October 22, 1832.

1018 *1868* wavering;   1023 *1868* indeed, so, I would lean on thee!
1024 *1868* me,   1025 *1868* come,   1026 *1868* seem, dying,
1027 *1868* giant: 1028 *1868* to me!   1030 *Lowell* happy, free from
doubt,   *1868* happy, free from doubt

And unknown secrets will be trusted me
Which were denied the waverer once; but now
I shall be priest and prophet as of old.

Sun-treader, I believe in God and truth   1020
And love; and as one just escaped from death
Would bind himself in bands of friends to feel
He lives indeed, so, I would lean on thee!
Thou must be ever with me, most in gloom
If such must come, but chiefly when I die,   1025
For I seem, dying, as one going in the dark
To fight a giant: but live thou for ever,
And be to all what thou hast been to me!
All in whom this wakes pleasant thoughts of me
Know my last state is happy, free from doubt   1030
Or touch of fear. Love me and wish me well.

RICHMOND:
October 22, 1832.

1019 *as of old*: 'Hence, in a Roman mouth, the graceful name / Of prophet and of poet was the same': Cowper, *Table Talk*, 500–1, referring to the word 'vates'. Note the revision from 'lover'.

1026 *For I seem, dying*: this has combined with ll.994 and 1030 to mislead some critics. It does not mean that the speaker is dying, but that 'it seems to me that when I die I shall be . . .'

RICHMOND . . .*1832*: for Mill's objection, see p. 3.

INTRODUCTION TO 'PARACELSUS'

Much of what my later writings have been about—the clash of ability and aspirations, of will and possibility, at once the tragedy and the comedy of mankind and the individual—is already adumbrated here.

Ibsen.[1]

IN the preface to the first edition Browning stated that *Paracelsus* 'had not been imagined six months ago', i.e. by the middle of September 1834. In March and April of that year he had paid a brief visit to Russia with the Chevalier George de Benkhausen,[2] and soon after his return he met Comte Amédée de Ripert-Monclar, a French royalist of cultivated interests who spent his summers in England at this time, 'ostensibly for his pleasure, really—as he confessed to the Browning family—in the character of private agent of communication between the royal exiles and their friends in France'.[3] Mrs Orr further informs us that it was this young man, who was four years older than the poet and shared his intellectual tastes to such an extent as to create 'an immediate bond of union between them', who 'suggested the life of Paracelsus as a possible subject for a poem'.[4] On second thoughts he 'pronounced it unsuitable, because it gave no room for the introduction of love: about which, he added, every young man of their age thought he had something quite new to say'; but when Browning had considered the matter he 'decided, after the necessary study, that he would write a poem on Paracelsus, but treating him in his own way'.

When, three years later, Ripert-Monclar asked for details about his poems Browning stated that shortly after the publication of *Pauline* he had tired of the idea of producing a number

---

[1] Preface to the second edition of *Catiline* (1875).
[2] Maynard judges that 'The total stay in Russia could not have been much more than two weeks': *Browning's Youth*, p. 420 n. 246.
[3] *Life*, p. 67.
[4] Maynard (p. 124) states that this 'is neither confirmed nor denied by the evidence in Monclar's journals', which remain unpublished; but there seems no reason to reject Mrs Orr's explicit statement.

of compositions supposed to be by different writers, had destroyed some works inspired by it, and had begun a quite different poem which was clearly *Sordello*.[1] Almost all that we know of the writing of *Paracelsus*, which interrupted that of *Sordello*, derives from two further letters to Ripert-Monclar. 'Paracelsus is done!', Browning wrote excitedly on 5 December 1834. 'exegi monumentum[2]—good or ill, it is done—I have worked incessantly at it—not at the thing itself, that is; but at the big books of the great man & his friends, all a terrible bookmaking set; done—3000 verses in 3 months! but it has cost me some thought & more research . . . I shall publish it as soon as some few scenes, rather rough at present, get their final burnishing—I purposely forbear to enter into detail, because with the book I shall give a preface & notes'. He mentions that he has 'changed [his] conception' of *Sordello* and has therefore abandoned a tentative plan 'of sending them both into the world together'. On 2 March 1835 he wrote again: '"Paracelsus" is finished & ready to come out—I should tell you, that you would have heard of it long ere this, had I not been very ill for a month & more,—a horrible ulcerated sore throat which effectually put a stop to my labours—I am quite recovered now & have got thro' the job with proportionable dispatch—now, am I to understand, that your admirable desire to figure in the dedication-page as patron thereof, still continues undiminished? In the event of your silence on this head, I shall set it down as certain that you repent your precipitate good nature.—Tis an affair of some 4000 lines, done in 3 or 4 months, novel, as I think, in conception & execution at once, &, from its nature, not likely to secure an overwhelming auditory—*you* will make it out easily enough'. After repeating his desire to dedicate the poem to Ripert-Monclar, Browning comments: 'I shall be glad to have your strictures on my forthcoming work—'tis in some measure an experiment—I wonder whether I can explain it to you? Vediam un pò': The conditions of the *Drama* are well known:—Those of what is popularly termed the *Poem* no less so . . .'[3]

[1] Cf. introduction to *Sordello*.
[2] Horace, *Odes*, III. xxx. 1: 'I have completed a monument [more lasting than bronze]'.
[3] Cf. the preface to the first edition.

In a much later letter to Julia Wedgwood, Browning refer-
red to this bad throat as one of the only two illnesses he could
remember, adding: 'my mother nursed me . . ., and I wrote
"Paracelsus" as soon as I recovered: I remember I was a little
lightheaded one night, and fancied I had to go through a
complete version of the Psalms by Donne, Psalm by Psalm!'[1]
The letter to Ripert-Monclar of 5 December 1834 makes it
clear that some three-quarters of *Paracelsus* had in fact been
written in their first form before Browning fell ill. On his
recovery he must have worked extremely hard to complete
the poem so rapidly.

A letter to W. J. Fox dated 2 April reveals that Browning had
already been in correspondence with him about publication:

You will oblige me indeed by forwarding the introduction to
Moxon. I merely suggested him in particular, on account of his good
name and fame among author-folk . . . So I hope we shall come to
terms.

I also hope my poem will not turn out utterly unworthy your
kind interest, and more deserving your favour than anything of mine
you have as yet seen.[2]

A fortnight later Browning wrote to Fox again:

I lost no time in presenting myself to Moxon, but no sooner was Mr.
[Cowden] Clarke's letter perused than the Moxonian visage loured
exceedingly thereat—the Moxonian accent grew dolorous there-
upon:—"Artevelde" has not paid expenses by about thirty odd
pounds. Tennyson's poetry is *"popular at Cambridge,"* and yet of 800
copies which were printed of his last,[3] some 300 only have gone off:
Mr. M. hardly knows whether he shall ever venture again, &c. &c.,
and in short begs to decline even inspecting, &c. &c.

I called on Saunders and Otley at once, and, marvel of marvels, do
really think there is some chance of our coming to decent terms—I
shall know at the beginning of next week, but am not over-sanguine.

This letter throws a great deal of light on the poem. Remark-
ing that Fox 'must need very little telling from me, of the real
feeling I have of your criticism's worth', Browning refers to
his review of *Pauline* in a most significant sentence:

---

[1] *Robert Browning and Julia Wedgwood*, ed. Richard Curle (1937), pp. 101–2.
[2] *Life*, pp. 64–5.
[3] *Poems* ('1833', published December 1832).

not a particle of your article has been rejected or neglected by your observant humble servant, and very proud shall I be if my new work bear in it the marks of the influence under which it was undertaken . . .

But such as it is, it is very earnest and suggestive—and likely I hope to do good; and though I am rather scared at the thought of a *fresh eye* going over its 4,000 lines—discovering blemishes of all sorts which my one wit cannot avail to detect, fools treated as sages, obscure passages, slipshod verses, and much that worse is,—yet on the whole I am not much afraid of the issue, and I would give something to be allowed to read it some morning to you—for every rap o' the knuckles I should get a clap o' the back, I know.

I have another affair on hand, rather of a more popular nature, I conceive,[1] but not so decisive and explicit on a point or two—so I decide on trying the question with this:—I really shall *need* your notice, on this account; I shall affix my name and stick my arms akimbo; there are a few precious bold bits here and there, and the drift and scope are awfully radical—I am 'off' for ever with the other side, but must by all means be 'on' with yours—a position once gained, worthier works shall follow—therefore a certain writer[2] who meditated a notice (it matters not laudatory or otherwise) on 'Pauline' in the 'Examiner' must be benignant or supercilious as he shall choose, but in no case an idle spectator of my first appearance on any stage (having previously only dabbled in private theatricals) and bawl 'Hats off!' 'Down in front!' &c., as soon as I get to the proscenium; and he may depend that tho' my 'Now is the winter of our discontent' be rather awkward, yet there shall be occasional outbreaks of good stuff—that I shall warm as I get on, and finally wish 'Richmond at the bottom of the seas,' &c. in the best style imaginable.

Excuse all this swagger, I know you will . . .[3]

In the event neither Saunders and Otley nor John Murray[4] would accept *Paracelsus*: it was Effingham Wilson who 'was induced to publish the poem, but more, we understand, on the ground of radical sympathies in Mr. Fox and the author than on that of its intrinsic worth'.[5] Robert Browning Sr. paid the

[1] *Sordello*.
[2] John Stuart Mill: see p. 3.
[3] *Life*, pp. 66–7. The quotations from *Richard III* (I. i. 1 and IV. iv. 464) are a reminder of the impression made on Browning by Kean's acting of the part.
[4] Maynard, p. 428 n. 51.
[5] *Life*, p. 67. Wilson was a bookseller who had recently begun publishing on a small scale. One of his first publications had been Tennyson's *Poems, Chiefly Lyrical* (1830).

expenses of publication, and on 30 July the poet was able to send Ripert-Monclar a presentation copy: 'Do me the honor to accept the accompanying poem', he wrote. '. . . I have only to beseech you to criticize it as a *whole* & not in *detail*: I shall be glad to have your opinion about it'. This was an advance copy, not 'properly bound & burnished', and only just received. The poem was published on 15 August, and cost 6s. od. In 1842 Browning gave the MS to John Forster, 'my early Understander', and it is now printed opposite the final text of 1888.[1]

In suggesting Paracelsus as a subject for a poem Ripert-Monclar—to whom Browning is almost certain to have mentioned that he was writing on Sordello, and who must have been struck by his new friend's interest in the role of the exceptional man in the development of mankind—was drawing Browning's attention to an enigmatic figure about whom he had every opportunity of learning from his father's library.[2] He is likely already to have been familiar with the article in the *Biographie Universelle,* virtually certain to have read the entry in Jeremy Collier's *Great Historical, Geographical, Genealogical and Poetical Dictionary* (1701), the work which was much later to provide an epigraph for *Jocoseria.*[3] Whether or not he was yet aware of Donne's interest in Paracelsus,[4] or Shelley's, he was no doubt reminded of the man who aspired to be the Luther of Medicine when he attended medical lectures at London University.[5]

The brief account of Paracelsus in an article on the 'History

---

[1] In *Works and Days from the Journal of Michael Field,* ed. T. and D. C. Sturge Moore (1933, p. 207) Katherine Bradley (one half of 'Michael Field') states that, on 1 June 1895, she saw 'heaps and heaps of letters on the floor' of the 'Casa Browning' at Asolo and that Sarianna said that she had 'the proof sheets of *Paracelsus,* inscribed to his mother', apparently among these papers. It does not appear that Miss Bradley had any opportunity of looking at the proofs, and we have been unable to trace them.

[2] Griffin and Minchin, pp. 69 ff.

[3] 'I have the work, 2 vols folio', he wrote to Furnivall in 1884, 'and read it right through when I was a boy,—my Father gave it me many years after': *Trumpeter,* p. 101. Collier devotes half a column to Paracelsus (as against seven-and-a-half lines for Shakespeare), and his account is by no means unfavourable: 'He used to laugh at the ordinary way of practising Physick, and gloried to have overthrown the Method of Galen, which he saw was imperfect and doubtful, whereby he contracted the Hatred of the Physicians.'

[4] For Donne and Paracelsus see Joseph Anthony Mazzeo, *Renaissance and Seventeenth-Century Studies* (1964), pp. 60 ff.

[5] According to Sharp (p. 19), Browning told a friend that his father 'seemed to have known Paracelsus, Faustus, and even Talmudic personages, personally'.

and Present State of Chemical Science' which appeared in the *Edinburgh Review* for October 1829 may have caught Browning's eye, and is in any case of interest as the expression of an eminent chemist of the time.[1] The author recommends as 'the best edition' that 'published at Geneva, 1658, in three large folio volumes'[2], states that he 'appeared like a meteor towards the conclusion of the fifteenth century', and offers this general assessment:

The prodigious activity of Paracelsus, the arrogance of his style, the scurrility of his invectives, and even his reveries and absurdities, contributed to procure him a reputation, which was altogether unrivalled during his own lifetime. And as he was a zealous cultivator of Chemistry, and extolled chemical medicines to the skies, he threw a lustre upon the science of which it was before destitute . . . The invectives of Paracelsus against Galen and Avicenna, and their adherents and disciples, scurrilous and absurd as they are, were probably necessary to rouse the attention of mankind, and to induce medical men to abandon the jargon of the schools, and to apply themselves to anatomy and chemistry; the only true foundations on which a rational medical practice can be built.[3]

While Thomson points out that 'His opinions, as far as they are intelligible, are quite inconsistent with each other', and comments that 'Nothing can give us a more contemptible idea of the state of medicine in the sixteenth century, than the knowledge, that the writings of Paracelsus constitute an important era in its progress', he also remarks that 'If we compare the formulae of Paracelsus with those of Boyle, published a century and a half later, we will not have much cause to boast of the superiority of the nostrums of our own countryman, above those of the Basil professor'. He stresses the importance of opium in the medical practice of Paracelsus, and states that he 'consider[s] his treatise on *Minerals* as the most curious of all his works'.

While Browning retains certain of the principal events in the life of Paracelsus, however, his statement that 'The liberties I

[1] Thomas Thomson, Regius Professor of Chemistry at the University of Glasgow, 1818–52. For an estimate of his importance see J. B. Morrell, 'The Chemist Breeders: The Research Schools of Liebig and Thomas Thomson', *Ambix*, vol. xix, no. 1 (March 1972).
[2] Cf. Browning's 'Note', on p. 512 below.
[3] Vol. L [50], p. 258.

have taken with my subject are very trifling' is completely misleading. As Leigh Hunt pointed out, 'an imaginary character, and to a large extent also an imaginary history, are bestowed upon the famous empiric';[1] while three personages are added who have no basis in history.

The addition of an admiring friend (Festus) was a natural step; as was that of his wife, Michal. The fact that Paracelsus retains their love from his student days onwards renders him more sympathetic to the reader, while they act as a chorus, commenting on his spectacular career and reminding the over-reacher (the Marlovian term is appropriate) of the dangers of his course. As for possible parallels between Browning and his protagonist, we need not quarrel with DeVane's carefully-qualified statement that 'We may read, with caution, a good deal of the character and aspirations of the young Browning in Paracelsus.' It is less certain that we are wise 'to see a dim reflection of Browning's own career at London in the account of Paracelsus' erratic education at Würzburg'.[2] When Mrs Betty Miller pushes her suggestion that Festus and Michal represent the attitude of Browning's parents towards their gifted son to the point of conjecturing that 'This inner equation seems to have governed the choice of names: Festus, Father: Michal, Mother', she illustrates the danger of such attractive speculations.[3]

The fact that Browning was undeterred by Ripert-Monclar's objection that the subject offered no opportunity 'for the introduction of love' relates to two noteworthy features of the poem. First, while Browning follows the usual biographical accounts in refraining from portraying Paracelsus as the lover of any particular woman, there is no suggestion at all that he is impotent. Michal expects him to be loved by 'some woman' as beautiful as he is wise,[4] while the pleasures to which he stoops in his later disillusionment would seem to include those of licentious sexuality. The tradition that Paracelsus had been castrated simply gave Browning an

[1] *Leigh Hunt's London Journal*, 21 November 1835, p. 406 b. Cf. p. 137n.
[2] Maynard, p. 280.
[3] *Robert Browning: A Portrait* (1952), pp. 4 ff. Lee and Locock had earlier pointed out, much more cautiously, that 'Festus may be a sketch of Browning's father in certain of his aspects': p. 23.
[4] iii. 67–8.

opportunity of presenting him as one of those 'luminaries of
the world' of whom Shelley had written in the preface to
Alastor, those who 'keep aloof from sympathies with their
kind' in their single-minded devotion to a superhuman goal.
But, secondly, Browning introduces a character who is par-
ticularly associated with love, the poet Aprile, to whom some
of the finest verse is given (e.g. ii. 420 ff.), yet about whom
almost every critic has felt uneasy. In fact he is not a character
at all, in any naturalistic sense. It is significant that Paracelsus
meets him in 'the house of a Greek Conjurer' and believes, in
his disordered state of mind, that he has 'compelled' him from
his 'lair', as if he were a spirit whom he had summoned from
another realm. It is not merely that 'all the *events*, (and inter-
est), take place in the *minds* of the actors', as Browning was
later to write of *Luria*:[1] Aprile has no reality or importance
except in relation to Paracelsus: they are two 'halves of one
dissevered world' (ii. 634): Paracelsus calls him

> My strange competitor in enterprise,
> Bound for the same end by another path,   (iii. 380–1)

and at ii. 624–6 he draws the parallel between them:

> I too have sought to KNOW as thou to LOVE—
> Excluding love as thou refusedst knowledge.
> Still thou hast beauty and I, power.

He comes to realize that it is only the illusion of power which
he possesses, however, and it is in comparing himself with
Aprile that Paracelsus comes to full understanding, as he
approaches the moment of death and looks back at an earlier
time when he had 'prayed to die':

> A strange adventure made me know, one sin
> Had spotted my career from its uprise;
> I saw Aprile—my Aprile there!
> And as the poor melodious wretch disburthened
> His heart, and moaned his weakness in my ear,
> I learned my own deep error; love's undoing
> Taught me the worth of love in man's estate,
> And what proportion love should hold with power
> In his right constitution.   (v. 849–57)

---

[1] Kintner, i. 381.

It is a theme which is prominent in much of Browning's poetry, not least in *Sordello*.[1]

The life and work of Paracelsus offered Browning an opportunity of dealing with two of his most constant preoccupations, the 'incidents in the development of a soul', on the one hand, and the moral and intellectual development of mankind, on the other.

Browning agreed with Fox that 'The most deeply interesting adventures, the wildest vicissitudes, the most daring explorations, the mightiest magic, the fiercest conflicts, the brightest triumphs, and the most affecting catastrophes, are those of the spiritual world', and accepted his view that 'The knowledge of mind is the first of sciences'.[2] While he shared Carlyle's passionate interest in Heroes, and in their role in the development of mankind,[3] Browning had a particular interest in men of great potential who had striven only to fail, who had 'aspired' without ever completely 'attaining'. As Fox had written in the review of *Pauline* which meant so much to Browning, 'The abasement of a mighty spirit, brooding over the wreck of character produced by its own mistaken daring, may be invested with all the touching sublimity of the historical incident of Marius . . . amid the ruins of Carthage'.[4] Forster, who believed that Browning's presentation of Paracelsus was not only 'perfectly new' but one which would be found, 'in all general respects, a sufficient solution of one of the most extraordinary problems contained in the history of men of science and letters', went on to claim that Paracelsus 'was to the physical creation what Rousseau was to the moral. Nature intended them both, in their respective sphere, for heroes; the world made them both cowards. . . Much of their knowledge [he continued] in both cases appears to have been intuitive. . . The Secret they appear to have had, but in the shape of a vast perception unexpressed, uncomprehended by their narrow

---

[1] Cf. 'Browning's Conception of Love as Represented in *Paracelsus*', by William O. Raymond, in *The Infinite Moment* (2nd ed., Toronto, 1965), p. 156.

[2] *The Monthly Repository for 1833* (NS vol. vii), p. 252–3.

[3] Carlyle's lectures *On Heroes, Hero-Worship, and the Heroic in History* were not published until 1841, but the importance of the Hero is stressed in much of his earlier work.

[4] loc. cit., p. 252.

thought, but felt and known, even in every shift and change of the spirit they bore. Both of them, as was natural in such circumstances, were men of brilliant excuses'.[1] Paracelsus is the first in the series of imaginary characters inspired by historical personages which includes Andrea del Sarto, Fra Lippo Lippi, and Bishop Blougram.

While the poem is a psychological study of considerable depth and penetration it also, as Forster pointed out, 'embraces in its development . . . many of the highest questions, and glances with . . . a masterly perception at some of the highest problems, of man's existence'.[2] It is Browning's first contribution to the debate on Progress which had gathered force in the later part of the previous century and which was to continue throughout his own lifetime. In view of Paracelsus's interest in mineralogy it is fascinating to realize that Lyell's *Principles of Geology* had appeared in three parts between 1830 and 1833, and that Darwin was on his momentous voyage on HMS *Beagle* while the poem was being written. It is not surprising that Browning later became tired of being asked to comment on his attitude to Darwin, but it is interesting to notice his statement to Furnivall that 'all that seems *proved* in Darwin's scheme was a conception familiar to me from the beginning: see in *Paracelsus* the progressive development from senseless matter to organized, until man's appearance (*Part* v)'.[3] Browning's beliefs derived from Lamarck and other earlier thinkers whose work frequently reached him at second-hand through the medium of poetry and other imaginative writing. Those who wish to pursue the question may turn to J. B. Bury's classic study, *The Idea of Progress* (which stresses the importance of French thinkers), to Georg Roppen's useful work, *Evolution and Poetic Belief*, and to many other studies. It is no disparagement to the imaginative power of Browning's speculations on such matters to comment that it is the fact that he presents them as part of a psychological study of an intricate

---

[1] *The New Monthly Magazine, 1836: Part the First*, pp. 291, 306.
[2] Ibid., p. 290.
[3] *Trumpeter*, p. 34. Cf. Maynard, pp. 338 ff. As Georg Roppen remarks, 'Browning's teleology, like that of Tennyson, is as much a development of eighteenth-century speculations about cosmic transition and change as an anticipation of the modern evolutionary theory, which, in any case, Lamarck had clearly stated': *Evolution and Poetic Belief* (1956), p. 122.

and enigmatic personality that invests them with their deepest interest.

Unusual as it is, *Paracelsus* is very much a poem of the 1830s. In 1828, influenced by the spirit of the age, Browning had enrolled as a student of German, and Maynard has suggested that the lectures of Professor Ludwig von Mühlenfels may have contributed to the intellectual background of the poem.[1] Carlyle's *Sartor Resartus*, with its injunction to 'Close thy *Byron*; open thy *Goethe*',[2] had completed its serial publication in August 1834. Many writers have noticed the affinity between *Paracelsus* and *Faust* (as between Paracelsus and Faust),[3] and the first complete translation of Part I of Goethe's masterpiece,[4] that of Abraham Hayward, had appeared in 1833, to be followed by the verse-translations of John S. Blackie and John Anster in 1834 and 1835. Whether or not *Paracelsus* was influenced in any degree by Goethe, it could certainly be described as 'Faustish', to borrow an adjective from Byron.[5]

In later years Browning gave somewhat inaccurate accounts of the initial reception of *Paracelsus*, and it is important to notice that in 1837 he told Ripert-Monclar that it had been much more successful than he had expected.[6] In 1845 he wrote to Elizabeth Barrett:

---

[1] *Browning's Youth*, pp. 274 ff. In view of Browning's repeated and testy denial of German influence it is amusing to read Joseph Arnould's letter to him of 19 December 1847: 'My dear Browning do you know the German transcendental writers at all, especially Fichte! . . . formalized in Fichte's books I find what has long been hovering vaguely before my own mind as truth . . . DO READ THEM . . . I am sure you could find grand food for thought in them: to my mind the most satisfactory word which has yet been spoken about that which is of supreme interest to all men. You will find yourself in a school where Carlyle evidently has been a most earnest student: the manner even closely resembling Carlyle in his loftier & graver moods . . . Altogether I think *you* must read these works. Tell me about it when you next write . . . I should so like you to give me the benefit of your thoughts on such great subjects as that of the Progress of the Race as developed after Fichte's theory in his book . . . named Characteristics of the Present Age, which . . . contains his whole plan of world history . . .': Donald Smalley, 'Joseph Arnould and Robert Browning: New Letters . . .': PMLA lxxx (March, 1965), pp. 97–8.
[2] Book II, ch. ix, para. 14.
[3] On the former see Roppen, p. 114, and on the latter the first chapter of *Paracelsus: Magic into Science*, by Henry M. Pachter (New York, 1951).
[4] If we ignore Leveson Gower's unsatisfactory rendering.
[5] Used to describe *The Deformed Transformed*, in *Letters and Journals*, ed. R. E. Prothero, v (1901), p. 518.
[6] Unpublished letter (dated 9 August) in the collection of Professor Purdy.

"Paracelsus" . . . had been as dead a failure as [Talfourd's] "Ion" a brilliant success—for, until just before . . Ah, really I forget!—but I know that until Forster's notice in the "Examiner" appeared, *every* journal that thought worth while to allude to the poem at all, treated it with entire contempt . . beginning, I think, with the "Athenæum" which *then* made haste to say, a few days after its publication, "that it was not without talent but spoiled by obscurity and only an imitation of—Shelley!"—something to this effect, in a criticism of about three lines among their "Library Table" notices: and that first taste was a most flattering sample of what the "craft" had in store for me—since my publisher and I had fairly to laugh at *his* 'Book' . . . in which he was used to paste extracts from newspapers & the like—seeing that, out of a long string of notices, one vied with its predecessor in disgust at my "rubbish," as their word went: but Forster's notice altered a good deal—which I have to recollect for his good . . .[1]

In 1875 Browning wrote in similar terms, complaining to Forster of 'what I find is something like a common belief—that *Paracelsus* was welcomed with the warmest acknowledgements' and repeating 'the true story of everybody's silence or condemnation till the *Examiner* spoke up for it', an account repeated almost verbatim in a letter to George Grove the following year.[2] While his gratitude to Forster does him credit, it is clear that his expectations on this his 'first appearance on any stage' must have been exceptionally high, since Forster's enthusiastic review appeared just three weeks after the poem's publication, to be followed by an eleven-page review by Fox in the *Monthly Repository* for November, a generous and perceptive piece by Leigh Hunt (containing copious quotations) in the course of the same month, and then Forster's 'Evidences of a New Genius for Dramatic Poetry.—No. 1' in the *New Monthly Magazine* the following

---

[1] Kintner i. 312. As we now know, Elizabeth Barrett had written to Miss Mitford about the poem in July or August 1836: 'have you seen Paracelsus? I . . . would wish for more harmony and rather more clearness and compression—*concentration*—besides: but I do think and feel that the pulse of poetry is full and warm and strong in it . . . There is a palpable power—a height and depth of thought—and sudden repressed gushings of tenderness which suggest to us a depth beyond, in the affections': *Elizabeth Barrett to Miss Mitford*, ed. Betty Miller (1954), p. 10. Although she wishes 'that some passages . . . referring to the divine Being had been softened or removed' she concludes that 'the author is a poet in the holy sense'. Cf. p. 134.

[2] *New Letters*, pp. 230–1.

year.[1] On 26 May 1836, at the famous supper to celebrate the success of *Ion*, Wordsworth is said to have 'leaned across the table and remarked, "I am proud to drink your health, Mr. Browning!"'.[2] Later that year another distinguished writer who had been present, Walter Savage Landor, mentioned the poem with commendation in *A Satire on Satirists*:[3] a tribute which elicited a response in *Sordello* (iii. 951 ff.) and won the most irascible of authors a lifelong friend. When it is remembered that *Paracelsus* appeared at a time when poetry was little in demand we can only conclude that it achieved a most notable *succès d'estime*. Browning had aspired, and seemed well on the way to attaining. Elizabeth Barrett was not the only reader to see in the poem 'the expression of a new mind'.[4]

The Text

The manuscript of *Paracelsus* in the Forster Collection at the Victoria and Albert Museum is a handsome fair copy, written by Browning in a clear, regular hand on greyish paper, each leaf being approximately 27.5cm × 22cm. The original large sheets, folded once to make folio gatherings, were cut down the fold and rebound in 1969, when three misplaced leaves were correctly inserted. The ink is now a fairly dark brown, with occasional deletions and insertions in a similar or darker ink. These are probably by Browning, except on p. 65 (at the end of Part III), where they may be by the printer, since the name of the compositor, Stock, is inked in. Elsewhere, the compositors' names (J. Riggs, Child, and Stock) are usually pencilled in, along with figures in ink indicating signatures, in

---

[1] *The Examiner*, 6 September 1835, pp. 563–5; *Monthly Repository*, November 1835 (NS vol. ix), pp. 716–27: *Leigh Hunt's London Journal*, 21 November 1835, pp. 405–8. Litzinger and Smalley give extracts, and conclude that 'With the general reception of *Paracelsus*, Browning's hopes seemed on the way to fulfilment': p. 4.

[2] Griffin and Minchin, p. 77. Two sonnets 'To the Author of "Paracelsus"' were published in Part iii of the *New Monthly Magazine* for 1836 (p. 48). They were the anonymous work of Fanny Haworth.

[3] 'Did *Paracelsus* spring from poet's brain [?]', line 67 demands rhetorically; while a footnote comments, no doubt with reference to Forster or Leigh Hunt: '*Paracelsus* has found a critick capable of appreciating him. It is not often that the generous are so judicious, nor always that the judicious are so generous'.

[4] Kintner, i. 316.

a sequence lacking L and N. The pencilled alterations of punc-
tuation in Parts I and III and the first leaf of Part IV, look like
house-styling, and may well be those of the printer: most of
them correspond with, or are in the same style as, the punctua-
tion of the first edition.

We decided to print a transcript of the MS rather than the
first edition for comparison with the edition of 1888, because
the first edition (1835) radically alters the punctuation, and
hence the tone and pace of the poem. It will be obvious from
our transcript that Browning's own pointing was unconven-
tional, relying mainly on dots, dashes, and commas. When a
mark of punctuation has been altered by the author himself (as
far as we can tell), we have printed his revised version—typi-
cally, a dash replacing a series of dots. We have not reproduced
the printers' alterations. We include the few substantive
changes, the original version within angled brackets, and the
revision within square brackets. Italics represent underlining.

The edition of 1835 follows the MS closely in substantives;
hence its variants are logically printed below the MS trans-
cript. The list is selective. *1835* normally prints 'mass'd', for
example, instead of 'massed', represents a series of dots or
dashes by a single dash, and frequently omits a dash following
some other punctuation mark: such variants are so numerous
and so habitual that they do not seem worth recording, but we
do aim to show the more significant changes—especially the
new sentence divisions, heavier pointing, and removal of
upper case initials for key words such as 'Truth' and 'Knowing'.
Browning was not pleased with the printing of the first edition:
in presenting what is now the Ashley Library copy to his friend
J. Westland Marston, Browning wrote, beneath the date 'April
21. 1844,' the comment '(Errors of the press—past calculation!)'

The text of 1835 shows that Browning must have changed
the wording of the MS slightly in about a dozen passages,
presumably in proof. Changes which seem almost certain to
be his are at ii. 399, iii. 885, *v*. 173, 759, 805, and 863, all
clarifying the sense or improving the sound. In addition, the
variants at ii. 481, iii. 124, 641a, and 765 are acceptable and
could be authorial revisions. Misprints corrected in later edi-
tions occur at i. 42, 360, 394, and *v*. 485. Two misprints caused
by misreading of handwriting ('heeds' for 'needs' at ii. 514 and

'affections' for 'affection' at iii. 8) have been corrected by the present editors: 'decries' for 'descries' at iii. 348 may also be a misprint, but the editors considered (perhaps wrongly) that Browning himself would have corrected such a distinctive word had he thought it necessary. Changed punctuation in *1835* sometimes distorts the sense, but in most cases revisions after 1835 have removed the need to consider emendation. An exception is the superfluous comma at the end of v. 714, first introduced in 1835; here we have restored the reading of the MS.

Paracelsus was thoroughly revised—indeed almost rewritten—and expanded for the two-volume collected edition of 1849. Browning was evidently known to be contemplating revision as early as 1846, for Arnould wrote to him on December 6th of that year: 'All success to the revision of Paracelsus & the Bells & Pomegranates: . . . . I say run the risk of all things for the sake of being clear; . . . . but, of course don't let us miss one of the characteristic features or well known hues which have long since settled so deeply into all our hearts:—in fact I know you will not do this.'[1] Browning himself consistently underestimated the extent of his revision. His motive for bringing out a new edition, he wrote to Moxon on 24 February 1847, was the 'real good' he could do to '*Paracelsus*, *Pippa*, and some others; good, not obtained by cutting them up and reconstructing them, but by affording just the proper revision they ought to have had before they were printed at all.'[2]

Interesting evidence exists, showing the nature and method of Browning's reworking. The Berg Collection in New York Public Library contains a copy of the first edition of *Paracelsus*, inscribed by Browning on the half-title; '(First corrections, made at Pisa, in the Spring of 1847.)' An inscription on the title-page reads 'S. A. Browning. (To Frederick Locker from RB)'. Browning's revisions, extending through the whole poem, are written in ink in the margins, between the lines, and in other available spaces—consequently the hand is sometimes cramped, and alterations difficult to decipher. A few long

---

[1] Quoted in D. Smalley, 'Joseph Arnould and Robert Browning', PMLA 1965, p. 95.
[2] Hood, *Letters* (1933), p. 14.

passages are written on slips of paper stuck in, but allowing the original text, sometimes with preliminary revisions, to appear. Some pages show signs of erased pencil notes. Almost all the revisions of the 1849 text are represented in some way in the Berg copy. They do not always tally precisely in punctuation, and there are several verbal differences. The copy also contains a handful of lines and phrases which were not used in 1849. It is of unusual interest, since it shows Browning in the process of composition, and we have recorded its substantive variants in our notes. He negated some of his revisions, either by straightforward deletion, or by adding 'stet' marks beneath the original words. We have described such readings as 'rejected'. We do not record Berg readings which agree substantially with those of 1849, nor isolated deletions which remain obstinately illegible.

The Berg copy was almost certainly not used by the printers to set up the new 1849 edition; Browning probably made further alterations in a revised fair copy. It would therefore be unwise to regard it as a reliable source of emendations. Nevertheless it may be used with caution to support emendation where all other texts are unsatisfactory. For example, it shows that Browning altered 'Some twenty years ago' to 'So many years ago' (iii. 18), presumably because he had changed '1507' to '1512' in Part I; but *1849* and subsequent editions retain the inconsistent 'twenty years'. Our emendation is based on the Berg revision. We have also used the evidence of the Berg copy to support our removal of 'it' from ii. 434: sense, grammar, and metre all strongly suggest that the word is a misprint.

Another revised copy of the first edition exists in Yale University Library. As far as p. 90 (iii. 377) revisions were originally made in pencil in a neat sloping handwriting that may be Browning's, but these have been obscured by writing in a more upright, rather clumsy hand, presumably copying the underlying notes. Occasionally, as on p. 21, and on the back of one of the inserted slips, a few lines in the original hand can still be deciphered. Slips are attached, as in the Berg copy, but these are written by the copyist. The insertions, unlike those in the Berg copy, do not include minor deletions and revisions, and they are incomplete, representing perhaps two-thirds of the changes made in this section of the 1849 edition. They may sometimes indicate a genuine authorial variant, but they also contain obviously nonsensical or non-metrical readings which probably derive from the copyist's failure to decipher the original hand. For example, at the foot of page 30, the copyist writes what looks like 'I have my belief' for *1849*'s 'Than my belief' (i. 606), 'hand' for 'home' at i. 108, and 'ride' for 'rise' at i. 112. The last two *may* be authorial, but seem more likely to be misreadings. Delenda are often carelessly or incompletely indicated, and many of the marginal insertions are, for no obvious reason, underlined. The copyist's hand contains some peculiarities, such as a long-tailed 'r', and this fact, added to the complications of the palimpsest, makes accurate transcription difficult. From p. 91 onwards, the notes are those of the copyist only. Unlike the earlier insertions, these could derive (with a few inaccuracies and omissions) from a printed copy of *1849*. It will be obvious that this Yale copy is of dubious value in an analysis of the transmission of the text or of Browning's revisions; we have therefore included its variants in an appendix instead of in our textual notes.

Yale University also possesses a copy of the first edition ('Copy 3') with a few corrections in what may be Browning's hand; on page 27, for example, ' "Apart for all reward?" ' is corrected to ' "Apart from all reward?" ' (i. 543). A copy of the first edition in the Sterling Library of the University of London has Browning's signature on the fly-leaf, and nine minor emendations: for example, 'not seldom' is changed to 'but seldom' at iii. 298. The Lowell copy in the Houghton Library, Harvard, inscribed in Browning's hand, 'To George Cattermole Esq, with the Author's sincere regard. June 5, 1837', also contains corrections. Most of these coincide with the corrections in the Sterling Library copy, and are incorporated in later editions. Both copies also alter 'improved' to 'approved' in l. i. 310e—part of a passage omitted in 1849. An undated fragment in the Forster collection at the Victoria and Albert Museum contains six lines of verse ('I am no trumpet. . . .') in Elizabeth Barrett Browning's handwriting, followed by ll. v. 186–192 of *Paracelsus* ('Oh, emptiness of fame!') in the hand of Browning. These lines were added to the poem in 1849, and the text agrees substantially with that edition, except that 'Who' is underlined in l.188, and l.190 has been altered from 'To gaze on glooms' to its present reading.

Our textual notes, in conjunction with the parallel texts, show how extensive Browning's revisions for *1849* were. We number the manuscript lines not as an independent sequence, but to show their correspondence with our accepted text (based on that of 1888). Thus lines which were omitted in 1849, and which occur only in the manuscript or *1835*, are marked as extra, using lower case letters of the alphabet, so that they can be readily identified. Where *1849* or later editions introduce new matter, we use the formula, 'No equivalent in *MS* or *1835*.' It may be useful to draw attention to some of the most interesting of these additions. At i. 400–14 Festus's persuasion is eloquently extended. At ii. 281–96 Browning added a sixteen-line proem to the song, 'Lost, lost!' In *1849* the proem is headed 'Aprile, from within'. It is possible that Browning intended this direction to apply to the song, not the proem (which is on a separate slip of paper in *Berg*), and that the compositor mistakenly placed it before the new material. The edition of 1863 retains this placing, but restores the wording of *1835* ('A voice from within')—perhaps implying that the extra lines are Paracelsus' comment on the 'voice'—and adds inverted commas for the song. Other notable additions in *1849* are the picturesque description of Aprile's appearance in the light of the setting sun (ii. 407–17); the sudden introduction of an orthodox Christian interpretation of God's love after ii. 649 (six lines discarded in subsequent editions); a reference to heaven's 'beatitudes', also modified later, in the additional lines at iii. 378–86); a curious line 'And let the next world's knowledge dawn on this', occurring only in 1849 (after iii. 579); and 17 lines (iv. 434–49) linking Paracelsus's song to the searching questions of Festus. Paracelsus's two long speeches, beginning 'What have I done?' (v. 158) were much altered and expanded. Interestingly, nearly 50 lines of his last great speech (v. 643–90) were left almost intact.

Revisions made in 1849 can be identified by reference to the text and notes printed on the right hand page. The text of *1849* is substantially the same as that of *1888* except where a variant is given in the textual footnotes. Thus if the 1888 text differs in substantives from that of the MS, the reader can assume that the difference arises from a revision made in 1849 unless the footnotes indicate otherwise.

Browning was evidently dissatisfied with his 1849 version of the poem. He wrote to Moncure Daniel Conway on 17th September 1863, referring to the new three-volume edition of that year, that there were 'no changes of importance in any of the poems—merely verbal corrections, nor many of these:—in the instance of *Paracelsus*, the few changes are simply a return to the original reading, which I had polished a little, in the second edition, and done no good to.'[1] Arnould, on the other hand, had liked most of the alterations, though he had reservations: 'I need not say that my creed is still rather with 'Paracelsus' as he was, than as he is;' he wrote on 25 April 1850.[2] In fact, though Browning wrote dismissively of the 'few changes' in his revision for *1863*, his recension was both careful and extensive. He removed some ambiguities and repetitions, and, on the whole, made the punctuation heavier; and, as he acknowledged in his letter, he frequently restored both the phrasing and punctuation of the first edition, or based his revisions on it in preference to *1849*. Hence many of the variants recorded in our notes are the unique readings of *1849*, which forms a kind of cul-de-sac in the progress of the poem. The text of *1863* is generally reliable, though it has a few obvious 'errors of the press'. A reversion to an inferior reading, 'Needs', occurs at i. 76, where we have preferred the text of *1849*.

After 1863 there were few major alterations. As usual, the fourth edition (that of 1865) has to be treated with caution. It introduces a handful of genuine substantive changes (for example, 'until you teach' for 'until you have taught' at iii. 901, 'new-hearted' for 'and untired' at i. 394); but it also introduces quite a large number of misprints. Marks of punctuation and even whole words are dropped—such as the key-word 'ill' at iv. 664; some words are mis-spelt, and occasionally word-order is changed. The edition of 1868 corrected the grosser errors, but missed others. Where we consider the variants originating in 1865 to be clearly inferior, we have restored the

---

[1] *New Letters* (1951), p. 157.
[2] PMLA (1965), p. 100.

readings of 1863; for example, 'whence' has been restored at v.
831, 'temple-courts' at ii. 94, and 'wants' at ii. 447.

Most of the alterations made in 1868 and 1888 were correc-
tions of misprints, or slight adjustments of punctuation. Ver-
bal changes are few and insignificant. When Browning was
preparing his works for the 1888 edition he intended that there
should be 'no alterations except of the most trifling nature',[1]
and he evidently decided that the much-revised *Paracelsus*
(unlike *Pauline*) needed little attention. In fact *1888* corrects
most of the misprints of *1868*, but not 'heart-strings' at ii. 379.
We have emended, since the metaphor seems to depend on the
'heart-springs' of earlier editions. Similarly, at v. 890, we have
restored the reading 'light-springs', obviously preferable to
the 'life-springs' introduced in *1868*. We have also corrected
about a dozen minor errors in *1888*, such as 'ere' for 'e'er' at iii.
74. Nevertheless, *1888* was on the whole well-printed, and was
only slightly revised by Browning in the Dykes Campbell
copy. The 1889 edition incorporates all but one of his correc-
tions, but loses a few end-of-line marks of punctuation; some
copies have 'toil' for 'tell' at iii. 725. Our basic text is that of
1888, emended according to the Dykes Campbell revisions.[2]

---

[1] Letter to Mrs. Charles Skirrow, 24 Jan. 1888. (*New Letters*, p. 355.)
[2] In the MS an engraving of a full-length 'portrait' of Paracelsus holding his sword
Azoth serves as a frontispiece. Above it is written, in Browning's hand, '(Parturiunt
madido quae nixu proela, recepta: Sed quae scripta manu sunt—veneranda magis.)',
and in the right-hand margin, 'To *John Forster Esq* (my early Understander) with true
thanks for his generous & seasonable public Confession of Faith in me. RB. *Hatcham,
Surrey, 1842.*' A second engraving, 'Effigies Paracelsi Medici celeberrimi', follows
Part III, and a third, with the lines 'Hic est cui magni mysteria cognita mundi: Et dare
qui potuit de salis arte salem.', is inserted after Part IV.

PARACELSUS

INSCRIBED TO

AMÉDÉE DE RIPERT-MONCLAR

BY HIS AFFECTIONATE FRIEND

R. B.

LONDON: *March* 15, 1835.

The dedication is present in all editions except *1849*. In *1835* it reads: 'INSCRIBED TO THE COMTE A. DE RIPERT-MONCLAR, BY HIS AFFECTIONATE FRIEND, ROBERT BROWNING.'

BROWNING'S PREFACE TO THE
PARACELSUS MANUSCRIPT

I am anxious that the Reader should not, ⟨—⟩ at the very out-
set—mistaking my performance for one of a class with which it has
nothing in common—judge it by principles on which it was never
moulded, & subject it to a standard to which it was never meant to
conform. : I therefore anticipate his discovery that it is an attempt,
probably more novel than happy, to reverse the method usually
adopted by writers whose aim it is to set forth any phaenomenon of
the mind or the passions by the operation of persons & events; & that
instead of having recourse to an external machinery of incidents to
create & evolve the crisis I desire to produce, I have ventured to
display somewhat minutely the Mood itself in its rise & progress,
& have suffered the agency by which it is influenced & determined,
to be generally discernible in its effects alone, & subordinate
throughout if not altogether excluded: & this for a reason. I have
endeavoured to write a Poem, not a Drama;—the canons of the
Drama are well known, & I cannot but think that, inasmuch as they
have immediate regard to stage-representation, the peculiar advan-
tages they hold out are really such only so long as the purpose for
which they were at first instituted is kept in view. I do not very well
understand what is called a Dramatic Poem, wherein all those restric-
tions only submitted to on account of compensating good in the
original scheme, are scrupulously retained as tho' for some special
fitness in themselves,—& all new facilities placed at an author's
disposal by the vehicle he selects, as pertinaciously rejected. It is
certain, however, that a work like mine depends more immediately
on the intelligence & sympathy of the Reader for its success—indeed
were my scenes stars it must be his co-operating fancy which,
supplying all chasms, shall connect the scattered lights into one
constellation—a Lyre or a Crown. I trust for his indulgence towards
a poem which had not been imagined six months ago; & that even
should he think slightingly of the present (an experiment I am in no
case likely to repeat) he will not be prejudiced against other produc-
tions which may follow in a more popular, & perhaps less difficult
form.

15. *March 1835*

{Commas are pencilled in after 'discovery' (l. 5), and 'passions' (l. 8);
the colon after 'conform.' (l. 5) is deleted in pencil. In the first edition

(1835) the text is substantially that of the MS, except that lower case initials are used for 'reader', 'mood', 'poem' (l. 13) and 'drama'. The preface was not printed in editions after 1835.}

PERSONS.

AUREOLUS PARACELSUS, *a student.*[1]
FESTUS *and* MICHAL, *his friends.*
APRILE, *an Italian poet.*[2]

[1] *a student*: added in *1863*.
[2] an Italian poet: added in *1849* ('*Poet*'). *1835* has a note (based on *MS*) after the list of
Persons: '*N.B.—For the localities and dates, see the note at the end.*'

PARACELSUS

I.   PARACELSUS ASPIRES.

Scene,   *Würzburg. a garden in the Environs.* 1507.
          Festus, Paracelsus, Michal.

P*l.*   Come close to me, dear Friends; still
        closer—thus;
       Close to the heart which,—tho' long time roll
        by
       Ere it again beat quicker, pressed to yours,
       As now it beats . . . perchance a long, long
        time . . . .
       At least henceforth your memories shall make   5
       Quiet & fragrant as befits their home.
       Nor shall my memory want a home in
        yours:—
       Alas, that it requires too well such free
       Forgiving love as shall embalm it there!
—   For if you would remember me aright . .   10
. .   As I was born to be . . you must forget
       All fitful, strange & moody waywardness

1835 1 friends;   2 which, though   7 yours.—   8 Alas!

PARACELSUS.

PART I.

PARACELSUS ASPIRES.

Scene.—*Würzburg; a garden in the environs.* 1512.

Festus, Paracelsus, Michal.

Paracelsus. Come close to me, dear friends; still
   closer; thus!
Close to the heart which, though long time roll
   by
Ere it again beat quicker, pressed to yours,
As now it beats—perchance a long, long
   time—
At least henceforth your memories shall make   5
Quiet and fragrant as befits their home.
Nor shall my memory want a home in
   yours—
Alas, that it requires too well such free
Forgiving love as shall embalm it there!
For if you would remember me aright,   10
As I was born to be, you must forget
All fitful strange and moody waywardness

---

10 *1849* aright—   11 *1849* be—

Würzburg: Browning follows tradition in making Paracelsus visit Würz-
burg. Historically, the date of the visit is uncertain. The revision to '1512' from
'1507' (*1835*) was probably prompted by Leigh Hunt's objection: 'At this time,
according to his real history, Paracelsus was only a boy of fourteen; but the
strain in which he here speaks, and still more perhaps the sentiments, approach-
ing to wonder and reverence, with which he seems to be already regarded by
his two gentle friends, would better suit a date of life a few years more
advanced': *Leigh Hunt's London Journal* no. 86, 21 November 1835 (p. 406b).
   5 *your memories*: my memories of you.
   12 *moody waywardness*: cf. Wordsworth, 'A Farewell', 41–2: 'And O most
constant, yet most fickle Place, / That hast thy wayward moods'.

Which e'er confused my better spirit . . . to
  dwell
Only on moments such as these, dear Friends;
My heart no truer . . . but my words & ways   15
More true to it: as Michal, some months hence,
Will say this Autumn was a pleasant time
For some few sunny days—& overlook
Its bleak wind, hankering after pining leaves:—
Autumn would fain be sunny . . I would look   20
Liker my nature's truth . . . & both are frail,
And both beloved for all their frailty! . .

M/. Aureole! . .
P/. Drop by drop! . . she is weeping like a
  child!
Not so . . . I am content . . . more than
  content . . .
Nay Autumn wins you best by this its mute   25
Appeal to sympathy for its decay . . .
Look up, sweet Michal, nor esteem the less
The stained and drooping vines their grapes
  bow down—
Those creaking trees bent with their fruit . . . &
  see
That apple-tree with a rare after-birth   30
Of peeping blooms sprinkled its wealth
  among—
And for the winds . . what wind that ever
  raved
Shall vex that ash that overlooks the rest
So proud it wears its berries . . . Ah! at length
The old smile meet for her, the lady of this   35
Sequestered nest!—this kingdom limited
Alone by one old populous green wall
Tenanted by the ever-busy flies,

1835 13 spirit,   14 friends;   15 truer,   18 days; and   19
leaves.   21 truth; and   31 among;   34 berries.   36 nest! This king-
dom,   37 wall,

Which e'er confused my better spirit, to
 dwell
Only on moments such as these, dear friends!
—My heart no truer, but my words and ways   15
More true to it: as Michal, some months hence,
Will say, "this autumn was a pleasant time,"
For some few sunny days; and overlook
Its bleak wind, hankering after pining leaves.
Autumn would fain be sunny; I would look   20
Liker my nature's truth: and both are frail,
And both beloved, for all our frailty.
   Michal.   Aureole!
   Paracelsus. Drop by drop! she is weeping like a
   child!
Not so! I am content—more than
 content;
Nay, autumn wins you best by this its mute 25
Appeal to sympathy for its decay:
Look up, sweet Michal, nor esteem the less
Your stained and drooping vines their grapes
 bow down,
Nor blame those creaking trees bent with their
 fruit,
That apple-tree with a rare after-birth   30
Of peeping blooms sprinkled its wealth
 among!
Then for the winds—what wind that ever
 raved
Shall vex that ash which overlooks you both,
So proud it wears its berries? Ah, at length,
The old smile meet for her, the lady of this 35
Sequestered nest!—this kingdom, limited
Alone by one old populous green wall
Tenanted by the ever-busy flies,

20 *1849* sunny— 22 *1849* And both beloved for all their frailty! *1863,*
1865 And both beloved, for all their frailty. 23 *1849* by drop!— 24 *1849*
than content— 26 *1849* decay! 33 *1849* ash that overlooks 34 *1849*
Ah! at length, 36 *1849* nest! This

35–6 *the lady of this / Sequestered nest!*: Leigh Hunt remarked that 'There is
much both in the diction and the versification which has a harsh, awkward, and
disappointing effect at first' (p. 406a); but this enjambement was not revised.

Grey crickets, & shy lizards, & quick spiders,
All families of the silver-threaded moss . . .   40
—Which look thro', near, this way,—& it
   appears
A stubble-field, or a cane-brake—a marsh
Of bulrush whitening in the sun: laugh now!
Fancy the crickets, each one in his house,
Looking out & wondering at the world: . . or
   best,   45
The painted snail, with his gay shell of dew,
Travelling to see [the] glossy balls high up
Hung by the caterpillar, like gold lamps.

M/. In truth, we have lived carelessly &
       well!
P/. And shall, my perfect Pair! . . each, trust me,
       born   50
For the other— —nay your very hair when
   mixed
Is of one hue— —for where beside this nook
Shall you two walk, when I am far away,
And wish me prosperous fortune?— —stay,
   —that plant
Shall never wave its tangles lightly & softly   55
As a Queen's languid & imperial arm
Which scatters crowns among her lovers, . . but
   you
Shall be reminded to predict some great
Success to me: . . . Ah, see! the sun sinks broad
Behind S.t Saviour's . . wholly gone, at last!   60
F/. Now, Aureole, stay those wandering eyes
       awhile—

1835   41 Which look through, near, this way, and   42 a crane-
brake—   45 world—   50 pair—   52 hue.   54 fortune? . . . Stay!
that plant   57 lovers,   59 me.   61 awhile:

Grey crickets and shy lizards and quick spiders,
Each family of the silver-threaded moss—   40
Which, look through near, this way, and it
      appears
A stubble-field or a cane-brake, a marsh
Of bulrush whitening in the sun: laugh now!
Fancy the crickets, each one in his house,
Looking out, wondering at the world—or
      best,   45
Yon painted snail with his gay shell of dew,
Travelling to see the glossy balls high up
Hung by the caterpillar, like gold lamps.
        Michal. In truth we have lived carelessly and
            well.
        Paracelsus. And shall, my perfect pair!—each,
            trust me, born   50
For the other; nay, your very hair, when
      mixed,
Is of one hue. For where save in this nook
Shall you two walk, when I am far away,
And wish me prosperous fortune? Stay: that
      plant
Shall never wave its tangles lightly and softly,   55
As a queen's languid and imperial arm
Which scatters crowns among her lovers, but
      you
Shall be reminded to predict to me
Some great success! Ah see, the sun sinks broad
Behind Saint Saviour's: wholly gone, at last!   60
        Festus. Now, Aureole, stay those wandering
            eyes awhile!

42 *1849* stubble-field, or a cane-brake—a marsh *Berg* {rejected} stubble-field, a
cane-brake, or a marsh   48 *1849* lamps!   49 *1849* well!   50 *1849*
pair—   53 *1865* you too walk,   54–5 *1849* Stay! Whene'er | That plant
shall wave its tangles   57 *1849* among her lovers, you *Berg* {rejected} among
her lovers, each

39 *quick spiders*: Elizabeth Barrett quoted this phrase in a letter in 1846:
Kintner ii. 755. 'I suspect . . .', Browning had written to her a few months
before, 'you have found out by this time my odd liking for "vermin"—you
once wrote "*your* snails"': Kintner i. 356.

—   You are ours to-night, at least—& while you
        spoke
      Of Michal & her tears, ⟨it seemed {?}⟩ [I
        thought] that none
      Could willing leave what he so seemed
        to love . . .
      But that last look destroys my dream . . . that
        look!   65
      As if where'er you gazed there stood a star!
      How far was Würzburg with its church & spire
      And garden-walls & all that they contain
      From that look's far alighting?

P/.   I but spoke
      And looked alike from simple joy to see   70
      The beings I best love, so well shut in
      From all rude chances like to be my lot,
      That, far from them, my weary spirit, disposed
      To lose awhile its cares in soothing thoughts
      Of them, their pleasant features, looks, &
        words . . .   75
      Needs never hesitate—nor apprehend
      Incroaching trouble may have reached them
        too,—
      Nor have recourse to Fancy's busy aid
      Even to frame a wish in their behalf
      Beyond what they possess already here,—   80
      But, unobstructed, may at once forget
      Itself in them,—assured how well they are.

——   This Festus knows, beside, he holds me one
      Whom quiet & its charms arrest in vain—
      One scarce aware of all the joys he quits . . .   85
      Too filled with airy hopes to make account
      Of soft delights his own heart garners up . . . .

1835 62 You are ours to-night at least;   71 love   72 lot;   75 and
words,   76 hesitate,   77 Encroaching . . . . reach'd them too;   80
here;   83 This Festus knows;   84 vain;   85 quits;   87 up:

You are ours to-night, at least; and while you
   spoke
Of Michal and her tears, I thought that
   none
Could willing leave what he so seemed to
   love:
But that last look destroys my dream—that
   look   65
As if, where'er you gazed, there stood a star!
How far was Würzburg with its church and spire
And garden-walls and all things they contain,
From that look's far alighting?
    Paracelsus.   I but spoke
And looked alike from simple joy to see   70
The beings I love best, shut in so well
From all rude chances like to be my lot,
That, when afar, my weary spirit,—disposed
To lose awhile its care in soothing thoughts
Of them, their pleasant features, looks and
   words,—
                           75
Need never hesitate, nor apprehend
Encroaching trouble may have reached them
   too,
Nor have recourse to fancy's busy aid
And fashion even a wish in their behalf
Beyond what they possess already here;   80
But, unobstructed, may at once forget
Itself in them, assured how well they fare.
Beside, this Festus knows he holds me one
Whom quiet and its charms arrest in vain,
One scarce aware of all the joys I quit,   85
Too filled with airy hopes to make account
Of soft delights his own heart garners up:

63–4 *1849* Of Michal and her tears, the thought came back | That none could
leave what he so seemed to love: {*1865* as *1888* except 'Could willingly leave' in
line 64.}   65 *1849* that look!   68 *1889* contain. {faulty type}   *76
{Reading of *1849.*} *1863–89* Needs never   78 *1849* Fancy's   79 *1849* To
fashion   82 *1849* they are.   83 *1849* knows, he thinks me   84 *1849*
charms attract in vain,   87 *1849* delights which free hearts garner up: *Berg*
{rejected} which each {?} heart garners

..   Whereas behold how much our sense of all
That's beautiful, is one!—& when he
    learns
That every common sight he can enjoy   90
Affects me as himself—that I have just
As varied appetite for joys derived
From common things—a stake in life, in short,
Like his—& which a rash pursuit of aims
That it affords not would as soon
    destroy— — —.   95
He may convince himself, that, knowing this,
I shall act well advised: & last, because
Tho' Heaven & earth & all things were at
    stake
Sweet Michal must not weep, our parting Eve.

F/.   True:—& the eve is deepening & we
    sit   100
As little anxious to begin our talk
As tho' tomorrow I could hint of it
As we paced arm in arm the cheerful town
At sundawn—or could whisper it by fits
(Trithemius busied with his class the while)   105
In ⟨the⟩ [that] dim chamber where the
    noon-streaks peer
Half frightened by the awful tomes around—
—   Or in some grassy lane unbosom all
From even-blush to midnight . . . . but
    to-morrow!
— — I have full leave to tell my inmost mind?   110
—   We have been brothers & henceforth the
    world

.

1835 89 beautiful is one! And   91 himself;   93 things;   94 his; and
95 destroy;—   99 weep our parting eve.   104 sun-dawn;   107 around;

Whereas behold how much our sense of all
That's beauteous proves alike! When Festus
  learns
That every common pleasure of the world   90
Affects me as himself; that I have just
As varied appetite for joy derived
From common things; a stake in life, in short,
Like his; a stake which rash pursuit of aims
That life affords not, would as soon
  destroy;—   95
He may convince himself that, this in view,
I shall act well advised. And last, because,
Though heaven and earth and all things were at
  stake,
Sweet Michal must not weep, our parting eve.
  Festus. True: and the eve is deepening, and we
  sit   100
As little anxious to begin our talk
As though to-morrow I could hint of it
As we paced arm-in-arm the cheerful town
At sun-dawn; or could whisper it by fits
(Trithemius busied with his class the while)   105
In that dim chamber where the noon-streaks
  peer
Half-frightened by the awful tomes around;
Or in some grassy lane unbosom all
From even-blush to midnight: but,
  to-morrow!
Have I full leave to tell my inmost mind?   110
We have been brothers, and henceforth the
  world

---

92 *1849* varied appetites   97 *1849* advised: 99 *1849* eve!   102 *1849* I
could open it   104 *1849* sun-dawn; and continue it   105 *1849* (Old
Tritheim busied   108 *1849* And here at home unbosom all the rest   109
1849 but, to-morrow! . . .   111 *1849* We two were brothers,

---

104 *sun-dawn*: as in *Sordello* ii. 17.
105 *Trithemius*: for the Abbot Tritheim see Browning's note (2) on p. 505
below, as well as all writers on Paracelsus. The most authoritative modern
work is *Paracelsus: An Introduction to Philosophical Medicine in the Era of the
Renaissance*, by Walter Pagel (Basel and New York, 1958).
109 *even-blush*: the only example in *OED*.

Will be between us;—all my freest mind?— —
Tis the last night, dear Aureole!

P/.   Oh, say on!
—   Devise some test of love—some arduous feat
To be performed for you—say on,—if night   115
Be spent the while, the better:—recall how oft
My wondrous plans & dreams & hopes &
    fears
Have—never wearied you . . oh, no! . . as I
Recall, & never vividly as now,
Your true affection born when Einsiedeln   120
And its green hills were all the world to us,—
And still increasing to this night which ends
My further stay at Würzburg . . . Oh you shall
Be very proud one day! . . . say on, dear Friend;
Talk volumes, I shall still be in arrear.   124a

F/.   In truth? . . 'tis for my proper peace, indeed,   125
Rather than yours . . for vain it looks, to seek
To stay your course— —the last hopes I
    conceived
Are fading even now:—old stories tell
Of some far embassy despatched to win
The favour of an Eastern king,—& how   130
The gifts it proffered were but dazzling dust
Shed from the ore-beds native to the clime;—
Just so, the value of repose & love
—   I meant should tempt you—better far than I
You seem to comprehend . . . & still desist   135
No whit from projects where they have no part:

1835 112 us . . . . all my freest mind? . . .   113 on;   115 on; if   117
plans, and dreams, and hopes, and fears,   122 this night,   124
friend;   128 now.   134 you,   136 part.

Will rise between us:—all my freest mind?
'T is the last night, dear Aureole!
   Paracelsus.   Oh, say on!
Devise some test of love, some arduous feat
To be performed for you: say on! If night   115
Be spent the while, the better! Recall how oft
My wondrous plans and dreams and hopes and
    fears
Have—never wearied you, oh no!—as I
Recall, and never vividly as now,
Your true affection, born when Einsiedeln   120
And its green hills were all the world to us;
And still increasing to this night which ends
My further stay at Würzburg. Oh, one day
You shall be very proud! Say on, dear friends!
   Festus. In truth? 'T is for my proper peace,
    indeed,   125
Rather than yours; for vain all projects seem
To stay your course: I said my latest hope
Is fading even now. A story tells
Of some far embassy despatched to win
The favour of an eastern king, and how   130
The gifts they offered proved but dazzling dust
Shed from the ore-beds native to his clime.
Just so, the value of repose and love,
I meant should tempt you, better far than I
You seem to comprehend; and yet desist   135
No whit from projects where repose nor love
Has part.

114 *1849* love—   115 *1849* you—   117 *1849* plans, and dreams, and hopes, and fears,   118 *1849* you . . . oh, no!   121 *1849* to us,   122 *1849* this night,   123 *1849* Würzburg . . .   129 *1849* despatched to buy *1863–8* despatched to win   131 *Berg* {rejected} proffer'd {illegible words} us dust   132 *1849* his clime: *Berg* {inserts, but deletes, a line after 132:} Not novel pleasure to be dazzled with!   135 *1849* comprehend—   137 *1849–68* Have part.

125 *proper*: own.
128 *A story*: untraced.

P/.   Alas! as I forbode; this weighty talk
     Has for its end no other than to revive 137a
F/.   A solitary briar the bank puts forth
     To save our swan's nest floating out to sea.
P/.   Dear Festus, hear me;— —what is it you wish?   140
     That I should lay aside my heart's pursuit,
     Abandon the sole ends for which I live,
     Reject God's great commission . . . & so die!
..   And still I listen for your true love's sake.
     Yet how has grown that love? even in a long   145
     And patient cherishing of the selfsame spirit
     It now would quell . . . as tho' a mother should
       hope
     To stay the lusty manhood of the child
     Once weak upon her knees: I was not born
     Informed & fearless from the first, but shrank   150
     From aught which marked me out apart from
       Men . .
     I would have lived their life, & striven their
       strife,
     Eluding Destiny, if that might be,—
     But you first guided me thro' doubt & fear
     And taught me to know them & know
       myself;—   155
     And now that I am strong & full of hope
—   That I can from my soul reject all aims
     Save those your earnest words made plain to
       me;—
     Now, that I touch the brink of my design,—

1835 137 I forbode,   140 hear me.   149 knees.   151 mark'd . . . .
men.   152 and . . . . strife—   156 hope;

Paracelsus. Once more? Alas! As I foretold.
　Festus. A solitary briar the bank puts forth
To save our swan's nest floating out to sea.
　Paracelsus. Dear Festus, hear me. What is it you
　　wish?   140
That I should lay aside my heart's pursuit,
Abandon the sole ends for which I live,
Reject God's great commission, and so die!
You bid me listen for your true love's sake:
Yet how has grown that love? Even in a long   145
And patient cherishing of the self-same spirit
It now would quell; as though a mother
　hoped
To stay the lusty manhood of the child
Once weak upon her knees. I was not born
Informed and fearless from the first, but shrank   150
From aught which marked me out apart from
　men:
I would have lived their life, and died their
　death,
Lost in their ranks, eluding destiny:
But you first guided me through doubt and fear,
Taught me to know mankind and know
　myself;   155
And now that I am strong and full of hope,
That, from my soul, I can reject all aims
Save those your earnest words made plain to
　me,
Now that I touch the brink of my design,

137 *1849* I forbode! *1863, 1865* I forebode.   143 *1849* commission—   158
1849 to me;   159 *1849* Now,

　143 *God's great commission:* cf. *Paradise Lost,* vii. 118–19: 'such commission
from above / I have received'. The general conception is central to Browning's
life and work.
　151 *apart from men:* cf. Shelley, 'Prince Athanase' (in *Posthumous Poems,* 1824),
31–3: 'His soul had wedded wisdom, and her dower / Is love and justice,
clothed in which he sate / Apart from men, as in a lonely tower'.
　155 *to know mankind:* cf. Pope, *An Essay on Man,* ii. 1–2: 'Know then thyself,
presume not God to scan; / The proper study of Mankind is Man'.

—   When I would have a triumph in their eyes,   160
       A glad cheer in their voices . . . Michal weeps,
       And Festus ponders gravely!

F/.   When you shall
       Have learned my purpose . . . .

P/.   Learned it? . . I can say
       Beforehand all this conference will produce:—
—   'Tis this way, Michal, that he uses;—first,   165
       Or he declares, or I, the leading points
       Of our belief in what is Man's true End
       And God's apparent Will . . . no two faiths ever
       Agreed as ours agree:—next, each allows
       These points are no mere visionary truths: 169a
       But, once determined, it remains alone   169b
       To act upon them straight as best we may:—   170
       Accordingly, I venture to submit
       My plan, in lack of better, for pursuing
       The path which God's will seems to authorize . . .
. .   A broad plan, vague & ill defined enough,   173a
       But courting censure & imploring aid:—   173b
       Well . . . he discerns much good in it—avows
       This motive worthy, that hope plausible,—   175
—   A danger, here, to be avoided—there,
       An oversight to be repaired—in fine,
       Our minds go every way together . . all good
       Approved by him, I gladly recognize,
       All he counts bad, I thankfully discard;   180
       And nought forbids me to look up at last
       For some stray comfort in his cautious
           brow— — —
       When, lo! I learn that, spite of all, there lurks
       Some innate & inexplicable germ
       Of failure in my schemes—so that at last   185

1835 164 produce.   167–8 man's true end | And God's apparent
will—   174 Well—he . . . . it,   177 repair'd: in fine   179 recog-
nize;   185 schemes;

When I would have a triumph in their eyes,   160
A glad cheer in their voices—Michal weeps,
And Festus ponders gravely!
    Festus.   When you deign
To hear my purpose . . .
    Paracelsus.   Hear it? I can say
Beforehand all this evening's conference!
'T is this way, Michal, that he uses: first,   165
Or he declares, or I, the leading points
Of our best scheme of life, what is man's end
And what God's will; no two faiths e'er agreed
As his with mine. Next, each of us allows
Faith should be acted on as best we may;   170
Accordingly, I venture to submit
My plan, in lack of better, for pursuing
The path which God's will seems to authorize.
Well, he discerns much good in it, avows
This motive worthy, that hope plausible,   175
A danger here to be avoided, there
An oversight to be repaired: in fine
Our two minds go together—all the good
Approved by him, I gladly recognize,
All he counts bad, I thankfully discard,   180
And nought forbids my looking up at last
For some stray comfort in his cautious brow.
When, lo! I learn that, spite of all, there lurks
Some innate and inexplicable germ
Of failure in my scheme; so that at last   185

168 *1849* will—   169 *1849* mine: 172 *1849* A plan,   173 *1849–68*
authorize: 174 *1849* Well—   176 *1849* A danger here, to be
avoided—there,   177 *1849* repaired: at last   179 *1849* recognize;   180
1849 discard;   182 *1849* brow—   185 *1849* my schemes;

172 *in lack of better*: for 'in lack of', cf. *Christmas-Eve and Easter-Day*
(*Christmas-Eve*, 39), and *The Ring and the Book*, vii. 1832.

It all amounts to this—the sovereign proof
That we devote ourselves wholly to God
Is in a life as tho' no God there were:—
. .   A life which prompted by the sad & blind
Folly of Man, Festus abhors the most,   190
But which these tenets sanctify at once,
Tho' to less subtle wits it seems the same
Consider it how they may:

M/.   Is it so, Festus?
He speaks so calmly & kindly . . is it so?

P/.   Reject those glorious visions of God's
love   195
And Man's design—laugh loud that he should
send
Vast longings to direct us; . . or find out
How else they may be satiated:—but this
Ambiguous warfare wearies:—

F/.   Not so much   200
That you will grant no last leave to your friend
—   And for his own sake, not for yours?—I wish
To send my soul in good hopes after you—
Never to sorrow that uncertain words
Erringly apprehended—a new creed   205
Ill understood, begot rash trust in you—
Had share in your undoing — — —

P/.   Choose your party:—
Hold or renounce:—but meanwhile blame me
not
Because I dare to act on your own views
—   Nor shrink when they point onward—nor spy
out   210
A peril where they most ensure success:—

F/.   Prove that to me—but that:—that you abide

1835 190 man, Festus abhors the most—   191 once—   193 may.   196
man's design;   199 wearies . . .   206 understood—   207 undo-
ing.   211 success . . .

It all amounts to this—the sovereign proof
That we devote ourselves to God, is seen
In living just as though no God there were;
A life which, prompted by the sad and blind
Folly of man, Festus abhors the most;   190
But which these tenets sanctify at once,
Though to less subtle wits it seems the same,
Consider it how they may.
    Michal.   Is it so, Festus?
He speaks so calmly and kindly: is it so?
    Paracelsus. Reject those glorious visions of
        God's love   195
And man's design; laugh loud that God should
    send
Vast longings to direct us; say how soon
Power satiates these, or lust, or gold; I know
The world's cry well, and how to answer it.
But this ambiguous warfare . . .
    Festus.   . . . Wearies so   200
That you will grant no last leave to your friend
To urge it?—for his sake, not yours? I wish
To send my soul in good hopes after you;
Never to sorrow that uncertain words
Erringly apprehended, a new creed   205
Ill understood, begot rash trust in you,
Had share in your undoing.
    Paracelsus.   Choose your side,
Hold or renounce: but meanwhile blame me not
Because I dare to act on your own views,
Nor shrink when they point onward, nor
    espy   210
A peril where they most ensure success.
    Festus. Prove that to me—but that! Prove you
    abide

188 *1849* as though there were no God: 190 *1849* Lusts of the world, Festus
abhors the most—   191 *1849* once;   *193 *1849–68,1889* Festus? *1888* Fes-
tus {corrected in DC}   194 *1849* kindly—   199 *1849–65* answer
it!   205 *1849* apprehended—a new creed,   206 *1849* understood—
207 *1849* And shared in your undoing.   207 *1849* side:

Within their warrant—nor presumptuous boast
God's labour laid on you;—that all you covet
A mortal may expect;—& most of all   215
That the strange course you now affect, will
    lead
To its attainment . . . & I bid you speed!
And count the minutes 'till you venture forth.
You will smile,—but I had gathered from slow
    thought,
Much musing on the fortunes of my friend,   220
Matter I deemed could not be urged in vain;
But it all leaves me at my need—in shreds
And fragments I must venture what remains:—

Ml. Ask at once, Festus, wherefore he should
    scorn . . .

Fl. Stay, Michal;—Aureole, I speak
    guardedly   225
And gravely, . . knowing well, whate'er your
    error,
This is no ill-considered choice of your's,
No sudden fancy of an ardent boy;—

. . Not from your own confiding words alone
Am I aware your passionate heart has long   230
Nourished, & has at length matured a plan
To give yourself up wholly to one End: 231a

. . . I will not speak of Einsiedeln,—'twas as
I had been born your elder by some years
Only to watch you fully from the first:—
In all beside, our mutual tasks were fixed   235
Even then—'twas mine to have you in my view
As you had your own soul:—accordingly
I could go further back, & trace each bough   237a
Of this wide-branching tree even to its birth—   b

— Each full-grown passion to its outspring
    faint,—   c
But I shall only dwell upon the intents   d

1835 219 smile; but . . . . thought—   220 friend—   222 need: 223
remains.   227 ill-consider'd choice of yours—   228 boy.   231a
end.   232 Einsiedeln;   237b birth;   237c faint;

Within their warrant, nor presumptuous boast
God's labour laid on you; prove, all you covet
A mortal may expect; and, most of all,   215
Prove the strange course you now affect, will
   lead
To its attainment—and I bid you speed,
Nay, count the minutes till you venture forth!
You smile; but I had gathered from slow
   thought—
Much musing on the fortunes of my friend—   220
Matter I deemed could not be urged in vain;
But it all leaves me at my need: in shreds
And fragments I must venture what remains.
   Michal. Ask at once, Festus, wherefore he
     should scorn . . .
   Festus. Stay, Michal: Aureole, I speak
     guardedly   225
And gravely, knowing well, whate'er your
   error,
This is no ill-considered choice of yours,
No sudden fancy of an ardent boy.
Not from your own confiding words alone
Am I aware your passionate heart long since   230
Gave birth to, nourished and at length matures
This scheme. I will not speak of Einsiedeln,
Where I was born your elder by some years
Only to watch you fully from the first:
In all beside, our mutual tasks were fixed   235
Even then—'t was mine to have you in my view
As you had your own soul and those intents

---

227 *1849* yours—   232 *1865* scheme,

   222 *But it all leaves me*: 'These touches of nature are continual throughout the
poem & bring its madness within the range of sympathies': Domett.

Which filled you when, to crown your dearest
    wish,
With a tumultuous heart you left with me
Our childhoods' home to join the favoured few   240
Whom famed Trithemius condescends to teach
A portion of his lore . . . . & not the dullest
Of those so favoured—whom you now
    despise—
Was earnest as you were,—resolved like you
To grasp all, & retain all, & deserve   245
By patient toil a wide renown like his: . . .
. . .   Now, just as well have I descried the growth   246a
Of this new ardour which supplants the old:—
I watched it—'twas significant & strange
In one, matched to his soul's content at length
With rivals in the search for Wisdom's prize,   250
To see the sudden pause—the total change—
From contest that transition to repose . . .
From pressing onward as his fellows pressed
To a blank idleness, yet most unlike
The dull stagnation of a soul content,   255
Once foiled, to leave betimes a thriveless quest:
That careless bearing, free from all pretence
Even of contempt for what it ceased to seek—
—   Smiling humility, praising much yet waiving
What it professed to praise . . yet not so well   260
Secured but that rare outbreaks—fierce & brief
Revealed the hidden scorn—as quickly
    curbed . . .
. .   That ostentatious show of past defeat—
That ready acquiescence in contempt— —
I deemed no other than the letting go   265

1835 243 favour'd, whom you now despise,   244 were; resolved, like
you,   246 his.   251 pause, the total change,   252 From contest, that
transition to repose—   254 idleness;   255–6 content— | Once
foil'd—   261 outbreaks, fierce and brief,

Which filled it when, to crown your dearest wish,
With a tumultuous heart, you left with me
Our childhood's home to join the favoured few   240
Whom, here, Trithemius condescends to teach
A portion of his lore: and not one youth
Of those so favoured, whom you now
          despise,
Came earnest as you came, resolved, like you,
To grasp all, and retain all, and deserve   245
By patient toil a wide renown like his.
Now, this new ardour which supplants the old
I watched, too; 't was significant and strange,
In one matched to his soul's content at length
With rivals in the search for wisdom's prize,   250
To see the sudden pause, the total change;
From contest, the transition to repose—
From pressing onward as his fellows pressed,
To a blank idleness, yet most unlike
The dull stagnation of a soul, content,   255
Once foiled, to leave betimes a thriveless quest.
That careless bearing, free from all pretence
Even of contempt for what it ceased to seek—
Smiling humility, praising much, yet waiving
What it professed to praise—though not so well   260
Maintained but that rare outbreaks, fierce and
          brief,
Revealed the hidden scorn, as quickly
          curbed.
That ostentatious show of past defeat,
That ready acquiescence in contempt,
I deemed no other than the letting go   265

---

241 *1849* Whom, here at Würzburg, Tritheim deigns to teach   242 *1849* and
not the best   244 *1849* you came;   247 *1849* And this new ardour which
supplants the old, *1863–8* Now, this . . . . old,   250 *1849* Wisdom's   254
1849 idleness;   261 *1849* fierce as brief,   262 *1849* curbed—

256 *thriveless*: a favourite word: see, e.g., iii. 712 and v. 581, and *Sordello*, ii.
371. It occurs more than once in the *Emblems* of Quarles (I. xii. 25, III. vi. 10,
e.g.), which Browning described as his 'childhood's pet book' (Griffin and
Minchin, p. 31).

His shivered sword, of one about to spring
Upon his foe's throat . . . but it was not thus:—
Not that way looked your brooding purpose
 then;—
But after-signs disclosed, & you confirmed,
That you prepared to task to the uttermost   270
Your strength, in furtherance of a certain aim
Which,—while it bore the name your rivals
 gave
To their most puny efforts, was so vast
In scope that it included their best flights,
Combined them, & desired to gain one prize   275
In place of many—the Secret of the World

— Of Man, & Man's true purpose, path, & fate:—
That you, . . not nursing as a lovely dream
This purpose, with the Sages of old Time . . .
Have struck upon a way to this, if all   280
You trust be true, which following, heart &
 soul,
You, if a Man may, dare aspire to KNOW:—
And that this aim shall differ from a host
Of aims alike in character & kind,
Mostly in this;—that in itself alone   285
Shall its reward be . . . not an alien end
Blending therewith . . no hope nor fear nor joy
Nor woe shall elsewhere move you, but this pure
Devotion shall sustain or shall undo you,—

— This you intend;—

P/.   You shall not state it thus . . . 290
.. I should not differ from the dreamy crew
You speak of:—I profess no other share
In the selection of my lot, than in
My ready answer to the will of God
Who summons me to be his organ—he   295

1835 273 efforts— 276–7 the secret of the world— | Of man, and man's
. . . . and fate: 279 sages of old Time, 282 man . . . . KNOW: 284
kind— 287–8 hope, nor fear, nor joy, | Nor woe, shall . . . . you; 289
undo you: 290 intend. | You . . . . thus: 292 speak of. 295 organ:

His shivered sword, of one about to spring
Upon his foe's throat; but it was not thus:
Not that way looked your brooding purpose
    then.
For after-signs disclosed, what you confirmed,
That you prepared to task to the uttermost   270
Your strength, in furtherance of a certain aim
Which—while it bore the name your rivals
    gave
Their own most puny efforts—was so vast
In scope that it included their best flights,
Combined them, and desired to gain one prize   275
In place of many,—the secret of the world,
Of man, and man's true purpose, path and fate.
—That you, not nursing as a mere vague dream
This purpose, with the sages of the past,
Have struck upon a way to this, if all   280
You trust be true, which following, heart and
    soul,
You, if a man may, dare aspire to KNOW:
And that this aim shall differ from a host
Of aims alike in character and kind,
Mostly in this,—that in itself alone   285
Shall its reward be, not an alien end
Blending therewith; no hope nor fear nor joy
Nor woe, to elsewhere move you, but this pure
Devotion to sustain you or betray:
Thus you aspire.
    Paracelsus.   You shall not state it thus: 290
I should not differ from the dreamy crew
You speak of. I profess no other share
In the selection of my lot, than this
My ready answer to the will of God
Who summons me to be his organ. All   295

277 *1849* fate: 280 *1849* struck upon a way *Berg* {rejected} struck on a real
way   285 *1849* this,—to seek its own reward *1863,1865* this,—that in itself
alone,   286–7 *1849* In itself only, not an alien end | To blend there-
with;   293–4 *1849* than this, | A ready answer   295 *1849* organ:

Whose innate strength supports him shall
   succeed
No better than the Sages:—

               Such [the] aim, [then,]
God sets before you;—& 'tis, doubtless, need
That he appoint no less the way of Praise
Than the desire to praise;—for, tho' I hold   300
With you, the setting forth such praise to be
The natural end & service of a Man,—
And that such praise seems best attained when he
Attains the general welfare of his ⟨k⟩ Kind, ...
Yet, *that*, the *instrument*, is not the *end*:—   305
There is a curse upon the earth—let Man   305a
Presume not to serve God apart from such
Appointed channel as he wills shall gather
Imperfect tributes—for that sole obedience
Valued perchance:—He seeks not that his altars
Blaze—careless how, so that they do but
   blaze   310
—   Tho' I doubt much if he consent that we   310a
Discover this great secret—I know well   b
You will allege no other comprehends   c
The work in question save its labourer: d
—   I shall assume the Aim approved—& you   e
That I am implicated in the issue   f
Not simply as your friend, but as yourself—   g
—   As tho' it were my task, that you perform,   h
And some plague dogged my heels till it were
   done . . .   i

1835 297 sages.   299 way of praise   302 man—   304 kind—   305
end.   305a earth; let man   309 perchance.   310 blaze.—   310b
secret I know well   310e the aim improved;   310i done.

Whose innate strength supports them shall
  succeed
No better than the sages.
  Festus.   Such the aim, then,
God sets before you; and 't is doubtless need
That he appoint no less the way of praise
Than the desire to praise; for, though I hold   300
With you, the setting forth such praise to be
The natural end and service of a man,
And hold such praise is best attained when man
Attains the general welfare of his kind—
Yet this, the end, is not the instrument.   305
Presume not to serve God apart from such
Appointed channel as he wills shall gather
Imperfect tributes, for that sole obedience
Valued perchance! He seeks not that his altars
Blaze, careless how, so that they do but blaze.   310

297 *1849–65* than your sages.   303 *1849* And think such praise is best . . . .
man *Berg* And ⟨that⟩ [think] such praise seems best . . . . ⟨he⟩ [man]   308
1849 tributes—   309 *1849–68* perchance.   310 *1849* Blaze—careless

302 *The natural end*: perhaps a reminiscence of the 'Larger Catechism' of the
Church of Scotland. '*Question 1*: What is the chief [and highest] end of man?
Answer. Man's chief [and highest] end is to glorify God, and [fully] to enjoy
him for ever'. In the 'Shorter Catechism' the words bracketed above are
omitted. Browning's mother was baptized into the Church of Scotland:
Maynard, p. 27. Domett comments: 'the true visionary. Talk of the Carlyle
school—the missions & the men of one idea—the truly great'.
  310 *careless how*: a Greek construction.

— — Suppose this owned, then,—you are born to
        KNOW,—   311
    (You will heed well your answers for my faith
    Shall meet implicitly what they affirm)—
    I cannot think you have annexed to such
    Selection aught beyond a stead-fast will,   315
    An intense purpose—gifts that would induce
    Scorn or neglect of ordinary means
    And instruments of success: no destiny
    Dispenses with endeavour:—now, dare you
        search
    Your inmost heart, & candidly avow   320
    Whether you have not rather wild desire
    For this distinction, than a full assurance
    That it exists,—or whether you discern
    The path to the fulfilment of your purpose
    Clear as that purpose, & again, that purpose   325
    Clear as your yearning to be singled out
    For its possessor— —dare you answer this?

P/. (*After a pause*)—No, I have nought to fear! who
        will may know
    The secrets't workings of [my] soul—what
        though
    It be so?—if indeed the strong desire   330
    Eclipse the ⟨true⟩ aim [in me]? . . if splendour
        break
    Upon the outset of my path alone,
    And duskest shade succeed? what fairer seal
    Shall I require to my authentic mission
    Than this fierce energy—this instinct striving   335
    Because its nature is to strive—enticed
    By the security of no broad course
    Where error is not, but success is sure . . .
—   How know I else such glorious fate my own

1835 311 Suppose this own'd then; you are born to KNOW.   319
endeavour.   323 exists; or   325 purpose—and again,   327 posses-
sor.   328 *pause*.) No;   329 of my soul.   335 energy?—   336
strive?—   337 course—   338 sure.

Suppose this, then; that God selected
   you
To KNOW (heed well your answers, for my faith
Shall meet implicitly what they affirm)
I cannot think you dare annex to such
Selection aught beyond a steadfast will,   315
An intense hope; nor let your gifts create
Scorn or neglect of ordinary means
Conducive to success, make destiny
Dispense with man's endeavour. Now, dare you
   search
Your inmost heart, and candidly avow   320
Whether you have not rather wild desire
For this distinction than security
Of its existence? whether you discern
The path to the fulfilment of your purpose
Clear as that purpose—and again, that purpose   325
Clear as your yearning to be singled out
For its pursuer. Dare you answer this?
   Paracelsus [*after a pause*]. No, I have nought to
     fear! Who will may know
The secret'st workings of my soul. What
   though
It be so?—if indeed the strong desire   330
Eclipse the aim in me?—if splendour
   break
Upon the outset of my path alone,
And duskest shade succeed? What fairer seal
Shall I require to my authentic mission
Than this fierce energy?—this instinct striving   335
Because its nature is to strive?—enticed
By the security of no broad course,
Without success forever in its eyes!
How know I else such glorious fate my own,

---

316 *1849* hope,   318 *1849* success—   323 *1849* existence;   335
1849–65,1888,1889 Than this   *1868* Then this   338 *1849* With no success

331 *Eclipse the aim in me?*: 'the true enthusiast—nay monomaniac who *reasons well* in support of his mad position': Domett.

But in the restless irresistible force   340
That works within me—is it for human will
To institute such impulses?—still less
To disregard their promptings . . . what should I
Do, kept among you all—your loves, your cares
Your life— —all to be mine? Be sure that God   345
Ne'er dooms to waste the strength he deigns
     impart . . . .—
Ask the gier-eagle why [she] stoops at once
Into the vast and unexplored abyss—
What fullgrown power informs her from the
     first,
Why she not marvels, strenuously beating   350
The silent boundless regions of the sky!—
Be sure they sleep not whom God needs;—nor
     fear
Their holding light his charge, when every hour
That finds that charge delayed is a new death:
— — Thus for the faith in which I trust;—& hence   355
I can abjure so well the secret Arts
These pedants strive to learn—the Magic
     they
So reverence— —I shall scarcely seek to know
If it exist: too intimate a tie
Connects me with our God:—a sullen fiend   360
To do my bidding—fallen & hateful sprites
To help me— —what are these, at best, beside
God every where,—sustaining & directing
So that the earth shall yield her secrets up

1835 341 me?   343 promptings?   344 all; your loves, your cares,   346
impart.   348 abyss!   349 first!   354 death.   356 arts   357
magic   358 reverence.   360 God. A sullen friend

But in the restless irresistible force   340
That works within me? Is it for human will
To institute such impulses?—still less,
To disregard their promptings! What should I
Do, kept among you all; your loves, your cares,
Your life—all to be mine? Be sure that God   345
Ne'er dooms to waste the strength he deigns
    impart!
Ask the geier-eagle why she stoops at once
Into the vast and unexplored abyss,
What full-grown power informs her from the
    first,
Why she not marvels, strenuously beating   350
The silent boundless regions of the sky!
Be sure they sleep not whom God needs! Nor
    fear
Their holding light his charge, when every hour
That finds that charge delayed, is a new death.
This for the faith in which I trust; and hence   355
I can abjure so well the idle arts
These pedants strive to learn and teach; Black
    Arts,
Great Works, the Secret and Sublime, forsooth—
Let others prize: too intimate a tie
Connects me with our God! A sullen fiend   360
To do my bidding, fallen and hateful sprites
To help me—what are these, at best, beside
God helping, God directing everywhere,
So that the earth shall yield her secrets up,

343 *1849–65* promptings?   347 *1849–68* gier-eagle   352 *1849* Nor fear
Berg {rejected} Why fear   354 *1849* death. *Berg* {rejected} death?

347 *the geier-eagle*: cf. Leviticus 11:18 and Deuteronomy 14:17. See too
Shelley, *The Revolt of Islam*, 2911: 'Swift as an eagle stooping from the plain'.
348 *the vast and unexplored abyss*: cf. *Paradise Lost*, i. 21 ('vast Abyss') and
Johnson, *Rambler* 137, para. 7 ('unexplored abysses of truth').
360–1 *A sullen fiend / To do my bidding*: a 'familiar'.
362 *beside*: 'the meaning of the whole passage is obscured by the use of
"beside" in the sense of "compared to" . . .': Domett.
364 *the earth shall yield*: a Biblical phrase: cf. Psalms, 67:6: 'Then shall the
earth yield her increase'.

And every object shall be charged to strike,   365
To teach, to gratify & to suggest?— —
And I am young, Festus,—happy & free!
I can devote myself—I have a life
To give—I who am singled out for this—
Think, think,—the wide East, where old wisdom
          sprung   370
—   The bright South where she dwelt—the
          populous North
— —   All are passed o'er—it lights on me!—'tis time
New hopes should animate the world—new
          light
Should dawn from new revealings to a race
Weighed down so long, forgotten so long—so
          shall   375
The Heaven reserved for us at last, receive
No creatures whom unwonted splendours blind,
But ardent to confront the unclouded blaze
Whose beams not seldom lit their
          pilgrimage,
Not seldom glorified their life below.   380
F/.   My words have their old fate & make faint stand
          ⟨Beside⟩ [Against] your glowing periods—I
          renounce
All hope of learning further on this head,   382a
And what I next advance holds good as well   b
With one assured that all these things are true;   c
For might not such seek out a fast retreat   383
After approved example? there to have   385
Calm converse with the great Dead, soul to soul,
—   Who laid up treasure with the like intent,—
To lift himself into their airy place—
To fill out full their unfulfilled careers—

1835 368 myself;   369 To give; I, who am singled out for this.   370–1
Think, think; the wide east, where old Wisdom sprung; | The bright south,
where she dwelt; the populous north,   372 me. 'T is   375 long; so
376 heaven . . . . at last receive   382 periods;   382a head;   383
retreat—   384 {No equivalent in MS or 1835.}   385 example—   386
dead—soul to soul—   387 intent?   388 place,   389 careers,

And every object there be charged to strike,   365
Teach, gratify her master God appoints?
And I am young, my Festus, happy and free!
I can devote myself; I have a life
To give; I, singled out for this, the One!
Think, think! the wide East, where all Wisdom
    sprung;   370
The bright South, where she dwelt; the hopeful
    North,
All are passed o'er—it lights on me! 'T is time
New hopes should animate the world, new
    light
Should dawn from new revealings to a race
Weighed down so long, forgotten so long; thus
    shall   375
The heaven reserved for us at last receive
Creatures whom no unwonted splendours blind,
But ardent to confront the unclouded blaze
Whose beams not seldom blessed their
    pilgrimage,
Not seldom glorified their life below.   380
    Festus. My words have their old fate and make
      faint stand
Against your glowing periods. Call this, truth—
Why not pursue it in a fast retreat,
Some one of Learning's many palaces,
After approved example?—seeking there   385
Calm converse with the great dead, soul to soul,
Who laid up treasure with the like intent
—So lift yourself into their airy place,
And fill out full their unfulfilled careers,

365 *1849* object shall be charged   370 *1849* east, where old Wisdom   375
1849 forgotten so long; so shall   376 *1849,1863* for us,   *378 *1849–68,1889*
blaze *1888* blaze. {corrected in DC}   383 *1849, 1865–89* a fast retreat, *1863* a
vast retreat,   385 *1849* example;   387 *1849* intent?

  366 *her master*: i.e. Paracelsus himself.
  374 *revealings*: cf. Shelley, *The Cenci*, IV. i. 38: 'No doubt divine revealings
may be made'.
  386 *Calm converse with the great dead*: cf. Thomson, *The Seasons, Winter*,
431–2: 'There studious let me sit, / And hold high converse with the mighty
dead'; and Shelley, 'Hymn to Intellectual Beauty', 52: 'Hopes of high talk with
the departed dead'.

—   Unraveling the knots their baffled skill   390
          Pronounced inextricable, but surely left
          Far less confused—a fresh eye, a fresh hand
          Might do much— —at their vigour's waning-point
          Succeeding with new-breathed & untired force
          As at old games a runner snatched the torch   395
          From runner still:— —such one might well do
              this:
— —   But you have linked to this your enterprize
          An arbitrary & most perplexing scheme
          Of seeking it in strange [&] untried paths,—

1835 392 confused?   393 Might do much at their vigour's waning-
point—   394 and untried force—   396 still? Such . . . . this.   397 this,
your enterprize,   399 paths;   400–14 {No equivalent in *MS* or *1835*.}

Unravelling the knots their baffled skill   390
Pronounced inextricable, true!—but left
Far less confused. A fresh eye, a fresh hand,
Might do much at their vigour's waning-point;
Succeeding with new-breathed new-hearted force,
As at old games the runner snatched the torch   395
From runner still: this way success
    might be.
But you have coupled with your enterprise,
An arbitrary self-repugnant scheme
Of seeking it in strange and untried paths.
What books are in the desert? Writes the sea   400
The secret of her yearning in vast caves
Where yours will fall the first of human feet?
Has wisdom sat there and recorded aught
You press to read? Why turn aside from her
To visit, where her vesture never glanced,   405
Now—solitudes consigned to barrenness
By God's decree, which who shall dare impugn?
Now—ruins where she paused but would not
    stay,
Old ravaged cities that, renouncing her,
She called an endless curse on, so it came: 410
Or worst of all, now—men you visit, men,
Ignoblest troops who never heard her voice
Or hate it, men without one gift from Rome
Or Athens,—these shall Aureole's teachers be!

392 *1849* confused?   394 *1849* new-breathed and earnest force, *1863* new-
breathed and untired force, *1865* new-breathed, new-hearted force,   395
1849–65 a runner   401 *Berg* {rejected} The secret of its yearnings in those
caves   403 *1849* Wisdom sate *1863,1865* Wisdom sat   405 *Berg* to ⟨follow⟩
[visit], where   407 *Berg* By ⟨her⟩ [God's] decree,   409 *Berg* cities,
⟨whom⟩ [that], renouncing   410 *1849* so it came— *Berg* ⟨and⟩ [so] it
came,—   411 *1849* men you visit, men, *Berg* men, ⟨mere living⟩ [you
visit—]   412 *1849,1863* troops that never heard her voice, *1865* troops who
never heard her voice, *Berg* {rejected} men that never . . . . voice,   413 *Berg*
from ⟨Greece⟩ [Rome]   414 *1849* Or Athens,—these *Berg* Or ⟨Rome,⟩
[Athens—] ⟨and⟩ these

395 *the runner snatched the torch*: a familiar image in classical literature: see,
e.g., Plato, *Laws*, 776 B ('handing on the torch of life from one generation to
another'), and Lucretius, *De rerum natura*, ii. 79.
   400 *What books are in the desert?*: Johnson wrote that Pope 'studied in the
academy of Paracelsus, and made the universe his favourite volume': *Lives of
the English Poets*, ed. George Birkbeck Hill (1905), iii. 216.

Rejecting past example, practice, precept,   415
That so you may stand aidless & alone:—
—— If in this wild rejection you regard
Mankind & their award of fame,—'tis clear
Whate'er you may protest, knowledge is not
Paramount in your love—or for her sake   420
You would collect all help from every source;
—   Friend, foe, assistant, rival, all would merge
In the broad class of those who shewed her
    haunts
And those who shewed ⟨it⟩ [them] not:—
P/.   What shall I say?— —
—   Festus, from childhood I have been possessed   4-5
By a fire—by a true fire— —or faint or fierce
As from without some Master, so it seemed,
Repressed or urged its current;—this but ill
Expresses what I would convey— —but rather
I will believe an Angel ruled me thus,   430
Than that my soul's own workings, own high
    nature
So became manifest;—I knew not then
What whispered in the evening & spoke out
At midnight:—if some mortal, born too soon,
Were laid away in some great trance,—the ages   435
Coming & going all the while,—until
His true time's advent—& could then record
The words ⟨t⟩They spoke who kept watch by
    his bed,
Then I might tell more of the breath so light
Upon my eyelids—& the fingers light   440
Among my hair;—youth is confused, yet never
So dull was I, but when that Spirit passed

1835   415 precept—   420 love;   421 source—   424 show'd them
not.   426 true fire, or . . . . fierce,   427 master, so it seem'd,   430
angel   432 manifest.   434 midnight.   437 advent, and   440
eyelids, and   441 hair. Youth is confused;   442 I but when that spirit
pass'd

Rejecting past example, practice, precept,   415
Aidless 'mid these he thinks to stand alone:
Thick like a glory round the Stagirite
Your rivals throng, the sages: here stand you!
Whatever you may protest, knowledge is not
Paramount in your love; or for her sake   420
You would collect all help from every source—
Rival, assistant, friend, foe, all would merge
In the broad class of those who showed her
      haunts,
And those who showed them not.
      Paracelsus.   What shall I say?
Festus, from childhood I have been possessed   425
By a fire—by a true fire, or faint or fierce,
As from without some master, so it seemed,
Repressed or urged its current: this but ill
Expresses what I would convey: but rather
I will believe an angel ruled me thus,   430
Than that my soul's own workings, own high
      nature,
So became manifest. I knew not then
What whispered in the evening, and spoke out
At midnight. If some mortal, born too soon,
Were laid away in some great trance—the ages   435
Coming and going all the while—till dawned
His true time's advent; and could then record
The words they spoke who kept watch by his
      bed,—
Then I might tell more of the breath so light
Upon my eyelids, and the fingers light   440
Among my hair. Youth is confused; yet never
So dull was I but, when that spirit passed,

---

419 *1849,1863* Whate'er you   422 *1849* Rival or helper, friend. foe, all would
merge   *429 {Reading of *1863–68.*} *1849* what I would convey— *1888,1889*
what would I convey: 437 *1849* advent,   440 *1849–65* fingers warm *Berg*
{rejected} fingers felt

---

417 *the Stagirite*: Aristotle. A 'glory' is a halo.

I turned to him, scarce consciously, as turns
A water-snake when fairies cross his sleep:—
—   And having this within me & about me   445
When Einsiedeln, its hills & lakes & plains
Confined me, what oppressive joy was mine
When life grew plain—& I first viewed [the
        thronged]
The evermoving concourse of mankind! . . .
Believe that ere I joined them,—ere I knew   450
The purpose of the pageant—or the place
Consigned to me within its ranks,—while yet
Wonder was freshest & delight most pure, . . .
. . .   'Twas then that least supportable appeared
A station with the brightest of the crowd   455
A portion with the proudest of them all! . .
—   And from the tumult in my breast, this only
Could I collect . . . that I must thenceforth die
Or elevate myself far, far above
The gorgeous spectacle;—what seemed a
        longing   460
To trample on yet save Mankind at once—
—   To make some unexampled sacrifice
In their behalf—to wring some wondrous good
From Heaven or earth for them—to perish,
        winning
Eternal weal in the act . . as who should dare   465
Pluck out the angry thunder from its cloud
That, all its gathered flame discharged on him,
No storm might threaten Summer's azure
        weather . . .
—   Yet never to be mixed with them, so much
As to have part even in my own work,—share   470

1835 447 me—   448 plain, and . . . . view'd the throng'd,   451
pageant,   453 pure—   455 crowd;   461 mankind   465 act:
469 them

I turned to him, scarce consciously, as turns
A water-snake when fairies cross his sleep.
And having this within me and about me   445
While Einsiedeln, its mountains, lakes and woods
Confined me—what oppressive joy was mine
When life grew plain, and I first viewed the
    thronged,
The everlasting concourse of mankind!
Believe that ere I joined them, ere I knew   450
The purpose of the pageant, or the place
Consigned me in its ranks—while, just awake,
Wonder was freshest and delight most pure—
'T was then that least supportable appeared
A station with the brightest of the crowd,   455
A portion with the proudest of them all.
And from the tumult in my breast, this only
Could I collect, that I must thenceforth die
Or elevate myself far, far above
The gorgeous spectacle. I seemed to
    long   460
At once to trample on, yet save mankind,
To make some unexampled sacrifice
In their behalf, to wring some wondrous good
From heaven or earth for them, to perish,
    winning
Eternal weal in the act: as who should dare   465
Pluck out the angry thunder from its cloud,
That, all its gathered flame discharged on him,
No storm might threaten summer's azure
    sleep:
Yet never to be mixed with men so much
As to have part even in my own work, share   470

---

449 *1849* The ever-moving concourse   450 *1849* them—   452 *1849* Consigned to me within its ranks—while yet   456 *1849* all!   458 *1849* collect—that .... die, *1863,1865* collect, that .... die,   461 *1849* mankind—   463 *1849* behalf—   464 *1849* them—   470 *1849* work—

---

444 *A water-snake*: water-snakes are mentioned several times in Shelley, e.g. in 'The Sensitive Plant' iii. 69. Cf. *Christmas-Eve and Easter-day*, (*Christmas-Eve*, 504, 780).
470 *to have part*: to share with others.

In my own largess,—once the feat achieved
I would withdraw from their officious praise,
—   Would gently put aside their profuse thanks
—   Like some Knight traversing a wilderness
Who, on his way, may chance to free a
⟨illegible word⟩ [tribe]   475
Of Desert-people from their dragon-foe,
When all the swarthy Race press round to kiss
His feet & choose him for their King, & yield
Their poor tents pitched among the sand-hills
for
His realm—. & he points smiling to his scarf   480
Heavy with riveld gold, his burgonet
Gay set with twinkling stones—& to the East
Where these must be displayed . . .

F/.   Good:—let us hear
No more about your nature "which first shrank
"From all that marked you out apart from
men."   485

P/.   I touch on it:—I would but
analyse
That first mad impulse . . 'twas as brief as fond;
For as I gazed again upon the show
I soon distinguished here & there a Shape
Palm-wreathed & radiant, forehead & full eye:—   490
Well pleased was I their state should thus at once
Interpret my own thoughts:—"Behold the clue
"To all—" I rashly said—"& all I pine
"To do, ⟨t⟩These have accomplished—we are
peers!
"They ⟨k⟩Know & therefore rule— —I too will
⟨k⟩Know!"   495

1835 471 largess.   474,476, etc. knight . . . . desert-people etc.   480
realm; and he points, smiling, to his scarf,   481 gold—his bur-
gonet,   489 shape   490 eye.   493 "To all," I rashly said, "and   494
these have accomplish'd: 495 know, and therefore rule . . . I too will
know!'

In my own largess. Once the feat achieved,
I would withdraw from their officious praise,
Would gently put aside their profuse thanks:
Like some knight traversing a wilderness,
Who, on his way, may chance to free a
tribe   475
Of desert-people from their dragon-foe;
When all the swarthy race press round to kiss
His feet, and choose him for their king, and yield
Their poor tents, pitched among the sand-hills,
for
His realm: and he points, smiling, to his scarf   480
Heavy with riveled gold, his burgonet
Gay set with twinkling stones—and to the East,
Where these must be displayed!
    Festus.   Good: let us hear
No more about your nature, "which first shrank
"From all that marked you out apart from
men!"   485
    Paracelsus. I touch on that; these words but
analyse
The first mad impulse: 't was as brief as fond,
For as I gazed again upon the show,
I soon distinguished here and there a shape
Palm-wreathed and radiant, forehead and full eye. 490
Well pleased was I their state should thus at once
Interpret my own thoughts:—"Behold the clue
"To all," I rashly said, "and what I pine
"To do, these have accomplished: we are
peers.
"They know and therefore rule: I, too, will
know!"   495

---

*473 {Reading of *1849*.} *1863–89* thanks.   487 *1849* That first mad impulse—
'twas . . . . fond;   494 *1849* peers!

481 *riveled*: OED rules that this here means 'Twisted; coiled', a rare usage. Its
other example is Marlowe and Nashe, *Dido Queen of Carthage*, 754: 'Ile giue
thee tackling made of riueld gold', here probably echoed.
   burgonet: a type of helmet, with a visor.
   487 *fond*: foolish.
   494 *we are peers*: cf. ii. 306 and v. 160; 'Childe Roland', 195 ('all the lost
adventurers my peers'); and 'Prospice', 17–18 ('my peers The heroes of old').

—   You were beside me, Festus, as you say . .
       You saw me plunge in their pursuits whom fame
       Is lavish to attest the Lords of Mind,
       Not pausing to make sure the prize in view
       Would satiate my cravings when obtained . .   500
. .   But as they strove, I strove:—then came a slow
       And strangling failure— —we aspired alike
       Yet not the meanest plodder Tritheim deems
       A marvel, but was all-sufficient, well content,
       And staggered only at his own strong wits,   505
—   While I was restless, nothing satisfied,
       Distrustful, most perplexed— — —I would slur
         over
       That struggle— —suffice it, that I loathed
         myself
       As weak compared with them, yet felt somehow
       A mighty power was brooding, taking shape   510
       Within me—& this lasted till one night
       When, as I sate revolving it & more,
       A still voice from without said "See'st thou not
       "Desponding child, whence springs defeat &
         loss?
—   Even from thy strength:—know better: hast
         thou gazed   515
       Presumptuous on Wisdom's countenance,
       No veil between, & can thy faultering hands

1835 496 say;   497 Fame   498 lords of mind,   502 failure.   505
wits;   507 perplex'd.   508 struggle;   511 me; and   515 strength.
517 between; and . . . . faltering   518 {No equivalent in MS or 1835.}

You were beside me, Festus, as you say;
You saw me plunge in their pursuits whom fame
Is lavish to attest the lords of mind,
Not pausing to make sure the prize in view
Would satiate my cravings when obtained,   500
But since they strove I strove. Then came a slow
And strangling failure. We aspired alike,
Yet not the meanest plodder, Tritheim counts
A marvel, but was all-sufficient, strong,
Or staggered only at his own vast wits;   505
While I was restless, nothing satisfied,
Distrustful, most perplexed. I would slur
    over
That struggle; suffice it, that I loathed
    myself
As weak compared with them, yet felt somehow
A mighty power was brooding, taking shape   510
Within me; and this lasted till one night
When, as I sat revolving it and more,
A still voice from without said—"Seest thou not,
"Desponding child, whence spring defeat and
    loss?
"Even from thy strength. Consider: hast thou
    gazed   515
"Presumptuously on wisdom's countenance,
"No veil between; and can thy faltering hands,
"Unguided by the brain the sight absorbs,

---

497 *1849* Fame   498 *1849–65* mind;   499 *1849* Not pausing *Berg* ⟨Not pausing⟩ [I paused not]   500 *1849* Would satiate . . . . obtained— *Berg* Would ⟨satiate⟩ [satisfy]. . . . obtained—,   503–4 *1849* Yet not the meanest plodder Tritheim schools | But faced me, all-sufficient, all-content,   505 *1849* own strong wits;   512 *1865* it more and more,   514 *1849* whence came defeat   516 *1849–65* Wisdom's   517 *1849* can thy hands which falter   518 *1849* by thy brain the mighty sight   *Berg* by the brain that mighty sight   *1863–65* by thy brain the sight absorbs

---

497 *in their pursuits*: in pursuit of them.
512 *revolving it*: cf. Shelley, 'Hymn to Mercury', xi 5: 'Revolving in his mind some subtle feat'.
517 *No veil between*: possibly a reminiscence of Schiller's poem, 'Das verschleierte Bild zu Saïs' ('The Veiled Image at Saïs').

Pursue as well the toil their earnest blinking,
Whom radiance ne'er distracts, so clear descries?   520
—   If thou wouldst share their fortune, choose their
          eyes
"Unfed by splendor;—let each task present
"Its petty good to thee—waste not thy gifts
"In profitless waiting for the God's descent,
"But have some idol of thine own to dress   525
"With their array:—Know, not for Knowing's
          sake,
"But to become a star to Men for ever;
"Know! for the gain it gets, the praise it brings,
"The wonder it inspires, the love it breeds . . .
"Look one step onward & secure that step"   530
And I smiled as one never smiles but once,
Then first discovering my aim's extent
Which sought to comprehend the works of God,
—   And God himself—& all God's intercourse
With our own mind;—& how such shewed
          beside   535
My fellow's studies— —whose true worth I saw
But smiled not, well aware who stood by
          me— —
And softer came the Voice—"There *is* a way—
—   "'Tis hard for flesh to tread therein, imbued
"With weakness— —hopeless, if indulgence
          first   540
"Ha⟨s⟩[ve] ripened inborn sins to strength—wilt
          thou
"Adventure for my sake & for thy ⟨k⟩Kind's
"Apart for all reward?"— —& last it breathed

1835 521 "If thou   522 splendour.   523 thee.   524 gods'   526
array. Know, ... knowing's   527, 528 men for ever. | "Know,
for   529 breeds.   530 step."   531 once;   534 himself, and   536
studies, whose . . . . saw,   537 me.   538 voice—   541 "Have ripen'd
. . . . strength: 542 thy kind's,

"Pursue their task as earnest blinkers do
"Whom radiance ne'er distracted? Live their life   520
"If thou wouldst share their fortune, choose their
     eyes
"Unfed by splendour. Let each task present
"Its petty good to thee. Waste not thy gifts
"In profitless waiting for the gods' descent,
"But have some idol of thine own to dress   525
"With their array. Know, not for knowing's
     sake,
"But to become a star to men for ever;
"Know, for the gain it gets, the praise it brings,
"The wonder it inspires, the love it breeds:
"Look one step onward, and secure that step!"   530
And I smiled as one never smiles but once,
Then first discovering my own aim's extent,
Which sought to comprehend the works of God,
And God himself, and all God's intercourse
With the human mind; I understood, no
     less,   535
My fellows' studies, whose true worth I saw,
But smiled not, well aware who stood by
     me.
And softer came the voice—"There is a way:
"'T is hard for flesh to tread therein, imbued
"With frailty—hopeless, if indulgence
     first   540
"Have ripened inborn germs of sin to
     strength:
"Wilt thou adventure for my sake and man's,
"Apart from all reward?" And last it breathed—

519–21 *1849* "Continues to absorb, pursue their task | "On earth like these
around thee—what their sense | "Which radiance ne'er distracted, clear
descries? | "If thou wouldst share their fortune, choose their life, | *Berg* {after
line 519} . . . . like those {?} around thee, *all* their sense,   527 *1849,1863*
ever.   529 *1849,1863* breeds.   530 *1849,1863* step."   531 *1849–65*
once;   536 *1849* fellow's   537 *1863,65* Who stood   538 *1849* way—

---

519 *blinkers*: people of little spiritual perception. Cf. *Sordello*, v. 14.
527 *to become a star*: cf. *Adonais*, 494: 'The soul of Adonais, like a star'.

"Be happy, my good soldier—I am by thee
"Be sure, even to the end!"— —I answered not,   545
Knowing Him:—as he spoke I was endued
With comprehension and a steadfast will,
And when He ceased, my fate was sealed
          forever:—
— — If there took place no special change in me
How comes it all things wore a different hue   550
Thenceforward?—pregnant with vast
          consequence,
Teeming with grand results,—loaded with
          fate,—
So that when quailing at the mighty range
Of secret truths yearning for birth, I haste
To contemplate undazzled some one Truth—   555
Its bearings & effects alone,—at once
What was a speck, expands into a star—
Demanding life to be explored alone,—
Till I near craze:. I go to prove my soul!
I see my way as birds their trackless way   560
— — I shall arrive!— —what time, what circuit first,
I ask not— —but unless God send his hail
Or blinding fire-balls, sleet or stifling snow,
In some time, his good time, I shall arrive:—
He guides me & the bird:—in his good time!   565
M/.   Vex him no further, Festus—it is so!

1835 544 soldier; I am by thee,   546 him. As he spoke,   547 will;   548
he   ceased,   my . . . .   seal'd   for   ever.   551   consequence—   552
results—loaded with fate;   555 truth,   557 star,   559 craze.   562
not: 564 time—his good time—I shall arrive: 565 bird.   566 Festus;

"Be happy, my good soldier; I am by thee,
"Be sure, even to the end!"—I answered not,   545
Knowing him. As he spoke, I was endued
With comprehension and a steadfast will;
And when he ceased, my brow was sealed his
    own.
If there took place no special change in me,
How comes it all things wore a different hue   550
Thenceforward?—pregnant with vast
    consequence,
Teeming with grand result, loaded with
    fate?
So that when, quailing at the mighty range
Of secret truths which yearn for birth, I haste
To contemplate undazzled some one truth,   555
Its bearings and effects alone—at once
What was a speck expands into a star,
Asking a life to pass exploring thus,
Till I near craze. I go to prove my soul!
I see my way as birds their trackless way.   560
I shall arrive! what time, what circuit first,
I ask not: but unless God send his hail
Or blinding fireballs, sleet or stifling snow,
In some time, his good time, I shall arrive:
He guides me and the bird. In his good time!   565
    Michal. Vex him no further, Festus; it is so!

---

546 *1849* Knowing Him. As He spoke,   *1863,1865* Knowing Him. As he
spoke,   548 *1849–65* He . . . . His own.   551 *1849* consequence—
552 *1849* results—loaded with fate;   *1863* results, loaded with fate?   560
1849 trackless way—   562 *1863,1865* His hail   564 *1849* time—his good
time—   *1863,1865* time, His good time,   565 *1863,1865* In His   566
1865 is it so!

---

    548 *my brow was sealed his own*: cf. Revelation 7:3: '. . . till we have sealed the
servants of our God in their foreheads'.
    559 *I go to prove my soul!*: 'Gordon [of Khartoum] . . . was wont to declare
that nothing in all nonscriptural literature was so dear to him, nothing had so
often inspired him in moments of gloom' as lines 559–65: Sharp, p. 69. Cf. *NQ*
vol. 201 (1956), p. 540.
    563 *fireballs*: in 1528 Paracelsus visited Ensisheim to examine a meteoric
stone which had fallen in 1492. His 'Lib[ri] Meteororum' are in vol. ii of
Bitiskius, pp. 293–341. On p. 320a he describes 'Lapis Ensishemii fulminalis'.
    566 *Vex him no further*: 'dramatic & true The woman takes his enthusiasm
first': Domett.

F/.   Just thus you answer ever— —this would
          hold
        Were it [the] trackless air & not a path
        Inviting you, distinct with foot-prints yet
        Of many a mighty spirit gone that way— —   570
        You may have purer views, for aught I know,
        But they were famous in their day—the proofs
        Remain:—at least accept the light they lend.

P/.   Their light!—the sum of all is briefly
          this:
        They laboured after their own fashion— —the
          fruits   575
        Are best seen in a dark & groaning earth
        Given over to a blind & endless strife
        With evils their best lore cannot abate— — —
— —   No, I reject & spurn them utterly
        And all they teach:—shall I still sit beside   580
        Their dry wells, with white lip & filmed eye
        While in the distance heaven is blue above
        Mountains where sleep the unsunned tarns?—

F/.   And yet
        As strong delusions have prevailed, ere now—
—   Men have set out as gallantly to seek   585
        Their ruin— —I have heard of such . . yourself
        Avow all hitherto have failed & fallen,—

M/.   Nay, Festus, when but as the pilgrims
          faint
        For the drear way, do you expect to see
        Their city dawn amid the clouds afar!   590

P/. —   Ay, sounds it not like some old well known
          tale?
—   For me, I estimate their works & them
        So rightly, that at times I wellnigh dream
        I too have spent a life the selfsame way,—

1835 567 ever.   570 way.   571 know;   573 Remain.   575 fash-
ion;   578 abate.   579 No; I reject and . . . . utterly,   580
teach.   581 with white lips and filmed eye,   584 prevail'd ere
now: 586 ruin; I . . . . such—   587 fail'd and fallen.

Festus. Just thus you help me ever. This would
    hold
Were it the trackless air, and not a path
Inviting you, distinct with footprints yet
Of many a mighty marcher gone that way.   570
You may have purer views than theirs, perhaps,
But they were famous in their day—the proofs
Remain. At least accept the light they lend.
    Paracelsus. Their light! the sum of all is briefly
    this:
They laboured and grew famous, and the
    fruits   575
Are best seen in a dark and groaning earth
Given over to a blind and endless strife
With evils, what of all their lore abates?
No; I reject and spurn them utterly
And all they teach. Shall I still sit beside   580
Their dry wells, with a white lip and filmed eye,
While in the distance heaven is blue above
Mountains where sleep the unsunned tarns?
    Festus.   And yet
As strong delusions have prevailed ere now.
Men have set out as gallantly to seek   585
Their ruin. I have heard of such: yourself
Avow all hitherto have failed and fallen.
    Michal. Nay, Festus, when but as the pilgrims
    faint
Through the drear way, do you expect to see
Their city dawn amid the clouds afar?   590
    Paracelsus. Ay, sounds it not like some old
    well-known tale?
For me, I estimate their works and them
So rightly, that at times I almost dream
I too have spent a life the sages' way,

---

570 *1849* mighty spirit gone   575 *1849* laboured, and grew famous;   578
1849 With evils, which of all your Gods abates?   584 *1849* now: 586 *1849*
ruin; I have heard of such—   590 *1849* dawn afar amid the clouds?

    568 *the trackless air:* cf. *Pauline,* 178 n.
    583 *tarns:* small mountain lakes (originally a Northern word).
    590 *Their city dawn amid the clouds:* cf. *Sordello,* v. 11 n.

— Tread once again an old life's course—
   perchance   595
 I perished in an arrogant self-reliance
 An age ago . . & in that act, a prayer
 For one more chance went up so earnest,—so
 Imbued with better light let in by Death,
 So free from all past sin— —that it was heard: 599a
— That life was blotted out . . not so completely 600
 But scattered wrecks enough remain to wake
 Dim memories; as now, when once more
   seems
 The goal in sight again: . . . All which is foolish
 Indeed & only means the form I bear,
 The earth I tread, are not more clear to 605
   me.

F/. And who am I to challenge & dispute
 That clear belief?— —I will devest all fear.

M/. Then Aureole is God's commissary! he
   shall
 Be great & grand— —& all for us!

P/.   No, sweet! 610
 Not great or grand:—If I can serve Mankind
 Tis well— —but there our intercourse must
   end:—
 I never will be served by those I serve!

F/. Look well to this: *here* is a plague-spot,
   veil it,
 Disguise it how you will:—'tis true, you utter 615

1835 595 course. 597 ago; and 599 Death— 599a heard . . . 604
Indeed, and only means—the form I bear, 606 {No equivalent in *MS* or
1835} 611 grand. If . . . . mankind 613 serve.

And tread once more familiar paths.
    Perchance   595
I perished in an arrogant self-reliance
Ages ago; and in that act, a prayer
For one more chance went up so earnest, so
Instinct with better light let in by
    death,
That life was blotted out—not so completely   600
But scattered wrecks enough of it remain,
Dim memories, as now, when once more
    seems
The goal in sight again. All which, indeed,
Is foolish, and only means—the flesh I wear,
The earth I tread, are not more clear to me   605
Than my belief, explained to you or no.
    Festus. And who am I, to challenge and dispute
That clear belief? I will divest all fear.
    Michal. Then Aureole is God's commissary! he
    shall
Be great and grand—and all for us!
    Paracelsus.   No, sweet!   610
Not great and grand. If I can serve mankind
'T is well; but there our intercourse must
    end:
I never will be served by those I serve.
    Festus. Look well to this; here is a plague-spot,
    here,
Disguise it how you may! 'T is true, you utter   615

---

597 *1849* An age ago;   599 *1849* Death,   602 *1849* Dim memories; as now, when seems once more *1863,65* Dim memories, as now, when seems once more *1868* Dim memories, as now, when once more seems   603 *1849* again: 608 *1849* I put away all fear.   610 *Berg* {rejected} Be great and famed {?}— and . . . . | No, sweet! *1863,1865* Be great and grand—and . . . . | No, Sweet!   611 *1849* Not great and grand If I can serve mankind *Berg* {rejected} Not great or famed. If I can serve my race   612 *1849* well—

---

599 *better light let in by death*: Browning was interested in the vision of life and its meaning which may come to a dying man: see l 765–9 below, and v. 487–8, 507–9.

608 *divest*: put off (rare: the previous example in OED is dated 1673).

609 *God's commissary*: cf. Donne, 'To Sʳ Henry Wotton', 11, and *Infinitati Sacrum, Metempsychosis*, 'The Progresse of the Soule', 31.

614 *a plague-spot*: cf. *Sordello*, i. 567–9.

This scorn while by our side & loving us . .
Tis but a spot as yet;—but it will break
Into a hideous blotch if overlooked:—
How can that course be safe which from the
    first
Produces carelessness to human love?   620
—   I know:—you have abjured the helps which
    men
Who overpass their kind, as you would do,
Have humbly sought . . I dare not thoroughly
    probe
This matter, lest I learn too much:—let be,
That popular praise would little instigate   625
Your efforts— —or particular approval
Reward you; put reward aside;—you shall
Go forth upon your arduous task alone,
None shall assist you—none partake your
    toil—
None share your triumph:—still you must
    retain   630
Some one to trust your glory to,—to share
Your rapture with;—had I been chosen like
    you
I should encircle [me] with love—should raise
A rampart of kind wishes— —it should seem
Impossible [for] me to fail, so watched   635
By gentle friends who made my cause their
    own;
—   They should ward off fate's envy— —the great
    boon,
Extravagant when claimed by me alone,
Being a gift to them as well as me:—
If ease seduced or danger daunted me,   640

1835 618 overlook'd.   621 I know you have abjured   623 sought.
630 triumph—   631 glory to;   632 with.   634 wishes;   637 Fate's
envy—   639 me.

This scorn while by our side and loving us;
'T is but a spot as yet: but it will break
Into a hideous blotch if overlooked.
How can that course be safe which from the
    first
Produces carelessness to human love?   620
It seems you have abjured the helps which
    men
Who overpass their kind, as you would do,
Have humbly sought; I dare not thoroughly
    probe
This matter, lest I learn too much. Let be
That popular praise would little instigate   625
Your efforts, nor particular approval
Reward you; put reward aside; alone
You shall go forth upon your arduous task,
None shall assist you, none partake your
    toil,
None share your triumph: still you must
    retain   630
Some one to cast your glory on, to share
Your rapture with. Were I elect like
    you,
I would encircle me with love, and raise
A rampart of my fellows; it should seem
Impossible for me to fail, so watched   635
By gentle friends who made my cause their
    own.
They should ward off fate's envy—the great
    gift,
Extravagant when claimed by me alone,
Being so a gift to them as well as me.
If danger daunted me or ease seduced,   640

---

623 *1849* sought—   624 *1849* much: 626 *1849* nor particular approval
Berg [n]or particular ⟨approval⟩ [applause]   630 *1849* triumph—   636
1849 own;   637 *1849* Fate's

---

619 *How can that course be safe*: Domett notes that Browning here 'hints at one
of the *morals* (if you will have such) of the poem'.
635 *so watched*: cf. *Pauline*, 9: 'To one so watched, so loved and so secured'.

How calmly their sad eyes should gaze
    reproach!— —
M/.   O Aureole, can I sing tho' all alone,
Without first calling, in my fancy, both
To listen by my side— —even I!—& you?—
Do you not feel this?—say that you feel this!—   645
P/.   I feel 'tis pleasant, that my aims, at
    length
Allowed their weight, should be supposed to
    need
A further strengthening in these goodly helps!
Once more (since I am forced to speak as one   648a
Who has full liberty at his discretion)   b
My course allures for its own sake— — —its
    sole
Intrinsic worth, & ne'er shall boat of mine   650
Adventure forth for gold & apes at once:—
Your sages say "if human, therefore weak":—
If weak, more need to give myself entire
To my pursuit;—& by its side, all else— —
— — No matter:—I deny myself but little   655
In waiving all assistance save its own,
And I regret it;—there's no sacrifice
To make;—the sages threw so much away
While I must be content with gaining all.
F/.   But do not cut yourself from human weal! . .   660
. .   You cannot thrive— — —a man that dares
    affect
To spend his life in service to his kind
For no reward of theirs—nor bound to them
By any tie!—nor do so, Aureole!
There are strange punishments for such . . .
    although   665
No visible good flow thence, give up some part

1835 650 worth; and   656 its own—   663 theirs,   664 tie; nor   665
such;

How calmly their sad eyes should gaze
      reproach!
      Michal. O Aureole, can I sing when all alone,
Without first calling, in my fancy, both
To listen by my side—even I! And you?
Do you not feel this? Say that you feel this!   645
      Paracelsus. I feel 't is pleasant that my aims, at
            length
Allowed their weight, should be supposed to
      need
A further strengthening in these goodly helps!
My course allures for its own sake, its
      sole
Intrinsic worth; and ne'er shall boat of mine   650
Adventure forth for gold and apes at once.
Your sages say, "if human, therefore weak:"
If weak, more need to give myself entire
To my pursuit; and by its side, all else . . .
No matter! I deny myself but little   655
In waiving all assistance save its own.
Would there were some real sacrifice to make!
Your friends the sages threw their joys away,
While I must be content with keeping mine.
      Festus. But do not cut yourself from human
            weal!   660
You cannot thrive—a man that dares
      affect
To spend his life in service to his kind
For no reward of theirs, unbound to them
By any tie; nor do so, Aureole! No—
There are strange punishments for such. Give
      up   665
(Although no visible good flow thence) some
      part

645 *1849* this?—say   649 *1849–1865* sake—   656 *1849* own—   658
Berg {rejected} The sages proudly threw so much away,   660 *1849*
weal?   663 *1849,1863* nor bound to them

651 *for gold and apes*: cf. 1 Kings 10:22: '. . . once in three years came the navy
of Tharshish, bringing gold, and silver, ivory, and apes, and peacocks'.
652 '*if human, therefore weak*': cf. the Latin proverb, *humanum est errare*.

Of your renown to another;—so you shall
Hide from yourself that all is for yourself:
Say,—say almost to God—"I have done all
"For her,— —not for myself!"— —

P/.   And who but late,   670
Was to rejoice in my success like you?
Whom should I love but you?

F/.   Nay, I know not:
But know this, you, that tis no will of mine
You should abjure the lofty claims you make
—   And this the cause . . . I will no longer seek   675
To overlook the truth . . . that there would be
A monstrous spectacle upon the earth,—
Beneath the pleasant sun,—among the trees—
A being knowing not what love is:—hear
     me;—
You are endowed with faculties which have   680
Annexed to them as 'twere a dispensation
To summon meaner spirits to do their will,
To gather round them at their need,—inspiring
Such with a love which *they* can never feel,
Passionless midst their passionate
     votaries;— — —   685
I know not if you joy in this or no,
Or ever dream that common men live wholly
On objects you so lightly prize, which make
Their hearts' sole wealth: the soft affections seem
Beauteous at most to you, which they must taste   690
Or die: & this strange quality accords
I know not how, with you—sits well upon
That luminous brow—(—tho' in another it
     were

1835 668 for yourself.   670 her—not for myself!"   674 make;   676
truth;   678 sun, among the trees,   679 is. Hear me;   683 need;
684 feel—   685 votaries.   692 you;   693 brow: though

Of the glory to another; hiding thus,
Even from yourself, that all is for yourself.
Say, say almost to God—"I have done all
"For her, not for myself!"
  Paracelsus.   And who but lately 670
Was to rejoice in my success like you?
Whom should I love but both of you?
  Festus.   I know not:
But know this, you, that 't is no will of mine
You should abjure the lofty claims you make;
And this the cause—I can no longer seek 675
To overlook the truth, that there would be
A monstrous spectacle upon the earth,
Beneath the pleasant sun, among the trees:
—A being knowing not what love is. Hear
  me!
You are endowed with faculties which bear 680
Annexed to them as 't were a dispensation
To summon meaner spirits to do their will
And gather round them at their need; inspiring
Such with a love themselves can never feel,
Passionless 'mid their passionate
  votaries.   685
I know not if you joy in this or no,
Or ever dream that common men can live
On objects you prize lightly, but which make
Their heart's sole treasure: the affections seem
Beauteous at most to you, which we must taste 690
Or die: and this strange quality accords,
I know not how, with you; sits well upon
That luminous brow, though in another it
  scowls

670 *1849* "For her—not for myself!" | And who, *1863,1865* "For her, not for myself!" | And who, 673 *1849* 'tis no wish of mine 675 *1849* Although I can no longer seek, indeed, 676 *1849* that there will be 684 *1849* feel—

670 *"For her*: this and other passages make it evident that Browning's Paracelsus is not castrated.
684–5 *they . . . their*: 'it had been better perhaps—*you & yours*': Domett (referring to 1835 text).

An eating brand—a shame:—I dare not blame
    you:
The rules of right & wrong thus set aside   695
There's no alternative . . . I judge you one
Of higher order—under other laws
Than bind us,—therefore curb not one bold
    glance!
Tis best aspire— —once mingled with us
    all . . . . .

M/.   Stay with us, Aureole! cast those hopes
    away   700
And stay with us—an angel warns me, too,
Man should be humble . . . you are very proud!
And God, dethroned, has doleful plagues for
    such!
Warns me to have in dread no quick repulse
No slow defeat— —but a complete success!   705
You will find all you seek, & perish so!

P/.   (*After a pause*)—Are these the barren firstfruits I
    should fear?
Is love like this the natural lot of all?
How many years of hate might one such hour
O'erballance? dearest Michal, dearest Festus,   710
What shall I say, if not that I desire
Well to deserve that love, & will, dear Friends,
In swerving nothing from my high resolves:
See—the great moon! & ere the mottled owls
Were wide awake, I should have made all sure   715
For my departure that remains to do;—   715a
So answer not, while I run lightly o'er   b
The topics you have urged to-night:—it seems   c
We acquiesce at last in all save only
If I am like to compass what I seek
In the untried career I chuse; & then,

1835 694 shame.   696 alternative.   698 us;   699 aspire.   701
us: 702 humble;   703 And God dethroned   705 defeat,   712
friends,   713 resolves.   714 See, the . . . . and 'ere   715c to-night.

An eating brand, a shame, I dare not judge
   you.
The rules of right and wrong thus set aside,   695
There 's no alternative—I own you one
Of higher order, under other laws
Than bind us; therefore, curb not one bold
   glance!
'T is best aspire. Once mingled with us
   all . . .
   Michal. Stay with us, Aureole! cast those hopes
     away,   700
And stay with us! An angel warns me, too,
Man should be humble; you are very proud:
And God, dethroned, has doleful plagues for
   such!
—Warns me to have in dread no quick repulse,
No slow defeat, but a complete success: 705
You will find all you seek, and perish so!
   Paracelsus [*after a pause*]. Are these the barren
     firstfruits of my quest?
Is love like this the natural lot of all?
How many years of pain might one such hour
O'erbalance? Dearest Michal, dearest Festus,   710
What shall I say, if not that I desire
To justify your love; and will, dear friends,
In swerving nothing from my first resolves.
See, the great moon! and ere the mottled owls
Were wide awake, I was to go. It seems   715
You acquiesce at last in all save this—
If I am like to compass what I seek
By the untried career I choose; and then,

694 *1849* brand—a shame. I dare not judge you: 704 *1849* He warns me not
to dread a quick repulse, | Nor slow defeat, but a complete success!   707
1849 first fruits of my life?   712 *1849* To merit this your love;

694 *An eating brand*: cf. iv. 139, and *Sordello*, iv. 138.

If that career, making but small account
Of much of life's delight, will offer joys   720
Sufficient to sustain my soul—for thus
I understand these fond fears just expressed:
And first:—the lore you praise & I neglect,
The labours & the precepts of old sages,
I have not slightly disesteemed— —but then   725
Truth is within ourselves . . it takes no rise
From outward things, whate'er you may believe;
There is an inmost centre in us all
Where truth abides in fullness; & around,
Wall within wall the gross flesh hems it in—   730
Perfect & true Perception—which is Truth;—
A baffling & perverting carnal mesh
Which blinds it, & makes Error: &, "to *know*"
Rather consists in opening out a way
Whence the imprisoned splendor may dart forth,   735
Than in effecting entry for the light
Supposed to be without: watch narrowly
The demonstration of a Truth, its birth,
And you shall trace the Effluence to its spring
And source within us, where broods radiance
    vast   740
To be elicited ray by ray, as chance
Shall favour;—*chance*—for hitherto
Even as we know not how those beams are
    born,
As little know we what unlocks their lair;—
For Men have oft grown old among their books   745
And died, casehardened in their ignorance,
Whose careless youth had promised what long
    years
Of unremitted labour ne'er performed:

1835 722 express'd.   725 disesteem'd.   726 ourselves;   730 within
wall, the . . . . in,   731 perception—which is truth;   733 error: and, "*to
know*"   737 without.   738 truth,   739 effluence   745 men

If that career, making but small account
Of much of life's delight, will yet retain   720
Sufficient to sustain my soul: for thus
I understand these fond fears just expressed.
And first; the lore you praise and I neglect,
The labours and the precepts of old time,
I have not lightly disesteemed. But, friends,   725
Truth is within ourselves; it takes no rise
From outward things, whate'er you may believe.
There is an inmost centre in us all,
Where truth abides in fulness; and around,
Wall upon wall, the gross flesh hems it in,   730
This perfect, clear perception—which is truth.
A baffling and perverting carnal mesh
Binds it, and makes all error: and to KNOW
Rather consists in opening out a way
Whence the imprisoned splendour may escape,   735
Than in effecting entry for a light
Supposed to be without. Watch narrowly
The demonstration of a truth, its birth,
And you trace back the effluence to its spring
And source within us; where broods radiance
     vast,
                                                       740
To be elicited ray by ray, as chance
Shall favour: chance—for hitherto, your sage
Even as he knows not how those beams are
     born,
As little knows he what unlocks their fount:
And men have oft grown old among their books   745
To die case-hardened in their ignorance,
Whose careless youth had promised what long
     years
Of unremitted labour ne'er performed:

721 *1849–65* soul—   725 *1849* slightly disesteemed.   727 *1849*
believe: 729 *1849,1863* around   731 *1849* truth;   733 *1849–68* Blinds
it,   735 *1849* inprisoned splendour   744 *1849* fount; *1863–68* fount.

728 *an inmost centre*: 'The old Platonic & new transcendental notion. Beauti-
ful in poetry, perhaps *not so true* in philosophy': Domett. Cf. *Pauline*, 274.
746 *case-hardened*: hardened on the surface.

While, contrary, it has chanced some idle day
To Autumn loiterers just as fancy-free   750
As the midges in the sun, has oft brought forth
A Truth, produced mysteriously as cape
Of cloud grown out of the invisible mist:—
Hence, may not Truth be lodged alike in all,
The lowest as the highest?—some slight film   755
The interposing bar which binds a soul,—
Some film removed the happy outlet whence
It issues proudly: seeing that the soul   759
Is deathless (we know well)— —but oftener
    cooped   759a
A prisoner & a thrall, than a throned Power . . .   b
That it strives weakly in the child—is loosed   760
In manhood, clogged by sickness, back
    compelled
By age & waste, set free at last by death;—
That not alone when life flows still do Truth   765
And Power emerge, but also when strange
    chance
Affects its current: in unused conjuncture,
Where sickness breaks the body—hunger,—
    watching,
Excess, or languor—oftenest death's approach—
Peril, deep joy or woe:—one man shall crawl   770

1835 750 To autumn {*MS* underlines 'To' in pencil, and has 'That' in the
margin.}   751 has oft {*MS* has 've' written in margin, indicating 'correc-
tion' to 'have oft'}   752 truth—   753 mist.   754 truth   756
soul?   757 {No equivalent in *MS* or *1835*}   759 proudly?   759b
power;   760 child,   763–4 {No equivalent in *MS* or *1835*}   765,766
truth| And power   768 Where sickness {Possibly 'When' is intended in the
MS}   770 woe.

While, contrary, it has chanced some idle day,
To autumn loiterers just as fancy-free   750
As the midges in the sun, gives birth at last
To truth—produced mysteriously as cape
Of cloud grown out of the invisible air.
Hence, may not truth be lodged alike in all,
The lowest as the highest? some slight film   755
The interposing bar which binds a soul
And makes the idiot, just as makes the sage
Some film removed, the happy outlet whence
Truth issues proudly? See this soul of ours!
How it strives weakly in the child, is loosed   760
In manhood, clogged by sickness, back
     compelled
By age and waste, set free at last by death:
Why is it, flesh enthrals it or enthrones?
What is this flesh we have to penetrate?
Oh, not alone when life flows still, do truth   765
And power emerge, but also when strange
     chance
Ruffles its current; in unused conjuncture,
When sickness breaks the body—hunger,
     watching,
Excess or languor—oftenest death's approach,
Peril, deep joy or woe. One man shall crawl   770

---

750 *1849* That autumn   751 *1849* sun, have oft given vent   756 *1849* binds
it up,   764 *Berg* {rejected} What is this flesh? How may we pierce through
it?   769 *1849* approach—

749 *contrary*: on the contrary: as in *Sordello*, i. 57.
749 *it has chanced*: 'Goethe says this somewhere': Domett.
some idle day: the subject of 'gives birth' (751).
761 *clogged*: cf. iv. 404 and n., and *Sordello* ii. 401.
763 *enthrals*: imprisons. Cf. *Sordello*, vi. 560.
767 *unused*: archaic, as OED notes.
769 *death's approach*: cf. 599 n., above.
770 *One man*: Mrs. Orr (*Handbook*, p. 350) states that these lines were
inspired by Christopher Smart. In 1887 Browning asked Furnivall to enquire
whether the British Museum Library 'possesses a copy of the "Song to
David", published as a small paper-bound book nearly sixty years ago:'
Trumpeter, p. 144. As Peterson points out, editions of the poem with a few
notes appeared in 1819 and 1827. It was probably the 1827 ed. which Browning
bought: cf. Maynard, p. 450. The third of the *Parleyings with Certain People of
Importance in their Day* is 'With Christopher Smart'.

Thro' life, surrounded with all stirring things,
Unmoved— —& he goes mad—& from the
　　wreck
Of what he was, by his wild talk alone
You first collect how great a spirit he hid—　　774
— 　Seeing all this, why should I pine in vain　　774a
Attempts to win some day the august form　　b
Of Truth to stand before me, & compel　　c
My dark unvalued frame to change its nature　　d
And straight become suffused with light . . at
　　best　　e
For my sole good . . leaving the world to seek　　f
Salvation out as it best may, or follow　　g
The same long thorny course: No, I will learn　　h
How to set free the soul alike in All,　　775
By searching out the laws by which the Flesh
Accloys the Spirit . . we may not be doomed
To cope with seraphs, but at least the rest
Shall cope with us—. make no more Giants, God!
But elevate the Race at once!—we ask　　780
But to put forth our strength, our human
　　strength,
— 　All starting fairly, all equipped alike
Gifted alike & eagle-eyed, true-hearted . . .
See if we cannot beat thy angels yet!—
— 　Such is my task— —I go to gather this　　785
Mysterious knowledge, here & there dispersed
About the world, long lost or ever-hidden—
And why should I be sad, or lorn of hope?
Why ever make Man's good distinct from God's?
Or, finding they are one, why have mistrust?　　790

1835　772 mad; and　　774 hid.　　774h course?　　775 in all,　　776
flesh　　777 spirit.　　779 us. Make no more giants, God!　　780 race at
once!　　783 true-hearted.　　785 task.　　787 ever-hidden;　　789 man's

Through life surrounded with all stirring things,
Unmoved; and he goes mad: and from the
    wreck
Of what he was, by his wild talk alone,
You first collect how great a spirit he hid.
Therefore, set free the soul alike in all,   775
Discovering the true laws by which the flesh
Accloys the spirit! We may not be doomed
To cope with seraphs, but at least the rest
Shall cope with us. Make no more giants, God,
But elevate the race at once! We ask   780
To put forth just our strength, our human
    strength,
All starting fairly, all equipped alike,
Gifted alike, all eagle-eyed, true-hearted—
See if we cannot beat thine angels yet!
Such is my task. I go to gather this   785
The sacred knowledge, here and there dispersed
About the world, long lost or never found.
And why should I be sad or lorn of hope?
Why ever make man's good distinct from God's,
Or, finding they are one, why dare mistrust?   790

---

772 *1849–65* Unmoved—and he goes mad;   777 *1849* Bars in the
spirit!   779 *1849* God!   784 *1849* thy angels *1863* the angels   789
1849,1863 God's?

---

777 *Accloys*: clogs, chokes, as in *The Faerie Queene*, II. vii. 15, and in the
Philosophicall Poems of Henry More (1647), p. 76. For Browning and More see
Sordello, i. 757 n. In 'Jochanan Hakkadosh' (in *Jocoseria*) we find 'custom the
accloyer' (l. 294).
    778 *to cope with seraphs*: perhaps a reference to the story of Jacob and the
angel: Genesis 32:24 ff.
    788 *lorn of hope*: cf. Keats, 'Hyperion', i. 118: 'lorn of light'.

Who shall succeed if not one pledged like me?
Mine is no mad attempt to build a world
Apart from his, like those who set themselves
To find the nature of the spirit they bore,
And, taught betimes that all their gorgeous
    dreams   795
And beauteous fancies hopes & aspirations   795a
Were born only to wither in this life,   796
Refused to curb or moderate their longings,   796a
Or fit them to this narrow sphere, but chose
To figure & conceive another world
And other frames meet for their vast desires,
And all a dream!—thus was life scorned; but
    life   800
Shall yet be crowned . . twine amaranth! I am
    Priest!
And all for yielding with a lively spirit
A poor existence—parting with a youth
Like theirs who squander every energy
Convertible to good on painted toys,   805
Breath-bubbles, gilded dust! & tho' I spurn
All adventitious aims, from empty praise
To love's award, yet whoso deems such helps
Important & concerns himself for me,
May know even these will follow with the
    rest—   810
As in the steady rolling Mayne, asleep
Yonder, is mingled & involved a mass   812
Of schistous particles of ore . . & even   812a
My own affections, laid to rest awhile,

Who shall succeed if not one pledged like me?
Mine is no mad attempt to build a world
Apart from his, like those who set themselves
To find the nature of the spirit they bore,
And, taught betimes that all their gorgeous
    dreams   795
Were only born to vanish in this life,
Refused to fit them to its narrow sphere,
But chose to figure forth another world
And other frames meet for their vast desires,—
And all a dream! Thus was life scorned; but
    life   800
Shall yet be crowned: twine amaranth! I am
    priest!
And all for yielding with a lively spirit
A poor existence, parting with a youth
Like theirs who squander every energy
Convertible to good, on painted toys,   805
Breath-bubbles, gilded dust! And though I spurn
All adventitious aims, from empty praise
To love's award, yet whoso deems such helps
Important, and concerns himself for me,
May know even these will follow with the
    rest—   810
As in the steady rolling Mayne, asleep
Yonder, is mixed its mass of schistous ore.
My own affections, laid to rest awhile,

793 *1849–65* His,   797 *1849* to this narrow sphere,   800 *1849* Still, all a
dream!   803 *1849* existence—   *804 {Reading of *1849–65*} *1868–89* Like
those who   *813 {Reading of *1849–68*} *1888,1889* affections laid

797 *its narrow sphere*: as in *Pauline*, 594, and *Sordello*, i. 563.
801 *amaranth*: an imaginary flower, supposed never to fade, as in *Sordello*, i.
371.
812 *schistous ore*: 'schist' in geology means 'A crystalline rock whose compo-
nent minerals are arranged in a more or less parallel manner' (OED). Paracel-
sus's scientific interests render the image appropriate. In the article referred to
above (p. 114), Professor Thomas Thomson wrote: 'We consider his treatise
on *Minerals* as the most curious of all his works' (p. 259). Note the frequent
references to mineralogy in the poem.

Will waken purified, subdued alone
By all I have achieved, . . till then—till
then— — —   815
Ah! the time-wiling . . loitering of a page
Thro' bower & over ⟨hall,⟩ [lawn,] till eve shall
    bring
The stately lady's presence whom he
    loves . . . .
The broken sleep of the fisher whose rough
    coat
Enwraps the queenly pearl— —these are faint
    types!   820
See, see, they look on me—I triumph now!
Tell me, Festus, Michal, but one thing—I have
    told
All I shall e'er disclose to mortal: . . . now,
Do you believe I shall accomplish this?
F/.   I do believe!
M/.   And I, dear Aureole!   825
P/.   Those words shall never fade from out my
    brain: . .
Tis earnest of the end:— —shall never fade!
Are there not, Festus, are there not dear Michal
Two points in the adventure of the diver . .
One—when, a beggar he prepares to plunge   830
One—when a prince he rises with his pearl,?
Festus, I plunge!

1835 815 achieved;   816 the time-wiling loitering   823 mortal . . .
now,   826 brain.   827 'Tis . . . . end—   829 diver: 830 One—
when a beggar . . . . plunge?

Will waken purified, subdued alone
By all I have achieved. Till then—till
   then . . .   815
Ah, the time-wiling loitering of a page
Through bower and over lawn, till eve shall
   bring
The stately lady's presence whom he
   loves—
The broken sleep of the fisher whose rough
   coat
Enwraps the queenly pearl—these are faint
   types!   820
See, see, they look on me: I triumph now!
But one thing, Festus, Michal! I have
   told
All I shall e'er disclose to mortal: say—
Do you believe I shall accomplish this?
   Festus. I do believe!
   Michal.   I ever did believe!   825
   Paracelsus. Those words shall never fade from
     out my brain!
This earnest of the end shall never fade!
Are there not, Festus, are there not, dear Michal,
Two points in the adventure of the diver,
One—when, a beggar, he prepares to plunge,   830
One—when, a prince, he rises with his pearl?
Festus, I plunge!
   Festus.   We wait you when you rise!

---

815 *1849* achieved;   821 *1849* See how they look   822 *1849* Michal!—
829 *1849–65* diver: 830 *1849* plunge?   832 *1849* *Fest.* I wait you when
you rise!

816 *time-wiling*: not in OED.

832 *when you rise!*: 'Rejecting love & sympathy as needless at least to his own
happiness—taking his *desire* for proof of his *destiny*—rejecting the past & what
it achieved as worthless, the source of truth being within—& above all, making
faith in the cause a substitute for all rational means—he determines to pierce
the mystery of man & evil. It is the start [?] & youth of an enthusiast': Domett.

2   PARACELSUS ATTAINS.

Scene, *Constantinople. "The House of the Greek."* 1521

Paracelsus.

Over the waters in the vapourous West
The sun goes down as in a sphere of gold
Behind the arm of the city, which between
Athwart the splendour black & crooked runs   5
Like a Turk verse along a scimetar— — —
There lie, sullen memorial, & no more
Possess my aching sight:—'tis done at last!
Strange!. & the juggles of a sallow cheat
Have won me to this act—'tis as yon cloud   10
Should voyage unwrecked o'er many a
      mountain-top
And break upon a molehill;—I have dared
Come to a pause at last—& scan for once

PART II.

PARACELSUS ATTAINS.

SCENE.—*Constantinople; the house of a Greek Conjurer.* 1521.

PARACELSUS.

Over the waters in the vaporous West
The sun goes down as in a sphere of gold
Behind the arm of the city, which between,
With all that length of domes and minarets,
Athwart the splendour, black and crooked runs   5
Like a Turk verse along a scimitar.
There lie, sullen memorial, and no more
Possess my aching sight! 'T is done at last.
Strange—and the juggles of a sallow cheat
Have won me to this act! 'T is as yon cloud   10
Should voyage unwrecked o'er many a
      mountain-top
And break upon a molehill. I have dared
Come to a pause with knowledge; scan for once

1849 SCENE.—*Constantinople.*—*"The House of the Greek-conjuror."* 1521.   3
1849 Behind the outstretched city,   7–8 *1849* There lie, thou saddest writing,
and awhile | Relieve my aching sight.   10 *1849* Could win me to this act!

Constantinople: see the tradition recorded in the *Biographie Universelle* that
Paracelsus visited Constantinople 'for the purpose of obtaining the secret of the
tincture of Trismegistus from a Greek who inhabited that capital': p. 502
below.
    1521: 'The time, it will be recollected, trembles on the dawn of the Reforma-
tion, when liberty of thought was rising in the world, and men's brains were
busy, and their spirits stirring with curiosity and zeal. *A great time!*': John
Forster, *New Monthly Magazine*, 1836, Part I, p. 292.
    PARACELSUS: he is alone to line 339.
    3 *the city, which between*: between the water and the setting sun.
    7 *sullen memorial*: he has been writing: see l. 20 ff.
    9 *juggles*: cf. *Pauline*, 681 n.

The heights already reached, without regard
To the extent above—fairly compute　　15
All I have clearly gained, for once excluding
A brilliant future to supply & perfect
All half-gains, & conjectures, & crude hopes—
— And all because a fortune-teller wills
His credulous seekers should inscribe thus much　　20
Within this roll— —& here amid the scrawled
Uncouth recordings of the dupes of this
Old arch-genethliac, lie my life's results!　　25

A few blurred characters suffice to note
A stranger wandered long in many lands
And reaped the fruit he coveted in a few
Discoveries,—as appended here & there,—
The fragmentary produce of those toils　　30
In a dim heap, fact & surmise to-gether
Confusedly massed as when acquired—he was
Intent on gain to come too much to stay
And scrutinize whate'er was gained—the whole

1835 15 above;　21 roll: and here amid the scrawl'd　22–3 {No equival-
ent in *MS* or *1835*.}　32 mass'd, as when acquired;　34 gain'd:

The heights already reached, without regard
To the extent above; fairly compute   15
All I have clearly gained; for once excluding
A brilliant future to supply and perfect
All half-gains and conjectures and crude hopes:
And all because a fortune-teller wills
His credulous seekers should inscribe thus much   20
Their previous life's attainment, in his roll,
Before his promised secret, as he vaunts,
Make up the sum: and here amid the scrawled
Uncouth recordings of the dupes of this
Old arch-genethliac, lie my life's results!   25

A few blurred characters suffice to note
A stranger wandered long through many lands
And reaped the fruit he coveted in a few
Discoveries, as appended here and there,
The fragmentary produce of much toil,   30
In a dim heap, fact and surmise together
Confusedly massed as when acquired; he was
Intent on gain to come too much to stay
And scrutinize the little gained: the whole

16–26 *1849* What I have clearly gained; for once excluding
          My future which should finish and fulfil
          All half-gains, and conjectures, and mere hopes—
          And this, because a fortune-teller bids
          His credulous enquirers write thus much,
          Their previous life's attainment, in his book,
          Before his promised secret, as he vaunts,
          Make that life perfect: here, accordingly,
          'Mid the uncouth recordings of such dupes,
          —Scrawled in like fashion, lie my life's results!

          These few blurred characters suffice to note
1863, *1865* as *1888*, except 'hopes— | And all,' 'much,' 'here, amid'   *1868* as
1888 except 'much,' 'here, amid'
32–4 *1849* Confusedly massed, as when acquired; himself | Too bent on
gaining more to calmly stay | And scrutinize the little which he gained:

14 *The heights already reached*: cf. the French note to *Pauline*, 811.
   25 *arch-genethliac*: a genethliac is one who calculates nativities: cf. *Hudibras* II.
iii. 689.
   29 *Discoveries*: for a modern assessment of his originality see Pagel, op. cit.,
pp. 344 ff.

Slipt in the blank space twixt an ideot's gibber   35
And a mad lover's ditty . . there it lies.

And yet those blottings chronicle a life
— — A whole life, & my life! no thing to do,
No problem for the fancy, but a life
Spent & decided,—wasted past retrieve   40
Or worthy beyond a peer— —stay, what does
    this
Remembrancer set down concerning "life".? . .
"'Time fleets, youth fades, life is an empty
    dream'
"—It is the echo of time—he whose heart beat
"First underneath a human heart, whose speech   45
"Was copied from a human tongue—can never
"Recall when he was living yet knew it not:
"Nevertheless long seasons pass o'er him
"Until, one hour's experience shows what
    nothing
"It seemed could clearer show—& ever after   50
"An altered brow & eye & gait & speech
"Attest that *now* he *knows* this adage true
"'Time fleets, youth fades, life is an empty
    dream'"

1835 38 nothing to do,   40 and decided, wasted past retrieve—   41
peer.   44 "It is the echo of time: 46 tongue,   50 show, and   51
"An alter'd brow, and eye, and gait, and speech

Slipt in the blank space 'twixt an idiot's gibber   35
And a mad lover's ditty—there it lies.

And yet those blottings chronicle a life—
A whole life, and my life! Nothing to do,
No problem for the fancy, but a life
Spent and decided, wasted past retrieve   40
Or worthy beyond peer. Stay, what does
    this
Remembrancer set down concerning "life"?
"'Time fleets, youth fades, life is an empty
    dream.'
"It is the echo of time; and he whose heart
"Beat first beneath a human heart, whose speech   45
"Was copied from a human tongue, can never
"Recall when he was living yet knew not this.
"Nevertheless long seasons pass o'er him
"Till some one hour's experience shows what
    nothing,
"It seemed, could clearer show; and ever after,   50
"An altered brow and eye and gait and speech
"Attest that now he knows the adage true
"'Time fleets, youth fades, life is an empty
    dream.'"

---

36 *1849* And a mad lover's ditty—lies the whole!   38 *1849* A whole
life,—mine! No thought to turn to act,   *1863, 1865* A whole life,—and my
life! Nothing to do,   40 *1849* past recall,   41–42 *1849* Stay, turn the page |
And take its chance,—thus: what, concerning "life" | Does this remembrancer
set down?—"We say   *43 {Reading of *1849–68*} *1888, 1889* dream,'   44
1849 "'Tis the mere echo   48 *1849* seasons come and go,   49 *1849* what
nought,   50 *1849* "He deemed, could . . . . after

35 *in the blank space*: in the conjuror's 'roll' (21).
36 *a mad lover's ditty*: 'Aprile's?': Domett.
37 *chronicle a life*: the phrase Browning used when revising *Pauline*, l. 884, in
1888.
42 *Remembrancer*: a notebook or commonplace-book.
43 *'Time fleets*: cf. Ovid, *Fasti*, vi. 771–2, rather closer than Horace, *Odes*, ii.
14.
45 *Beat . . . beneath a human heart*: in the womb.

Ay, my brave chronicler, & this same hour
As well as any:—now, let my time be!   55

Now!—I can go no farther— —well or ill
Tis done— —I must desist & take my chance—
I cannot keep at this— —'tis no back-
    shrinking,—
For let but some assurance beam, some close
To this my toil appear, & I proceed   60
At any price, tho' closing it, I die: . . . .
But here I pause:—the old Greek's prophecy
Is like to turn out true—I shall not quit
His chamber till I know what I desire.   64

An end,—a rest! strange how the notion once   66
Encountered, gathers strength by
    moments—rest!
Where has it kept so long?— —this throbbing
    brow
To cease—this beating heart to cease—all cruel
And gnawing thoughts to cease! to dare let down 70
My strung, so high-strung brain—to dare
    unnerve
My harassed o'ertasked frame— —to know my
    place,
My portion, my reward—even my failure,
Assigned—made sure forever!—to lose myself
Among the common creatures of the world,—   75
To draw some gain from having been a Man,—
Neither to hope nor fear— — —to live at
    length!

1835 56 *Now*! I can go no farther; well or ill—   57 'T is done. I . . .
chance;   58 this; 'tis no back shrinking—   61 though closing it, I die
. . .   65 {No equivalent in *MS* or *1835*.}   66 end, a rest! . . . . notion,
once   67 moments.   73 reward,   74 Assign'd, made sure for
ever!—   75 world—   76 man—

Ay, my brave chronicler, and this same hour
As well as any: now, let my time be!   55

Now! I can go no farther; well or ill,
'T is done. I must desist and take my chance.
I cannot keep on the stretch: 't is no
    back-shrinking—
For let but some assurance beam, some close
To my toil grow visible, and I proceed   60
At any price, though closing it, I die.
Else, here I pause. The old Greek's prophecy
Is like to turn out true: "I shall not quit
"His chamber till I know what I desire!"
Was it the light wind sang it o'er the sea?   65

An end, a rest! strange how the notion, once
Encountered, gathers strength by moments!
    Rest!
Where has it kept so long? this throbbing brow
To cease, this beating heart to cease, all cruel
And gnawing thoughts to cease! To dare let
    down   70
My strung, so high-strung brain, to dare unnerve
My harassed o'ertasked frame, to know my
    place,
My portion, my reward, even my failure,
Assigned, made sure for ever! To lose myself
Among the common creatures of the world,   75
To draw some gain from having been a man,
Neither to hope nor fear, to live at length!

54 *1849* same time   55 *1849* any: let my hour speak now!   56 *1849* or
ill—   57 *1849* chance;   59–61 *1849* For let the least assurance dawn, some
end | To my toil seem possible, and I proceed | At any price, by any
sacrifice: 62 *1849* pause: 63 *1849* true—   65 *1849* sung it,   67
1849 Admitted, gains strength every moment! Rest!   68–70 *1849* Where
kept that thought so long? this throbbing brow | To cease—this beating heart
to cease—its crowd | Of gnawing thoughts to cease!—   71 *1849*
brain—   72 *1849* frame—to. . . . place, *1863*,65 frame, to. . . . place!   73
1849—My portion, ... my failure even,   74 *1849* ever!—   75 *1849*
world—   76 *1849* man—   77 *1849* fear—

71 *unnerve*: relax.

Even in failure, rest!—but rest, in Truth   78
And power & recompense— — —   79

Tis little wonder truly—things go on   79a
And at their worst they end or mend—'tis time   b
To look about with matters at this pass:—   c
Have I insensibly sunk as deep . . . has all   80
Been undergone for this? *this*, the request
My labour qualified me to present
With no fear of refusal?—had I gone
Slightingly thro' my task & therefore judged
It fit to moderate my hopes,—nay, were it   85
My sole concern to exculpate myself . . .
..   To flounder thro' the scrape—I could not chuse
An humbler mood to wait for the event!
—   No, no, there needs not this—no, after all
At worst I have performed *my* share of the task: 90
—   The rest is God's concern— —mine, merely
            this,—
To know that I have obstinately held
By my own work:—the mortal whose brave
            foot
Has trod so far the Temple-courts unscathed
That he descries at length the shrine of shrines,   95
Must let no sneering of the daemons' eyes
Which he could pass unquailing, fasten now
Upon him, fairly past their power—no—no
He must not stagger & fall down at last,
Having a charm to baffle them; behold   100

1835 78 truth,   79a truly;   81 *this* the request   85 hopes;   89 this;
no, after all,   90 task.   94 temple-courts   96 demon's eyes,   98
power; no, no,

Even in failure, rest! But rest in truth
And power and recompense . . . I hoped that
   once!

What, sunk insensibly so deep? Has all   80
Been undergone for this? This the request
My labour qualified me to present
With no fear of refusal? Had I gone
Slightingly through my task, and so judged fit
To moderate my hopes; nay, were it now   85
My sole concern to exculpate myself,
End things or mend them,—why, I could not
   choose
A humbler mood to wait for the event!
No, no, there needs not this; no, after all,
At worst I have performed my share of the task: 90
The rest is God's concern; mine, merely this,
To know that I have obstinately held
By my own work. The mortal whose brave
   foot
Has trod, unscathed, the temple-courts so far
That he descries at length the shrine of shrines,   95
Must let no sneering of the demons' eyes,
Whom he could pass unquailing, fasten now
Upon him, fairly past their power; no, no—
He must not stagger, faint, fall down at last,
Having a charm to baffle them; behold,   100

78 *1849* Oh, were it but in failure, to have rest!   79 {No equivalent in
1849}   80–1 *Berg* What: sunk insensibly so deep? such toil, | And under-
gone   81 *1849* this? Was this the prayer   84 *1849* Carelessly
through   87 *1849* And lessen punishment,—I could not chuse   88 *1849*
An humbler mood to wait for the decree!   *90 {Reading of *1849,1889*.}
1863–68 task; *1888* task·   91 *1849* concern—   *94 {Reading of *1849–63*}
1865–89 temple-court
97–100 *1849* Whose wrath he met unquailing, follow sly
               And fasten on him, fairly past their power,
               If where he stands he dares but stay; no, no—
               He must not stagger, faint and fall at last,
               —Knowing a charm to baffle them; behold,
line after 98 *Berg* If, where he stands he ⟨will⟩ [dares] but stay; no, no,

87 *End things or mend them*: proverbial. In his *Journal* for 30 August 1759 John
Wesley wrote: 'I . . . determined to mend them or end them'.

He bares his front—a mortal ventures thus
Serene amid the echoes, beams & glooms!—
If he be Priest henceforth—if he wake up
The God of the place to ban & blast him
    there,—
Both well! . . what's failure or success to me?   105
I have subdued my life to the one purpose
Whereto I ordained it . . . there alone I spy
No doubt— —that way I may be satisfied:
Yes, well have I subdued my life!. beyond
The obligation of my strictest vows,   110
The contemplation of my wildest bond,
Which gave my nature freely up, in truth,
But in its actual state— —consenting fully
All passionate impulses its soil was formed
To rear, should wither—but forseeing not   115
The tract doomed to perpetual barrenness
Would seem one day, remembered as it was
Beside [the] parched sand-tract which now it is,
Already strewn with faint blooms, viewless
    then . . .
I ne'er engaged to root up loves so frail   120

1835 101 front: 103 priest henceforth, if he wake up,   104 god . . . .
there.   107 ordain'd it;   108 doubt; that . . . . satisfied.   115 wither;
but foreseeing   119 then.

He bares his front: a mortal ventures thus
Serene amid the echoes, beams and glooms!
If he be priest henceforth, if he wake up
The god of the place to ban and blast him
    there,
Both well! What 's failure or success to me?   105
I have subdued my life to the one purpose
Whereto I ordained it; there alone I spy,
No doubt, that way I may be satisfied.

Yes, well have I subdued my life! beyond
The obligation of my strictest vow,   110
The contemplation of my wildest bond,
Which gave my nature freely up, in truth,
But in its actual state, consenting fully
All passionate impulses its soil was formed
To rear, should wither; but foreseeing not   115
The tract, doomed to perpetual barrenness,
Would seem one day, remembered as it was,
Beside the parched sand-waste which now it is,
Already strewn with faint blooms, viewless
    then.
I ne'er engaged to root up loves so frail   120

---

101 *1849* front—   103 *1849* henceforth, or if he wake   104 *1849* there,—
106–8 *1849* I have subdued my life to the one end | Ordained life; there alone I
cannot doubt, | That only way I may be satisfied.   110 *1849–65*
vows,   112 *1849* Which gave, in truth, my nature freely up,
113–18 *1849* In what it should be, more than what it was—
    Consenting that whatever passions slept,
    Whatever impulses lay unmatured,
    Should wither in the germ,—but scarce foreseeing
    That the soil, doomed thus to perpetual waste,
    Would seem one day, remembered in its youth
    Beside the parched sand-tract which now it is,

---

104 *to ban and blast him there*: cf. *Hamlet* III. ii. 252: 'With Hecat's ban thrice
blasted'.
105 *Both well!*: i.e. it is all one whether such an adventurer succeeds and
becomes a priest or awakens the deity of the temple and is destroyed.
107 *I spy,*: it is tempting to remove the comma, so reverting to *MS*. We have
resisted the temptation, rightly or wrongly, because the comma makes some
sort of sense, Browning twice revised after writing the *MS* version, *1863* is
usually reliable, and Browning let the comma stand in subsequent editions.
119 *viewless*: invisible.

I felt them not—yet now, tis very plain
Some soft spots had their birth in me at first,
If not love, say, like love:—there was a time
When yet this wolfish hunger after knowledge
Set not remorselessly its claims aside. . . .　　125
This heart was human once, or why recall
Einsiedeln, even now—& Würzburg whom the
　　Mayne
⟨The Mayne⟩ Forsakes her course to fold as
　　with an arm? . .

And Festus . . my poor Festus—with his praise,
And counsel & grave fears— —where is he
　　now?　　　　　　　　　　　　　130
With the sweet maiden, long [ago] his
　　bride,— — —
I surely loved ⟨him{?}⟩ [them]—that last night,
　　at least,
When we— —gone! gone! the better:—I am
　　saved
The sad review of an ambitious youth
Choked by vile lusts unnoticed in their birth　　135
Which have grown up & wound around a Will
Till action was destroyed:—No, I have gone
Purging my path successively of aught
Wearing the distant likeness of such loves:
— 　I have made life consist of one idea: . .　　140
Ere *that* was master . . up 'till that was born
I bear a memory of a pleasant life
Whose small events I can recall even to
The morn [I ran] over the grassy fields
Startling the flocks of nameless birds, to tell　　145
Poor Festus, leaping all the while for joy,
To leave all trouble for my future plans
For I had just determined to become

1835　121 not,　　122 first—　　125 aside;　　127 now, and Würz-
burg,　　129 Festus—my poor Festus,　　131 bride?　　136 a will　　137
destroy'd.　　139 loves.　　141 E're *that* was master—up 'till *that* was born

I felt them not; yet now, 't is very plain
Some soft spots had their birth in me at first,
If not love, say, like love: there was a time
When yet this wolfish hunger after knowledge
Set not remorselessly love's claims aside.   125
This heart was human once, or why recall
Einsiedeln, now, and Würzburg which the
  Mayne
Forsakes her course to fold as with an
  arm?

And Festus—my poor Festus, with his praise
And counsel and grave fears—where is he
  now   130
With the sweet maiden, long ago his
  bride?
I surely loved them—that last night, at
  least,
When we . . . gone! gone! the better. I am
  saved
The sad review of an ambitious youth
Choked by vile lusts, unnoticed in their birth,   135
But let grow up and wind around a will
Till action was destroyed. No, I have gone
Purging my path successively of aught
Wearing the distant likeness of such lusts.
I have made life consist of one idea: 140
Ere that was master, up till that was born,
I bear a memory of a pleasant life
Whose small events I treasure; till one morn
I ran o'er the seven little grassy fields,
Startling the flocks of nameless birds, to tell   145
Poor Festus, leaping all the while for joy,
To leave all trouble for my future plans,
Since I had just determined to become

122 *1849* first—   125 *1849* aside;   130 *1849* now?   131 *1849* Or the
sweet   133 *1849* better: 139 *1889* (some copies) lusts   147 *1849* for
futurity,

The greatest & most glorious being on earth:
But since that hour, all life has been
    forgotten:—   150
Tis as one day— —one only step between
The outset & the end: one tyrant, all
Absorbing aim fills up the interval:
—   One vast unbroken chain of thought kept up
Throughout a course apparently adverse   155
To its existence—life, death, light & shadow,
The shews of the world . . were bare
    receptacles
Or indices of truth to be wrung thence
Not ministers of sorrow or delight— —
A wondrous natural robe in which I went: 160
For some one truth would dimly beacon me
From mountains rough with pines, & flit &
    wink
Oer dazzling wastes of frozen snow—&
    tremble
Into assured light in some branching mine
Where ripens swathed in fire the liquid gold,   165
Yet all was then o'erlooked, tho' noted now:—
So much is good then, in this working sea   170
Which parts me from that happy strip of land;
But o'er that happy strip a sun shone too!

1835 149 earth.   150 forgotten.   152 one tyrant all-   153 inter-
val—   156 existence: 157 world,   163 O'er . . . . snow, and   165
Where ripens, swathed in fire, the liquid gold—   166 now.   167–9 {No
equivalent in *MS* or *1835*.}   171 land.

The greatest and most glorious man on earth.
And since that morn all life has been
      forgotten;   150
All is one day, one only step between
The outset and the end: one tyrant all-
Absorbing aim fills up the interspace,
One vast unbroken chain of thought, kept up
Through a career apparently adverse   155
To its existence: life, death, light and shadow,
The shows of the world, were bare
      receptacles
Or indices of truth to be wrung thence,
Not ministers of sorrow or delight:
A wondrous natural robe in which she went.   160
For some one truth would dimly beacon me
From mountains rough with pines, and flit and
      wink
O'er dazzling wastes of frozen snow, and
      tremble
Into assured light in some branching mine
Where ripens, swathed in fire, the liquid gold—   165
And all the beauty, all the wonder fell
On either side the truth, as its mere robe;
I see the robe now—then I saw the form.
So far, then, I have voyaged with success,
So much is good, then, in this working sea   170
Which parts me from that happy strip of land:
But o'er that happy strip a sun shone, too!

152–3 *all-* / *Absorbing*: an enjambement in Donne's manner.
   158 *indices of truth*: pointers to truth.
   164 *some branching mine*: cf. i. 812 n.
   166 *And all the beauty, all the wonder*: cf. 'Fra Lippo Lippi', 283.
   170 *this working sea*: cf. Dryden, *Aurungzebe*, IV. i. 295 ('A working Sea'), and Pope, *Odyssey*, xii. 265.

And fainter gleams it as the waves grow rough,
And still more faint as the sea widens . . last,
I sicken on a dead gulf streaked with light   175
From its own putrefying depths alone!—
Then—God was pledged to take me by the
    hand,—
Now—any miserable juggle can bid
My pride depart—all is alike at length,
God may take pleasure in confounding us   180
By hiding secrets in the scorned & base . . .
I am here, in short: so little have I paused
Throughout . . I never glanced behind to know
If I had kept my primal light from wane,
And thus insensibly am—what I am!   185

Oh, bitter, very bitter!
                    And more bitter
To ⟨hear{?}⟩ [fear] a deeper curse, an inner
    ruin,
Plague beneath plague . . the last turning the
    first
To light beside its darkness: let me weep
My youth & its brave hopes all dead & gone.   190
In tears which burn . . would I were sure to
    win

1835 174 widens.   177 hand;   179 depart. All . . . . length: 183
Throughout.   186 Oh, bitter;   187 ruin—   189 darkness.   190
hopes, all dead and gone,   191 burn.

And fainter gleams it as the waves grow rough,
And still more faint as the sea widens; last
I sicken on a dead gulf streaked with light   175
From its own putrefying depths alone.
Then, God was pledged to take me by the
     hand;
Now, any miserable juggle can bid
My pride depart. All is alike at length:
God may take pleasure in confounding pride   180
By hiding secrets with the scorned and base—
I am here, in short: so little have I paused
Throughout! I never glanced behind to know
If I had kept my primal light from wane,
And thus insensibly am—what I am!   185

Oh, bitter; very bitter!
                         And more bitter,
To fear a deeper curse, an inner
     ruin,
Plague beneath plague, the last turning the
     first
To light beside its darkness. Let me weep
My youth and its brave hopes, all dead and gone, 190
In tears which burn! Would I were sure to
     win

176 *1849* putrifying depths alone!   177 *1849* Then—
178–83 *1849* Now—any miserable juggler bends
     My pride to him. All seems alike at length:
     Who knows which are the wise and which the fools?
     God may take pleasure in confounding pride
     By hiding secrets with the scorned and base—
     He who stoops lowest may find most—in short,
     I am here; and all seems natural; I start not:
     And never having glanced behind to know
1863, 1865 {as *1888* except 'Throughout.' in line 183} 185 *1849* Am thus
insensibly grown—what I am!   187 *1849* ruin—   189 *1849* darkness.
Better weep

187 *an inner ruin*: 'the purity of his aims lost': Domett.

Some startling secret in their stead—a tincture
Of force to flush old age with youth, or breed
Gold, or imprison moonbeams till they change
To opal-shafts . . . only that, hurling it   195
Indignant back, I might convince myself
My Aim's remained supreme & pure as ever!
Even now, why not desire, for mankind's sake
That if I fail, it may be for some fault,—
That tho' I sink, another may succeed?—   200
—   I cannot! O God I am despicable!
Shut out this hideous ⟨murrain {?}⟩ [mockery]
    from my heart!

T'was politic in you, Aureole, to reject
Single rewards— —to ask them in the
    lump . . .
At all events, once launched, to hold straight
    on;   205
For now 'tis all or nothing—mighty profit
Your gains will bring if they stop short of such
Full consummation! as a man, you had
A certain share of strength, & that is gone
Already in the getting these you boast . . .   210
Do not they seem to laugh as who should say
"Great Master, we are here, indeed,—dragged
    forth

1835 192 stead!   195 opal shafts!   197 aims remain'd   199 fault;
204 rewards, to . . . . lump;   206 nothing.   210 boast.   211–12
laugh, as who should say– | "Great master, we are here indeed; dragg'd forth

Some startling secret in their stead, a tincture
Of force to flush old age with youth, or breed
Gold, or imprison moonbeams till they change
To opal shafts!—only that, hurling it   195
Indignant back, I might convince myself
My aims remained supreme and pure as ever!
Even now, why not desire, for mankind's sake,
That if I fail, some fault may be the cause,
That, though I sink, another may succeed?   200
O God, the despicable heart of us!
Shut out this hideous mockery from my
      heart!

'T was politic in you, Aureole, to reject
Single rewards, and ask them in the
      lump;
At all events, once launched, to hold straight
      on: 205
For now 't is all or nothing. Mighty profit
Your gains will bring if they stop short of such
Full consummation! As a man, you had
A certain share of strength; and that is gone
Already in the getting these you boast.   210
Do not they seem to laugh, as who should say—
"Great master, we are here indeed, dragged
      forth

192 *1849* stead!—   197 *1849* My aims remained as ever supreme and
pure!   199 *1849* cause,—   209 *1849* strength,   212 *1849* indeed;

   192 *a tincture*: 'Alchemy. A supposed spiritual principle or immaterial sub-
stance whose character or quality may be infused into material things . . .; the
quintessence, spirit, or soul of a thing. *Universal tincture*, the Elixir. *Obs*.': OED,
'Tincture', 6. 'The remedy by which, according to Paracelsus, *rejuvenation*
(regeneration) could be accomplished is something entirely different from
what it has been supposed to be by his critics . . . "The *Materia Tincturæ* is the
greatest treasure in the world"': Franz Hartmann, *The Life of Paracelsus* (2nd
ed., 1896), 249–50 (and see p. 250 n.). See also Pachter, op. cit.
   197 *My aims*: the word 'aim' occurs six times in *Pauline*, ten in this poem. The
plural is even more frequent.
   203 *Aureole*: the stress is on the first syllable here, as elsewhere, so 'politic'
should be slightly slurred. Paracelsus is addressing himself, mockingly.

"To light—this hast thou done—be glad! now,
    seek
"[The] Strength to use, which thou hast spent
    in getting!"

And yet 'tis much, surely 'tis very much   215
Thus to have emptied youth of all its gifts
To feed a fire meant to hold out till Morn
Arrived with inexhaustible light—& lo,
I have heaped up my last— —& Day dawns
    not!
And I am left with grey hair, faded hands   220
And furrowed brow—ha, have I after all
Mistaken the wild nursling of my breast . . .
Was she who glided thro' my room, of
    nights—
Who laid my head on her soft knees, &
    smoothed   225
The damp locks— —whose sly soothings just
    began
When my sick spirit craved repose awhile . . .
God! was I fighting Sleep off, for Death's sake?

God! Thou art Mind!—unto the Master-Mind,
Mind should be precious . . . spare my mind
    alone!   230
All else I will endure: if, as I stand
Here, with my gains, thy thunder smite me
    down
I bow me—'tis thy will—thy righteous will . .
I o'erpass life's restrictions & I die . . .

1835 213 "To light: this thou hast done;   214 "The strength to use   217
morn   218 light;   219 last, and day   221 brow. Ha, have I, after
all,   222 breast?   223 {No equivalent in *MS* or *1835*.}   224 through
my room of nights;   226 locks;   230 precious.   233 me; 't is thy will,
thy righteous will;   234 restrictions, and I die:

"To light; this hast thou done: be glad! Now,
    seek
"The strength to use which thou hast spent in
    getting!"

And yet 't is much, surely 't is very much,   215
Thus to have emptied youth of all its gifts,
To feed a fire meant to hold out till morn
Arrived with inexhaustible light; and lo,
I have heaped up my last, and day dawns
    not!
And I am left with grey hair, faded hands,   220
And furrowed brow. Ha, have I, after all,
Mistaken the wild nursling of my breast?
Knowledge it seemed, and power, and
    recompense!
Was she who glided through my room of nights,
Who laid my head on her soft knees and
    smoothed   225
The damp locks,—whose sly soothings just
    began
When my sick spirit craved repose awhile—
God! was I fighting sleep off for death's sake?

God! Thou art mind! Unto the master-mind
Mind should be precious. Spare my mind alone!   230
All else I will endure; if, as I stand
Here, with my gains, thy thunder smite me
    down,
I bow me; 't is thy will, thy righteous will;
I o'erpass life's restrictions, and I die;

---

215 *1849* And yet 'tis surely much, 'tis   218 *1849* Arrive with   220 *1849*
While I am   223 *1849–65* Power, and Recompense!   224 *1849*
nights,—   228 *1849–65* Sleep . . . Death's   229 *1849–65* Mind! . . . .
Master-Mind

---

    220 *grey hair*: 'The "grey hair, faded hands, and furrowed brow" ascribed to
the Paracelsus of eight-and-twenty, are not derived from history, but from the
"scattered hair, sered by the autumn of strange suffering," and the "listless
hands" of [the poet in] *Alastor*'; Griffin and Minchin, p. 67. Taurello Saling-
uerra notices similar premature signs of aging in Sordello: *Sordello*, v. 360 ff.

And if no trace of my career remain   235
Save a thin corpse at pleasure of the wind
In these bright chambers level with the air,
See thou to it: but if my spirit fail—
My once proud spirit forsake me at the last,
Hast thou done well by me? So do not thou!   240
Crush not my mind, dear God, tho' I be
   crushed . . .
Hold me before the frequence of thy Seraphs
And say "I crushed him lest he should disturb
My law . . Men must not know their strength:
   behold,
Weak & alone, how he had raised himself!"   245

But if delusions trouble me, & Thou,—
—   Not seldom felt with rapture in thy help
And stay, throughout my wanderings,—dost
   intend
To work Man's welfare thro' my weak
   Endeavour . . .
To crown my mortal forehead with a beam   250
From thine own blinding crown—to smile, &
   guide
⟨His⟩ [This] puny hand, & let the work so
   framed
Be styled ⟨his⟩ [my] work—, hear me! I covet
   not
An influx of new power, an angel's soul . .

And if no trace of my career remain   235
Save a thin corpse at pleasure of the wind
In these bright chambers level with the air,
See thou to it! But if my spirit fail,
My once proud spirit forsake me at the last,
Hast thou done well by me? So do not thou!   240
Crush not my mind, dear God, though I be
     crushed!
Hold me before the frequence of thy seraphs
And say—"I crushed him, lest he should disturb
"My law. Men must not know their strength:
     behold,
"Weak and alone, how he had raised himself!"   245

But if delusions trouble me, and thou,
Not seldom felt with rapture in thy help
Throughout my toils and wanderings, dost
     intend
To work man's welfare through my weak
     endeavour,
To crown my mortal forehead with a beam   250
From thine own blinding crown, to smile, and
     guide
This puny hand and let the work so
     wrought
Be styled my work,—hear me! I covet
     not
An influx of new power, an angel's soul:

*244 {Reading of *1849–68*} *1888,1889* behold   245 *1849* how near he
raised   246 *1849* me—and Thou, *1863,1865* me, and Thou,   248 *1849*
Throughout my toil   249 *1849* endeavour—   251 *1849* crown—   252
1849 hand, and . . . . work so framed   *1863,1865* hand, and . . . . work so
wrought

237 *these bright chambers*: the opening lines of Part II suggest that Paracelsus is
looking out from a turret or an elevated building of some sort. There is a clear
reminiscence of *Epipsychidion* 515–17: 'And I have fitted up some chambers
there / Looking towards the golden Eastern air, / And level with the living
winds . . .'
  242 *the frequence of thy seraphs*: 'Crowd; concourse; assembly' (Johnson): cf.
Paradise Regained, i. 128: 'frequence . . . Of angels'.
  246 *But if delusions*: Paracelsus becomes more and more over-excited until he
hears the '*voice*' at 281.
  thou: God (cf. 241).

It were no marvel then—but I have gone   255
Thus far, a Man—let me conclude, a Man!
Give but one hour of my first energy
—   Of that invincible faith, but only one!
— — I should go over with an eagle-glance
The truths I have, & spy some certain way   260
To mould them & complete them & pursue
them . . .

(After a pause)
Yet God is good:—I started, sure of that—
And why dispute it now?—I'll not believe
But some undoubted warning long ere this
Had reached me . . a labarum was not deemed   265
Too much for the old founder of these walls:—
—   Then, if [my] life have not been natural
It has been monstruous . . yet till late, my
course
So ardently engrossed me, that delight,—
A pausing & reflecting joy,—'tis plain,   270
Could find no place in it: tis true, I am worn,
But who clothes summer, who is Life itself?
—   And then tho' after-life to please me now
Must have no likeness to the past, what hinders   275
Reward from springing out of ⟨t⟩ Toil, as
changed
As bursts the flower from earth & root &
stalk?

1835 256 Thus far a man; let me conclude a man!   258 faith—   261 To
mould them, and complete them, and pursue them!   262 good: I started
sure of that,   265 me: 266 walls.   267 my life has not   268 mon-
strous: yet, till late,   271 it. 'T is true, I am worn;   273 {No equivalent in
MS or *1835*.}   277 earth, and root, and stalk?

It were no marvel then—but I have reached   255
Thus far, a man; let me conclude, a man!
Give but one hour of my first energy,
Of that invincible faith, but only one!
That I may cover with an eagle-glance
The truths I have, and spy some certain way   260
To mould them, and completing them,
    possess!

Yet God is good: I started sure of that,
And why dispute it now? I 'll not believe
But some undoubted warning long ere this
Had reached me: a fire-labarum was not deemed   265
Too much for the old founder of these walls.
Then, if my life has not been natural,
It has been monstrous: yet, till late, my
    course
So ardently engrossed me, that delight,
A pausing and reflecting joy, 't is plain,   270
Could find no place in it. True, I am worn;
But who clothes summer, who is life itself?
God, that created all things, can renew!
And then, though after-life to please me now
Must have no likeness to the past, what hinders   275
Reward from springing out of toil, as changed
As bursts the flower from earth and root and
    stalk?

258 *1849* Of that invincible faith—one only hour!   265–6 *1849* Had reached me: stars would write his will in heaven, | As once when a labarum was not deemed | Too much for the old founder of these walls.   270–1 *1849* A pausing and reflecting joy, 't is plain, | Though such were meant to follow as its fruit, | Could find no place in it. True, I am worn;   272 *1849* who clothes summer, who is Life *1863,1865* Who clothes summer, Who is Life

262 *God is good*: cf. *Pauline*, 1020.
265 *Had reached me*: would have reached me (otherwise).
   a fire-labarum: 'An allusion to Constantine's vision of a fiery cross during his struggle with Maxentius, A.D. 312. The "labarum", or Standard of the Cross, was afterwards adopted throughout the Roman army': Lee and Locock.
268 *monstrous*: cf. i. 677.

—   What use were punishment, unless some sin
      Were first detected?—let me know that first!
      No man could ever offend as I have
          done   280

What use were punishment, unless some sin
Be first detected? let me know that first!
No man could ever offend as I have
   done . . .   280

                [*A voice from within.*]

I hear a voice, perchance I heard
Long ago, but all too low,
So that scarce a care it stirred
If the voice were real or no:
I heard it in my youth when first   285
The waters of my life outburst:
But, now their stream ebbs faint, I hear
That voice, still low, but fatal-clear—
As if all poets, God ever meant
Should save the world, and therefore lent   290
Great gifts to, but who, proud, refused
To do his work, or lightly used

---

280 {Omitted from *1849*.}   Before 281: *1849* (*Aprile, from within*)   283
1849 So that scarce a thought was stirred   284 *1849* If really spoke the voice
or no: *1863,1865* If the voice was real or no: 285 *1849* youth, *Berg* (That
{illegible word}) [I heard it] in my youth,   287 *Berg* But now (that life)
[their stream]   *1849–65* But now their stream   288 *Berg* (That) [The] voice,
still low,   *1849* The voice, still low, *1863–68* That voice, still low   289 *Berg*
Poets [that {i.w.}] God (ever) meant   *1849* Poets, that God meant *1863,1865*
Poets, God ever meant

281 *I hear a voice*: in *1835* Paracelsus immediately hears ll. 297 ff., the sad song
of his 'peers', those who have failed to utter in song the message which would
have freed the world. In *1849*, no doubt for clarity's sake, Browning added the
introductory ll. 281–96, clearly spoken by Aprile, who goes on to repeat ll. 297
ff. as a song which he has heard. Ll. 289 ff. introduce God, as do the words 'God
who gave / Our powers, and man they could not save!' (338–9: see textual
notes). In *1863* Browning altered 'Aprile, from within' back to 'A voice from
within', which may mean that he intended the voice *not* to be Aprile's.
   Domett comments on 'Lost, lost! yet come' (as directly introduced in 1835):
' 'Tis most likely Aprile, singing *to himself* the song he fancies in the mouths of
the spirits of those whose imagination has ruined them—its excess having
prevented them from turning it to the good of mankind & *working it prop-
erly*.—Such were the Shelleys—Keats's & c'.
   Pottle discusses the lyric on pp. 58–60 of his *Shelley and Browning*, pointing
out that it is 'very Shelleyan in style' and suggesting that 'It seems to have been
modeled on the lyric interludes of *Prometheus Unbound*, especially the choruses
of the Furies in Act I'. It is also evident that Browning knew the lyrics in
Manfred. Maynard has an interesting discussion of the additions made in
1849 in *Browning's Youth*, p. 231.
   286 *outburst*: a favourite verb in Browning, though OED terms it 'rare'.

(a voice from within,)
Lost, Lost!—yet come,
With our wan troop make thy home
Come, come,—for we
Will not breathe, so much as breathe   300
Reproach to thee!
Lost one, come! the last
Who, living, hast life o'erpast   305
And, all together we
Will ask for us & ask for thee
Whose trial is past whose lot is cast
With those who watch but work no more,—
Who gaze on Life, but live no more: . .   310
Yet we chose thee a birth-place   315
Where the richness ran to flowers . . .
Could'st not sing one song for us?   317
Not make one blossom ours,
Not one of the sweet race?

1835 298 home: 299 Come, come! for we   302, 303 {No equivalent in
MS or *1835*.}   308 past,   310 life, but. . . . more: 311–14 {No equiv-
alent in *MS* or *1835*.}   318 ours—   320–2 {No equivalent in *MS* or
1835.}

Those gifts, or failed through weak
    endeavour,
So, mourn cast off by him for ever,—
As if these leaned in airy ring   295
To take me; this the song they sing.

"Lost, lost! yet come,
With our wan troop make thy home.
Come, come! for we
Will not breathe, so much as breathe   300
Reproach to thee,
Knowing what thou sink'st beneath.
So sank we in those old years,
We who bid thee, come! thou last
Who, living yet, hast life o'erpast.   305
And altogether we, thy peers,
Will pardon crave for thee, the last
Whose trial is done, whose lot is cast
With those who watch but work no more,
Who gaze on life but live no more.   310
Yet we trusted thou shouldst speak
The message which our lips, too weak,
Refused to utter,—shouldst redeem
Our fault: such trust, and all a dream!
Yet we chose thee a birthplace   315
Where the richness ran to flowers:
Couldst not sing one song for grace?
Not make one blossom man's and ours?
Must one more recreant to his race
Die with unexerted powers,   320

293 *Berg* thro' (slack) [weak] endeavour,—   294 *Berg* (Now {?}) [?]
mourn, cast off by (God) [him] forever,—   *1849* And mourn, cast off by him
forever,—   *1863,1865* So, mourn cast off by Him for ever,—   296 *1849*
To call me;   298 *1849* home: 301 *1849,1863* thee!   302 *1849* beneath:
303 *1849* So we sank in those   305 *1849* Who, a living man, hast life o'erpast,
{*1863* as *1888* except 'o'erpast,', *1865* as *1888* except 'o'erpast'}   306 *1849*
And all together we.   307 *1849–68* Will pardon ask for   309 *1849* watch,
but work no more—   310 *1849* Who gaze on life, but live no more: 311
1849 And yet we   312 *1849* God's message which *Berg* God's message (out)
[which],   314 *1849* and all,   315 *1849* So we chose thee a bright birth-
place   316 *1849* flowers—   *1863–68* flowers;   318 *1849* Nor make

Anguish! ever & for ever,   323
Still beginning, ending never!
Yet, lost & last one, come!   325
How coulds't understand, alas,
What our pale ghosts strove to say
As their shades did glance & pass
Before thee, night & day—   329
O come, come!
How shall we clothe, how arm the spirit   332
Who next shall thy post inherit . .

And join us, leaving as he found
The world, he was to loosen, bound?
Anguish! ever and for ever;
Still beginning, ending never.
Yet, lost and last one, come!   325
How couldst understand, alas,
What our pale ghosts strove to say,
As their shades did glance and pass
Before thee night and day?
Thou wast blind as we were dumb: 330
Once more, therefore, come, O come!
How should we clothe, how arm the spirit
Shall next thy post of life inherit—

322 *Berg* ⟨w⟩ he was to ⟨free, fast⟩ [loosen,] bound?   324 *1849–68*
never!   330 *1849* Thou wert blind,   332 *1849* How shall we better arm the
spirit   *1863–68* How shall we clothe, how arm the spirit   333 *1849–65* Who
next shall thy post of life inherit—

323 *Anguish! ever and for ever*: cf. *Prometheus Unbound*, I. 23: 'alas, pain, pain
ever, for ever!'
332 *we*: 'the "white brows lit up with glory—poets all" mentioned after-
wards': Domett, quoting 646.
333 *of life*: in life.

How guard him from thy speedy ruin?
Tell us of thy sad undoing   335
Here, where we sit, ever pursuing
Our weary task, ever renewing
Sharp sorrow, far from . . .

(Aprile enters—)—

A/.   Ha, ha, our King that wouldst be, here at last?   340

How guard him from thy speedy ruin?
Tell us of thy sad undoing   335
Here, where we sit, ever pursuing
Our weary task, ever renewing
Sharp sorrow, far from God who gave
Our powers, and man they could not
     save!"

APRILE *enters*.

Ha, ha! our king that wouldst be, here at last?   340
Art thou the poet who shall save the world?

334 *1849* thy ruin?   Before 340 *1849* APRILE *enters*.   A spirit better armed,
succeeding me?   341 *Berg* Poet (that) [who] shall   *1849–65* Poet who shall

334–6 *ruin . . . pursuing*: Pottle points out (p. 60 ff.) that Shelley uses this pair
of rhymes on half-a-dozen occasions (as also that the conventional rhyme
'spirit/inherit' occurs in Shelley). In his 'Preface to the New Edition' in 1965 he
quotes H. C. Wyld's authority for the fact that 'down to the thirties of the last
century, -*in* and not -*ing* was the almost universal pronunciation among all
classes of speakers'.

334 *thy speedy ruin*: cf. the preface to *Alastor*: 'The Poet's self-centred seclu-
sion was avenged by the furies of an irresistible passion pursuing him to speedy
ruin'.

APRILE *enters*: Aprile remains present to the end of Part II. Thereafter he is not
seen again, although he remains important in the mind of Paracelsus. On this
first appearance he seems almost like a spirit summoned by Paracelsus, 'com-
pelled' from his 'lair' (346), and it is significant that he meet in 'the house of a
Greek Conjurer'. They are the two 'halves of one dissevered world' (634), a
Platonic notion dear to Browning's favourite Donne. Initially each mistakes
the nature of the other. Aprile thinks Paracelsus a man destined to succeed
where he himself has failed, and assumes that he is to be The Great Poet:
Paracelsus thinks that Aprile may be 'the sage I only seemed to be', his destined
successor. Whereas Aprile calls Paracelsus his 'dear master' and asks him to
sing to him, Paracelsus (who is on the verge of madness) is aggressive and
envious.

Domett comments: 'Aprile is a poet (in imagination at least) who with the
same desire as Paracelsus, that of piercing the secret of man & procuring his
happiness—would have his object effected by *love* & poetry as the other by
knowledge & science. But he has overlooked the *means* as Paracelsus did—&
seduced by the delights of indulging his imagination, has neglected the *labour*
necessary to turn even that faculty to good account (which is a noble moral) &
to man's advantage. "Many are poets but without the name" says Byron. [*The
Prophecy of Dante*, iv. 10]. Shelley except in the latter particular was in actual life
almost such a being as Aprile. His ideas of the regeneration of mankind were
much the same—& of the means to be used—Aprile is an idealized & *unwriting*
Shelley. For he cannot "unbosom & embody" what is within him—nor
"wreak his thoughts upon expression". All was to be done by an intense &
universal *love* as by a similar knowledge in Parac. case'.

Leigh Hunt describes Aprile as 'a mad poet, to whom is given the affected
and misformed name of Aprile, which, as well as we can gather from the verse,
the author seems to intend that we should pronounce in three syllables, with
the accent on the second', a 'contrivance for a man's name' which he describes
as 'abominable': loc. cit. p. 406b.

...   Thy hand to mine . . . stay—fix thine eyes on
       mine,
       Thou wouldst be King?—still fix thine eyes on
       mine— — —

P/.   Ha, ha, why crouchest not?—am I not
       King?
       So torture is not wholly unavailing!   345
       Have my fierce spasms compelled thee from
       thy lair?
       Ay, look on me!—shall I be King or no?
       I scarcely trusted God with the surmise   352
       That thou would'st come— —& thou did'st
       hear the while!

A/.   Thine eyes are lustreless to mine,—my hair
       Is soft, nay silkensoft—to talk with thee   355
       Flushes my cheek . . & thou art ashy-pale . . .
       Truly thou hast laboured, hast withstood their
       lips
—   Their kisses . . . yes, 'tis like thou hast attained!
       Tell me, dear Master, wherefore now thou
       comest?
       I thought thy solemn songs would have their
       meed   360
       In after-time—that I should hear the earth
       Exult in thee, & echo with thy praise
       While I was laid forgotten in my grave.
P/.   Ah, fiend, I know thee, I am not thy dupe!

Thy hand to mine! Stay, fix thine eyes on
   mine!
Thou wouldst be king? Still fix thine eyes on
   mine!
   Paracelsus. Ha, ha! why crouchest not? Am I not
    king?
So torture is not wholly unavailing!   345
Have my fierce spasms compelled thee from thy
   lair?
Art thou the sage I only seemed to be,
Myself of after-time, my very self
With sight a little clearer, strength more firm,
Who robes him in my robe and grasps my crown 350
For just a fault, a weakness, a neglect?
I scarcely trusted God with the surmise
That such might come, and thou didst hear the
   while!
   Aprile. Thine eyes are lustreless to mine; my
    hair
Is soft, nay silken soft: to talk with thee   355
Flushes my cheek, and thou art ashy-pale.
Truly, thou hast laboured, hast withstood her lips,
The siren's! Yes, 't is like thou hast attained!
Tell me, dear master, wherefore now thou
   comest?
I thought thy solemn songs would have their
   meed   360
In after-time; that I should hear the earth
Exult in thee and echo with thy praise,
While I was laid forgotten in my grave.
   Paracelsus. Ah fiend, I know thee, I am not thy
    dupe!

---

342 *1849–65* mine. Stay, fix thine eyes on mine.   347 *1849* Sage   350 *1849*
Who robs me of my prize and takes my place   356 *1849* ashy-pale,   357
1849 True, thou hast   364 *1849* Not so! I know   *1863* Ah, fiend, I know

---

  345 *So torture*: Paracelsus is raving.
  351 *For just a fault*: Paracelsus fears that Aprile is to attain the kingship he
himself has sought but failed to reach, on account of 'a fault'.
  353 *and thou didst hear*: as if he had summoned Aprile up.
  360 *thy solemn songs*: cf. *Alastor*, 567: 'its solemn song'.

Thou art ordained to follow in my
    track— — —   365
To reap my sowing, as I disdained to reap
The harvest left by sages long since gone . . . .
I am to be degraded, after all,   370
To an aspirant after Fame, not Truth . . .
. . .   To all but envy of thy fate, be sure!
A/.   Nay, sing them to me; I shall envy not:
Thou shalt be king—sing thou & I will sit
Beside & call deep silence for thy songs,   375
And worship thee, as I had ne'er been meant
To fill thy throne . . . but none shall ever
    know:
Sing to me; for already thy wild eyes
Unlock my heartsprings, as some chrystal-shaft
Reveals by some chance blaze its parent fount   380
After long time— —so thou revealest my soul!
. .   All will flash forth at last, with thee to hear!
P/.   (His secret! I shall get his secret . . fool!)—I am
The mortal who aspired to KNOW . . . & Thou?
A/.   I would LOVE infinitely, & be loved!   385
P/.   Poor slave! I am thy King indeed:
A/.   Thou deemest
That,—born a spirit dowered even as thou,
Born for thy fate,—because I could not curb
My yearnings to possess at once the full
Enjoyment— —⟨& {?}⟩ [but] neglected all the
    means   390

1835 365 track,   366 sowing—   367 gone.   368, 369 {No equivalent
in *MS* or *1835*.}   371 fame, not truth—   374 king. Sing thou,
and   377 throne. But . . . . know!   386 king indeed.   387
That—born a spirit,   388 fate—   390 Enjoyment; but

Thou art ordained to follow in my
    track,   365
Reaping my sowing, as I scorned to reap
The harvest sown by sages passed away.
Thou art the sober searcher, cautious striver,
As if, except through me, thou hadst searched or
    striven!
Ay, tell the world! Degrade me after all,   370
To an aspirant after fame, not truth—
To all but envy of thy fate, be sure!
    Aprile. Nay, sing them to me; I shall envy not:
Thou shalt be king! Sing thou, and I will sit
Beside, and call deep silence for thy songs,   375
And worship thee, as I had ne'er been meant
To fill thy throne: but none shall ever know!
Sing to me; for already thy wild eyes
Unlock my heart-springs, as some crystal-shaft
Reveals by some chance blaze its parent fount   380
After long time: so thou reveal'st my soul.
All will flash forth at last, with thee to hear!
    Paracelsus. (His secret! I shall get his
    secret—fool!)
I am he that aspired to KNOW: and thou?
    Aprile. I would LOVE infinitely, and be loved!   385
    Paracelsus. Poor slave! I am thy king indeed.
    Aprile.   Thou deem'st
That—born a spirit, dowered even as thou,
Born for thy fate—because I could not curb
My yearnings to possess at once the full
Enjoyment, but neglected all the means   390

After 365 *1849* Even as thou sayest, succeeding to my place,   366 *1849*
sowing—   368 *Berg* the ⟨spare{?}⟩ [cautious] striver—   *369 {Reading
of *1863–68*}   *1849* thou had'st *1888,1889* thou hast   374 *1849* I will
stand   377 *1849* throne—   *379 {Reading of *1849–1865*}   *1868–89*
heart-strings,   381 *1849* time—so . . . . soul!   383 *1849* (His secret! my
successor's secret—fool!)   390 *1849* Enjoyment; yet neglected

366 *As I scorned to reap*: Paracelsus's scorn for earlier medical authorities
caused great scandal: see p. 502 below.
373 *sing them to me*: Aprile still regards Paracelsus as a poet.
379 *as some crystal-shaft*: cf. i. 739 ff.

Of realizing even the frailest joy,—
Gathering no fragments to appease my want
Yet nursing up that want till thus I die . . . .
That I cannot conceive thy safe sure March,
—   Triumphing o'er the perils that o'erwhelm me,   395
Neglecting nought below for aught above,
Despising nothing & ensuring all . . .
. .   That I could not, my time to come again,
Lead my own spirit securely as thine own;
Listen, & thou shalt see I know thee well: 400
I would ⟨l⟩ Love infinitely . . . Ah,—lost, lost,
        How shall I look on all of ye
        With your gifts even yet on
           me . . . .
P/.   (Ah,—tis some moonstruck creature after all!   405
Such fond fools as are like to haunt this
    den: . .).

1835 391 joy;   394 safe, sure march,   399 Lead this my spirit   401 love
infinitely . . . Ah, lost! lost!   402 {No equivalent in *MS* or *1835*.}   407–
417 {No equivalent in *MS* or *1835*.}

Of realizing even the frailest joy,
Gathering no fragments to appease my want,
Yet nursing up that want till thus I die—
Thou deem'st I cannot trace thy safe sure march
O'er perils that o'erwhelm me, triumphing,   395
Neglecting nought below for aught above,
Despising nothing and ensuring all—
Nor that I could (my time to come again)
Lead thus my spirit securely as thine own.
Listen, and thou shalt see I know thee well.   400
I would love infinitely . . . Ah, lost! lost!
        Oh ye who armed me at such cost,
        How shall I look on all of ye
        With your gifts even yet on me?
    Paracelsus. (Ah, 't is some moonstruck creature
        after all!   405
Such fond fools as are like to haunt this den:
They spread contagion, doubtless: yet he seemed
To echo one foreboding of my heart
So truly, that . . . no matter! How he stands
With eve's last sunbeam staying on his hair   410
Which turns to it as if they were akin:
And those clear smiling eyes of saddest blue
Nearly set free, so far they rise above
The painful fruitless striving of the brow
And enforced knowledge of the lips, firm-set   415
In slow despondency's eternal sigh!
Has he, too, missed life's end, and learned the
        cause?)

391 *1849* realising . . . . joy;   399 *1849* own: 403 *1849* Your faces shall I
bear to see   404 *1849* on me?—   410,411 *1849 Berg* {rejected} With one
{?} last sunbeam . . . . | That turns   413 *Berg* {rejected} they fare {?}
above   414 *1849* of that brow   415 *1849* And enforced knowledge of
those lips, firm-set   *Berg* {rejected} And awful {?deeper} knowledge of that
mouth, firm-set   416 *Berg* {rejected} In calm defeat's resigned eternal sigh!

394 *thy safe sure march*: Aprile still misunderstands Paracelsus.
402 *Oh ye*: this line was added in 1849 in an attempt at clarification.
406 *this den*: the conjuror's house.
417 *life's end*: as in *Pauline*, 445.

I charge thee, by thy fealty, be calm!
Tell me what thou wouldst be & what I am!

A/.　　　I would Love infinitely & be loved!　　　　　　420
First, I would carve in stone or cast in brass
The forms of Earth:—no ancient Hunter lifted
Up to the Gods by his renown,—no
　　⟨n⟩ Nymph
Supposed the sweet soul of a woodland tree
Or sapphirine spirit of a twilight star　　　　　　425
Should be too hard for me; no shepherd-king
Regal for his white locks . . no youth who
　　stands
Silent & very calm amid the throng,
His right-hand ever hid beneath his robe,
Until the tyrant pass,—no law-giver,　　　　　　430
No swan-soft woman rubbed with lucid oils
Given by a God for love of her,—too hard.
Every passion sprung from Man, conceived by
　　Man
Would I express & clothe in its fit form,—
Or show, repressed by an ungainly form,—　　　　435
Or blend with others struggling in one form,—

1835 418 calm;　　419 be, and what I am.　　420 love infinitely, and be loved.　　421 First: I . . . . stone, or cast in brass,　　422 earth. No ancient hunter　　423 gods by his renown; no nymph　　427 locks;　　430 pass; no law-giver;　　432 god for love of her—　　433 man, conceived by man,　　435 show repress'd . . . . form,　　436 form.

I charge thee, by thy fealty, be calm!
Tell me what thou wouldst be, and what I am.
   Aprile. I would love infinitely, and be loved.   420
First: I would carve in stone, or cast in brass,
The forms of earth. No ancient hunter lifted
Up to the gods by his renown, no
   nymph
Supposed the sweet soul of a woodland tree
Or sapphirine spirit of a twilight star,   425
Should be too hard for me; no shepherd-king
Regal for his white locks; no youth who
   stands
Silent and very calm amid the throng,
His right hand ever hid beneath his robe
Until the tyrant pass; no lawgiver,   430
No swan-soft woman rubbed with lucid oils
Given by a god for love of her—too hard!
Every passion sprung from man, conceived by
   man,
Would I express and clothe in its right form,
Or blend with others struggling in one form,   435
Or show repressed by an ungainly form.

---

418 *1849* Be calm, I charge thee, by thy fealty!   422 *1849* hunter, raised   423 *1849* renown;   427 *1849* Regal with his   430 *1849* lawgiver;   433 *1849* Each passion   *434 { Editors' emendation, supported by *Berg* and *Yale.*}   *1849–89* clothe it in

421 *I would carve in stone*: cf. the speeches of the young sculptor, Jules, in Part II of *Pippa Passes*. Browning himself was an enthusiastic amateur sculptor: see Henry James, *William Wetmore Story and his Friends* (1903), ii. 68, 113, 117. Browning greatly admired Rodin, who gave lessons to 'Pen'.

422 *No ancient hunter*: probably Orion, who after his death 'was placed in heaven, where one of the constellations still bears his name': Lemprière. Cf. *Pauline*, 323 n.

423 *no nymph*: perhaps Daphne, who was changed into a laurel (cf. *Pauline*, 321–2 n) to save her from the attentions of Apollo (*Metamorphoses*, i. 452 ff).

425 *Or sapphirine spirit*: perhaps Ariadne (ibid. viii. 172 ff.), whose crown was set in the sky by Bacchus. Cf. Donne, 'Elegie: Death', 21: 'She was too Saphirine'.

426 *no shepherd-king*: perhaps Endymion.

427 *no youth*: Hood suggests that this may be a reference to the slaying of Hipparchus by Harmodius and Aristogiton, a suggestion supported by *Pippa Passes* ii. 61.

430 *no lawgiver*: possibly Solon.

—   O if you marveled at some mighty Spirit
          With a fit frame to execute his will,
—   Even unconsciously to work his will, . . .
          You should be moved no less beside some
               strong   440
          Rare spirit, fettered to a stubborn body,
          Endeavouring to subdue it & inform it
          With its own splendour!—All this I would do,
          And I would say, this done, "His sprites
               created,
          "God grants to each a sphere to be his world,   445
          "Appointed with the various objects needed
          "To satisfy his own peculiar wants;
          "So, I create a world for these my shapes
          "Fit to sustain their beauty & their strength!"
—   And at the word, I would contrive & paint   450
          Woods, valleys, rocks & plains, dells, sands &
               wastes
          Lakes which when morn breaks on their
               quivering bed
          Blaze like a wyvern flying round the sun,—
—   And ocean-isles so small, the dog-fish tracking
          A dead whale, who should find them, would
               swim thrice   455
          Around them, & fare onward— — —all to
               hold
          The offspring of my brain—nor these alone . . .
          Bronze labyrinths, palace, pyramid & crypt
          Baths, galleries, courts, temples & terraces
          Marts, theatres & wharfs— —all filled with
               ⟨m⟩ Men!   460

Oh, if you marvelled at some mighty spirit
With a fit frame to execute its will—
Even unconsciously to work its will—
You should be moved no less beside some
    strong   440
Rare spirit, fettered to a stubborn body,
Endeavouring to subdue it and inform it
With its own splendour! All this I would do:
And I would say, this done, "His sprites
    created,
"God grants to each a sphere to be its world,   445
"Appointed with the various objects needed
"To satisfy its own peculiar wants;
"So, I create a world for these my shapes
"Fit to sustain their beauty and their strength!"
And, at the word, I would contrive and paint   450
Woods, valleys, rocks and plains, dells, sands and
    wastes,
Lakes which, when morn breaks on their
    quivering bed,
Blaze like a wyvern flying round the sun,
And ocean isles so small, the dog-fish tracking
A dead whale, who should find them, would
    swim thrice   455
Around them, and fare onward—all to
    hold
The offspring of my brain. Nor these alone:
Bronze labyrinth, palace, pyramid and crypt,
Baths, galleries, courts, temples and terraces,
Marts, theatres and wharfs—all filled with
    men,   460

437 *1849* For, if you marvelled   438 *1849* execute his will—   439 *1849* Ay,
even unconsciously to work his will—   443 *1849* would do,   444 *1849*
this done, "God's sprites being made,   445 *1849* "He grants   *447
{Reading of *1863*}   *1849* "To satisfy its spiritual desires;   *1865–89* "To satisfy
its own peculiar want;   453 *1849* sun;   457 *1849* alone—   458 *1849*
labyrinths, palace, pyramid,   460 *1849* theatres, and . . . . men!   *1863,1865*
theatres and . . . . men!

442 *and inform it*: a reference to the Aristotelian theory according to which
soul represents form and body represents matter.
453 *a wyvern*: 'a winged dragon with two feet like those of an eagle, and a
serpent-like, barbed tail' OED.

Men every where:—& this performed, in turn,
When those who looked on pined to hear the
  hopes
And fears & hates & loves which moved the
  crowd,
I would throw down the pencil as the chisel
And I would Speak,—no thought which ever
  stirred   465
A human breast should be untold; all passions
All soft emotions,—from the turbulent stir
Within a heart fed with desires like mine . . .
To the last comfort shutting the tired lids
Of him who sleeps the sultry noon away   470
Beneath the tent-tree by the wayside-well:—
And this, in language as the need should be,—
Now,—poured at once forth in a burning flow,
Now,—piled up in a grand array of words:—
This done,—to perfect & consummate all,   475
Even as a luminous haze links star to star
I would supply all chasms with
  ⟨m⟩ Music,—breathing
Mysterious motions of the soul, no way
To be defined save in strange melodies:
— — Last, having thus revealed all I could love,   480
Having received all love bestowed on them,—

1835 463 fears, and hates,   465 speak: no . . . . stirr'd   473 Now pour'd
474 Now piled up in a grand array of words.   477 music, breathing   479
melodies.   481 bestow'd on it,

Men everywhere! And this performed in turn,
When those who looked on, pined to hear the
   hopes
And fears and hates and loves which moved the
   crowd,
I would throw down the pencil as the chisel,
And I would speak; no thought which ever
   stirred   465
A human breast should be untold; all passions,
All soft emotions, from the turbulent stir
Within a heart fed with desires like mine,
To the last comfort shutting the tired lids
Of him who sleeps the sultry noon away   470
Beneath the tent-tree by the wayside well:
And this in language as the need should be,
Now poured at once forth in a burning flow,
Now piled up in a grand array of words.
This done, to perfect and consummate all,   475
Even as a luminous haze links star to star,
I would supply all chasms with music,
   breathing
Mysterious motions of the soul, no way
To be defined save in strange melodies.
Last, having thus revealed all I could love,   480
Having received all love bestowed on it,

463 *1849* fears, and hates, and . . . . crowd,—   466 *1849* untold; no pas-
sions,   467 *1849* No soft emotions,   468 *1849* mine—   473 *1889* {some
copies} flow.   478 *1849* Mysterious notions of *Berg* Mysterious motions
of   481 *1849* And having received

465 *And I would speak*: after Sculpture and Painting, Language, used
dramatically (lines 462–3).
  471 *tent-tree*: 'a species of screw-pine': OED.
  475 *consummate*: stressed on the second syllable, as in Johnson.
  477 *music*: cf. *Pauline*, 365 ff. In his youth, Browning may seriously have
thought of becoming a musician: Maynard, p. 140. Later he told Ripert-
Monclar that music had been his chief interest for many years of his life (ibid.)
He always regarded music as the highest of the arts.
  478 *Mysterious motions of the soul*: Elizabeth Barrett expressed Browning's
own view when she wrote to him that 'all the Arts are mediators between the
soul & the Infinite': Kintner, i. 526.

I would die: having preserved throughout my
    course
God full on me, as I was full on Men:
He would approve my prayer—"I have gone
    thro'
"The loveliness of Life,—create for me   485
"If not for Men,—or take me to thyself,
"Eternal, infinite Love!"
                       If thou hast ne'er
Conceived this mighty Aim, this full Desire
Thou hast not passed my trial, & thou art
No king of mine!

P/.   Ah me!
A/.   But thou art here!   490
Thou dids't not gaze like me upon that End
Till thine own powers for compassing the bliss
Were blind with glory:—nor grow mad to
    grasp
At once the prize long patient toil should claim;
Nor spurn all granted short of that—& I   495
Would do as thou, if that might be; Nay,
    listen:—
Knowing ourselves, our world,—our task so
    great,
Our time so brief—'tis clear if we refuse
The means so limited, the tools so rude
To execute our purpose, life will fleet   500
And we shall fade & nothing will be done:
We will be wise in time: what tho' our work

1835 483 men.   485 life,   486 men—   488 aim, this full desire.
490 mine.   491 end   495 that. And I   496 nay, listen—   498
brief;   501 fade, and . . . . done.

I would die: preserving so throughout my
   course
God full on me, as I was full on men:
He would approve my prayer, "I have gone
   through
"The loveliness of life; create for me   485
"If not for men, or take me to thyself,
"Eternal, infinite love!"
                     If thou hast ne'er
Conceived this mighty aim, this full desire,
Thou hast not passed my trial, and thou art
No king of mine.
    Paracelsus.   Ah me!
    Aprile.   But thou art here!   490
Thou didst not gaze like me upon that end
Till thine own powers for compassing the bliss
Were blind with glory; nor grow mad to
   grasp
At once the prize long patient toil should claim,
Nor spurn all granted short of that. And I   495
Would do as thou, a second time: nay,
   listen!
Knowing ourselves, our world, our task so
   great,
Our time so brief, 't is clear if we refuse
The means so limited, the tools so rude
To execute our purpose, life will fleet,   500
And we shall fade, and leave our task undone.
We will be wise in time: what though our work

482 *1849* I would die: so preserving through my course   484–5 *1849* And He
would grant my prayer—"I have gone through | "All loveliness of life; make
more for me,   486 *1849* men—or . . . . thyself,   *1863,1865* men, or . . . .
Thyself,   487 *1849–65* Love!"   494 *1849* claim;   496 *1849* lis-
ten—   498 *1849* brief,—   502 *1849* Rather, grow wise in time:

483 *God full on me*: 'a favourite phrase of Browning's, suggested by the
metaphor of sunlight', as Lee and Locock remark. 'The poet thinks of himself
as storing and reflecting upon his fellow-men the light of God's love'.
   497 *our task so great*: cf. the first aphorism of Hippocrates, 'ars longa, vita
brevis'.

Be fashioned in despite of their ill service,
Be crippled every way? 'Twere little praise
Did full resources wait on our good will   505
At every turn: . . let all be as it is:—
Some say the earth is even so contrived—
That tree & flower, a vesture gay, conceal
A bare & skeleton framework:—had we means
Answering to our mind! . . but now I seem   510
Wrecked on a savage isle—how rear thereon
My palace?—branching palms the props shall
    be,
Fruit glossy mingling; gems are for the East,—
Who needs them? I can pass them: serpent
    scales
And painted bird's down, furs & fishes' skins   515
Must help me; & a little here & there
Is all I can aspire to: still my art
Shall show its birth was in a gentler clime:
"Had I green jars of malachite, this way
"I'd range them: where those sea-shells glisten
    above,   520
"Cressets should hang, by right: this way we
    set
"The purple carpets, as these mats are laid
"Woven of fern & rush & blossoming-flag."

1835 506 turn. Let all be as it is.   507 contrived   511 isle.   513
east;   514 Who heeds them? I can pass them. Serpent's scales,   515 birds'
down, furs,   518 clime.   523 and blossoming flag."

Be fashioned in despite of their ill-service,
Be crippled every way? 'T were little praise
Did full resources wait on our goodwill   505
At every turn. Let all be as it is.
Some say the earth is even so contrived
That tree and flower, a vesture gay, conceal
A bare and skeleton framework. Had we means
Answering to our mind! But now I seem   510
Wrecked on a savage isle: how rear thereon
My palace? Branching palms the props shall
      be,
Fruit glossy mingling; gems are for the East;
Who needs them? I can pass them. Serpents'
      scales,
And painted birds' down, furs and fishes' skins   515
Must help me; and a little here and there
Is all I can aspire to: still my art
Shall show its birth was in a gentler clime.
"Had I green jars of malachite, this way
"I'd range them: where those sea-shells glisten
      above,   520
"Cressets should hang, by right: this way we
      set
"The purple carpets, as these mats are laid,
"Woven of fern and rush and blossoming flag."

---

509 *1849* framework: 510 *1849* That answered to our mind!   *514
{Editors' emendation.}   *1849* Who heeds them? I can waive them. Serpent's
scales,   *1863–89* Who heeds them? I can pass them. Serpents' scales,   515
1849 Birds' feathers, downy furs, and fishes' skins   523 *1849* "Woven of
mere fern

503 *their ill-service*: that provided by the limited means and rude tools which
are all that we have.
511 *a savage isle*: an image for this world, contrasted with his 'own home'
(526).
512 *My palace?*: 'All this exquisite metaphor of building a palace with
nothing but what *nature* affords on a savage island all describes the case of one
who has none of the artificial & acquired means of displaying the riches of his
imagination': Domett.
521 *Cressets should hang*: cf. the description of Pandaemonium, *Paradise Lost* i.
726 ff. A cresset is a torch, sometimes on a cross.
523 *flag*: the common iris with purple flowers: cf. preceding line, and *Pauline*,
776.

Or if, by fortune, some completer grace
Be spared to me, some fragment, some slight
　　sample　　　　　　　　　　　　　　　　　525
Of the prouder workmanship my own Home
　　boasts,
Some trifle little heeded there, but *here*
The one perfection of the place,—how gladly
Would I enshrine the relic—cheerfully
Foregoing all the marvels out of reach!　　　530
Could I retain one strain of all the Psalm
Of the angels . . . one word of the fiat of God,
To let my followers know what such things
　　are! . . .
— — I would adventure nobly for their sakes;
When nights were still & still the moaning sea　535
And far away I could descry the Land
Whence I departed, whither I return, . .
I would dispart the waves & stand once more
At home, & load my bark & hasten back
And fling my gains to them, worthless or true,　540
"Friends," I would say, "I went far, far for
　　them
"Past the high rocks the haunt of doves—the
　　mounds
"Of red earth from whose sides strange trees
　　grow out,
"Past tracts of milk-white minute blinding
　　sand,
"Till, by a mighty moon, I tremblingly　　　545
"Gathered these magic herbs, berry & bud,

1835 526 home　　　530 reach—　　　531–2 psalm | Of the angels—one . . . .
　　God—　　　536 land　　　540 true.　　　542 doves,

Or if, by fortune, some completer grace
Be spared to me, some fragment, some slight
   sample   525
Of the prouder workmanship my own home
   boasts,
Some trifle little heeded there, but here
The place's one perfection—with what joy
Would I enshrine the relic, cheerfully
Foregoing all the marvels out of reach!   530
Could I retain one strain of all the psalm
Of the angels, one word of the fiat of God,
To let my followers know what such things
   are!
I would adventure nobly for their sakes:
When nights were still, and still the moaning sea,   535
And far away I could descry the land
Whence I departed, whither I return,
I would dispart the waves, and stand once more
At home, and load my bark, and hasten back,
And fling my gains to them, worthless or true.   540
"Friends," I would say, "I went far, far for
   them,
"Past the high rocks the haunt of doves, the
   mounds
"Of red earth from whose sides strange trees
   grow out,
"Past tracts of milk-white minute blinding
   sand,
"Till, by a mighty moon, I tremblingly   545
"Gathered these magic herbs, berry and bud,

---

526 *1849* Of my own land's completer workmanship,   529 *1849*
relic—   532 *1849* angels—one . . . . God—   *535 {Reading of
1865–1868,1889}   *1849,1863* still, the moaning sea,   *1888* still the moaning sea
{corrected to 'sea,' in DC.}   540 *1849* And fling my gains before them, rich
or poor—   *1863–8* And fling my gains to them, worthless or true—

---

538 *dispart*: cf. iii. 99. The phrase 'dispart the wave' occurs in *Balaustion's
Adventure*, 516.

"In haste— —not pausing to reject the weeds
"But happy, plucking them at any price:
"To me, who have seen them bloom in their
   own soil
"They are scarce lovely:—plait & wear them,
   you!   550
"And guess from what they are, the springs
   that fed them
"The stars that sparkled o'er them, night by
   night,
"The snakes that travelled far to sip their dew!"
Thus for my higher loves— —& thus even
   weakness
Would win me honour:—but not these alone   555
Should claim my care,—for common life, its
   wants
And ways would I set forth in beauteous
   hues, . .
The lowest hind should not possess a hope
A fear, but I'd be by him, saying better
Than he, his own hearts' language—I would
   live   560
For ever in the thoughts I thus explored,
As a discoverer's memory is attached
To all he finds—they should be [mine]
   henceforth,
Imbued with me, though free to all before,—
For clay, once cast into my soul's rich mine   565
Should come up crusted oer with gems: nor
   this
Would need a meaner spirit, than the first:
—   Nay, 'twould be but the selfsame spirit, clothed

1835 548 happy plucking . . . . price.   551 are the springs that fed
them,   554 loves; and   555 honour.   556 care;   557 ways, would
. . . . hues: 560 he his . . . . language.   563 finds: ·564 before;

"In haste, not pausing to reject the weeds,
"But happy plucking them at any price.
"To me, who have seen them bloom in their
    own soil,
"They are scarce lovely: plait and wear them,
    you!   550
"And guess, from what they are, the springs that
    fed them,
"The stars that sparkled o'er them, night by
    night,
"The snakes that travelled far to sip their dew!"
Thus for my higher loves; and thus even
    weakness
Would win me honour. But not these alone   555
Should claim my care; for common life, its
    wants
And ways, would I set forth in beauteous
    hues:
The lowest hind should not possess a hope,
A fear, but I'd be by him, saying better
Than he his own heart's language. I would
    live   560
For ever in the thoughts I thus explored,
As a discoverer's memory is attached
To all he finds; they should be mine
    henceforth,
Imbued with me, though free to all before:
For clay, once cast into my soul's rich mine,   565
Should come up crusted o'er with gems. Nor
    this
Would need a meaner spirit, than the first;
Nay, 't would be but the selfsame spirit, clothed

---

547 *1849* haste—551–2 *1849* springs that fed— | "The stars   566 *1849* gems:

551 *And guess, from what they are*: '—his "own home & gentler clime", the heaven he revels in, but is obliged to content himself with the small [?] powers *nature* gives for that purpose': Domett.
554 *Thus for my higher loves*: 'such for those kindred spirits who c^d. sympathise with & appreciate the wealth of his imagination; he w^d. also deck common life with rare glory': Domett.

In humbler guise,—but still the selfsame spirit:
As one spring wind unbinds the mountain
    snow   570
And comforts violets in their hermitage.

. . .   But, Master, Poet, who hast done all this,
How did'st thou 'scape the ruin I have met?
Did'st thou, when nerving thee to this attempt,
Ne'er range thy mind's extent, as some wide
    Hall,   575
Dazzled by shapes that filled its length with
    light,
Shapes clustered there, to rule thee, not obey,—
That will not wait thy summons—will not rise
Singly,—nor when thy practised eye & hand
Can well transfer their loveliness,—but are   580
By thee forever, bright to thy despair!
Didst thou ne'er gaze on each by turns,—&
    ne'er
Resolve to single out *One*,—tho' the rest
Should vanish, & to give that One, entire
In beauty, to the world—& to forget   585
Its peers whose number baffles mortal
    power;—
— And, this determined, wert thou ne'er seduced
By memories & regrets & passionate love
To glance once more farewel . . . & did their
    eyes
Fasten thee, brighter & more bright, until   590
Thou could'st but stagger back unto their feet
And laugh that Man's applause or welfare ever

1835 569 guise, but . . . . spirit—   572 But master, poet,   575
hall,   577 cluster'd there to rule thee, not obey—   578 sum-
mons,   581 despair?   583 *one*, though   584 and to give that
one,   585 world; and   586 Its peers, whose number baffles mortal
power?   588 By memories, and regrets, and passionate love,   589
farewell? and   592 man's

In humbler guise, but still the selfsame spirit:
As one spring wind unbinds the mountain
   snow   570
And comforts violets in their hermitage.

But, master, poet, who hast done all this,
How didst thou 'scape the ruin whelming me?
Didst thou, when nerving thee to this attempt,
Ne'er range thy mind's extent, as some wide
   hall,   575
Dazzled by shapes that filled its length with
   light,
Shapes clustered there to rule thee, not obey,
That will not wait thy summons, will not rise
Singly, nor when thy practised eye and hand
Can well transfer their loveliness, but crowd   580
By thee for ever, bright to thy despair?
Didst thou ne'er gaze on each by turns, and
   ne'er
Resolve to single out one, though the rest
Should vanish, and to give that one, entire
In beauty, to the world; forgetting, so,   585
Its peers, whose number baffles mortal
   power?
And, this determined, wast thou ne'er seduced
By memories and regrets and passionate love,
To glance once more farewell? and did their
   eyes
Fasten thee, brighter and more bright, until   590
Thou couldst but stagger back unto their feet,
And laugh that man's applause or welfare ever

---

569 *1849* spirit—   573 *1849* ruin I have met?   577 *1849* obey—   583
1849 single out *one, Berg* single out one, {indicated by wavy line under
one,}   587 *1849* determined, wert thou   592 *1849* welfare once

572 *poet*: to the end Aprile regards Paracelsus as a poet, although he has been
told that Knowledge has been his aim. For him, as it seems, all great men are
poets, and 'God . . . the perfect poet' (648).

Could tempt thee to forsake them: . . or when
   years
Had passed, & still their love possessed thee
   wholly,
When from without some murmur startled thee   595
Of darkling mortals famished for one ray
Of thy so hoarded luxury of light,
Did'st thou ne'er strive even yet to break their
   spells . . .
. . .   To prove that even yet thou could'st fulfil
Thy early mission, long ago renounced,—   600
And, to that end, select some shape once more
— — —And did not mist-like influences, thick films,
Faint memories of the rest, so long before
Thine eyes, fast float, confuse thee, bear thee off
As whirling snowdrifts blind a man who treads   605
A mountain-ridge, with guiding spear, thro'
   storm:—
Dids't not perceive, spoiled by the subtle ways   606a
Of intricate but instantaneous thought,   b
That common speech was useless to its ends,   c
That language, wedded from the first to
   Thought   d
Will strengthen as it strengthens . . but,
   divorced,   e
Will dwindle while Thought widens more &
   more? . .   f
Say, though I fell I had excuse to fall,—
Say I was tempted sorely,—say but this
Dear Lord, Aprile's Lord!
P/.   Clasp me not thus

1835 593 them?   594 pass'd, and . . . . wholly;   598 Didst . . . .
spells,   601 more?   606 A mountain ridge, ... through storm?
606c ends—   606d thought,   606e strengthens;   606f dwindle,
while thought   607 fell, I had . . . . fall;   608,609 sorely. Say but this, |
Dear Lord, Aprile's lord!

Could tempt thee to forsake them? Or when
    years
Had passed and still their love possessed thee
    wholly,
When from without some murmur startled thee   595
Of darkling mortals famished for one ray
Of thy so-hoarded luxury of light,
Didst thou ne'er strive even yet to break those
    spells
And prove thou couldst recover and fulfil
Thy early mission, long ago renounced,   600
And to that end, select some shape once more?
And did not mist-like influences, thick films,
Faint memories of the rest that charmed so long
Thine eyes, float fast, confuse thee, bear thee off,
As whirling snow-drifts blind a man who treads   605
A mountain ridge, with guiding spear, through
    storm?
Say, though I fell, I had excuse to fall;
Say, I was tempted sorely: say but this,
Dear lord, Aprile's lord!
    Paracelsus.   Clasp me not thus,

---

594 *1849* passed, and . . . . wholly;   603 *1849* rest,

593 *Could tempt thee to forsake them?*: 'A vivid & powerful picture of the *love* of
day-dreaming the delights of the imagination preventing the production of
works of imagination—An exquisite commentary on the lines—"the beings
of the mind are not of clay. Essentially immortal they create &c a *more beloved*
existence"': Domett, quoting *Childe Harold's Pilgrimage*, IV. v.
   600 *Thy early mission*: 'just as Paracelsus page 51 wishes for some great
acquisition to prove his desires still pure & high': Domett, referring to ii.
196–7.
   606 *with guiding spear*: like Childe Roland (l. 123).

Aprile!—that the truth should reach me thus!   610
We are weak dust . . . nay, clasp not or I faint!

A/.   My King! & envious thoughts could outrage
          thee!

—   Lo, I forget my ruin & rejoice
In thy success, as thou: let our God's praise
Go bravely thro' the world at last!—what care   615
Thro' me or thee? I feel thy breath . . .
          why,—tears?
Tears in the darkness— —& from thee to me?

P/.   Love me henceforth Aprile, while *I*
          learn
To love—& merciful God forgive us both!
We wake at length from weary dreams . . but
          both   620
Have slept in fairy-land— —tho' dark & drear
Appears the world before us, we no less
Wake with our wrists & ancles jewelled still: .
I, too, have sought to KNOW as thou to LOVE
Excluding love as thou refused'st knowledge: . .   625
Still thou hast beauty & I power: we wake:
What penance canst devise for both of us?

A/.   I hear thee faintly . . the thick darkness!
          even
Thine eyes are hid: 'tis as I knew . . I speak
And now I die . . but I have seen thy face!   630
O dear soul, think of me, . . & sing of me . . .
    . .   But to have seen thee, & to die so soon!

P/.   Die not, Aprile . . . we must never part . . .
Are we not halves of one dissevered world

1835 611 dust. Nay, clasp not,   612 My king! and   614 thou!   616
why tears?   619 To love; and, merciful God, forgive us both!   620
dreams;   621 fairy-land. Though   623 still.   624 LOVE—   625
knowledge.   626 power.   629 hid. 'T is as I knew: I speak,   630
die.   633 Aprile: we must never part.

Aprile! That the truth should reach me thus!   610
We are weak dust. Nay, clasp not or I faint!
   Aprile. My king! and envious thoughts could
     outrage thee?
Lo, I forget my ruin, and rejoice
In thy success, as thou! Let our God's praise
Go bravely through the world at last! What care   615
Through me or thee? I feel thy breath. Why,
   tears?
Tears in the darkness, and from thee to me?
   Paracelsus. Love me henceforth, Aprile, while I
     learn
To love; and, merciful God, forgive us both!
We wake at length from weary dreams; but
   both   620
Have slept in fairy-land: though dark and drear
Appears the world before us, we no less
Wake with our wrists and ankles jewelled still.
I too have sought to KNOW as thou to LOVE—
Excluding love as thou refusedst knowledge.   625
Still thou hast beauty and I, power. We wake:
What penance canst devise for both of us?
   Aprile. I hear thee faintly. The thick darkness!
     Even
Thine eyes are hid. 'T is as I knew: I speak,
And now I die. But I have seen thy face!   630
O poet, think of me, and sing of me!
But to have seen thee and to die so soon!
   Paracelsus. Die not, Aprile! We must never part.
Are we not halves of one dissevered world,

---

610 *1849* Aprile! . . .   612 *1849–65* thee!   616 *1849* breath . . .
why,   617 *1849* darkness—   628 *1849* faintly . . . the   633 *1849* Aprile:

   615 *What care*: what does it matter whether God is praised through Aprile or
through Paracelsus?
   616 *Why, tears?*: 'How beautiful this emotion, if the *causes* of it had been more
ordinary ones, & more easily sympathised with by the mass. He congratulates
Paracelsus on *his* success, who has failed so bitterly. Nothing would revive &
increase the grief of a person so circumstanced so soon': Domett.
   618–19 *while I learn / To love*: cf. the preface to *Alastor*, quoted above on p.
116.
   634 *halves of one dissevered world*: cf. Plato, *Symposium*, 189–93. Browning
alludes to the notion again in *Fifine at the Fair*, sect. 39.

Whom this strange chance unites once more?
   part? never!   635
Till thou, the Lover, know,—& I, the Knower,
Love——until both are saved!—Aprile,
   hear!
God! he will die upon my breast: Aprile!

A/.   To speak but once & die! yet by his
   side: 640
Hush, hush—
          Ha, go you ever girt
With Phantoms, Powers? . . . I have created
   such,
But these seem real as I: . .

P/.   Whom can you see
Thro' the accursed darkness? . . .

A/.   —Stay, I know
I know them: who should know them well as
   I?   645
White brows—lit up with glory—Poets all!

P/.   Let him but live, & I have my
   reward!

A/.   Yes, I see now—God is the PERFECT POET:
Who in his person, acts his own creations.
Had you but told me this at first! . . hush,
   hush   650

1835 636 the lover, know; and I, the knower, 637 saved.   638 {No equivalent in *MS* or *1835*.}   639 God, he . . . . breast! Aprile!   640–1 To speak but once, and die! yet by his side. | Hush! Hush! | Ha! go you 642 phantoms, powers? I have 644 Through . . . darkness? | *Apr.* Stay; I know, 646 White brows, lit up with glory; poets all! 648 Yes; I . . . . POET, 650 Hush! hush!

Whom this strange chance unites once more? Part?
    never!   635
Till thou, the lover, know; and I, the knower,
Love—until both are saved. Aprile, hear!
We will accept our gains, and use them—now!
God, he will die upon my breast! Aprile!
    Aprile. To speak but once, and die! yet by his
    side.   640
Hush! hush!
                Ha! go you ever girt about
With phantoms, powers? I have created
    such,
But these seem real as I.
    Paracelsus.   Whom can you see
Through the accursed darkness?
    Aprile.   Stay; I know,
I know them: who should know them well as
    I?   645
White brows, lit up with glory; poets all!
    Paracelsus. Let him but live, and I have my
    reward!
    Aprile. Yes; I see now. God is the perfect poet,
Who in his person acts his own creations.
Had you but told me this at first! Hush!
    hush!   650

---

635 *1863* Part   *636 {Reading of *1849–1865*}   *1868–1889* Till thou   638
Berg We will accept {'We' not clear: 'He' might be intended.}   643 *1849* as
I!   *1863,65* as I?   648 *1849* now—God is the PERFECT POET, *1863* now. God is
the PERFECT POET, *1865* now. God is the perfect Poet,   649–650 (6 lines
inserted in *1849*; not in later editions.}
649 Who in creation acts his own conceptions.
  A Shall man refuse to be aught less than God?
  B Man's weakness is his glory—for the strength
  C Which raises him to heaven and near God's self,
  D Came spite of it: God's strength his glory is,
  E For thence came with our weakness sympathy
  F Which brought God down to earth, a man like us.
650 Had you but told me this at first! . . . Hush! hush!
649C–D *Berg* {rejected} That raises him . . . . self, | Rose spite of it:
649E–F *Berg* {rejected} (i. w.) For thence rose with our weakness sympathy |
Making God walk the earth.   649 *1863,1865* Who in His person acts His
own creations.

---

   643 *But these seem real as I*: 'The dying man mistakes vision for reality':
Domett.

P/. Live! for my sake . . because of my
  great sin
  To help my brain oppressed by ⟨your {?}⟩
  [these] wild words
  And their deep import— —Live! 'tis not too
  late,—
  I have a quiet home ⟨afar⟩ for us—& friends,—
  Michal shall smile on you— —hear you? lean
  thus   655
  And breathe my breath— —I shall not lose one
  word
  Of all your speech—one little word, Aprile!

A/. No, no—crown *me*? I am not one of
  you!
  Tis he, the King you seek . . I am not one . . .

P/. Thy spirit, at least, Aprile!—let *me*
  love! . . .   660

I have attained, & now I may depart.

1835 653 import. Live! . . . . late: 654 home for us, and friends. 656
breath: 657 word, Aprile. 659 'T is he, the king, you seek. 660
Aprile, let *me* love! . . . 661 I HAVE ATTAIN'D, AND NOW I MAY DEPART. {The
double rule in the MS has probably been misinterpreted to mean small capi-
tals.}

Paracelsus. Live! for my sake, because of my
    great sin,
To help my brain, oppressed by these wild
    words
And their deep import. Live! 't is not too
    late.
I have a quiet home for us, and friends.
Michal shall smile on you. Hear you? Lean
    thus,   655
And breathe my breath. I shall not lose one
    word
Of all your speech, one little word, Aprile!
    Aprile. No, no. Crown me? I am not one of
        you!
'T is he, the king, you seek. I am not one.
    Paracelsus. Thy spirit, at least, Aprile! Let me
        love!   660

I have attained, and now I may depart.

---

653 *1849* late: 655 *1849* you . . .   656 *1849* breath: 657 *1849* speech— no
little word, Aprile!   658 *1849* No, no . . .   659 *1849* one . . .   660 *1849*
Give me thy spirit, at least! Let me love, too! {*1865* as *1888* except 'let'}

   660 *Thy spirit, at least, Aprile!* Aprile dies, but remains of great importance in
the mind of Paracelsus. See, in particular, iii. 379 ff, and Part V.
   661 *I have attained*: 'He has attained to the knowledge that something more
than knowledge is requisite to the renovation of mankind—& reached the
close of his toil, in that line': Domett.

3. PARACELSUS.

Scene, *a chamber in the House of Paracelsus at Basil. 1526.*

Paracelsus, Festus.

P/.   Heap logs & let the blaze laugh out:
F/.   True, true,—
      Tis very fit all Time & Chance & change
      Have wrought since last we sate thus, face to
          face
      And soul to soul— —all cares,—far-looking
          fears
      Vague apprehensions—all vain fancies bred   5
      By your long absence— — —should be cast
          away,
      Forgotten in this glad unhoped renewal
      Of our affection:
P/.   Oh, omit not aught

1835 1 logs, and . . . . out. | True, true;   2 'T is . . . time, and chance, and change   5 apprehensions,   6 absence,   8 Of our affections.

PART III.

PARACELSUS.

SCENE.—*Basil; a chamber in the house of*
PARACELSUS. 1526.

PARACELSUS, FESTUS.

Paracelsus. Heap logs and let the blaze laugh out!
Festus.   True, true!
'T is very fit all, time and chance and change
Have wrought since last we sat thus, face to
      face
And soul to soul—all cares, far-looking
      fears,
Vague apprehensions, all vain fancies bred   5
By your long absence, should be cast
      away,
Forgotten in this glad unhoped renewal
Of our affection.
Paracelsus.   Oh, omit not aught

1849 SCENE—*A chamber in the house of Paracelsus at Basil.* 1526.
1 *1863* True, true   2 *1849* 'Tis very fit that all, time, chance, and
change *Berg* {rejected} 'Tis fit that all which time and chance, and
change   *8 {Editors' emendation.}   *1849–89* Of our affections.

PART III:
    'He tries mankind—& wins worldly reputation from the wrecks of his first
knowledge. But a mocking proud bitterness is the highest mood of mind
which is left him—& utter hopelessness; but yet determined (in failure) to do
what good he can to men—while they *let* him': Domett.
SCENE.—*Basil . . . 1526*: this follows the date given in the *Biographie Universelle*:
see p. 502 below.
FESTUS: the reason for his presence in Basil is explained at 952 ff.
    2 *time*: cf. *Prometheus Unbound*, II. iv. 119: 'Fate, Time, Occasion, Chance,
and Change'.

Which witnesses your own & Michals own
Affection—spare not that! forget alone   10
The honours & the glories & what not
That [you] are pleased to tell profusely out.

F/.   Nay, even your honours in a certain
       sense: . .
The wondrous Paracelsus—the dispenser
Of life—the commissary of fate—the idol   15
Of Princes— —is no more than Aureole
       still,—
Still Aureole & my friend, as when we parted
Some twenty years ago, when I restrained
As I best could the promptings of my spirit
Which secretly advanced you, from the first,   20
To the pre-eminent rank which since, your
       own
Adventurous ardour, nobly triumphing,
Has won for you.

P/.   — —Yes, yes . . . & Michal's face
Still wears that quiet & peculiar light
Like the dim circlet floating round a pearl?   25

F/.   Just so:
P/.   And yet her calm sweet
       countenance
Though saintly was not sad—for she would
       sing
Alone . . does she still sing alone? bird-like,
Not dreaming you are near: her carols dropt
In flakes thro' that old leafy bower built under   30

Which witnesses your own and Michal's own
Affection: spare not that! Only forget   10
The honours and the glories and what not,
It pleases you to tell profusely out.
    Festus. Nay, even your honours, in a sense, I
      waive:
The wondrous Paracelsus, life's dispenser,
Fate's commissary, idol of the schools   15
And courts, shall be no more than Aureole still,
Still Aureole and my friend as when we parted
So many years ago, and I restrained
As best I could the promptings of my spirit
Which secretly advanced you, from the first,   20
To the pre-eminent rank which, since, your
    own
Adventurous ardour, nobly triumphing,
Has won for you.
    Paracelsus.   Yes, yes. And Michal's face
Still wears that quiet and peculiar light
Like the dim circlet floating round a pearl?   25
    Festus. Just so.
    Paracelsus.   And yet her calm sweet
      countenance,
Though saintly, was not sad; for she would
    sing
Alone. Does she still sing alone, bird-like,
Not dreaming you are near? Her carols dropt
In flakes through that old leafy bower built under 30

9–12 *1849* Which witnesses your own and Michal's love! | I bade you not spare
that! Forget alone | The honours and the glories, and the rest, | You seemed
disposed to tell profusely out.   14 *1849* Paracelsus—Life's *1863* Paracelsus,
Life's   16 *1849* Courts, shall . . . . still—   *18 {Editors' emendation,
supported by *Berg*.}   *Berg* So ⟨me twenty⟩ [many] years ago, ⟨when⟩ [and] I
restrained *1849–89* Some twenty years ago, and I restrained   19 *1849* As I
best could . . . . spirit,   28 *1849* Alone . . Does she still

  15 *Fate's commissary*: see i. 609 n.
  18 *many years ago*: the Berg copy (above) shows that Browning realized that
his revision of '1507' to '1512' in the stage-direction at the beginning of Part I
required a revision here; but it was not incorporated in the printed eds.

The sunny wall at Würzburg, from her lattice
Among the trees above . . while I unseen
Sate conning some rare roll from Tritheim's
   shelves,
Much wondering notes so simple could divert
My mind from study . . . those were happy
   days!   35
Respect all such as sing when all alone.

F/.   Scarcely alone . . . her children, you may
   guess,
Are wild beside her . . .

P/.   Ah, those children quite
Unsettle the pure picture in my mind:—
A girl—she was so perfect, so distinct, . .   40
No change, no change!—not but this added
   grace
May blend & harmonize with its compeers,
And Michal may become her mother-hood;
But 'tis a change—& I detest all change,
And most a change in aught I loved long since: 45
But Michal . . . you have said she thinks of me?

F/.   O very proud will Michal be of you!
Imagine how we sate, long winter-nights,
Scheming & wondering—shaping your
   presumed
Adventure, or devising your reward;   50
Shutting out fear as long as hope might be

. . .   For it was strange how, even when most secure

The sunny wall at Würzburg, from her lattice
Among the trees above, while I, unseen,
Sat conning some rare scroll from Tritheim's
    shelves
Much wondering notes so simple could divert
My mind from study. Those were happy
    days.   35
Respect all such as sing when all alone!
    Festus. Scarcely alone: her children, you may
      guess,
Are wild beside her.
    Paracelsus.   Ah, those children quite
Unsettle the pure picture in my mind:
A girl, she was so perfect, so distinct: 40
No change, no change! Not but this added
    grace
May blend and harmonize with its compeers,
And Michal may become her motherhood;
But 't is a change, and I detest all change,
And most a change in aught I loved long since.   45
So, Michal—you have said she thinks of me?
    Festus. O very proud will Michal be of you!
Imagine how we sat, long winter-nights,
Scheming and wondering, shaping your
    presumed
Adventure, or devising its reward;   50
Shutting out fear with all the strength of hope.
For it was strange how, even when most secure

---

35 *1849* days!   36 *1849* all alone.   37 *1849* Scarcely alone—   38 *1849*
her . . .   39 *1865,1868* Unsettled   40 *1849* A girl—she . . . . distinct
. . . *1863–68* A girl, she . . . . distinct.   44 *1849* change—and   45 *1849*
since!   46 *1849* So, Michal . . .   49 wondering—   50 *1849* Adven-
tures, or devising their reward;   52 *1849* Though it was strange

   33 *some rare scroll*: as Abbot, Tritheim insisted that there was no manual work
which his monks could undertake of comparable importance to that of trans-
cribing manuscripts. Over the years he built up in the convent a library of two
thousand manuscripts and printed books, a collection which rendered it fam-
ous. See the *Biographie Universelle*.
   52 *even when most secure*: cf. 'Bishop Blougram's Apology', 182 ff.

In our domestic peace, a certain dim
And flitting shade could sadden all;—it seemed
A restlessness of heart—a silent yearning   55
A sense of something wanting, incomplete,—
Not to be put in words, perhaps avoided
By mute consent,—but felt no less when traced
To point to one so loved & so long lost.

—   Not but, to balance fears, were glowing
          hopes . . .   60
How you would laugh should I recount them
     now!

—   I still predicted your return at last
With gifts beyond the greatest of them all,
All Tritheim's wondrous troop—did one of
     which
Attain renown by any chance, I smiled   65
As well aware of who would prove his peer:
Michal was sure that long ere this some being
As beautiful as you were brave, had
     loved . . . . .

P/.   Far-seeing truly to discern as
          much
In the fantastic projects & day-dreams   70
Of a raw, restless boy.

F/.   —   —   Oh no, the sunrise
Well warranted our faith in this full Noon:
Have I forgotten the anxious voice that said
"Festus, have thoughts like these e'er shaped
     themselves   75
"In other brains than mine— —have their
     possessors
"Existed in like circumstance— —were they
     weak
"As I—or ever constant from the first,

In our domestic peace, a certain dim
And flitting shade could sadden all; it seemed
A restlessness of heart, a silent yearning,   55
A sense of something wanting, incomplete—
Not to be put in words, perhaps avoided
By mute consent—but, said or unsaid, felt
To point to one so loved and so long lost.
And then the hopes rose and shut out the
    fears—   60
How you would laugh should I recount them
    now!
I still predicted your return at last
With gifts beyond the greatest of them all,
All Tritheim's wondrous troop; did one of
    which
Attain renown by any chance, I smiled,   65
As well aware of who would prove his peer.
Michal was sure some woman, long ere this,
As beautiful as you were sage, had
    loved . . .
    Paracelsus. Far-seeing, truly, to discern so
    much
In the fantastic projects and day-dreams   70
Of a raw restless boy!
    Festus.   Oh, no: the sunrise
Well warranted our faith in this full noon!
Can I forget the anxious voice which said
"Festus, have thoughts like these e'er shaped
    themselves
"In other brains than mine? have their
    possessors   75
"Existed in like circumstance? were they
    weak
"As I, or ever constant from the first,

---

*61 *1849–68* now!   *1888,1889* now {Emended in DC to 'now!'}   63 *1849* the greatest vaunt of all,   65 *1849* smiled—   *66 *1849–68,1889* peer.   *1888* peer {corrected in DC.}   68 *Berg* {rejected} as you were wise,   71 *1849* *Fest.* Say, one whose sunrise   *75 {Reading of *1849–68*}   *1888,89* these ere shaped   76 *1849* mine—   77 *1849* circumstance—   78 *1849* "As I—

67 *some woman:* cf. i. 670 n.

"Despising youth's allurements & rejecting
"As spider-films the shackles I endure?
"Is there hope for me?"— —& I answered
    gravely   80
As an acknowledged elder, calmer, wiser
More gifted mortal . . . O you must remember,
For all your glorious . . . . .

P/.   Glorious? ay, to wit this hair,
These hands . . . nay touch them, they are
    mine! recall
With all the said recallings, times when thus   85
To lay them by your own ne'er turned you pale
As now:—most glorious are they not?

F/.   Why . . . why . . .
Something must be subtracted from success
So wide, no doubt:—he would be scrupulous
    truly
Who should object such drawbacks: . .
    still—still, Aureole,   90
You *are* changed—very changed . . . 'twere
    losing nothing
To look well to it: you must not be stolen
From the enjoyment of your wellwon meed.

P/.   My Friend!—you seek my pleasure, past a
    doubt:
You will best gain your point by talking, not   95
Of me, but of yourself.

F/.   Have I not said
All touching Michal & my children? sure
You know, by this, full well how Annchen
    looks
Gravely, while one disparts her thick brown
    hair,—
And Aureole's glee when some stray gannet
    builds   100

1835 82 mortal.   84 These hands—nay, touch them, they are mine—recall
87 now. Most glorious,   89 doubt. He . . . . scrupulous, truly,   90
drawbacks. Still, still Aureole,   91 very changed.   94 My friend! you
99 hair;

"Despising youth's allurements and rejecting
"As spider-films the shackles I endure?
"Is there hope for me?"—and I answered
    gravely   80
As an acknowledged elder, calmer, wiser,
More gifted mortal. O you must remember,
For all your glorious . . .
    Paracelsus.   Glorious? ay, this hair,
These hands—nay, touch them, they are mine!
    Recall
With all the said recallings, times when thus   85
To lay them by your own ne'er turned you pale
As now. Most glorious, are they not?
    Festus.   Why—why—
Something must be subtracted from success
So wide, no doubt. He would be scrupulous,
    truly,
Who should object such drawbacks. Still, still,
    Aureole,   90
You are changed, very changed! 'T were losing
    nothing
To look well to it: you must not be stolen
From the enjoyment of your well-won meed.
    Paracelsus. My friend! you seek my pleasure,
    past a doubt:
You will best gain your point, by talking, not   95
Of me, but of yourself.
    Festus.   Have I not said
All touching Michal and my children? Sure
You know, by this, full well how Aennchen
    looks
Gravely, while one disparts her thick brown
    hair;
And Aureole's glee when some stray gannet
    builds   100

---

80 *1849* I answered grave   86 *1849* pale,   87 *1849* Why . . . why . . .   91
1849 You are changed—   95 *1849* By talking, not of me, but of your-
self,   96 *1849* You will best gain your point.

Amid the birch-trees by the lake— —small
 hope
Have I that he will honour,—the wild imp!—
His namesake;—sigh not!—'tis too much to
 ask
That all we love should reach the same proud
 fate:
But you are very kind to humour me   105
By shewing interest in my quiet life;
You, who of old could never tame yourself
To tranquil pleasures, must at heart
 despise . . . . .

P/. Festus, strange secrets are let out by Death
Who blabs so oft the follies of this world: 110
I, as you know, am Death's familiar oft:
I helped a man to die, some few weeks since,
Warped even from his go-cart to one end—
To live on Princes' smiles—reflected from
A mighty herd of favourites:—no mean trick   115
He left untried, & truly well nigh wormed
All traces of God's finger out of him.
He died, grown old:—& just an hour before,—
Having lain long with blank & soulless eyes,
He sate up suddenly, & with natural voice   120
Said, that in spite of thick air & closed doors
God told him it was June; & he knew well
Without such telling, harebells grew in June;
And that all kings could ever give or take

1835 101 lake.   103 namesake. Sigh not!   104 fate.   111 oft.   114
prince's smiles,   115 favourites.   118 old; and . . . . before—   119
eyes—   124 And all that kings

Amid the birch-trees by the lake. Small
  hope
Have I that he will honour (the wild imp)
His namesake. Sigh not! 't is too much to
  ask
That all we love should reach the same proud
  fate.
But you are very kind to humour me   105
By showing interest in my quiet life;
You, who of old could never tame yourself
To tranquil pleasures, must at heart despise . . .
  Paracelsus. Festus, strange secrets are let out by
    death
Who blabs so oft the follies of this world: 110
And I am death's familiar, as you know.
I helped a man to die, some few weeks since,
Warped even from his go-cart to one end—
The living on princes' smiles, reflected from
A mighty herd of favourites. No mean trick   115
He left untried, and truly well-nigh wormed
All traces of God's finger out of him:
Then died, grown old. And just an hour before,
Having lain long with blank and soulless eyes,
He sat up suddenly, and with natural voice   120
Said that in spite of thick air and closed doors
God told him it was June; and he knew well,
Without such telling, harebells grew in June;
And all that kings could ever give or take

102 *1849* honour, the wild imp,   103 *1849–65* namesake!   109 *1849–1865*
Death,   111 *1849–1865* Death's   116 *1849* untried; and truly well
nigh   117 *1849* him.   118 *1849* old; and . . . . before—   119 *1849*
eyes—

103 *Sigh not!*: 'all through—never *one* speaks without the *listener* being also
before the reader': Domett.
  111 *death's familiar*: 'familiar' has a slightly sinister connotation, meaning not
only 'An intimate; one long acquainted', but also 'A demon supposed to attend
at call' (both Johnson).
  117 *God's finger*: biblical: cf. Exodus viii. 19 and Luke xi. 20. Paracelsus
himself wrote: 'It was the book of Nature, written by the finger of God, which
I studied': Hartmann, p. 20. The phrase occurs on several other occasions in
Browning, notably in 'Abt Vogler', 49.

Would not be precious as those blooms to
    him: 125
Just so, allowing I am passing wise,
It seems to me much worthier argument
Why pansies*—eyes that laugh—are
    lovelier
Than violets—eyes that dream—(your Michal's
    choice)
Than all fools find to wonder at in me   130
Or in my fortunes: & be very sure
I say this from no prurient restlessness—
—   No self-complacency itching to vary
And turn & view its pleasure from all points,
And, in this instance, willing other Men   135
Should be at pains to demonstrate to it
The realness of the very joy it lives on . . . .
What should delight me like the news of friends
Whose memories were a solace to me oft,
As mountain-baths to wild fowls in their flight?   140
Oftener that you had wasted thought on me
Had you been sage, & rightly valued bliss,—
But there's no taming nor repressing hearts:
God knows I need such! . . . so you heard me
    speak?

---

*/ Citrinula (flammula) herba P.° multùm familiaris. Dorn.
1835 125 him.   128 pansies,* eyes that laugh,   129 violets, eyes . . . .
choice)—   133 No self-complacency—itching to vary,   135 men
137 on.   142 bliss;

Would not be precious as those blooms to
    him.   125
Just so, allowing I am passing sage,
It seems to me much worthier argument
Why pansies,* eyes that laugh, bear beauty's
    prize
From violets, eyes that dream—(your Michal's
    choice)—
Than all fools find to wonder at in me   130
Or in my fortunes. And be very sure
I say this from no prurient restlessness,
No self-complacency, itching to turn,
Vary and view its pleasure from all points,
And, in this instance, willing other men   135
May be at pains, demonstrate to itself
The realness of the very joy it tastes.
What should delight me like the news of friends
Whose memories were a solace to me oft,
As mountain-baths to wild fowls in their flight?   140
Ofter than you had wasted thought on me
Had you been wise, and rightly valued bliss.
But there's no taming nor repressing hearts:
God knows I need such!—So, you heard me
    speak?

* Citrinula (flammula) herba Paracelso multum familiaris.—DORN.

126 *1849* passing wise,   128, 129 *Berg* {rejected} that laugh, in loveliness |
Pass violets,   131 *1849* fortunes: 132 *1849* restlessness—   133 *1849*
self-complacency—   *Berg* {rejected} self-complacency, that, itching
134 *1849–1865* Vary, and view its pleasure   135, 136 *1849* And, in this matter,
willing other men | Should argue and demonstrate to itself   136 *1863–68*
Should be   138 *1849* What joy is better than the news of friends   141 *1849*
Yes, ofter than you wasted   142 *1849* If you were sage, and rightly valued
bliss!   *1863,65* Had you been wise, and rightly valued bliss!

  125 *precious as those blooms*: cf. *Pauline*, 131 ff.
  128 *pansies**: 'citrinula [little flame], a plant much associated with Paracel-
sus'. Referring to this note in a letter to Elizabeth Barrett, Browning called the
pansy 'Paracelsus' *own*', adding: 'they usually ornament his pictures with it':
Kintner, ii. 742. Two pansies appear in the decorative border of one of the three
engravings of Paracelsus with which he illustrated the MS of the poem. As he
knew Johnson's *Dictionary* so well, he may have remembered the quotation
from [Walter] Harte given there: 'And in the pansy's life God's providence
discern'd'. Gerard Dorn was a German chemist who was one of the principal
disciples of Paracelsus. Browning may be quoting from *Lexicon Chymicum*,
authore Gulielmo Johnsonio (ed. of 1652), which has the same comment on
'Citrinula'.

F/.   Speak? when?
P/.   When but this morning at my
                   class?   145
               There was noise & crowd enough—I saw you
                   not:
               Surely you know I am engaged to fill
               The chair here? that 'tis part of my proud fate
               To lecture to as many thick-sculled youths
               As please to throng the ⟨t⟩ Theatre each day   150
               To my great reputation & no small
               Peril of benches long unused to crack
               Beneath such honour?
F/.   I was there, indeed:—
               I mingled with the throng: shall I avow
               Small care was mine to listen?—I was intent   155
               On gathering from the murmurs of the crowd
               A full corroboration of my hopes:
               What can *I* learn about your powers?—but *they*
               Know, care for nought beyond your actual
                   state,
               Your actual value— —yet they worship you!   160
               Those various natures whom you sway as
                   one:—
               But ere I go, be sure I shall attend . . . .
P/.   Stop, o' God's name: the thing's by no means
                   yet
               Past remedy,—shall I read this morning's
                   labour?
               At least, in substance? nought so worth the
                   gaining   165
               As an apt scholar: thus then, with all due
               Precision & emphasis; . . (you, besides, are
                   clearly
               Guiltless of understanding more a whit
               The subject, than your stool,—allowed to be

1835 146 enough.   150 theatre each day,   153 indeed.   157
hopes.   159 state—   160 value.   161 one.   164 remedy.   167
and emphasis—

Festus. Speak? when?
Paracelsus   When but this morning at my
    class?   145
There was noise and crowd enough. I saw you
    not.
Surely you know I am engaged to fill
The chair here?—that 't is part of my proud fate
To lecture to as many thick-skulled youths
As please, each day, to throng the theatre,   150
To my great reputation, and no small
Danger of Basil's benches long unused
To crack beneath such honour?
    Festus.   I was there;
I mingled with the throng: shall I avow
Small care was mine to listen?—too intent   155
On gathering from the murmurs of the crowd
A full corroboration of my hopes!
What can I learn about your powers? but they
Know, care for nought beyond your actual
    state,
Your actual value; yet they worship you,   160
Those various natures whom you sway as
    one!
But ere I go, be sure I shall attend . . .
    Paracelsus. Stop, o' God's name: the thing 's by
    no means yet
Past remedy! Shall I read this morning's
    labour
—At least in substance? Nought so worth the
    gaining   165
As an apt scholar! Thus then, with all due
Precision and emphasis—you, beside, are
    clearly
Guiltless of understanding more, a whit,
The subject than your stool—allowed to be

155 *1849* I had small care to listen?—   159 *1849* state—   160 *1849* value;
and yet worship you! *Berg* value. [; and] Yet they worship you(!),   164
1849 morning's work   167 *1849* (you, besides, *1863,1865* you,
besides,   168 *1849* understanding a whit more

A notable advantage:)
F/.   Surely, Aureole,   170
You laugh at me!
P/.   *I* laugh? Ha ha! thank heaven
I charge you, if 'tbe so! for I forget
Much—& what laughter should be like: no less
However, I forego that luxury
Since it offends the friend who brings it back.   175
True, laughter like my own must echo
          strangely
To thinking men;—a smile were better far,—
So make me smile!—if the exulting look
You wore but now, be smiling, 'tis so long
Since I have smiled! alas, such smiles are born   180
Alone of hearts like yours,—& those old Herds'
Of ancient time, whose eyes—calm as their
          flocks—
Saw in the stars mere garnishry of heaven,
And in the earth a stage for altars only:—
Never change, Festus: I say, never change!   185
F/.   My God, if he be wretched after all!
P/.   When last we parted, Festus, you
          declared— —
Or Michal— —yes *her* soft lips whispered
          what
I have preserved: she told me she believed
I should succeed, (meaning, that in the search   190
I then engaged in, I should meet success)
And yet be wretched: now, she augured false.
F/.   Thank Heaven! but you spoke strangely! could
          I venture

1835 170 advantage) . . .   178–9 So make me smile, if the exulting look |
You wore but now be smiling. 'Tis so long   182 eyes, calm as their
flocks,   184 only.   187 declared,

A notable advantage.
    Festus.   Surely, Aureole,   170
You laugh at me!
    Paracelsus.   I laugh? Ha, ha! thank heaven,
I charge you, if 't be so! for I forget
Much, and what laughter should be like. No less,
However, I forego that luxury
Since it alarms the friend who brings it back.   175
True, laughter like my own must echo
    strangely
To thinking men; a smile were better far;
So, make me smile! If the exulting look
You wore but now be smiling, 't is so long
Since I have smiled! Alas, such smiles are born   180
Alone of hearts like yours, or herdsmen's souls
Of ancient time, whose eyes, calm as their
    flocks,
Saw in the stars mere garnishry of heaven,
And in the earth a stage for altars only.
Never change, Festus: I say, never change!   185
    Festus. My God, if he be wretched after all!
    Paracelsus. When last we parted, Festus, you
    declared,
—Or Michal, yes, her soft lips whispered
    words
I have preserved. She told me she believed
I should succeed (meaning, that in the search   190
I then engaged in, I should meet success)
And yet be wretched: now, she augured false.
    Festus. Thank heaven! but you spoke strangely:
    could I venture

---

170 *1849* advantage)...   173 *1849* Much—and . . . . like!   *1863,1865* Much,
and . . . . like!   176 *1849* echo strange   177 *1849* far—   178 *Berg* If
⟨the⟩ [that] exulting look,   181 *1849* yours, or shepherds old   184
1849–65 In earth a stage for altars, nothing more.   *186 *1849–68,1889*
all!   *1888* all {corrected in DC.}   188 *1849* —Or did your Michal's soft lips
whisper words *Berg* {rejected} Or were they Michal's soft lips whisper'd
what   189 *1849* preserved?   192 *Berg* And ⟨yet⟩ [still] be   193 *1849*
heaven! . . . . strangely!   *1863,1865* Heaven! . . . . strangely:

---

183 *garnishry*: a nonce-word, according to OED, which cites only this and
The Ring and the Book iv. 545.

To think bare apprehension lest your friend
Dazzled by your resplendent course should find   195
Henceforth less sweetness in his own, could
   move
Such earnest mood in you? fear not, dear
   Friend,
That I shall leave you, inwardly repining
Such lot was not my own . . . .

P/.   And this forever!
Forever! gull who may, they will be blind!   200
They will not look nor think—'tis nothing new
In *them*— —but surely *he* is not of them!
My Festus, do you know I reckoned *you*— —
Tho' all beside were sand-blind—you, my
   friend,
Would look at me, once close, with piercing
   eye   205
Untroubled by false glare that well confounds
A weaker vision; would remain serene
Tho' singular amid a gaping throng:
I feared you, or I had come, sure, long ere this
To Einsiedeln: . . . well,—error has no end,   210
And Rhasis is a sage & Basil boasts
A tribe of wits & I am wise & blest
Past all dispute! 'tis vain to fret at it:
I have vowed long ago my worshippers
Shall owe to their own deep sagacity   215
All further information, good or bad:
Small risk indeed my reputation runs

To think bare apprehension lest your friend,
Dazzled by your resplendent course, might find   195
Henceforth less sweetness in his own, could
    move
Such earnest mood in you? Fear not, dear
    friend,
That I shall leave you, inwardly repining
Your lot was not my own!
    Paracelsus.   And this for ever!
For ever! gull who may, they will be gulled!   200
They will not look nor think; 't is nothing new
In them: but surely he is not of them!
My Festus, do you know, I reckoned, you—
Though all beside were sand-blind—you, my
    friend,
Would look at me, once close, with piercing
    eye   205
Untroubled by the false glare that confounds
A weaker vision: would remain serene,
Though singular, amid a gaping throng.
I feared you, or I had come, sure, long ere this,
To Einsiedeln. Well, error has no end,   210
And Rhasis is a sage, and Basil boasts
A tribe of wits, and I am wise and blest
Past all dispute! 'T is vain to fret at it.
I have vowed long ago my worshippers
Shall owe to their own deep sagacity   215
All further information, good or bad.
Small risk indeed my reputation runs,

194 *Berg* {rejected} To think that apprehension   196 *1849–1865* own,
awakes   200 *1849* they will be blind!   201 *1849* think—   205 *1849*
eye,   *208 {Reading of *1849,1863.*}   *1865–89* singular   209 *1849* or had
come,   214 *1849* long since that my worshippers   216 *1849* bad: 217
1849 And little risk my reputation runs,

204 *sand-blind*: 'Having a defect in the eyes, by which small particles appear
to fly before them': Johnson. Cf. *The Merchant of Venice*, II. ii. 31 and 67.
    208 *singular*: alone, unique.
    211 *Rhasis*: under 'Razi, Mohammed Abou-Bekr Ibn Zacaria', the *Biographie
Universelle* devotes four pages to this Arab physician, who is remembered
above all for his treatise on Smallpox. It is characteristic of Paracelsus to have
attacked him, as his writings were widely used as textbooks.

Unless perchance the glance no[w] searching
  me
Be fixed much longer . . . for it seems to spell
Dimly the characters a simpler man   220
Might read distinct enough: old Eastern books
Say the fallen Prince of Morning some short
  space
Remained unchanged in seeming— —nay his
  brow
Was hued with triumph: every spirit then
Praising; *his* heart on flame the while: a tale!   225
Well, Festus, what discover you, I pray?

F/.   Some foul deed sullies then a life which
  else
Were raised above— — —

P/.   Good: I do well—most well!
Why strive to make them know & feel & fret
Themselves with what 'tis past their power to
  know,   230
Or feel, or comprehend? Still,—having nursed
The faint surmise that one yet walked the earth,
One, at least, not the utter fool of shew,
Not absolutely formed to be the dupe
Of shallow plausibilities alone;—   235
One who, in youth found wise enough to
  choose
That happiness his riper years approve,
Was yet so anxious for another's sake
That ere his Friend could rush upon a mad
And ruinous course, the converse of his own,   240

1835 221 enough.   222 prince of morning   225 while . . .   229 know,
and feel,   239 friend

Unless perchance the glance now searching
   me
Be fixed much longer; for it seems to spell
Dimly the characters a simpler man   220
Might read distinct enough. Old Eastern books
Say, the fallen prince of morning some short
   space
Remained unchanged in semblance; nay, his
   brow
Was hued with triumph: every spirit then
Praising, *his* heart on flame the while:—a tale!   225
Well, Festus, what discover you, I pray?
   Festus. Some foul deed sullies then a life
     which else
Were raised supreme?
   Paracelsus.   Good: I do well, most well!
Why strive to make men hear, feel, fret themselves
With what is past their power to
   comprehend?   230
I should not strive now: only, having nursed
The faint surmise that one yet walked the earth,
One, at least, not the utter fool of show,
Not absolutely formed to be the dupe
Of shallow plausibilities alone: 235
One who, in youth, found wise enough to
   choose
The happiness his riper years approve,
Was yet so anxious for another's sake,
That, ere his friend could rush upon a mad
And ruinous course, the converse of his own,   240

219, 220 *1849* longer—for it seems to spell, | Dimly,   223 *1849* unchanged in feature—nay,   224 *1849* Seemed hued   225 *1849* Praising;   *228 {Reading of *1863–68.*}   *1849* well—most well!   *1888,1889* well, most well   230 *1849–68* what 'tis *Berg* what ⟨t⟩ is   231 *1849* I would not 239 *1849* upon a course   240 *1849* Mad, ruinous, the converse of his own,

221 *Old Eastern books*: cf. *Paradise Lost*, i. 591 ff.
228 *supreme?*: 'admirable—Festus not taking his meaning[?]—failure': Domett.
233 *fool of show*: cf. (e.g.) 'The natural fool of fortune': *King Lear*, IV. vi. 192.
237 *approve*: "To make, or show, to be worthy of approbation': Johnson.

His gentle spirit had already tried
The perilous path, foreseen its destiny
And warned the weak one in such tender words
—   Such accents—his whole heart in every one—
That they oft served to comfort him, in hours   245
When they, by right, should have increased
   despair;— —
Having believed, I say, such happy One
Could never lose the light thus from the first
His portion,—I can not refuse to grieve
Even at my gain if it disturb our old   250
Relation,—if it make *me* out the wiser . . . .
Therefore, once more reminding him how well
He prophesied, I note the single flaw
That seems to cross his title: in plain words
You were deceived, & thus were you
   deceived:—   255
I have not been successful, & yet am
Most miserable; 'tis said at last; nor you
Give credit, lest you force me to believe
That common sense yet lives upon the world.
F/.   You surely do not mean to banter me?   260
P/.   You know,—or, (—if you have been wise
   enough
To cleanse your memory of such matters,—)
   knew,
As far as words of mine could make it clear,
That 'twas my purpose to find joy or grief
Alone in the fulfilment of my plan,   265
Or plot, or whatsoe'er it was:—rejoicing
Alone as it proceeded prosperously;—

His gentle spirit essayed, prejudged for him
The perilous path, foresaw its destiny,
And warned the weak one in such tender words,
Such accents—his whole heart in every tone—
That oft their memory comforted that friend   245
When it by right should have increased
     despair:
—Having believed, I say, that this one man
Could never lose the light thus from the first
His portion—how should I refuse to grieve
At even my gain if it disturb our old   250
Relation, if it make me out more wise?
Therefore, once more reminding him how well
He prophesied, I note the single flaw
That spoils his prophet's title. In plain words,
You were deceived, and thus were you
     deceived—   255
I have not been successful, and yet am
Most miserable; 't is said at last; nor you
Give credit, lest you force me to concede
That common sense yet lives upon the world!
     Festus. You surely do not mean to banter me?   260
     Paracelsus. You know, or—if you have been
          wise enough
To cleanse your memory of such matters—
     knew,
As far as words of mine could make it clear,
That 't was my purpose to find joy or grief
Solely in the fulfilment of my plan   265
Or plot or whatsoe'er it was; rejoicing
Alone as it proceeded prosperously,

---

241 *1849* His gentler spirit   245 *Berg* {rejected} That oft their memory
comforted the soul in hours {'soul' not clear. 'sad' may be the intended word.}
246 *1849* When rather it should have increased despair: *Berg* {rejected} When
such by right should have increased despair: 248 *1849* lose the wisdom
from 250–1 *1849* At even my gain if it attest his loss, | At triumph which so
signally disturbs | Our old relation, proving me more wise? 254 *1849* That
spoils his prophet's title: in plain words *Berg* {rejected} That seems to cross a
prophet's title: plainly, 257–8 *1849* Most wretched; there—'tis said at last;
but give | No credit, lest you force me to concede 259 *1849* the
earth. *1863,1865* the world. 261 *1849* or (if you 262 *1849* matters)
knew,

Sorrowing then only, when mischance retarded
Its progress: nor was this the scheme of one   269
Enamoured of a lot unlike the world's,   269a
And thus far sure from common casualty   b
(Folly of follies!) in that, thus; the Mind   c
Became the only arbiter of fate:—   d
No: what I termed, & might conceive my
    choice   e
Already had been rooted in my soul— —   f
Had long been part & portion of my self: g
Not to prolong a theme I thoroughly hate,—   270
I have since followed it with all my strength,
And having failed therein most signally,
Cannot object to ruin utter & drear
As all-excelling would have been the prize
Had fortune favoured me: I scarce have right   275
To vex your frank good spirit late so glad
In my supposed prosperity I know,—
And were I lucky in a glut of friends
Would well agree to let your error live,
And strengthen it with fables of success;—   280
But I'm in no condition to refuse
The transient solace of so rare a Godsend,
My solitary luxury, my one friend;
Accordingly I venture to put off
The wearisome vest of falsehood galling me,   285
Secure when he is by: I lay me bare
And at his mercy— — —but he is my friend!
Not that he needs retain his grave respect—
That answers not my purpose; for 'tis like,
Some sunny morning,—Basil being drained   290
Of its wise population—every corner
Of the Amphitheatre crammed with learned
    clerks—
Here Æcolampadius looking worlds of wit

1835 269 Its progress.   269b casualty—   269c thus, the mind   269d
fate.   269g myself.   271 strength;   275 favour'd me.   276
spirit,   277 prosperity, I know;   280 success.   283 luxury—   286
by.   291 population,   292 amphitheatre . . . . clerks,   293 Œcolam-
padius, looking . . . . wit;

Sorrowing then only when mischance retarded
Its progress. That was in those Würzburg days!
Not to prolong a theme I thoroughly hate,   270
I have pursued this plan with all my strength;
And having failed therein most signally,
Cannot object to ruin utter and drear
As all-excelling would have been the prize
Had fortune favoured me. I scarce have right   275
To vex your frank good spirit late so glad
In my supposed prosperity, I know,
And, were I lucky in a glut of friends,
Would well agree to let your error live,
Nay, strengthen it with fables of success.   280
But mine is no condition to refuse
The transient solace of so rare a godsend,
My solitary luxury, my one friend:
Accordingly I venture to put off
The wearisome vest of falsehood galling me,   285
Secure when he is by. I lay me bare,
Prone at his mercy—but he is my friend!
Not that he needs retain his aspect grave;
That answers not my purpose; for 't is like,
Some sunny morning—Basil being drained   290
Of its wise population, every corner
Of the amphitheatre crammed with learned
    clerks,
Here Œcolampadius, looking worlds of wit,

268 *1849* Sorrowing alone when any chance retarded   275 *1849* I scarce do right   276 *1849* spirit, late rejoiced *1863,1865* spirit, late so glad   277 *1849* By my supposed   278 *Berg* And, were I (lucky in) [troubled with] a glut of friends,   280 *1849* success: 282 *1849* so rare a chance,   283 *1849* luxury, my Festus—

293 *Œcolampadius:* see Browning's note, p. 507 below.

Here Castellanus as profound as he,
Munsterus here, Frobenius there . . all squeezed   295
And staring;—that the zany of the Shew,
Even Paracelsus, shall put off before them
His trappings with a grace not seldom judged
Expedient in such cases:—the grim smile
That will go round!—Is it not therefore best   300
To venture a rehearsal like the present
In a small way?—where are the signs I seek,
The first-fruits & fair sample of the scorn
Due to all Quacks? why, this will never do!

F/.   These are foul vapours, Aureole; nought   305
    beside!
The effect of watching, study, weariness,— —
Were there a spark of truth in the confusion
Of these wild words, you would not outrage
    thus
Your youth's companion: . . I shall ne'er regard
These wanderings, bred of faintness & much
    study.— — —   310
Tis not thus you would trust a trouble to me,

1835 294 Castellanus, as . . . . he;   295 there;   296 staring—that . . . .
show,   299 cases.   304 quacks?   306 weariness.   309 compan-
ion.   310 study.

Here Castellanus, as profound as he,
Munsterus here, Frobenius there, all squeezed   295
And staring,—that the zany of the show,
Even Paracelsus, shall put off before them
His trappings with a grace but seldom judged
Expedient in such cases:—the grim smile
That will go round! Is it not therefore best   300
To venture a rehearsal like the present
In a small way? Where are the signs I seek,
The first-fruits and fair sample of the scorn
Due to all quacks? Why, this will never do!
    Festus. These are foul vapours, Aureole;
      nought beside!   305
The effect of watching, study, weariness.
Were there a spark of truth in the confusion
Of these wild words, you would not outrage
    thus
Your youth's companion. I shall ne'er regard
These wanderings, bred of faintness and much
    study.   310
'T is not thus you would trust a trouble to me,

---

295 *1849* there,—all squeezed, *1863,65* there, all squeezed, 296–8 *1849* And
staring, and expectant,—then, I say, | 'Tis like that the poor zany of the show, |
Your friend, will choose to put his trappings off | Before them, bid adieu to cap
and bells | And motley with a grace but seldom judged   296 *Berg* {rejected}
the main zany   311 *1849* You would not trust a trouble thus to me,

294 *Castellanus*: Pierre Duchatel, 'en latin Castellanus', as the *Biographie
Universelle* notes, was 'attracted to Bâle by the great reputation of Erasmus,
who placed him with Frobenius, in the capacity of a corrector of the press, an
honourable situation at that time, when it was given only to men learned in the
ancient languages'. He created a great impression by his profound knowledge
of Greek and helped Erasmus with the classical editions on which he was
engaged. Later in life he became Bishop of Orléans and Grand Almoner of
France.
    295 *Munsterus . . . Frobenius*: Sebastian Münster (1489–1552) was a Hebrew
scholar and also a geographer and mathematician. Profoundly influenced by
Luther, he went to Bâle in 1529, and there taught Hebrew and then Theology
with much acclamation. Frobenius (Johannes Froben) set up as a printer in Bâle
in 1491, learned the classical languages, became a friend of Erasmus, and is
remembered as one of the great printers and encouragers of learning. See 480 n.
and 915 n, below.
    305 *foul vapours*: depressing illusions.
    306 *watching*: remaining awake.
    309 *regard*: 'To value; to attend to as worthy of notice': Johnson.

To Michal's friend:

P/.   I have said it, dearest Festus:
For the manner— —'tis ungracious
    probably—
—   You may have it told in broken sobs one day
And scalding tears, ere long—I thought it best   315
To keep that off as long as possible: . . . .
Do you wonder still?

F/.   No: it must oft fall out
That he whose labour perfects any work
Shall rise from it with eye so worn, that he
Least of all men can measure the extent   320
Of that he has accomplished;—he alone,
Who, nothing tasked is nothing weary, *he*
Can clearly scan the little he has done:—
But we,—the bystanders, untouched by toil,
We estimate aright . . . . .

P/.   This worthy Festus   325
Is one of them, at last! Tis so with all:
First they set down all progress as a dream,
And next, when he, whose quick discomfiture
Was counted on—accomplishes some few
And doubtful steps in his career,—behold   330
They look for every inch of ground to vanish
Beneath his tread, so sure they spy success!

F/.   Few, doubtful steps? . . . when death retires
      before
Your presence,—when the noblest of mankind
Broken in body, yet untired in Spirit   335
May thro' your skill renew their vigour, raise
The shattered frame to pristine stateliness . . . .

1835 312 friend.   313 ungracious, probably;   315 ere long.   316 pos-
sible.   321 accomplish'd.   325 We estimate aright. | *Par.* This, worthy
Festus,   329 on,   332 tread—   333 Few doubtful steps?   335
spirit,   337 shatter'd . . . . stateliness:

To Michal's friend.
   Paracelsus.   I have said it, dearest Festus!
For the manner, 't is ungracious
   probably;
You may have it told in broken sobs, one day,
And scalding tears, ere long: but I thought best   315
To keep that off as long as possible.
Do you wonder still?
   Festus.   No; it must oft fall out
That one whose labour perfects any work,
Shall rise from it with eye so worn that he
Of all men least can measure the extent   320
Of what he has accomplished. He alone
Who, nothing tasked, is nothing weary too,
May clearly scan the little he effects:
But we, the bystanders, untouched by toil,
Estimate each aright.
   Paracelsus.   This worthy Festus   325
Is one of them, at last! 'T is so with all!
First, they set down all progress as a dream;
And next, when he whose quick discomfiture
Was counted on, accomplishes some few
And doubtful steps in his career,—behold,   330
They look for every inch of ground to vanish
Beneath his tread, so sure they spy success!
   Festus. Few doubtful steps? when death retires
   before
Your presence—when the noblest of mankind,
Broken in body or subdued in soul,   335
May through your skill renew their vigour, raise
The shattered frame to pristine stateliness?

---

313 *1849* The manner is ungracious, probably;   *1863,1865* For the manner, 'tis
ungracious, probably;   314 *1849* More may be told   321 *1863* ac-
complished He alone,   *1865* accomplished. He alone,   323 *1849* Can clearly
scan   327 *1849* dream, *1865* dream   332 *1849* they judge success!
334 *Berg* Your presence?—When   335 *1849* subdued in mind,

---

315 *scalding tears*: as in Shelley, 'Julian and Maddalo', 477.

That Men in racking pain may purchase dreams
Of what delights them most—swooning at
     once
Into a sea of bliss—or rapt along   340
As in a flying sphere of turbulent light—
When we may look to you as one ordained
To free the flesh from fell disease, as frees
Our Luther's burning tongue the fettered
     soul,—
When . . . . .

P/.   And when & where the devil did you
     get   345
This notable news?

F/.   — Even from the common voice;
From those whose envy, daring not dispute
The wonders it descries, attributes them
To magic & such folly;—

P/.   Folly?— —why not
To magic, pray?—you find a comfort doubtless   350
In holding God ne'er troubles him about
Us or our doings:—once we were judged
     worth
The devil's tempting— — —I offend: forgive
     me,
And rest content: your prophecy on the whole
Was fair enough as prophesyings go,—   355
—   At fault a little in detail, but quite

1835 338 When men   340 bliss,   341 light: 344 soul: 348 it
decries,   349 folly.   354 content.   355 go;

When men in racking pain may purchase dreams
Of what delights them most, swooning at
  once
Into a sea of bliss or rapt along   340
As in a flying sphere of turbulent light?
When we may look to you as one ordained
To free the flesh from fell disease, as frees
Our Luther's burning tongue the fettered
  soul?
When . . .
  Paracelsus. When and where, the devil, did you
    get   345
This notable news?
  Festus.   Even from the common voice;
From those whose envy, daring not dispute
The wonders it decries, attributes them
To magic and such folly.
  Paracelsus.   Folly? Why not
To magic, pray? You find a comfort doubtless   350
In holding, God ne'er troubles him about
Us or our doings: once we were judged
  worth
The devil's tempting . . . I offend: forgive
  me,
And rest content. Your prophecy on the whole
Was fair enough as prophesyings go;   355
At fault a little in detail, but quite

---

339 *1849* most—   345 *1849* Rather, when and where, friend, did you get

338 *may purchase dreams*: a reference to his liberal use of laudanum (Brown-ing's note 5, on p. 509 below). The imagery which follows recalls that of dreams described by de Quincey and others.
343 *fell disease*: cf. Gray, 'Ode to Adversity', 40.
344 *Our Luther's burning tongue*: by this time Martin Luther had been con-demned at the Council of Worms and had broken with the Roman Catholic Church. Paracelsus was often compared with him: see 964 n. below.
349–50 *Why not / To magic, pray?*: 'That which gives healing power to a medicine is its "Spiritus" (an ethereal essence or principle), and it is only perceptible by the senses of the sidereal man. It therefore follows that Magic is a teacher of medicine far preferable to all written books. Magic power alone . . . is the true teacher, preceptor, and pedagogue, to teach the art of curing the sick': Hartmann, p. 54.

Precise enough in the main; & hereupon
I pay due homage: you guessed long ago
(The prophet) I should fail . . . . & I have failed.

F/. You mean to tell me, then,—the hopes which
fed   360
Your youth have not been realized as yet?

—   Some obstacle has barred them hitherto,—
Or that their innate . . .

P/.   As I said but now
You have a very decent prophet's fame
So you but shun these details;—little matters   365
Whether those hopes were mad & what they
sought
Safe & secure from all ambitious fools,—
Or whether my weak wits are overcome
By what a better spirit would scorn:—I fail.
And now methinks 'twere best to change the
theme.   370
I am a sad fool to have stumbled on it— —
I say confusedly what comes uppermost . . . .
But there are times when patience proves at
fault,—
As now;—this morning's strange encounter
—you
Beside me once again! you, whom I guessed   375
Alive, since hitherto, (with Luther's leave)
No friend have I among the saints above;

Precise enough in the main; and hereupon
I pay due homage: you guessed long ago
(The prophet!) I should fail—and I have failed.
   Festus. You mean to tell me, then, the hopes
      which fed   360
Your youth have not been realized as yet?
Some obstacle has barred them hitherto?
Or that their innate . . .
   Paracelsus.   As I said but now,
You have a very decent prophet's fame,
So you but shun details here. Little matter   365
Whether those hopes were mad,—the aims they
      sought,
Safe and secure from all ambitious fools;
Or whether my weak wits are overcome
By what a better spirit would scorn: I fail.
And now methinks 't were best to change a
      theme   370
I am a sad fool to have stumbled on.
I say confusedly what comes uppermost;
But there are times when patience proves at
      fault,
As now: this morning's strange encounter—
      you
Beside me once again! you, whom I guessed   375
Alive, since hitherto (with Luther's leave)
No friend have I among the saints at peace,

---

357 *1849* in the main; accordingly   365 *1849* Little matters   377 *1849* the
saints at rest,

   360–1 *the hopes which fed | Your youth*: Pottle rightly compares Shelley,
'Hymn to Intellectual Beauty', 53: 'poisonous names with which our youth is
fed'.
   365 *details*: stressed on the second syllable, as in Johnson.
   377 *the saints at peace*: Luther opposed the doctrine of the intercession of the
saints, i.e. the teaching that the spirits of those who are in blessedness may pray
for those who are still in this life.

(The poor mad poet is howling by this time:)   387
—   I could not quite repress the varied feelings
This meeting wakens,—they have had their
          way,   390
And now forget them:—do the rear-mice still
Hang like a fret-work on the gate, (or what
In my time, was a gate) fronting the road
From Einsiedeln to Lachen?
F/.   — Trifle not:
Answer me—for my sake alone:—you smiled   395
Just now, when I supposed some deed
          unworthy
Yourself, might blot the else so bright result—
But if your motives have continued pure,

1835 378–386 {No equivalent in *MS* or *1835*.}   387 time)—   390
wakens;   391 them,   395 alone.   397 Yourself might . . . . result;

To judge by any good their prayers effect.
I knew you would have helped me—why not he,
My strange competitor in enterprise,   380
Bound for the same end by another path,
Arrived, or ill or well, before the time,
At our disastrous journey's doubtful close?
How goes it with Aprile? Ah, they miss
Your lone sad sunny idleness of heaven,   385
Our martyrs for the world's sake; heaven shuts
     fast:
The poor mad poet is howling by this time!
Since you are my sole friend then, here or there,
I could not quite repress the varied feelings
This meeting wakens; they have had their vent,   390
And now forget them. Do the rear-mice still
Hang like a fretwork on the gate (or what
In my time was a gate) fronting the road
From Einsiedeln to Lachen?
          Festus.   Trifle not:
Answer me, for my sake alone! You smiled   395
Just now, when I supposed some deed, unworthy
Yourself, might blot the else so bright result;
Yet if your motives have continued pure,

---

378 *1849–65* effect— *Berg* ⟨produce⟩ [effect]— *1868* effect: 379 *1849*
helped me!—So would He,   *1863,1865* helped me!—Why not He.   380–2
Berg {rejected} My bright competitor in enterprize, | Fellow in travel by
another path, | Arrived, for good or ill, before the time,   383 *1849*
close— *Berg* ⟨end—⟩ [close—]   384 *1849* Ah, your heaven   385 *1849*
Receives not into its beatitudes   *Berg* {rejected} Extends not its beatitudes so
far   *1863,1865* Your lone, sad, sunny idleness of Heaven,   386 *1849* Mere
martyrs . . . . heaven   *1863,1865* Our martyrs . . . . Heaven *Berg* ⟨To him
and me—⟩ mere martyrs ⟨of⟩ [for] the world's sake—⟨him or me⟩   388
Berg ⟨So⟩ [Since] you are my sole friend ⟨in {?} heaven or earth;⟩ [then here or
there,]   390 *Berg* {rejected} Our meeting   394 *1849* Trifle not!   395
1849 Answer me—for . . . . alone.   *1863,1865* Answer me, for . . . . alone.

---

384 *Aprile*: because he, unlike Festus, is already dead. But having been
merely one of the 'martyrs for the world's sake', he is not in heaven.
387 *The poor mad poet*: the contemptuous manner in which he here refers to
Aprile throws light on the bitterness in the heart of Paracelsus, at this point:
Festus senses his mood. When he comes to the end of his own life Paracelsus
sees matters in a different light: cf. v. 110 ff.
391 *rear-mice*: bats.

Your earnest will, unfaultering— —if you still
Remain unchanged, & if in spite of all   399a
You have experienced the defeat you tell . . .   400
I say not, you would cheerfully resign
The contest— —mortal hearts are not so
  fashioned . . .
But surely you would ne'ertheless resign;
You sought not Fame, nor Gain, nor even
  Love—
No end distinct from Knowledge:—I repeat   405
Your very words:—once satisfied that
  Knowledge
Is a mere dream, you would announce as much,
Yourself the first:— —but how is the event?
You are defeated . . . & I find you *here*! . .
P/.   As tho' *"here"* did not signify
  defeat!   410
I spoke not of my labours *here*:—past doubt
I am quite competent to answer all   411a
Demands, in any such capacity,—   b
But of the break-down of my general aims:
For you—aware of their extent & scope—
To look on these sage lecturings, commended
By silly beardless boys, & bearded dotards,   415
As a fit consummation of those aims
Is worthy notice:—a professorship
At Basil! . . . since you see so much in it,—
Since 'tis but just my life should have been
  drained

1835 399 will unfaltering: 403 resign.   404,405 fame, nor gain, nor even
love; | No . . . . knowledge.   406 words: once . . . . knowledge   408
first.   411 *here*—past   413 you, aware . . . . scope,   417 notice—
418 Basil! Since . . . . it;

Your will unfaltering, and in spite of
    this,
You have experienced a defeat, why then   400
I say not you would cheerfully withdraw
From contest—mortal hearts are not so
    fashioned—
But surely you would ne'ertheless withdraw.
You sought not fame nor gain nor even
    love,
No end distinct from knowledge,—I repeat   405
Your very words: once satisfied that
    knowledge
Is a mere dream, you would announce as much,
Yourself the first. But how is the event?
You are defeated—and I find you here!
    Paracelsus. As though "here" did not signify
      defeat!   410
I spoke not of my little labours here,
But of the break-down of my general aims:
For you, aware of their extent and scope,
To look on these sage lecturings, approved
By beardless boys, and bearded dotards worse,   415
As a fit consummation of such aims,
Is worthy notice. A professorship
At Basil! Since you see so much in it,
And think my life was reasonably
    drained

399–402 *1849* Your earnest will unfaltering, if you still | Remain unchanged,
and if, in spite of this, | You have experienced a defeat that proves | Your aims
for ever unattainable— | I say not, you would cheerfully resign | The con-
test—mortal hearts are not so fashioned— *Berg* (l.402) not so ⟨fashion'd⟩
[made)] *1863,1865* Your will unfaltering, and in spite of this, | You have
experienced a defeat, why, then | I say not, you would cheerfully withdraw |
From contest—mortal hearts are not so fashioned— {*1865* has 'withdraw.' in
line 401.}   403 *1849* But sure you would resign it, ne'ertheless. *1863,1865*
But surely you would, ne'ertheless, withdraw.   404 *1849–65* fame, nor gain,
nor even love;   411 *1849* labours here— *1868* labours here   413 *1849*
That you, aware   414 *1849* Should look   415 *1849* dotards,—these
417 *1849–65* worthy notice!

---

410 *"here"*: in Basle, as a Professor.

Of its delights to render me a match   420
For duties arduous as such Post demands, ...
Far be it from me to deny my power
To fill the petty circle lotted out
Of infinite Space, or to deserve the host
Of honours thence accruing: so take notice: 425
This jewel dangling from my neck preserves
The features of a Prince my skill restored
To plague his people some few years to come
. . And all thro' a pure whim—he had eased the
      earth
For me, but that the droll despair which seized   430
The vermin of his household, tickled me:—
—   I came to see:—here, driveled the Physician
Whose most infallible nostrum was at
      fault,— —
There shook the Astrologer in his shoes, whose
      grand
Horoscope promised further score of
      years,— —   435
Here a monk fumbled at [the] sick man's nose
With some undoubted relic . . . a sudary
Of the Virgin,— —while some half-a dozen
      knaves
Of the same brotherhood (he loved them ever)
Were making active preparations for   440
Such a suffumigation as, once fired,
Had stunk the patient dead ere he could groan.
—   I cursed the Doctor, & upset the Wiper,
Brushed past the conjurer—vowed that the first
      gust

1835 421 post demands;   424 space,   425 notice.   427 prince   428
come: 429 And all through a pure whim.   431 me.   432–452
physician, {etc. Lower case initial letters.}   433 fault;   435 years;
438 Virgin; while some half-dozen   443 doctor, and . . . . wiper;   444
Brush'd past the conjurer; vow'd

Of life's delights to render me a match   420
For duties arduous as such post demands,—
Be it far from me to deny my power
To fill the petty circle lotted out
Of infinite space, or justify the host
Of honours thence accruing. So, take notice,   425
This jewel dangling from my neck preserves
The features of a prince, my skill restored
To plague his people some few years to come:
And all through a pure whim. He had eased the
          earth
For me, but that the droll despair which seized   430
The vermin of his household, tickled me.
I came to see. Here, drivelled the physician,
Whose most infallible nostrum was at
          fault;
There quaked the astrologer, whose
          horoscope
Had promised him interminable
          years;   435
Here a monk fumbled at the sick man's mouth
With some undoubted relic—a sudary
Of the Virgin; while another piebald
          knave
Of the same brotherhood (he loved them ever)
Was actively preparing 'neath his nose   440
Such a suffumigation as, once fired,
Had stunk the patient dead ere he could groan.
I cursed the doctor and upset the brother,
Brushed past the conjurer, vowed that the first
          gust

422 *1849,1863* Far be it from   424 *1849* From infinite   425 *1849* accru-
ing: 432 *1849* see: 438 *1849* while some other dozen knaves   440
1849 Were actively preparing   443 *1849–65* doctor, and upset the
brother;   444 *1849–65* conjurer;

423 *the petty circle lotted out*: cf. Henry More, *Philosophicall Poems*, p. 114: 'And
so of life they'll want their 'lotted fee'.
429–30 *He had eased the earth / For me*: he might have relieved the world of his
presence, so far as I was concerned . . .
437 *sudary*: 'a napkin or handkerchief used to wipe sweat or tears from the
face . . .; *esp.* such a napkin venerated as a relic of a saint': OED.

Of stench from the ingredients just alight   445
Would raise a cross-grained devil in my sword
Not easily laid:—& ere an hour the Prince
Slept as he never slept since Prince he was.
A day—& I was posting for my life
Placarded thro' the Town as one whose spite   450
Had near availed to stop the blessed effects
Of the Doctor's nostrum, which, well seconded
By the sudary, & most by the costly smoke,
—   Not leaving out the strenuous prayers sent up
Hard by, in the Abbey,—raised the Prince to
    life   455
To the great reputation of the Sage
Who, confident, expected all along
The glad event— —the Doctor's recompense . . .
Much largess from his Highness to the
    Monks,— —
And the vast solace of his loving people,   460
Whose general satisfaction to increase
The Prince was pleased no longer to defer
The burning of some dozen heretics
Remanded 'till God's mercy should be shown
Touching his sickness: last of all, were joined   465
Ample directions to all loyal folk
To seize myself, to swell the complement,
Who, doubtless some rank sorcerer, had
    endeavoured
To thwart these pious offices— — —obstruct
The Prince's cure, & frustrate all, by help   470
Of certain devils dwelling in his sword
By luck, the Prince in his first fit of thanks
Had forced this bauble on me as an earnest

1835 453 smoke—   455 abbey—raised the prince to life;   468
Who—doubtless . . . . sorcerer—   469 offices,   471 his sword: {MS
has 'my' written below 'his' in pencil.}

Of stench from the ingredients just alight   445
Would raise a cross-grained devil in my sword,
Not easily laid: and ere an hour the prince
Slept as he never slept since prince he was.
A day—and I was posting for my life,
Placarded through the town as one whose spite   450
Had near availed to stop the blessed effects
Of the doctor's nostrum which, well seconded
By the sudary, and most by the costly smoke—
Not leaving out the strenuous prayers sent up
Hard by in the abbey—raised the prince to
    life: 455
To the great reputation of the seer
Who, confident, expected all along
The glad event—the doctor's recompense—
Much largess from his highness to the
    monks—
And the vast solace of his loving people,   460
Whose general satisfaction to increase,
The prince was pleased no longer to defer
The burning of some dozen heretics
Remanded till God's mercy should be shown
Touching his sickness: last of all were joined   465
Ample directions to all loyal folk
To swell the complement by seizing me
Who—doubtless some rank sorcerer—
    endeavoured
To thwart these pious offices, obstruct
The prince's cure, and frustrate heaven by help   470
Of certain devils dwelling in his sword.
By luck, the prince in his first fit of thanks
Had forced this bauble on me as an earnest

---

465 {followed by additional line:} *1849* Touching his sickness, as a prudent
pledge | To make it surer: last of all were joined   468 *1849–65* sor-
cerer—had endeavoured

446 *a . . . devil in my sword*: cf. Browning's note (5), below, on p. 509.
449 *posting*: 'To post: To travel with speed': Johnson.
470 *frustrate*: stressed on the first syllable, as in Johnson.
473 *this bauble*: see line 426.

Of further favours: this one case may serve
To give sufficient taste of many such,   475
So let them pass:— — —those shelves support
   a pile
Of Patents, Licenses, Diplomas, got
In France & Spain & Italy, as well
As Germany:—they authorize my claims   478a
To honour from the world—nevertheless
I set more store by this Erasmus sends— —   480
He trusts me—our Frobenius is his friend
And him I raised (nay, read it) from the
   dead;— —
I weary you, I see . . I merely sought
To show there's no great wonder after all
That while I fill the class-room & attract   485
A crowd to Basil, I have leave to stay;
And that I need not scruple to accept
The utmost they can offer . . . if I love it:
For 'tis but right the world should be prepared
To treat especially the several wants   490
Of one like me, used up in serving her— —
Just as the mortal, whom the Gods in part
Devoured, received in place of his lost limb
Some virtue or other—cured disease, I think;—
You mind the fables we have read together.   495

Of further favours. This one case may serve
To give sufficient taste of many such,   475
So, let them pass. Those shelves support
      a pile
Of patents, licences, diplomas, titles
From Germany, France, Spain, and Italy;
They authorize some honour;
      ne'ertheless,
I set more store by this Erasmus sent;   480
He trusts me; our Frobenius is his friend,
And him "I raised" (nay, read it) "from the
      dead."
I weary you, I see. I merely sought
To show, there 's no great wonder after all
That, while I fill the class-room and attract   485
A crowd to Basil, I get leave to stay,
And therefore need not scruple to accept
The utmost they can offer, if I please:
For 't is but right the world should be prepared
To treat with favour e'en fantastic wants   490
Of one like me, used up in serving her.
Just as the mortal, whom the gods in part
Devoured, received in place of his lost limb
Some virtue or other—cured disease, I think;
You mind the fables we have read together.   495

---

476 *1849* So let them pass: *1863, 1865* So let them pass.   478 *1865* Italy   479
Berg honour: nevertheless,   482 *1849* dead" . . .   483 *1849* see;   486
1849–68 stay;   488 *1849–65* offer—

480 *this Erasmus sent*: 'Frobenium ab inferis revocasti', Erasmus wrote to
Paracelsus, 'hoc est dimidium mei' ('you have recalled Frobenius, who is half
of myself, from the dead)': the letter was available to Browning in the *Vitae
Germanorum Medicorum* of Melchior Adamus (Heidelberg, 1620, p. 37), and
elsewhere. Cf. p 509 n. below. It was early in 1527 that Paracelsus went to
Basle and cured a leg which Frobenius had been advised to have amputated.
492 *the mortal*: Pelops, whose limbs were served to the gods as food by his
father, Tantalus, king of Phrygia, who wished to 'try the divinity of the gods'.
Only Ceres, 'whom the recent loss of her daughter had rendered melancholy
and inattentive', ate of the meat. She ate a shoulder, 'and therefore when Jupiter
. . . restored him to life, he placed a shoulder of ivory instead of that which
Ceres had devoured. This shoulder . . . could heal by its very touch, every
complaint, and remove every disorder': Lemprière.

F/.   You do not think I comprehend a word:
        The time was, Aureole, when you were not
            slow
        To clothe the airiest thoughts in specious
            words;—
        But surely you must feel how vague and
            strange
        These speeches sound.
P/.   Well then: you know my hopes;   500
        I am assured at length, they may not be:
        That Truth is just as far from me as ever:
        That I have thrown my life away— —that
            sorrow
        On that account is vain & further effort
        To mend & patch what's marred beyond
            repairing   505
        As useless : & all this was taught to me
        By the convincing, good old fashioned method
        Of force—by sheer compulsion:—Is that plain?
F/.   Dear Aureole! can it be my fears were
            just!
        God wills not . . .
P/.   Now 'tis this I most admire—   510
        The constant talk men of your stamp keep up
        Of God's will,—as they style it . . . one would
            swear
        Man had but merely to uplift his eye,
        To see the will in question charactered
        On the heaven's vault: . . . 'tis hardly wise to
            moot   515
        Such topics:—doubts are many & faith is
            weak:—
        I know as much of any will of His

1835 502 truth . . . . ever;   503 away;   504 vain, and   508 compul-
sion.   512 will, as they style it;   515 vault.   516 topics: doubts . . . .
weak.

Festus. You do not think I comprehend a word.
The time was, Aureole, you were apt
     enough
To clothe the airiest thoughts in specious
     breath;
But surely you must feel how vague and
     strange
These speeches sound.
     Paracelsus.   Well, then: you know my hopts;   500
I am assured, at length, those hopes were vain;
That truth is just as far from me as ever;
That I have thrown my life away; that
     sorrow
On that account is idle, and further effort
To mend and patch what 's marred beyond
     repairing,   505
As useless: and all this was taught your friend
By the convincing good old-fashioned method
Of force—by sheer compulsion. Is that plain?
     Festus. Dear Aureole, can it be my fears were
          just?
God wills not . . .
     Paracelsus.   Now, 't is this I most admire— 510
The constant talk men of your stamp keep up
Of God's will, as they style it; one would
     swear
Man had but merely to uplift his eye,
And see the will in question charactered
On the heaven's vault. 'T is hardly wise to
     moot   515
Such topics: doubts are many and faith is
     weak.
I know as much of any will of God

---

496 *1849* word: 502 *1865* ever   504 *1849* is vain, and   506 *1849–65* was
taught to me   509 *1849* Dear Aureole! you confess my fears were
just? *1863, 1865* Aureole! can   514 *1849* To see   517 *1849, 1863* will of
God's, *1865* will of God's

---

510 *I most admire*: I find most astonishing.
517 *I know as much*: cf. 'Caliban upon Setebos'.

As knows some dumb & tortured brute of
    what
His stern lord wills from the bewildering blows
That plague him every way,—& there, of
    course,   520
Where least he suffers, longest he will stay:—
My case: & for such reasons I plod on . . .
Subdued, but not convinced: I know as little
Why I deserve to fail, as why I hoped
Better things in my youth . . . . I simply know   525
I am no master here but trained & beaten
Into the path I tread;—& here I stay
Until some further intimation reach me
Like an obedient drudge;—& though I like
The best to view the whole thing as a task   530
Imposed—which, dull or pleasant, must be
    done, ...
Yet, I deny not, there is made provision
Of joys which tastes less jaded might affect;—
Nay, some which please me too, for all my
    pride . . .
Pleasures that once were pains; the iron-ring   535
Festering about a slave's neck, grows at length
Into the flesh it eats— — —I hate no longer
A host of petty, vile delights—undreamed of
Or spurned, before:—such now supply the
    place
Of my dead Aims; as in the Autumn woods   540
Where tall trees flourished—from their very
    roots
Springs up a fungous brood, sickly & pale,
Chill mushrooms, coloured like a corpse's
    cheek . . . .

1835 521 stay: 523 convinced.   525 youth.   531 done—   537 eats.
538 delights, undream'd   540 aims: as . . . autumn

As knows some dumb and tortured brute what
    Man,
His stern lord, wills from the perplexing blows
That plague him every way; but there, of
    course,   520
Where least he suffers, longest he remains—
My case; and for such reasons I plod on,
Subdued but not convinced. I know as little
Why I deserve to fail, as why I hoped
Better things in my youth. I simply know   525
I am no master here, but trained and beaten
Into the path I tread; and here I stay,
Until some further intimation reach me,
Like an obedient drudge. Though I prefer
To view the whole thing as a task imposed   530
Which, whether dull or pleasant, must be
    done—
Yet, I deny not, there is made provision
Of joys which tastes less jaded might affect;
Nay, some which please me too, for all my
    pride—
Pleasures that once were pains: the iron ring   535
Festering about a slave's neck grows at length
Into the flesh it eats. I hate no longer
A host of petty vile delights, undreamed of
Or spurned before; such now supply the
    place
Of my dead aims: as in the autumn woods   540
Where tall trees used to flourish, from their
    roots
Springs up a fungous brood sickly and pale,
Chill mushrooms coloured like a corpse's
    cheek.

520 *1849* way, and there,   529 *1849* drudge: 530 *Berg* {rejected} To view
this matter {?} as a task imposed,   537 *1849* Part of the flesh it eats. I hate no
more

533 *affect*: like.
542 *fungous*: 'Excrescent; spongy; wanting firmness': Johnson. Pottle com-
pares Shelley, 'The Sensitive Plant', iii. 62–5.

F/. —　　If I interpret well your words, I own
　　　　It troubles me but little that your Aims   545
　　　　Vast in their dawning & most likely grown
　　　　Extravagantly since, have proved abortive:—
　　　　Perchance I am glad—you have the greater
　　　　　　praise;
—　　　Because they are too glorious to be gained,
　　　　You have not blindly clung to them & died   550
　　　　With them: you have not sullenly refused
　　　　To rise, because an angel worsted you
　　　　In wrestling, tho' the world has not your
　　　　　　peer:
　　　　And [tho'] too harsh & sudden is the change
　　　　To yield you pleasure, as yet,—still, you pursue   555
　　　　The ungracious path as though 'twere
　　　　　　rosy-strewn:
　　　　Tis well: & your reward, sooner or later
　　　　Will come from Him whom none e'er served in
　　　　　　vain.

P/.　　Ah! very fine:—for my part I
　　　　　　conceive
　　　　The very pausing from all further toil,   560
　　　　Which you find heinous . . would be as a seal
　　　　To the sincerity of all my deeds:
　　　　To be consistent I should die at once;—
　　　　I calculated on no after-life, . . .
　　　　Nay, was assured no such could be for me,   564a
　　　　Yet—(how crept in, how fostered, I know
　　　　　　not)—   565
　　　　Here am I with as passionate regret
　　　　For youth, & health, & love so vainly lavished,
　　　　As if their preservation had been first

1835 545 aims,   548 Perchance I am glad; you have the greater
praise,   549 Because . . . . gain'd—   551 them—   556 rosy-
strewn.   561 heinous,   564 after-life;

Festus. If I interpret well your words, I own
It troubles me but little that your aims,   545
Vast in their dawning and most likely grown
Extravagantly since, have baffled you.
Perchance I am glad; you merit greater
    praise;
Because they are too glorious to be gained,
You do not blindly cling to them and die;   550
You fell, but have not sullenly refused
To rise, because an angel worsted you
In wrestling, though the world holds not your
    peer;
And though too harsh and sudden is the change
To yield content as yet, still you pursue   555
The ungracious path as though 't were
    rosy-strewn.
'T is well: and your reward, or soon or late,
Will come from him whom no man serves
    in vain.
    Paracelsus. Ah, very fine! For my part, I
    conceive
The very pausing from all further toil,   560
Which you find heinous, would become a seal
To the sincerity of all my deeds.
To be consistent I should die at once;
I calculated on no after-life;
Yet (how crept in, how fostered, I know   565
    not)
Here am I with as passionate regret
For youth and health and love so vainly lavished,
As if their preservation had been first

---

544 *1849* If I interpret well what words I seize,   553 *1849, 1889* peer   555
1849 yet—still,   558 *1849–1865* from Him   561 *1849, 63* would be as a
seal   *1865* would become a seal!   567 *1849* For youth, and health, and love
so vainly lost,

552 *an angel worsted you*: a reference to the story of Jacob and the angel:
Genesis 32:24 ff.
556 *The ungracious path*: cf. Shelley, 'The Cyclops . . . Translated from . . .
Euripides', 117: 'they live in an ungracious land'.

And foremost in my thoughts . . . & this
   strange fact
Humbled me wondrously & had due force   570
In rendering me the less averse to follow
A certain counsel— — —a mysterious
   warning
— — You will not understand— —but 'twas
   a Man
Perishing in my sight, who summoned me   576
As I would shun the ghastly fate I saw
To serve my Race at once— —to wait no
   longer
That God should interfere in my behalf
Nor trust to Time— —but to distrust myself,   580
And give my gains imperfect as they were
To Men:— —I have not leisure to explain
How since, a singular series of events
Has raised me to the station you behold,
Wherein I seem to turn to most account   585
The sad wreck of the past, & to receive
Some feeble glimmering token that God views
And may approve my penance—therefore here
You find me— —doing good as best I may,
And if folks wonder much & profit little   590
'Tis not my fault— —only I shall rejoice
When my part in the farce is shuffled thro',
And the curtain falls:— —I must hold out 'till
   then.
F/.   Till when, dear Aureole?
P/.   Till I'm fairly thrust
From my proud eminence:— —fortune is
   fickle   595
And even Professors fall: should that arrive
I see no sin in ceding to my bent
Whatever that may be— —but not till then: 597a

1835 569 thoughts;   572 counsel, a . . . . warning—   573 man   574–5
{No equivalent in *MS* or *1835*}   578 race at once;   579,580 behalf— |
Nor trust to time;   582 men.   588 penance: 589 may;   591
fault;   595 eminence.   597a then.

And foremost in my thoughts; and this strange
   fact
Humbled me wondrously, and had due force   570
In rendering me the less averse to follow
A certain counsel, a mysterious warning—
You will not understand—but 't was a man
With aims not mine and yet pursued like mine,
With the same fervour and no more success,   575
Perishing in my sight; who summoned me
As I would shun the ghastly fate I saw,
To serve my race at once; to wait no
   longer
That God should interfere in my behalf,
But to distrust myself, put pride away,   580
And give my gains, imperfect as they were,
To men. I have not leisure to explain
How, since, a singular series of events
Has raised me to the station you behold,
Wherein I seem to turn to most account   585
The mere wreck of the past,—perhaps receive
Some feeble glimmering token that God views
And may approve my penance: therefore here
You find me, doing most good or least harm.
And if folks wonder much and profit little   590
'T is not my fault; only, I shall rejoice
When my part in the farce is shuffled through,
And the curtain falls: I must hold out till
   then.
   Festus. Till when, dear Aureole?
   Paracelsus.   Till I'm fairly thrust
From my proud eminence. Fortune is fickle   595
And even professors fall: should that arrive,
I see no sin in ceding to my bent.

571 *1849* In rendering me the more disposed to follow   574 *1849* mine, but
yet pursued like mine,   *Berg* like ⟨them,⟩ [mine,]   576 *1849* Who perished
in my sight; but summoned me   579, {followed by additional line:}   *1849*
'Till God should interfere in my behalf, | And let the next world's knowledge
dawn on this;   580 *1849* put pride away,   *Berg* ⟨cast⟩ [put] pride away,
583 *1849* How since, a strange succession of events   *1863, 1865* How since, a
singular series of events   589 *1849* me—doing . . . . harm:

573 *a man*: Aprile.

You little fancy what rude shocks apprize us
We sin—God's intimations rather fail
In clearness than in energy—'twere well   600
Did they but indicate the course to take
Like that to be forsaken: I would fain
Be spared a further sample . . . here I am
And here I stay, be sure, till forced to flit.

F/.   Be you but firm on that head—long ere
           then   605
All I expect will come to pass, I trust:
The cloud that wraps you will have
           disappeared.
At present, I see small chance of such event:
They praise you here as one whose Lore
           already
Divulged eclipses all the Past can show   610
But whose achiev[em]ents, marvellous as they
           be,
Are faint anticipations of a light
Which shall hereafter be revealed . . . when
           They
Dismiss their teacher, I shall be content
That he depart—

P/.   This favour at their hands   615
I look for earlier than your view of things
Would warrant;—of the crowd you saw to-day
Remove the herd whom sheer amazement
           brings
—   The novelty, nought else;—& next, the tribe
Whose innate blockish dullness just perceives   620
That unless miracles (as seem my works)
Be wrought in their behalf, they are not like
To puzzle the devil: & a numerous set

1835 599 sin: 600 energy: 602 forsaken.   605 head;   609–10 lore
. . . . past can show,   613 reveal'd. When they   615 depart.   617 war-
rant.

You little fancy what rude shocks apprise us
We sin; God's intimations rather fail
In clearness than in energy: 't were well   600
Did they but indicate the course to take
Like that to be forsaken. I would fain
Be spared a further sample. Here I stand,
And here I stay, be sure, till forced to flit.
   Festus. Be you but firm on that head! long ere
     then   605
All I expect will come to pass, I trust:
The cloud that wraps you will have
    disappeared.
Meantime, I see small chance of such event:
They praise you here as one whose lore,
    already
Divulged, eclipses all the past can show,   610
But whose achievements, marvellous as they
    be,
Are faint anticipations of a glory
About to be revealed. When Basil's
    crowds
Dismiss their teacher, I shall be content
That he depart.
   Paracelsus.   This favour at their hands   615
I look for earlier than your view of things
Would warrant. Of the crowd you saw to-day,
Remove the full half sheer amazement
    draws,
Mere novelty, nought else; and next, the tribe
Whose innate blockish dulness just perceives   620
That unless miracles (as seem my works)
Be wrought in their behalf, their chance is slight
To puzzle the devil; next, the numerous set

---

603 *1849–65* sample!   605 *1849* Remain but firm on that head;   *1863–68* Be
you but firm on that head;   609–10 *1849* They praise you here as one whose
lore, divulged | Already, eclipses all the past can show,   *1863, 1865* {as *1888*
except 'Past'}   619 *1849* The novelty,

  604 *to flit*: to move, migrate.
  623 *To puzzle the devil*: to get the better of the devil (to whom they rightly
belong).

Who bitterly hate established schools & help
A Teacher that oppugns them, 'till he once   625
Have planted his own doctrine, when the
    Teacher
May reckon on their rancour in his turn;
With a good sprinkling of sagacious knaves
Whose cunning runs not counter to the vogue
But seeks by flattery & crafty nursing   630
To force my system to a premature
Short-lived development:— —why swell the
    list?
Each has his end to serve, & his best way
Of pushing it: remove all these, remains
A scantling—a poor dozen at the best,   635
Worthy to look for sympathy & service,
And likely to draw profit from my pains
F/.   Tis no encouraging picture: still these
          few
Redeem their fellows— —once the germ
    implanted
The rest will fail not to succeed:
P/.   God grant it!   640
I would make some amends . . . the hate
    between us
Is of one side: should it prove otherwise,   641a
The luckless rogues have this excuse to urge,
That much is in my method & my manner,
My uncouth habits, my impatient spirit,
Which hinders of its influence & reception   645
My doctrine: much to say, small skill to speak:
— — It is, I fancy, some slight proof my old   646a
Devotion suffered not a looking-off

1835 625, 626 teacher   632 developement . . . Why   635 best—   637
pains.   639 fellows.   640 succeed.   641 amends: 641a Is on one
side.   646 speak . . .

Who bitterly hate established schools, and help
The teacher that oppugns them, till he once   625
Have planted his own doctrine, when the
    teacher
May reckon on their rancour in his turn;
Take, too, the sprinkling of sagacious knaves
Whose cunning runs not counter to the vogue
But seeks, by flattery and crafty nursing,   630
To force my system to a premature
Short-lived development. Why swell the
    list?
Each has his end to serve, and his best way
Of serving it: remove all these, remains
A scantling, a poor dozen at the best,   635
Worthy to look for sympathy and service,
And likely to draw profit from my pains.
    Festus. 'T is no encouraging picture: still these
      few
Redeem their fellows. Once the germ
    implanted,
Its growth, if slow, is sure.
    Paracelsus.   God grant it so!   640
I would make some amends: but if I
    fail,
The luckless rogues have this excuse to
    urge,
That much is in my method and my manner,
My uncouth habits, my impatient spirit,
Which hinders of reception and result   645
My doctrine: much to say, small skill to speak!
Those old aims suffered not a looking-off

624 *1849* schools, so help   625 *1849* them, and o'erthrows,   626 *1849* 'Till
having planted his own doctrine, he   630 *1849* and nursing craft,   *1863* and
crafty nursing   632 *1849* development . . .   635 *1849* scantling—a poor
. . . . best—   After 635: *1849* That really come to learn for learning's
sake;   639 *1849* Once implant the germ,   *647 *1849*, *1863* Those old aims
. . . . looking-off,   *1865* These old aims . . . . looking-off,   *1868–1889* These
old aims . . . . looking-off

647 *a looking-off*: not in OED. Cf. *Sordello*, III. 631.

Tho' for an instant, seeing that then alone
When I renounced it, & resolved to reap
Some present fruit— —to teach Mankind the
    truth   650
So dearly purchased—*then* I first discovered
Such teaching was an art requiring cares
And qualities peculiar to itself;—
That to possess was one thing . . . to display
Another. I had never dreamed of this: 655
Had but renown been present in my thoughts   655a
Or popular praise, I had soon found it out:—
One grows but little apt to learn these things.

F/.   If it be so,—which nowise I believe—
There needs no waiting fuller dispensation
To leave a labour to so little use: 660
Why not throw up the irksome charge at once?

P/.   A task, a task! . . .
                . . but wherefore hide the whole
Extent of degradation, once engaged
In the confessing vein? In spite of all
My fine talk of obedience, & repugnance,   665
Docility & what not, 'tis yet to learn
If when the task shall really be performed,
My inclinations free to choose once more . . .
I shall do aught but slightly modify
Its nature in the next career they try: 670
In plain words, I am spoiled:—my life still
    tends
As first it tended . . . I am broken & trained

1835 650 mankind   656 out.   658 so, which . . . . believe,   668
more,   670 try.   672 tended.

Though for an instant; therefore, only when
I thus renounced them and resolved to reap
Some present fruit—to teach mankind some
    truth   650
So dearly purchased—only then I found
Such teaching was an art requiring cares
And qualities peculiar to itself:
That to possess was one thing—to display
Another. With renown first in my
    thoughts,   655
Or popular praise, I had soon discovered it:
One grows but little apt to learn these things.
    Festus. If it be so, which nowise I believe,
There needs no waiting fuller dispensation
To leave a labour of so little use.   660
Why not throw up the irksome charge at once?
    Paracelsus. A task, a task!
                    But wherefore hide the whole
Extent of degradation, once engaged
In the confessing vein? Despite of all
My fine talk of obedience and repugnance,   665
Docility and what not, 't is yet to learn
If when the task shall really be performed,
My inclination free to choose once more,
I shall do aught but slightly modify
The nature of the hated task I quit.   670
In plain words, I am spoiled; my life still
    tends
As first it tended; I am broken and trained

---

655 *1849–65* Another. Had renown been in my thoughts,   656 *1849–65*
discovered it!   660 *1849–65* labour to so little   662–4 *1849* A task, a task!
. . . But wherefore hide from you | The whole extent of degradation, once |
Engaged in the confession? Spite of all   667–8 *1849* If when the old task
really is performed, | And my will free once more, to choose a new, {*1863* as
1888 except 'inclinations'}   670 *1849* hated one I quit.   672 *1849–65*
tended.

---

662 *A task, a task!*: I may not 'throw up the irksome charge' because I have
this new labour (that of teaching mankind 'some truth', at least).
    672 *broken*: broken in, like a horse.

To my old habits—they are part of me:
I know— —& none so well, my darling Ends
Are proved impossible— —no less— —no less   675
Even now what humours me, fond fool, as
  when
Their faint ghosts sit with me, & flatter me
And send me back content to my dull
  round? . .
How can I change this soul—this apparatus
Constructed solely for their purposes . .   680
So well adapted to their wants & uses,
To search, discover, & dissect & prove . . .
This intricate machine, whose most minute
And meanest motions have their charm to me
Tho' to none else—an aptitude I see—   685
An object I perceive—a use, a meaning
A property, a fitness, I explain
And I alone . . . how can I change my soul?—
And this wronged body, worthless save when
  tasked
Under that soul's dominion—used to care   690
For its bright ⟨m⟩ Masters cares, & to subdue
Its proper cravings . . not to ail nor pine
So He but prosper— — —whither drag this
  poor
Tried, patient body? God! how I essayed
To live like that mad Poet, for a while!— —   695
To Love alone!— —& how I felt too warped

1835 673 habits;   674 I know, and . . . . ends   675 impossible: no less, no
less.   679 soul?   680 purposes?   681 uses—   682 and dissect, and
prove: 684 their charms   691 master's   695,696 poet, for a while! |
To love alone! and

To my old habits: they are part of me.
I know, and none so well, my darling ends
Are proved impossible: no less, no less,   675
Even now what humours me, fond fool, as
        when
Their faint ghosts sit with me and flatter me
And send me back content to my dull
        round?
How can I change this soul?—this apparatus
Constructed solely for their purposes,   680
So well adapted to their every want,
To search out and discover, prove and perfect;
This intricate machine whose most minute
And meanest motions have their charm to me
Though to none else—an aptitude I seize,   685
An object I perceive, a use, a meaning,
A property, a fitness, I explain
And I alone:—how can I change my soul?
And this wronged body, worthless save
        when tasked
Under that soul's dominion—used to care   690
For its bright master's cares and quite subdue
Its proper cravings—not to ail nor pine
So he but prosper—whither drag this
        poor
Tried patient body? God! how I essayed
To live like that mad poet, for a while,   695
To love alone; and how I felt too warped

680 *1849–65* purposes   684 *1849* Least obvious motions   693 *1849* So the
soul prosper—whither . . . . poor,   *1863*, *1865* So he but prosper—whither
. . . . poor,   After 695: *1849* To catch Aprile's spirit, as I hoped,   696 *1849*
And love alone!   *1863* To love alone!
_____

680 *their purposes*: those of his 'darling ends.'
683 *This intricate machine*: cf. *Sordello*, ii. 994: 'The Body, the Machine for
acting Will'; and ibid. iii. 25.
685 *an aptitude*: a fitness for some particular purpose.
691 *its bright master's cares*: those of the soul.
692 *proper*: own.
696 *To love alone*: to do nothing but love.

And twisted & deformed! What should I do
Released from this sad drudgery but return
Faint as I am & halting— —blind & sore
To my old life & die as I begun!   700
I cannot feed on beauty, for the sake
Of beauty only— —nor can drink in balm
From lovely objects for their loveliness . . . .
My nature cannot lose her first impress
I still must hoard & heap & class all Truths   705
With One ulterior purpose—one intent— —
Would God translate me to his throne, believe
That I should only listen to his words
To further my own Aims! full well I know
Beauty is prodigally strown around,   710
And I were happy could I trample under
This mad & thriveless longing, & content me
With beauty for itself alone; — —alas!
I have addressed a frock of heavy mail
Yet may not join the troop of sacred
    Knights,—   715
And now the forest-creatures fly from me,
The grass-banks cool, the sunbeams warm no
    more!
Best follow, dreaming that ere night arrive
I shall o'ertake the company, & ride
Glittering as they!
F/.   —   I think I apprehend   720
What you would say: if you, in truth, design
To enter on such life again, seek not
To hide that much of all ⟨the⟩ [this]
    consciousness

1835 699 halting,   700 life—and   702 only;   703 loveliness;   704
impress;   705 hoard, and heap, and class all truths   706 With one ulterior
. . . . intent.   709 aims!   710 strewn   715 knights;

And twisted and deformed! What should I do,
Even tho' released from drudgery, but return
Faint, as you see, and halting, blind and sore,
To my old life and die as I began?   700
I cannot feed on beauty for the sake
Of beauty only, nor can drink in balm
From lovely objects for their loveliness;
My nature cannot lose her first imprint;
I still must hoard and heap and class all truths   705
With one ulterior purpose: I must know!
Would God translate me to his throne, believe
That I should only listen to his word
To further my own aim! For other men,
Beauty is prodigally strewn around,   710
And I were happy could I quench as they
This mad and thriveless longing, and content me
With beauty for itself alone: alas,
I have addressed a frock of heavy mail
Yet may not join the troop of sacred
      knights;   715
And now the forest-creatures fly from me,
The grass-banks cool, the sunbeams warm no
      more.
Best follow, dreaming that ere night arrive,
I shall o'ertake the company and ride
Glittering as they!
      Festus.   I think I apprehend   720
What you would say: if you, in truth, design
To enter once more on the life thus left,
Seek not to hide that all this consciousness

700 *1849* life—and die as I begun!   *1863,1865* life—and die as I began!   *1868* life and die as I Legan!   702 *1849–65* only;   704 *1849* her first intent;   708 *1849* his words   *1863, 1865* His words   709 *1849–65* aims!   712 *1849* longing, be content   713 *1849–65* alas!   717 *1849* more!   718 *1849* night arrives

701 *I cannot feed on beauty*: 'He has been trying to follow the poet's advice & mix love with knowledge—he cannot yet attain to it': Domett.
707 *translate*: 'To carry or convey to heaven without death': OED.
714 *addressed*: donned.

Of failure is assumed— —

P/.   My friend, my friend,

I tell . . . you listen;—I explain— —perhaps   725
You understand:— —there our communion
    ends.
Have you learnt nothing from to-days
    discourse?

—   When we would thoroughly know the sick
    man's state
We feel awhile the fluttering pulse—press soft
The hot brow—look upon the languid eye   730
And thence divine the rest . . must I lay bare
My heart—hideous & beating—or tear up
My vitals for your gaze, ere you will deem
Enough made known?—You! who are you,
    forsooth?

—   *That* is the crowning operation claimed   735
By the Arch-demonstrator—heaven the hall,
And earth the audience— —Let Aprile & you
Secure good places—'twill be worth the
    while . . .

F/.   Are you mad, Aureole? what can I have
    said
To call for this? . . I judged from your own
    words.—   740

P/.   Oh, doubtless! a sick wretch describes
    the ape
That mocks him from the bed-foot . . . & all
    gravely
You thither turn at once: or he recounts
⟨How sweet the gardens where he slept last
    night,— — —⟩

1835 724 assumed.   729,730 pulse, press soft | The hot brow, look . . . .
eye,   731 rest.   732 heart, hideous and beating,   736 arch-
demonstrator—   737 audience.   738 while.   742 bed-foot, and

Of failure is assumed!
   Paracelsus.   My friend, my friend,
I tell, you listen; I explain, perhaps   725
You understand: there our communion
   ends.
Have you learnt nothing from to-day's
   discourse?
When we would thoroughly know the sick man's
   state
We feel awhile the fluttering pulse, press soft
The hot brow, look upon the languid eye,   730
And thence divine the rest. Must I lay bare
My heart, hideous and beating, or tear up
My vitals for your gaze, ere you will deem
Enough made known? You! who are you,
   forsooth?
That is the crowning operation claimed   735
By the arch-demonstrator—heaven the hall,
And earth the audience. Let Aprile and you
Secure good places: 't will be worth the
   while.
   Festus. Are you mad, Aureole? What can I have
   said
To call for this? I judged from your own
   words.   740
   Paracelsus. Oh, doubtless! A sick wretch
   describes the ape
That mocks him from the bed-foot, and all
   gravely
You thither turn at once: or he recounts

---

724 *1849–65* assumed.   725 *1849* I speak, you listen;   *1888* {some copies}
1889 I toil, you listen;   738 *1849* places—'t will be worth your while.   741
1849 Oh, true! A fevered wretch   742 *1849* bed-foot, and you turn   743
1849 All gravely thither at once:

731–2 *Must I lay bare | My heart*: cf. *Pauline*, 124.
735 *That*: i.e. the laying-bare of one's heart. By 'the crowning operation'
Paracelsus is referring to the attendance of students and others in the tiered
operating theatre, a good image for the Last Day.

[The perilous journey he has late performed,]
And you are puzzled much how that could be!   745
You find me here—, half-stupid & half mad:—
..   It makes no part of my delight to search
Into these things,—much less to undergo
Another's scrutiny,—but so it chances
That I am led to trust my state to you   750
As calmly, as sincerely as I may;—   750a
—   And the event is, you combine, contrast
And ponder on my foolish words as tho'
They thoroughly conveyed all hidden *here*,
Here—loathsome with despair & hate & rage!
Is there no fear, no shrinking, or no shame?   755
Will you guess nothing? will you spare me
nothing?
Must I go deeper? Aye or No?
F/.   — — —Dear Friend . . . .
P/.   True:—I am brutal—'tis a part of it;—
A plague-fit:—you are not a lazar-haunter,
How should you know? well then, you think it
strange   760
I should profess to have failed utterly,
And yet propose an ultimate return
To courses void of hope: & this, because
You know not what Temptation is, nor how
Tis like to ply me in my sickliest part   765
..   You are to understand, that we, who make
Sport for the Gods, are hunted to the end:
There is not one sharp volley shot at us

1835 749 scrutiny;   753,754 *here*— | *Here*, loathsome with despair, and hate,
and rage!   757 Dear friend . . .   764 temptation   765 'Tis . . . . in the
sickliest part.   766 we who make   767 gods,

The perilous journey he has late performed,
And you are puzzled much how that could be!   745
You find me here, half stupid and half mad;
It makes no part of my delight to search
Into these matters, much less undergo
Another's scrutiny; but so it chances
That I am led to trust my state to
          you: 750
And the event is, you combine, contrast
And ponder on my foolish words as though
They thoroughly conveyed all hidden here—
Here, loathsome with despair and hate and rage!
Is there no fear, no shrinking and no shame?   755
Will you guess nothing? will you spare me
          nothing?
Must I go deeper? Ay or no?
     Festus.   Dear friend . . .
     Paracelsus. True: I am brutal—'t is a part of it;
The plague's sign—you are not a lazar-haunter,
How should you know? Well then, you think it
          strange   760
I should profess to have failed utterly,
And yet propose an ultimate return
To courses void of hope: and this, because
You know not what temptation is, nor how
'T is like to ply men in the sickliest part.   765
You are to understand that we who make
Sport for the gods, are hunted to the end:
There is not one sharp volley shot at us,

---

748 *1849–65* Into these things, much less to undergo   755 *1849* shrinking, or
no shame?   *1863, 1865* shrinking or no shame?   After 768 *1849* Which if we
manage to escape with life,

---

   759 *a lazar-haunter*: Johnson defines a lazar as 'One deformed and nauseous
with filthy and pestilential diseases'. OED has only this example of the com-
pound.
   765 *to ply*: 'to solicit importunately': Johnson.
   766–7 *who make / Sport for the gods*: cf. *King Lear*, IV. i. 37–8: 'As flies to
wanton boys are we to th' gods, / They kill us for their sport'.

Which 'scaped with life, 'tho hurt, we slacken
   pace
And gather by the wayside herbs & roots   770
To staunch our wounds, secure from further
   harm: . . .
We are assailed to life's extremest verge:
It will be well indeed if I return,
A harmless busy fool, to my old ways! . . .
I would forget hints of another fate   775
Significant enough, which silent hours
Have lately scared me with;—

F/.   Another! & what?

P/.   — —After all, Festus, you say well: I am
A Man yet—I need never humble me;— —
I would have been— —something I know not
   what,—   780
But tho' I cannot soar, I do not crawl:
There are worse portions than this one of
   mine,—
You say well . . .

F/.   Ah! . .

P/.   . . . & deeper degradation:
If the mean stimulants of vulgar praise
And vanity—should become the chosen food   785
Of a sunk mind,—should stifle even the wish
To find its early aspirations true . .
Should teach it to breathe falsehood like
   life-breath;—
An atmosphere of craft & trick & lies;—
Should make it proud to emulate or surpass   790

1835 771 harm . . .   772 verge.   777 with.   779 man . . . .
me;   780—something, I know not what;   782 mine;   785 van-
ity,   786 mind;   787 true;   788 life-breath—   789 craft, and trick,
and lies—

Which 'scaped with life, though hurt, we slacken
   pace
And gather by the wayside herbs and roots   770
To staunch our wounds, secure from further
   harm:
We are assailed to life's extremest verge.
It will be well indeed if I return,
A harmless busy fool, to my old ways!
I would forget hints of another fate,   775
Significant enough, which silent hours
Have lately scared me with.
    Festus.   Another! and what?
    Paracelsus. After all, Festus, you say well: I am
A man yet: I need never humble me.
I would have been—something, I know not
   what;   780
But though I cannot soar, I do not crawl.
There are worse portions than this one of
   mine.
You say well!
    Festus.   Ah!
    Paracelsus.   And deeper degradation!
If the mean stimulants of vulgar praise,
If vanity should become the chosen food   785
Of a sunk mind, should stifle even the wish
To find its early aspirations true,
Should teach it to breathe falsehood like
   life-breath—
An atmosphere of craft and trick and lies;
Should make it proud to emulate, surpass   790

---

769 *1849* Though touched and hurt, we straight may slacken pace *Berg*
{Rejected} Escaping with life, though hurt,   771 *1849* staunch . . . .
harm—   *1863* stanch . . . . harm: 772 *1849* No; we are chased to life's
extremest verge.   778 *1849* well: I stand   779 *1849* yet—   781 *1849*
crawl: 782 *1849* mine;   783 *1849* Ah! . . .   785 *1849–65* And vanity,
should   786 *1849–65* mind;   787 *1849–65* true;   790 *1849–65* to emu-
late or surpass

---

769 *Which 'scaped with life*: an absolute construction.
772 *extremest verge*: cf. *As You Like It*, II. i. 42.
775 *another fate*: exposure.

Base natures in the practices which woke
Its most indignant loathing once . . . . No, no.
Utter damnation is reserved for Hell!—
I *had* immortal feelings—such shall never
Be wholly quenched— —No—No— —
　　　　　My friend, you wear　　　795
A melancholy face, & certain 'tis,
There's little cheer in all this dismal work;
But 'twas not my desire to set abroach
Such memories & forbodings . . I foresaw
Where they would drive— —'twere better to
　　discuss　　　800
News of Lucerne or Zurich; or to tell
Of Egypt's flaring sky, or Spain's cork-
　　groves:—

F/.　I have thought: trust me, this mood will pass
　　away:
—　I know you, & the lofty spirit you bear,
And easily ravel out a clue to all:　　　805
These are the trials meet for such as you . . .
—　Nor must you hope exemption: to be mortal
Is to be plied with trials manifold.
Look round! The obstacles which kept the rest
From your ambition have been spurned by you　810
Their fears, their doubts . . the chains that bind
　　them best

1835 792 No, no:　795 quench'd—no, no.　799 forebodings.　800 drive;
802 cork-groves.　803 away.　806 you,　810 by you:　811 doubts,
the . . . . best,

Base natures in the practices which woke
Its most indignant loathing once . . . No, no!
Utter damnation is reserved for hell!
I had immortal feelings; such shall never
Be wholly quenched: no, no!
                         My friend, you wear 795
A melancholy face, and certain 't is
There's little cheer in all this dismal work.
But was it my desire to set abroach
Such memories and forebodings? I foresaw
Where they would drive. 'T were better we
     discuss   800
News from Lucerne or Zurich; ask and tell
Of Egypt's flaring sky or Spain's cork-
     groves.
     Festus. I have thought: trust me, this mood will
          pass away!
I know you and the lofty spirit you bear,
And easily ravel out a clue to all.   805
These are the trials meet for such as you,
Nor must you hope exemption: to be mortal
Is to be plied with trials manifold.
Look round! The obstacles which kept the rest
From your ambition, have been spurned by you; 810
Their fears, their doubts, the chains that bind them
     all,

---

794 *1849* feelings—   *1863,1865* feelings: 795 *1849* quenched—   796 *1849*
and truth to speak,   *1863, 1865* and, certain 't is   797 *1849* work;   798
1849–65 But 'twas not my desire   799 *1849* forebodings.   *1863, 1865* fore-
bodings: 800–2 *1849* Where they would drive; 'twere better you detailed |
News of Lucerne or Zurich; or I described | Great Egypt's flaring sky,   *Berg*
{rejected in l.802} Arabia's flaring sky,   *1863, 1865* Where they would drive.
'Twere better to discuss | News of Lucerne or Zurich; or to tell | Of Egypt's
flaring sky   803 *1849* I have thought now: yes, this mood will pass
away.   *1863, 1865* I have thought: trust me, this mood will pass away.   810
1849 Of men from your ambition, you have spurned;   *Berg* {rejected} From
your ambition were spurn'd by you long since;   811 *1849* bind them best,

---

  798 *to set abroach*: cf. *Romeo and Juliet* I. i. 102: 'Who set this ancient quarrel
new abroach?'
  805 *ravel out*: draw out.

Were flax before your resolute soul, which
   nought
Avails to awe, save these delusions bred
From its own strength—its selfsame strength
   disguised,
Mocking itself—be brave, dear Aureole! since   815
The rabbit has his shade to frighten him
The fawn a rustling bough,—mortals their
   cares,
And higher natures yet would slight & laugh
At these entangling fantasies, as you
At trammels of a weaker mind—but judge   820
Your mind's dimension by the shade it casts!
I know you:

P/.   And I know you, dearest Festus!
And how you love unworthily . . & how
All admiration renders blind.

F/.   You hold
That admiration blinds?

P/.   Aye, & alas!   825

F/.   Nought blinds you less than
   admiration:
Whether it be that all love renders wise
In its degree . . . from Love which blends with
   Love
— — Heart answering heart— — —to that which
   spends itself
In silent mad idolatry of some   830
Pre-eminent mortal—some great Soul of
   Souls—
Which ne'er will know how well it is
   adored: . . . .
. .   I say, such love is never blind,—but rather

1835 813–4 delusions, bred | From its own strength, its selfsame strength,
disguised—   815 itself.   820 mind;   822 you. | *Par.* And   823
unworthily; and   828 degree; from love . . . . love—   831 soul of
souls—   833 I say, ... blind;

Were flax before your resolute soul, which
   nought
Avails to awe save these delusions bred
From its own strength, its selfsame strength
   disguised,
Mocking itself. Be brave, dear Aureole! Since   815
The rabbit has his shade to frighten him,
The fawn a rustling bough, mortals their
   cares,
And higher natures yet would slight and laugh
At these entangling fantasies, as you
At trammels of a weaker intellect,—   820
Measure your mind's height by the shade it casts!
I know you.
   Paracelsus. And I know you, dearest Festus!
And how you love unworthily; and how
All admiration renders blind.
   Festus.   You hold
That admiration blinds?
   Paracelsus.   Ay and alas!   825
   Festus. Nought blinds you less than
   admiration, friend!
Whether it be that all love renders wise
In its degree; from love which blends with
   love—
Heart answering heart—to love which spends
   itself
In silent mad idolatry of some   830
Pre-eminent mortal, some great soul of
   souls,
Which ne'er will know how well it is
   adored.
I say, such love is never blind; but rather

813 *1849* awe, save these delusions, *1863, 1865* awe, save these delusions
814 *1849* strength, disguised— *1863, 1865* strength disguised—   817 *1849*
The fawn his rustling   818 *1849* And higher natures yet their power to laugh
820 *1849* intellect.   826 *1849–65* less than admiration will.   832 *1849*
Which ne'er will know . . . . adored:—   *Berg* (Which ne'er will) [Too high
to] know . . . . adored:—

Alive to every the minutest spot
That mars its object, & which Hate (supposed   835
So vigilant & searching) dreams not of:
Love broods on such: what then? in the first
    case
Is there no sweet strife to forget, to change,
To overflush those blemishes with all
The glow of goodness they cannot disturb?   840
To make those very defects an endless source
Of new affection grown from hopes & fears?
—   And in the last,—is there no gallant stand
Made even for much proved weak? no
    shrinking-back
Lest, (since all love assimilates the soul   845
To what it loves,) it should at length become
Almost a rival of its idol? Trust me,
If there be Fiends who seek to work our
    hurt,—
To ruin & drag down Earth's mightiest spirits
Even at God's foot,—twill be from such as
    Love   850
Their zeal will gather most to serve their cause;
And least from those who hate, who most
    essay
By contumely & scorn to blot the Light
Which will have entrance even to *their* hearts
. . .   For thence will our Defender tear the veil   855
And [show] within the heart, as in a shrine,
The giant image of Perfection, grown
In their despite, whose calumnies were
    spawned
In the untroubled presence of its eyes!

Alive to every the minutest spot
Which mars its object, and which hate (supposed   835
So vigilant and searching) dreams not of.
Love broods on such: what then? When first
    perceived
Is there no sweet strife to forget, to change,
To overflush those blemishes with all
The glow of general goodness they disturb?   840
—To make those very defects an endless source
Of new affection grown from hopes and fears?
And, when all fails, is there no gallant stand
Made even for much proved weak? no
    shrinking-back
Lest, since all love assimilates the soul   845
To what it loves, it should at length become
Almost a rival of its idol? Trust me,
If there be fiends who seek to work our
    hurt,
To ruin and drag down earth's mightiest spirits
Even at God's foot, 't will be from such as
    love,   850
Their zeal will gather most to serve their cause;
And least from those who hate, who most
    essay
By contumely and scorn to blot the light
Which forces entrance even to their hearts:
For thence will our defender tear the veil   855
And show within each heart, as in a shrine,
The giant image of perfection, grown
In hate's despite, whose calumnies were
    spawned
In the untroubled presence of its eyes.

---

836 *1849* dreams not of: 845 *1849* Lest, rising even as its idol sinks,   846
1849 It nearly reach the sacred place, and stand   *Berg* It [nearly] reach the sacred
place (too nearly?) and stand   847 *1849* of that idol?   854 *1849* Which will
have entrance even to their hearts;   855 *1849* Defender   857 *1849–65*
Perfection,   859 *1849–65* eyes!

---

858 *whose calumnies were spawned*: 'Browning & his poem & detractors—cap-
ital!': Domett.

True admiration blinds not: nor am I   860
So blind: I know your unexampled sins,
But I know too, what sort of soul is prone   861a
To errors of that stamp;—sins like to spring   b
From one alone, whose life has passed the
        bounds
Prescribed to life . . . compound *that* fault with
        God!
I speak of Men . . to common Men like me
The weakness you confess endears you more,   865
⟨As⟩ [Like] the far traces of decay in suns:—
I bid you have good cheer!

P/.   *Praeclarè! Optimè!*
Think of a quiet mountain-cloistered Priest
Instructing Paracelsus! yet 'tis so:
And that his flittering words should soothe me
        better   869a
Than fulsome tributes . . . not that ⟨'tis so⟩
        [that] strange:—   b
Come, I will show you where my merit lies: 870
I ne'er supposed that since *I* failed no other   a
Needs hope success . . . I act as though each
        one   b
Who hears me, may aspire; now mark me
        well:—   c
Tis in the advance of individual minds
That the slow crowd should ground their
        expectation
Eventually to follow,—as the sea
Waits ages in its bed, 'till some one wave
Of all the multitudinous mass extends   875
The empire of the whole, some feet perhaps,
Over the strip of sand which could confine
Its fellows, so long time:—thenceforth the rest,
Even to the meanest, hurry in at once,—

1835 861b stamp—   863 life.   864 men; to common men   865
more—   868 mountain-cloister'd priest   869b tributes: not that that is
strange: 870 lies.   870b success:

True admiration blinds not; nor am I   860
So blind. I call your sin exceptional;
It springs from one whose life has passed the
   bounds
Prescribed to life. Compound that fault with
   God!
I speak of men; to common men like me
The weakness you reveal endears you more,   865
Like the far traces of decay in suns.
I bid you have good cheer!
   Paracelsus.   *Præclare! Optime!*
Think of a quiet mountain-cloistered priest
Instructing Paracelsus! yet 't is so.
Come, I will show you where my merit lies.   870
'T is in the advance of individual minds
That the slow crowd should ground their
   expectation
Eventually to follow; as the sea
Waits ages in its bed till some one wave
Out of the multitudinous mass, extends   875
The empire of the whole, some feet perhaps,
Over the strip of sand which could confine
Its fellows so long time: thenceforth the rest,
Even to the meanest, hurry in at once,

---

861 *1849* blind: 865 *1849* The weakness you confess endears you
more—   *1863*, 65 The weakness you confess endears you more,   866 *1849*
suns: 873 *1849* follow—   875 *1849* Out of the multitude aspires, extends

863 *Compound that fault*: come to terms with God about that fault.
866 *the far traces of decay in suns*: an image which shows that Festus shares his
friend's scientific interests.
867 *Præclare! Optime!*: Splendid! Excellent!

And so much is clear gained: . . . I shall be glad   880
If all my labours, failing of aught else
Suffice to make such inroad— —to procure
A wider range for Thought: nay, they *do*
   this,—
For whatsoe'er my notions of true Knowledge
And a legitimate success . . . no less   885
I am not blind to my undoubted rank
When classed with others:—I precede my age:
And whoso wills, is very free to make
That use of me which I disdained to máke   888a
Of my forerunners—(vanity, perchance: b
But had I deemed their learning wonder-worth,   c
I had been other than I am)— —to mount   d
Those labours as a platform whence their own
May have a prosperous outset:—but, alas!   890
My followers . . . they are noisy as you heard,
But for intelligence— —the best of them
So clumsily wield the weapons I supply
And they extol,—that I begin to doubt
Whether their own rude clubs & pebble-stones   895
Would not do better service than my arms
Thus vilely swayed,—if error will not fall
Sooner before their aukward batterings
Than my more subtle warfare!

F/.   In that case
I would supply that art & would withold   900
The arms until their mystery was made known.

P/.   Content you; 'tis my wish; I have
   recourse
To the simplest training: day by day I seek
To wake the mood, the spirit which alone
Can make those arms of any use to them.   905

1835 880 gain'd.   883 thought: nay, they *do* this;   884 know-
ledge   885–6 success may be, | I am not   887 others.   900 art, and
would withhold   902 Content you, 't is   903 training.

And so much is clear gained. I shall be glad   880
If all my labours, failing of aught else,
Suffice to make such inroad and procure
A wider range for thought: nay, they do
    this;
For, whatsoe'er my notions of true knowledge
And a legitimate success, may be,   885
I am not blind to my undoubted rank
When classed with others: I precede my age:
And whoso wills is very free to mount
These labours as a platform whence his own
May have a prosperous outset. But, alas!   890
My followers—they are noisy as you heard;
But, for intelligence, the best of them
So clumsily wield the weapons I supply
And they extol, that I begin to doubt
Whether their own rude clubs and pebble-stones   895
Would not do better service than my arms
Thus vilely swayed—if error will not fall
Sooner before the old awkward batterings
Than my more subtle warfare, not half learned.
    Festus. I would supply that art, then, or
        withhold   900
New arms until you teach their mystery.
    Paracelsus. Content you, 't is my wish; I have
        recourse
To the simplest training. Day by day I seek
To wake the mood, the spirit which alone
Can make those arms of any use to men.   905

---

889 *1849, 1863* a platform, whence their own   *1865* a platform, whence his
own   890 *1849* outset: 891 *1849–65* heard,   892 *1849, 1863* But for
intelligence—   *1865* But for intelligence   900 *1849–65* then, and with-
hold   901 *1849–63* Its arms until you have taught their mystery.   *1865* Its
arms until you teach their mystery.

---

889 *a platform*: cf. 'une espèce de plateau' in the note to *Pauline*, 811.
900 *that art*: that of 'wield[ing] the weapons' he provides.

—— Of course they are for swaggering forth at once
With Hercule's club, Achilles shield, Ulysses'
Bow—a choice sight to scare the crows away! 910
F/. Pity you choose not, then, some other
method
Of coming at your point:—the marvellous art
At length established in the world bids fair
To remedy all hindrances like these:
Trust to Frobenius' Press the precious lore 915
Obscured by uncouth manner, or unfit
For raw beginners—let his types secure
A deathless monument to after-times;
Meanwhile enjoy & confidently wait
The ultimate effect: sooner or later 920
You shall be all-revealed.
P/.   An ancient question
In a new form; no more: thus: I possess
Two sorts of Knowledge,—one, vast shadowy
hints
Of the unbounded Aim I once pursued;—
The other, many secrets, made my own 925
While bent on nobler prize, & not a few
First principles which may conduct to much;
These last I offer to my followers here:—

1835 907 Hercules' club, Achilles' 908, 909 {No equivalent in *MS* or
1835} 912 point. 915 press 922 more. 923 knowledge—one,
vast, shadowy, hints 924 aim I once pursued— 928 here.

Of course they are for swaggering forth at once
Graced with Ulysses' bow, Achilles' shield—
Flash on us, all in armour, thou Achilles!
Make our hearts dance to thy resounding step!
A proper sight to scare the crows away!   910
   Festus. Pity you choose not then some other method
     method
Of coming at your point. The marvellous art
At length established in the world bids fair
To remedy all hindrances like these:
Trust to Frobenius' press the precious lore   915
Obscured by uncouth manner, or unfit
For raw beginners; let his types secure
A deathless monument to after-time;
Meanwhile wait confidently and enjoy
The ultimate effect: sooner or later   920
You shall be all-revealed.
   Paracelsus.   The old dull question
In a new form; no more. Thus: I possess
Two sorts of knowledge; one,—vast, shadowy,
     shadowy,
Hints of the unbounded aim I once pursued:
The other consists of many secrets, caught   925
While bent on nobler prize,—perhaps a few
Prime principles which may conduct to much:
These last I offer to my followers here.

907 *1849* Graced with Ulysses' club,   *Berg* ⟨Girt⟩ [Graced] with ⟨Hercules' club,⟩ [Ulysses' bow,]   918 *1849–65* after-times;   925 *1849* secrets, learned   927 *1849* First principles   928 *1849* These last   *Berg* {rejected} Which last

  907 *Ulysses' bow, Achilles' shield*: the former is described in the *Odyssey*, xxi., the latter in the *Iliad*, xviii. 478 ff.
  908 *thou Achilles*: he addresses one of his students ironically.
  912 *The marvellous art*: that of printing with movable types, first practised (in Europe) by Johann Gutenberg, who is known to have had a printing-press about 1450.
  915 *Frobenius' press*: Paracelsus published only a small part of his writings. For Frobenius, whom he described as his 'best friend', see 295 n and 480 n, above.

Now bid me chronicle the first of these,—
My ancient study,—& in effect, you bid me   930
Revert to the wild course I have abjured:—
And, for the principles, they are so
    simple
—   (Being chiefly of the overturning sort)
That one time is as proper to propound them   935
As any other—tomorrow at my class
Or half a century hence embalmed in print—
For if Mankind intend to learn at all
They must begin by giving faith to them
And acting on them: & I do not see   940
But that my lectures serve indifferent well:
No doubt these dogmas fall not to the earth
For all their novelty & rugged setting:
I think my class will not forget the day
I let them know the Gods of Israel,   945
Aëtius, Oribasius, Galen, Rhasis,
And Avicenna, & Averroës,
Were blocks!—
F/.   — —And that reminds me,—they said
    something

1835 931 abjured.   932 {No equivalent in MS or 1835.}   937 embalm'd in
print;   938 mankind   943 setting.   945 gods

Now, bid me chronicle the first of these,
My ancient study, and in effect you bid   930
Revert to the wild courses just abjured:
I must go find them scattered through the world.
Then, for the principles, they are so simple
(Being chiefly of the overturning sort),
That one time is as proper to propound them   935
As any other—to-morrow at my class,
Or half a century hence embalmed in print.
For if mankind intend to learn at all,
They must begin by giving faith to them
And acting on them: and I do not see   940
But that my lectures serve indifferent well:
No doubt these dogmas fall not to the earth,
For all their novelty and rugged setting.
I think my class will not forget the day
I let them know the gods of Israel,   945
Aëtius, Oribasius, Galen, Rhasis,
Serapion, Avicenna, Averröes,
Were blocks!
    Festus.   And that reminds me, I heard
       something

929 *1849*, *1863* Now   930 *1849–65* you bid me   937 *1849* print: *Berg*
print.   947 *1849–65* Averröes,—

941 *indifferent well*: a Shakespearian phrase: see, e.g., *Twelfth Night*, I. iii. 126.
945 *the gods of Israel*: an allusion to the story of the Golden Calf: Exodus
xxxii. 2 ff. Aëtius of Amida produced the *Tetrabiblos*, a compilation of the
principal writings of Galen and other early medical writers, with some new
material. He lived in the late fifth and early sixth centuries, his works being
printed a thousand years later. Oribasius was a Greek physician of the fourth
century who became a friend of Julian the Apostate and whose surviving
writings were similarly published in the sixteenth century. The printing of the
works of Galen, who lived in the second century, began in the fifteenth
(Paracelsus refers to him again at v. 179 ff.) After Hippocrates, he was the
greatest physician of antiquity. Rhasis, or Razi, was an Arab physician. The
Biographie Universelle tells us that Avicenna drew on his writings, that transla-
tions of his works were long influential in European universities, and that he
was the first to give a full and accurate account of smallpox. Serapion was a
Syrian physician of the tenth century. Avicenna, the great Arab physician, was
the author of Canons which were translated into Latin and began to be printed
in the fifteenth century. Averröes was an Arab philosopher and authority on
medicine of the twelfth century whose 'great reputation', as the *Biographie*
points out, 'is due above all to the fact that he was the first translator of the
works of Aristotle'.

About your waywardness: you burned their
   books
It seems instead of answering those sages   950
P/.   And who said that?
F/.   Some I met yesternight
With Æcolampadius: as you know, the purpose
Of this short stay at Basil, was to learn
His pleasure touching certain missives sent
For our Zuinglius & himself:—'twas he   955
Apprized me that the famous teacher here
Was my old friend— —
P/.   Ah! I forgot: you went . . . .
F/.   From Zurich with advices for the ear
Of Luther now at Wittemburg— —(you
   know,
I make no doubt, the differences of late   960
With Carolostadius—)—& returning sought
Basil & Æcolampadius.
P/.   Here's a case now,
Will teach you why I answer not, but burn
The books you mention: Pray, does Luther
   dream

1835 952 Œcolampadius.   955 himself.   957 friend.

About your waywardness: you burned their
   books,
It seems, instead of answering those sages.   950
   Paracelsus. And who said that?
   Festus.   Some I met yesternight
With Œcolampadius. As you know, the purpose
Of this short stay at Basil was to learn
His pleasure touching certain missives sent
For our Zuinglius and himself. 'T was he   955
Apprised me that the famous teacher here
Was my old friend.
   Paracelsus.   Ah, I forgot: you went . . .
   Festus. From Zurich with advices for the ear
Of Luther, now at Wittenberg—(you
   know,
I make no doubt, the differences of late   960
With Carolostadius)—and returning sought
Basil and . . .
   Paracelsus. I remember. Here 's a case, now,
Will teach you why I answer not, but burn
The books you mention, Pray, does Luther
   dream

---

959 *1849–68* Wittemburg—   964 *1849–68* mention:

949 *you burned their books*: see p. 502 below.
955 *Zuinglius*: in 1528 Zuinglius and Œcolampadius (Ulrich [Huldrych] Zwingli and Joannes Hausschein or Hussgen), leaders of the Reformation in Switzerland, published an answer to Luther's Confession of Faith. Later they met Luther and Melanchthon to confer at Marburg. They differed on the doctrine of the Real Presence. Of all the great reformers he, through his disciples, exercised the greatest influence on the nascent Church of England.
961 *Carolostadius*: Andreas Rudolf Bodenstein Carlstadt, one of the first reformers, who became an antagonist of Luther's.
964 *does Luther dream*: Paracelsus was often compared to Luther, and at times he would accept the comparison. As Pagel remarks, 'There are the obvious common traits in their behaviour—the coarse and boisterous language, the use of the vernacular which had to be moulded and reformed in order to convey something un-traditional and unheard of, the crass rejection of learned pre-decessors and authorities, theatrical acts designed to appeal to students and the illiterate mob—such as the burning of books or the display of "theses" in public places'. It is also true, however, in Pagel's words, that 'A deep gulf . . . divorces Paracelsus from Luther' (pp. 40–1), and on occasion Paracelsus would speak strongly against the great Reformer. According to the dubious evidence of Thomas Erastus, in his *De Medicina Nova*, p. 239, 'He would boast that one day he would put Luther and the Pope in their place just as decidedly as he was now doing with Galen and Hippocrates'.

His arguments convince by their own force   965
The crowds that own his doctrine? No, indeed:
His plain denial of established points
Ages had sanctified, & none supposed
Could be oppugned while earth was under him
And heaven above—which chance or change or
    time   970
Affected not . . . did more than the array
Of argument which followed: boldly deny!—
There is much breath-stopping, hair-stiffening
Awhile,—amazed glances—mute awaiting
The thunder-bolt which does not come,— —&
    next   975
Reproachful wonder & inquiry—those
Who else had never stirred, are able now
To find the rest out for themselves . . perhaps
To outstrip him who set the whole at
    work; . . .
. . .   As never will my wise class its instructor:—   980
—   And you saw Luther?
F/.   'Tis a wondrous Soul!
P/.   True: the so heavy chain which galled
    Mankind
Is shattered—& the noblest of us all
Must bow to the Deliverer— —nay, the
    worker
Of our own projects—we who long before   985
Had burst its trammels, but forgot the crowd
We would have taught still groaned beneath the
    load:—
This he has done & nobly: Speed that may!
Whatever be my chance or my despair
What benefits mankind must glad me too: 990

1835 970 chance, or change,   972 follow'd. Boldly deny!   974 Awhile,
amazed glances,   976 inquiry;   979 work,   980 As . . . . instructor
. . .   981 soul!   982 so-heavy chain which gall'd mankind   983 shat-
ter'd, and   984 deliverer —nay,   988 nobly.

His arguments convince by their own force   965
The crowds that own his doctrine? No, indeed!
His plain denial of established points
Ages had sanctified and men supposed
Could never be oppugned while earth was under
And heaven above them—points which chance or
    time   970
Affected not—did more than the array
Of argument which followed. Boldly deny!
There is much breath-stopping, hair-stiffening
Awhile; then, amazed glances, mute awaiting
The thunderbolt which does not come: and
    next,   975
Reproachful wonder and inquiry: those
Who else had never stirred, are able now
To find the rest out for themselves, perhaps
To outstrip him who set the whole at
    work,
—As never will my wise class its instructor.   980
And you saw Luther?
    Festus.   'T is a wondrous soul!
    Paracelsus. True: the so-heavy chain which
    galled mankind
Is shattered, and the noblest of us all
Must bow to the deliverer—nay, the
    worker
Of our own project—we who long before   985
Had burst our trammels, but forgot the crowd,
We should have taught, still groaned beneath their
    load:
This he has done and nobly. Speed that may!
Whatever be my chance or my mischance,
What benefits mankind must glad me too;   990

978 *1849–65* To find the rest out for themselves—perhaps *1868* To find
rest for themselves, perhaps 985 *1849* projects— 986 *1849* its tram-
mels, *1868* our trammels *987 {Reading of *1889*, based on Browning's
revision in DC.} *1849–88* the load: 989 *1849* or my despair,

    982 *the so-heavy chain*: cf. Shelley, Dedication to *The Revolt of Islam*, 58–9:
'when the mortal chain / Of Custom thou didst burst and rend in twain'.
    988 *Speed that may!*: let him succeed who may!

And Men seem made, tho' not as I believed,
For something better than the times can
   show;—
Witness these gangs of Peasants your new
   lights
From Suabia have possessed, whom Munzer
   leads,
And whom the Duke, the Landgrave, & the
   Elector   995
Will calm in blood— —well, well—'tis not my
   world!

F/.   Hark!
P/. —   —Tis the melancholy wind astir
Within the trees— —the embers too are grey,
 —   Morn must be near:
F/.   Best ope the casement: see
The night, late strewn with clouds & flying
   stars,   1000
Is blank & motionless;—how peaceful sleep
The tree-tops all together! like an asp
The wind slips whispering from bough to
   bough.
P/. —   Ay: you would gaze on a wind-shaken
   tree
By the hour, nor count time lost?

1835 991 men . . . . though   993 peasants   995, 996 duke, the landgrave,
and the elector | Will calm in blood! Well, well—. . . . world.   998
trees;   999 Morn . . . . near.   1005 lost.

And men seem made, though not as I believed,
For something better than the times
    produce.
Witness these gangs of peasants your new
    lights
From Suabia have possessed, whom Münzer
    leads,
And whom the duke, the landgrave and the
    elector   995
Will calm in blood! Well, well; 't is not my
    world!
Festus. Hark!
Paracelsus.   'T is the melancholy wind astir
Within the trees; the embers too are grey:
Morn must be near.
    Festus.   Best ope the casement: see,
The night, late strewn with clouds and flying
    stars,   1000
Is blank and motionless: how peaceful sleep
The tree-tops altogether! Like an asp,
The wind slips whispering from bough to
    bough.
    Paracelsus. Ay; you would gaze on a wind-
    shaken tree
By the hour, nor count time lost.

---

992 *1849* produce: 994 *1849* Munzer   996 *1849–65* Well, well—   998
1849 grey,   1002 *1849–65* The tree-tops all together!

993 *these gangs of peasants*: a reference to the Peasants' War of 1525. Thomas
Münzer was an Anabaptist who at first followed Luther but subsequently
adopted more extreme views and participated in the Peasants' War. He was
captured and beheaded.
    993–4 *your new lights / From Suabia*: for 'new lights', meaning 'novel doc-
trines' (a phrase particularly common in Scotland in the seventeenth and
eighteenth centuries), see OED, 'light', *sb.* 6d. Suabia, in the south west of
Germany, was the scene of some of the most violent episodes of the war.
    995 *the landgrave and the elector*: in Germany a landgrave was a count having
jurisdiction over a territory, an elector one of the princes entitled to take part in
the election of an Emperor.
    1002 *Like an asp*: the simile was probably suggested by the two words of the
same spelling: an asp is 'A small, venomous, hooded serpent', or alternatively
'A tree of the poplar family, . . . the leaves of which are specially liable to the
tremulous motion that characterizes all the poplars': OED.
    1003 *The wind slips whispering*: cf. *Prometheus Unbound*, III. iii. 18–19: 'the
ever-moving air, / Whispering without from tree to tree'.

F/.   So you shall gaze: 1005
Those happy times will come again . . .
P/.   Gone! Gone!
Those pleasant times! . . . does not the moaning
    wind
Seem to bewail that we have gained such gains
And bartered sleep for them?
F/.   It is our trust
That there is yet another world to mend   1010
All error & mischance.— — —
P/.   Another world!
And why this world, this common world to be
A make-shift,—a mere foil, how fair soever,
To some fine life to-come? Man must be fed
With Angels' food, forsooth; & some few traces   1015
Of a diviner nature which look out
Thro' his corporeal baseness warrant him
In a supreme contempt for all provision
For his inferior tastes . . . some straggling
    marks
Which constitute his essence, just as truly   1020
As here and there a gem, would constitute
The rock, their barren bed, a diamond.
—   But were it so—were Man all ⟨m⟩ Mind—the
          station
He gains is little enviable: . . . from God
Down to the lowest spirit ministrant   1025
Intelligence exists which casts *our* Mind
Into immeasurable shade . . . No, no:—
Love, Hope, Fear, Faith—these make
    Humanity:
These are its sign, & note, & character:—
— — —

1835 1015 angel's   1021 gem   1023 But . . . . man all mind—   1024
enviable.   1026 mind   1027 shade. No, no: 1028 Love, hope, fear,
faith—these make humanity;   1029 and character;

Festus.   So you shall gaze: 1005
Those happy times will come again.
   Paracelsus.   Gone, gone,
Those pleasant times! Does not the moaning
   wind
Seem to bewail that we have gained such gains
And bartered sleep for them?
   Festus.   It is our trust
That there is yet another world to mend   1010
All error and mischance.
   Paracelsus.   Another world!
And why this world, this common world, to be
A make-shift, a mere foil, how fair soever,
To some fine life to come? Man must be fed
With angels' food, forsooth; and some few traces 1015
Of a diviner nature which look out
Through his corporeal baseness, warrant him
In a supreme contempt of all provision
For his inferior tastes—some straggling
   marks
Which constitute his essence, just as truly   1020
As here and there a gem would constitute
The rock, their barren bed, one diamond.
But were it so—were man all mind—he
   gains
A station little enviable. From God
Down to the lowest spirit ministrant,   1025
Intelligence exists which casts our mind
Into immeasurable shade. No, no:
Love, hope, fear, faith—these make
   humanity;
These are its sign and note and
   character,

1006 *1849* again . . . | Gone! Gone!   1015 *1849–65* angel's   1018 *1849*
contempt for all   1022 *1849* bed, a diamond.   1029 *1849* sign, and note,
and character;

1025 *spirit ministrant*: cf. *Paradise Lost*, x. 87: 'dominations ministrant'.
1028: *Love, hope, fear, faith*: cf. 1 Corinthians 13:13: 'And now abideth faith,
hope, charity, these three; but the greatest of these is charity'.
1029 *note*: essential characteristic.

— —   And these I have lost! gone—shut from me
          forever   1030
          Like a dead friend, safe from unkindness more!
          See, morn at length— —the heavy darkness
          seems
          Diluted,—grey & clear without the stars,
  —   The shrubs bestir & rouse themselves, as
          though
          Some snake, that weighed them down all night,
          let go   1035
          His hold; & from the East, fuller & fuller
          Day, like a mighty river, flowing in;
          But clouded, wintry, desolate, & cold:
          Yet see how that broad prickly star-shaped
          plant
          Half down in the crevice spreads its woolly
          leaves   1040
          All thick & glistering with diamond dew:—
          And you depart for Einsiedeln this day,
          And we have spent all night in talk like
          this!— — —
          If you would have me better for your love
          Revert no more to these sad themes—
F/.   One favour,   1045
          And I have done:—I leave you, deeply moved:
          Unwilling to have fared so well, the while
          My Friend has changed so sorely: if this mood
          Shall pass away— —if light once more arise
          Where all is darkness now . . if you see fit   1050
          To hope, & trust again, & strive again,—

And these I have lost!—gone, shut from me for
 ever,   1030
Like a dead friend safe from unkindness more!
See, morn at length. The heavy darkness
 seems
Diluted, grey and clear without the stars;
The shrubs bestir and rouse themselves
 as if
Some snake, that weighed them down all night,
 let go   1035
His hold; and from the East, fuller and fuller,
Day, like a mighty river, flowing in;
But clouded, wintry, desolate and cold.
Yet see how that broad prickly star-shaped
 plant,
Half-down in the crevice, spreads its woolly
 leaves   1040
All thick and glistering with diamond dew.
And you depart for Einsiedeln this day,
And we have spent all night in talk like
 this!
If you would have me better for your love,
Revert no more to these sad themes.
  Festus.   One favour, 1045
And I have done. I leave you, deeply moved;
Unwilling to have fared so well, the while
My friend has changed so sorely. If this mood
Shall pass away, if light once more arise
Where all is darkness now, if you see fit 1050
To hope and trust again, and strive again,

1031 *1849–65* friend, 1032 *1849* See 1033 *1849–68* Diluted; *1036
{Reading of DC and *1889*} *1849–88* fuller and fuller 1037 *1849–65* river, is
flowing 1038 *1849* cold: 1042 *1849–65* day: 1048 *1849* My friend has
. . . . sorely: *Berg* {rejected} Aureole has . . . . sorely. 1049 *1849*
away— 1050 *1849* now— 1051 *1849* To hope, and . . . . strive
again; *1863*, *1865* To hope, and . . . . strive again.

You will remember—not our love alone—
But that my faith in God's desire that Man
Should trust on his support . . . as I must think
You trusted . . . . is obscured & dim thro'
    you,—   1055
For you are thus, & this is no reward;—
Will you not call me to your side, dear
    Aureole?

1835 1053 man   1054, 1055 support, as . . . . trusted, is obscured and dim
through you;

You will remember—not our love alone—
But that my faith in God's desire that man
Should trust on his support, (as I must think
You trusted) is obscured and dim through
    you: 1055
For you are thus, and this is no reward.
Will you not call me to your side, dear Aureole?

1053 *1849* desire for man   1054 *1849* To trust on his   *1863, 1865* Should . . .
His   1057 *1849* dear friend?

1057 *dear Aureole?*: below this concluding line Domett comments: 'Ill-
treated & rejected by the world—determines to know & enjoy—though in
bitter despair & pride letting things go as they may'.

4.   PARACELSUS ASPIRES.

Scene, *a House at Colmar in Alsatia. 1528.*
        Paracelsus, Festus.

P/.   (To John Oporinus his secretary) *Sic itur ad*
            astra! . . . . dear Von Visenburg
        Is scandalized & poor Torinus paralyzed,
        And every honest soul that Basil holds
        Aghast . . . & yet we live—as one may say—
        Just as tho Liechtenfels had never set   5
        So true a value on his sorry carcass—
        And learned Pütter had not frowned us
            dumb; . . .
        We live, & shall as surely start to-morrow
        For Nuremburg, as we drink speedy scathe
        To Basil in this mantling wine, suffused   10
        A delicate blush, no fainter tinge is born

1835 4 Aghast; and yet we live, as . . . . say,   6 carcass,   7 dumb.   8
live; and   9 Nuremburg   11 blush—

PART IV.

PARACELSUS ASPIRES.

SCENE.—*Colmar in Alsatia: an Inn.* 1528.

PARACELSUS, FESTUS.

Paracelsus [*to* JOHANNES OPORINUS, *his Secretary*].
  Sic itur ad astra! Dear Von Visenburg
Is scandalized, and poor Torinus paralysed,
And every honest soul that Basil holds
Aghast; and yet we live, as one may say,
Just as though Liechtenfels had never set   5
So true a value on his sorry carcass,
And learned Pütter had not frowned us
   dumb.
We live; and shall as surely start to-morrow
For Nuremberg, as we drink speedy scathe
To Basil in this mantling wine, suffused   10
A delicate blush, no fainter tinge is born

1849 SCENE.—*A House at Colmar, in Alsatia.* 1528.   *8 *1849–68* to-morrow
1888, 1889 to morrow   9 *1849–68* Nuremburg,   11 *1849* With a delicate
blush—

Colmar in Alsatia: see p. 504 below.
OPORINUS: ibid.
   1 *Sic itur ad astra!*: 'that is the way to the stars!': *Aeneid*, ix. 641.
   Von Visenburg: Wolfgang Wisenberg was a theologian who was censorious
about Paracelsus: Pagel, p. 49 n. 136.
   2 *Torinus*: Albanus Torinus, a pupil of Paracelsus who became Professor of
Theoretical Medicine at Basle.
   5 *Liechtenfels*: see Browning's last note on the poem, below. 'One *John
Lichtenfels*, a Canon, falling extream sick, promised him [Paracelsus] a consid-
erable Sum if he would recover him, which *Paracelsus* effected, but the other
refusing to pay was sued by him; but the Judges having ordered the Canon to
pay him only the usual Fee, he was so enraged thereat, that he forsoke the City
of *Basil* and retir'd into *Alsatia*': Jeremy Collier's *Great Dictionary*. Cf. l. 68, 76.
   7 *learned Pütter*: unidentified.

I' th' shut heart of a bud;— —pledge me, good
    John,—
"Basil—a hot plague ravage it, & Pütter
"Oppose the plague!"—even so? do you too
    share
Their panic . . . the reptiles! Ha, ha, faint thro'
    them   15
Desist for *them*! . . . they manage matters so
At Basil, 'tis like— —but others may find
    means
To bring the stoutest braggart of the tribe
Once more to crouch in silence—means to
    breed
A stupid wonder in each fool again   20
Now big with admiration at the skill
Which stripped a vain pretender of his
    plumes,—
And, that done, means to brand each slavish
    brow
So deeply-sure—so ineffaceably,
That, thenceforth, flattery shall not pucker it   25
So well but there the hideous stamp shall stay
To teach the Man they fawn on, who they are
Whom I curse soul & limb: & now dispatch
Dispatch, my trusty John, & what remains   30
To do—whate'er arrangements for our trip
Are yet to be completed, see you hasten
This night—we'll weather the storm at
    least—to-morrow
For Nuremburg!—Now leave us—this grave
    clerk

1835 13 "Basil;   17 like: 22 plumes;   24 deeply-sure,   27 man
they fawn on   28 {No equivalent in *MS* or *1835*.}   29 limb. And   30
John; and   31 do,   33 night; we'll . . . . least: 34 Nuremburg! Now
leave us;

I' the shut heart of a bud. Pledge me, good
    John—
"Basil; a hot plague ravage it, and Pütter
"Oppose the plague!" Even so? Do you too
    share
Their panic, the reptiles? Ha, ha; faint through
    these,   15
Desist for these! They manage matters so
At Basil, 't is like: but others may find
    means
To bring the stoutest braggart of the tribe
Once more to crouch in silence—means to
    breed
A stupid wonder in each fool again,   20
Now big with admiration at the skill
Which stript a vain pretender of his
    plumes:
And, that done,—means to brand each slavish
    brow
So deeply, surely, ineffaceably,
That henceforth flattery shall not pucker it   25
Out of the furrow; there that stamp shall stay
To show the next they fawn on, what they are,
This Basil with its magnates,—fill my cup,—
Whom I curse soul and limb. And now despatch,
Despatch, my trusty John; and what remains   30
To do, whate'er arrangements for our trip
Are yet to be completed, see you hasten
This night; we 'll weather the storm at least:
    to-morrow
For Nuremberg! Now leave us; this grave clerk

---

12 *1849* bud: 13 *1849* it, with Pütter   14 *1849* "To stop the
plague!"   15 *1849* panic—the . . . . through *them,*   *1863* panic, the . . . .
through *them,* 16–19 *1849* Desist for *them!*—while means enough exist | To
bow the stoutest braggart of the tribe | Once more in crouching silence—
means to breed   *1863* Desist for *them!* They manage matters so | At Basil 't is
like: but others may find means | To bring the stoutest braggart of the tribe |
Once more to crouch in silence—means to breed   *1865, 1868, 1889* as *1888*
{except that *1865* has no comma after 'Basil'.}   23 *1849* done, means   25
1849, 63 That thenceforth   26–28 *1849* Out of the furrow of that hideous
stamp | Which shows the next they fawn on, what they are, | This Basil with its
magnates one and all,   34 *1849–68* Nuremburg!

Has divers weighty matters for my ear—.
　　(*Oporinus goes out.*　　　　　　　　　　35
And spare my lungs—at last, my gallant Festus,
I have got rid of this arch-knave that dogs me
As a gaunt crow a gasping sheep,—& now
May give a loose to my delight; how kind
How very kind!—my first, best, only Friend!　　40
— 　Why this looks like fidelity:—embrace me,
— 　Not a hair silvered yet? Right: you shall live
Till I am worth your love—you shall be proud
And I— —but time will show: did you not
　　wonder?
I sent to you because our compact weighed　　45
Upon my conscience, (you recall the night
At Basil, which the Gods confound)—because
Once more, I aspire!— —& you are here! all
　　this
Is strange;—& strange my message?
F/.　　　　　　　　　　　　I confess
So strange that I must think your messenger　　50
Has mingled his own fancies with the words
Purporting to be yours . . . . .
P/.　　　　　　　　　　　　He said no more,
Tis probable, than the precious folks I leave
Have said more roughly fifty-fold—alack
Tis true: poor Paracelsus is exposed　　　　55
At last—a most egregious quack is he,
And those he overreached must spit their hate
On one who,—utterly beneath contempt,—
Could yet deceive their topping wits—He said
Bare truth, & at my bidding you are here　　60

1835 35 ear,　　36 lungs.　　38 sheep;　　39 delight. How kind,　　40 kind, my . . . . friend!　　41 Why . . . . fidelity. Embrace me:　　42 Not . . . . silver'd yet!　　43 love; you . . . . proud,　　44 show.　　46 conscience— 49 Is strange, and strange my message.　　52 yours.　　54 fifty-fold. Alack, 56 At last: a . . . . he;　　59 wits.　　60 truth; and

Has divers weighty matters for my ear: 35
                    [OPORINUS *goes out.*
And spare my lungs. At last, my gallant Festus,
I am rid of this arch-knave that dogs my heels
As a gaunt crow a gasping sheep; at last
May give a loose to my delight. How kind,
How very kind, my first best only friend!   40
Why, this looks like fidelity. Embrace me!
Not a hair silvered yet? Right! you shall live
Till I am worth your love; you shall be proud,
And I—but let time show! Did you not
        wonder?
I sent to you because our compact weighed   45
Upon my conscience—(you recall the night
At Basil, which the gods confound!)—because
Once more I aspire. I call you to my
        side:
You come. You thought my message strange?
        Festus.   So strange
That I must hope, indeed, your messenger   50
Has mingled his own fancies with the words
Purporting to be yours.
        Paracelsus.   He said no more,
'T is probable, than the precious folk I leave
Said fiftyfold more roughly. Well-a-day,
'T is true! poor Paracelsus is exposed   55
At last; a most egregious quack he proves:
And those he overreached must spit their hate
On one who, utterly beneath contempt,
Could yet deceive their topping wits. You heard
Bare truth; and at my bidding you come here   60

37 *1849* that follows me   41 *1849* Why .... me: 42 *1849* yet!
Right: 44 *1849–68* show.   47 *1849* confound)—   48 *1849* aspire! I call
.... side;   *1863–68* aspire. I call .... side;   53 *1849–68* folks   55 *1849*
'Tis true;   56 *1849* proves,

38 *As a gaunt crow*: proverbial: 'The crow bewails the sheep, and then eats it':
Herbert 458: Ray 6.
    37 *dogs my heels*: a Shakespearian phrase: cf., e.g., *Richard III*, IV. i. 40.
    42 *Not a hair silvered*: unlike Paracelsus himself: see ii. 220 and n.
    45 *our compact*: cf. iii. 1057.
    59 *topping*: 'Fine; noble; gallant. A low word': Johnson.

To speed me on my enterprise, as once
Your lavish wishes sped me; my own friend!
F/.   And now, what is your purpose, Aureole?
P/.   There is no lack of precedents in a
       case
      Like mine . . . . at least, if not precisely mine,   65
      The case of men cast off by those they sought
      To benefit— — —
F/.   They really cast you off? . . .
      I merely heard a vague tale of some priest
      Cured by your skill, who wrangled at the
       just
      Reward you claimed . . . & that the
       Magistrate   70
      The matter was referred to saw no cause
      To interfere— —nor you to hide your full
      Contempt of him— —nor he, again, to
       smother
      His wrath which raised so hot an opposition
      That Basil soon became no place for you.   75
P/.   The affair of Liechtenfels? The shallowest
       pretext,
      The last & silliest outrage!— —mere pretence!
—   I knew it—I foretold it from the first—
      How soon the stupid wonder you mistook
      For genuine loyalty, a cheering promise   80
      Of better things to come, would pall &
       pass . . .
      And every word comes true—Saul is among
      The prophets! just so long as I was pleased
      To play off all the marvels of my art—
      Fantastic gambols leading to no end,—   85
      I had huge praise, & doubtless might have
       grown

1835 62 sped me, my own friend?   65 Like mine,   70 claim'd; and . . . .
magistrate   72 interfere,   73 him;   77 outrage—mere pretence.
78 I knew it, I . . . . first,   80 loyalty—   81 come—would pall and pass;
82 true.

To speed me on my enterprise, as once
Your lavish wishes sped me, my own friend!
   Festus. What is your purpose, Aureole?
   Paracelsus.   Oh, for purpose,
There is no lack of precedents in a case
Like mine; at least, if not precisely mine,   65
The case of men cast off by those they sought
To benefit.
   Festus.   They really cast you off?
I only heard a vague tale of some priest,
Cured by your skill, who wrangled at your
   claim,
Knowing his life's worth best; and how the
   judge   70
The matter was referred to, saw no cause
To interfere, nor you to hide your full
Contempt of him; nor he, again, to
   smother
His wrath thereat, which raised so fierce a flame
That Basil soon was made no place for you.   75
   Paracelsus. The affair of Liechtenfels? the
   shallowest fable,
The last and silliest outrage—mere pretence!
I knew it, I foretold it from the first,
How soon the stupid wonder you mistook
For genuine loyalty—a cheering promise   80
Of better things to come—would pall and
   pass;
And every word comes true. Saul is among
The prophets! Just so long as I was pleased
To play off the mere antics of my art,
Fantastic gambols leading to no end,   85
I got huge praise: but one can ne'er keep
   down

---

62 *1849* friend?   67 *1849* benefit . . .   76 *1849* shallowest cause,   84
1849 the mere marvels of my art—   85 *1849* no end—

---

  82 *Saul*: see 1 Samuel 10:12: 'Therefore it became a proverb, Is Saul also
among the prophets?'

Grey in the exposition of such antics   86a
Had my stock lasted long enough;—but such   b
Was not my purpose— —one can ne'er keep
   down   c
Our foolish nature's weakness—there they
   flocked   87
Poor devils, jostling, swearing & perspiring
Till the walls rang again— — . . . & all for me!
I had a kindness for them,—which was right—   90
But then I stopped not 'till I tacked to that
A trust in them & a respect— —a sort
Of sympathy for them . . I, in short, began
To teach them, not amaze them; to impart
The spirit which should instigate the search   95
Of truth— —forthwith a mighty squadron
   straight
Filed off:—"the sifted chaff of the sack," I
   said,—
Redoubling my endeavours to secure
The rest; when lo! one man had tarried so long   100
Only to ascertain if I supported
This tenet or the other;—another loved
To hear impartially before he judged,
And now was satisfied;—one had all along
Spied error where his neighbours marveled
   most:—   106
—   This doctor set a school up to revive
The good old ways which could content our
   sires   110
Tho' not their squeamish sons;—the other
   worthy
Discovered divers verses of St John

1835 86c purpose: 89 again; and   90 them, which was right;   93
them: 96 truth.   96 {No equivalent in MS or 1835.}   105, 108, 109
{No equivalent in MS or 1835.}

Our foolish nature's weakness. There they
    flocked,
Poor devils, jostling, swearing and perspiring,
Till the walls rang again; and all for me!
I had a kindness for them, which was right;   90
But then I stopped not till I tacked to that
A trust in them and a respect—a sort
Of sympathy for them; I must needs begin
To teach them, not amaze them, "to impart
"The spirit which should instigate the search   95
"Of truth," just what you bade me! I spoke out.
Forthwith a mighty squadron, in disgust,
Filed off—"the sifted chaff of the sack," I said,
Redoubling my endeavours to secure
The rest. When lo! one man had tarried so long   100
Only to ascertain if I supported
This tenet of his, or that; another loved
To hear impartially before he judged,
And having heard, now judged; this bland
    disciple
Passed for my dupe, but all along, it seems,   105
Spied error where his neighbours marvelled
    most;
That fiery doctor who had hailed me friend,
Did it because my by-paths, once proved wrong
And beaconed properly, would commend again
The good old ways our sires jogged safely o'er,   110
Though not their squeamish sons; the other
    worthy
Discovered divers verses of St. John,

---

87 *1849* weakness: 100 *1849* The rest; when lo! one man had stayed thus
long   108 *Berg* {rejected} bye paths proved unsafe {altered to} bye paths
proved all wrong   109 *Berg* {rejected} would best commend

98 *chaff*: proverbial: 'Sift him grain by grain and he proveth but chaff': *Oxford
Dictionary of English Proverbs* (2nd ed., 1948).
    108 *by-paths*: cf. *II Henry IV*, IV. v. 185: 'by-paths and indirect crook'd ways'.
    109 *beaconed*: cf. *Epipsychidion*, 147–8: 'Thy wisdom speaks in me, and bids
me dare / Beacon the rocks on which high hearts are wrecked'.

Which read successively refreshed the soul
But muttered backwards cured the gout, the
    stone
The cholic & what not—*quid multa?*—the end   115
Was a clear class-room & a quiet leer
From grave folk, & a sour reproachful look
From those in chief who, cap in hand, installed
The new Professor scarce a year before,—
— — And a vast flourish about patient merit   120
Obscured awhile by flashy tricks, but sure
Sooner or later to emerge in splendour,—
Of which the example was some luckless wight
Whom my arrival had discomfited
But now, it seems, the general voice recalled   125
To fill my chair & so efface the stain
Basil had long incurred;— — —I sought no
    better:
— Nought but a quiet dismissal from my Post—
And from my heart I wished them better suited
And better served:—goodnight to Basil, then!   130
But fast as I proposed to rid the tribe
Of my obnoxious self, I could not spare them
The pleasure of a parting kick: . . .
F/.   You smile:— —
Despise them as they merit!
P/.   If I smile
Tis with as very contempt as ever turned   135
Flesh into stone: this courteous recompense,

Which, read successively, refreshed the soul,
But, muttered backwards, cured the gout, the
    stone,
The colic and what not. *Quid multa?* The end   115
Was a clear class-room, and a quiet leer
From grave folk, and a sour reproachful glance
From those in chief who, cap in hand, installed
The new professor scarce a year before;
And a vast flourish about patient merit   120
Obscured awhile by flashy tricks, but sure
Sooner or later to emerge in splendour—
Of which the example was some luckless wight
Whom my arrival had discomfited,
But now, it seems, the general voice recalled   125
To fill my chair and so efface the stain
Basil had long incurred. I sought no
    better,
Only a quiet dismissal from my post,
And from my heart I wished them better suited
And better served. Good night to Basil, then!   130
But fast as I proposed to rid the tribe
Of my obnoxious back, I could not spare them
The pleasure of a parting kick.
     Festus.   You smile:
Despise them as they merit!
     Paracelsus.   If I smile,
'T is with as very contempt as ever turned   135
Flesh into stone. This courteous recompense,

---

115 *1849* The cholic, and what not:— *1863,1865* The colic, and what
not.   116 *1849* class-room, with a quiet leer   122 *1849,1865–89* later *1863*
latter   127 *1849* better—   128 *1849* Nought but a quiet . . . .
post;   129 *1849* While from . . . . suited,   136 *1849* stone: this . . . .
recompense! *1863* stone. This . . . . recompense! *1865* stone. This . . . .
recompense

---

114 *muttered backwards*: the recital of a passage of Scripture backwards was
common in the practices of black magic.
115 *Quid multa?*: what need is there for me to expatiate?
120 *a vast flourish*: a great deal of eloquence.
133 *a parting kick*: 'the flying-sheet was mild compared to the chastisement
. . . which he drew up for the preface to his "Buch Paragranum." The Basel of
1528 is pilloried in these to all time': Stoddart, p. 139.

This grateful . . . Festus, were your nature fit
To be defiled— —your eyes, the eyes to ache
At festering blotches—eating poisoning blains,
The ulcerous barky scurf of leprosy   140
Which finds a Man, & leaves a hideous
     Thing
That cannot but be mended by
     hell-fire— — —
I would lay bare the heart of man to you;—
Which God cursed long ago,—which devils
     have made
Their pet-nest & their never-tiring home, ...   145
— — — O, Sages have found out that Man is born
For various ends,—to love, to know;—has ever
One stumbled in his search on any signs
Of a nature in him formed to *Hate*? . . to *Hate*?
. . . If that be Man's true object which evokes   150
His powers in fullest strength, be sure 'tis
     Hate;—
Yet Men have doubted if the best & bravest
Of Spirits can nourish him with Hate
     alone! . . .
I had not the monopoly of fools,
It seems, at Basil;—
F/.   But your plans—your plans!   155
I have yet to learn your purpose, Aureole!
P/.   Whether to sink beneath such ponderous
     shame—
To shrink in like a crushed snail—to endure

1835 138 defiled, your eyes   139 blotches,   141 man and leaves a hideous
thing   142 hell fire,   143 you,   145 pet nest and . . . . home.   146
O, sages . . . . man   147 ends—to love, to know.   149 form'd to *hate*?
To *hate*?   150 man's   151 hate: 152 men   153 spirits . . . . hate
alone.   155 Basil. | *Fest.* But your plans, your plans:

This grateful . . . Festus, were your nature fit
To be defiled, your eyes the eyes to ache
At gangrene-blotches, eating poison-blains,
The ulcerous barky scurf of leprosy   140
Which finds—a man, and leaves—a hideous
    thing
That cannot but be mended by hell
    fire,
—I would lay bare to you the human heart
Which God cursed long ago, and devils make
    since
Their pet nest and their never-tiring home.   145
Oh, sages have discovered we are born
For various ends—to love, to know: has ever
One stumbled, in his search, on any signs
Of a nature in us formed to hate? To hate?
If that be our true object which evokes   150
Our powers in fullest strength, be sure 't is
    hate!
Yet men have doubted if the best and bravest
Of spirits can nourish him with hate
    alone.
I had not the monopoly of fools,
It seems, at Basil.
        Festus.   But your plans, your plans!   155
I have yet to learn your purpose, Aureole!
        Paracelsus. Whether to sink beneath such
            ponderous shame,
To shrink up like a crushed snail, undergo

139–43 *1849* At gangrened blotches, eating poisonous blains, | The ulcered
barky scurf of leprosy | Which finds—a man, and leaves—a hideous thing |
That cannot but be mended by hell fire, | —I say that, could you see as I could
show, | I would lay bare to you these human hearts   144 *Berg* {rejected} and
devils make now   149 *1849* in him formed *Berg* in ⟨him⟩ [us]
form'd   152–4 {Omitted from *1849*}   155–6 *1849 Fest.* But I have yet to
learn your purpose, Aureole! | *Par.* What purpose were the fittest now for
me?   157 *1849* Decide! To sink   158 *1849* snail—

139 *eating*: cf. i. 694.
    poison-blains: not in OED. Johnson defines a blain as 'A pustule; a botch; a
blister'.

In silence & desist from further toil
And so subside into a monument   160
Of one their censure blasted? Or to bow
Cheerfully as submissively,—to lower
My old pretensions even as they dictate,
To drop into the rank their wit assigns me,
And live as they prescribe, & make that use   165
Of all my knowledge which their rules allow—
Proud to be patted now & then, & careful
To practise the fit posture for receiving
The amplest benefit from their hoofs appliance
When they shall condescend to tutor me?— —   170
— — Then one may feel resentment like a flame
Within—& deck false systems in truth's garb
And tangle & entwine mankind with error
And give them darkness for a dower, &
    falsehood
For a possession, ages: or one may mope   175
Into a shade, for thinking: or may drowse
Into a dreamless sleep & so die off:—
But I . . . now Festus shall divine . . . but I
Am merely setting out once more—embracing
My earliest aims again! what thinks he now?   180

F/.   Your aims? *The Aims?—to Know?*—& where is
            found
        The trust, the sure belief . . . .

P/.   Nay, not so fast;—
        The Aims, . . . but not the Means—you know
            they made me
        A laughing stock . . I was a fool—you know

1835 161 blasted; or   163 dictate—   169 hoofs' appliance,   170
me.   172 Within, and . . . . Truth's garb,   173 error;   176 shade for
thinking;   179 more,   181 *the aims?—to know?* and   183 *The aims—*
but not the means.   184 A laughing-stock: I was a fool;

In silence and desist from further toil,
And so subside into a monument   160
Of one their censure blasted? or to bow
Cheerfully as submissively, to lower
My old pretensions even as Basil dictates,
To drop into the rank her wits assign me
And live as they prescribe, and make that use   165
Of my poor knowledge which their rules allow,
Proud to be patted now and then, and careful
To practise the true posture for receiving
The amplest benefit from their hoofs' appliance
When they shall condescend to tutor me?   170
Then, one may feel resentment like a flame
Within, and deck false systems in truth's garb,
And tangle and entwine mankind with error,
And give them darkness for a dower and
    falsehood
For a possession, ages: or one may mope   175
Into a shade through thinking, or else drowse
Into a dreamless sleep and so die off.
But I,—now Festus shall divine!—but I
Am merely setting out once more, embracing
My earliest aims again! What thinks he now?   180
    Festus. Your aims? the aims?—to Know? and
        where is found
    The early trust . . .
    Paracelsus.   Nay, not so fast; I say,
The aims—not the old means. You know they
    made me
A laughing-stock; I was a fool; you know

161 *1849* blasted;   162 *1849* submissively—   163 *1849* dictates—   164
1849 her wits assign me, *Berg* {rejected} her wits assign,   166 *1849*
allow—   170 *1849* tutor me.   172 *1849* Prompting to deck false systems
in Truth's garb,   175 *1849* For a possession: or one may mope away   177
1849 sleep, and so die off: 178–80 *1849* But I, but I—now Festus shall
divine! | —Am merely setting out in life once more, | Embracing my old aims!
What thinks he now?   181 *1849* know?   183 *1849* You know what made
me

160 *a monument*: a perpetual reminder.
175 *mope*: 'To be stupid; to drowse; to be in a constant day-dream; to be
spiritless, inactive and inattentive': Johnson.

The when & the how—hardly those Means
    again! . . .   185
Not but they had their beauty— —who should
    know
Their passing beauty if not I?—but still
They were dreams, so let them vanish!—yet in
    beauty
If that may be,— —stay—(he
    sings)
      Heap cassia, sandal-buds, & stripes   190
        Of labdanum, & aloe-balls
      Smeared with dull nard an Indian wipes
        From out her hair . . . such balsam
          falls
      From tall trees where tired winds are fain,   195
      Spent with the vast & howling main,
      To treasure half their island-gain; . . .

      And strew faint sweetness from some old
      Egyptians fine worm-eaten shroud

1835 185 and the how: hardly those means again;   188 vanish: yet in
beauty,   189 be. Stay . . .   193 hair: 194 {No equivalent in MS or
1835.}   199 Egyptian's . . . . shroud,

The when and the how: hardly those means
   again!   185
Not but they had their beauty; who should
   know
Their passing beauty, if not I? Still, dreams
They were, so let them vanish, yet in
   beauty
If that may be. Stay: thus they pass in song!
                         [*He sings.*

Heap cassia, sandal-buds and stripes   190
   Of labdanum, and aloe-balls,
Smeared with dull nard an Indian wipes
   From out her hair: such balsam falls
   Down sea-side mountain pedestals,
From tree-tops where tired winds are fain,   195
Spent with the vast and howling main,
To treasure half their island-gain.

And strew faint sweetness from some old
   Egyptian's fine worm-eaten shroud

---

186 *1849* beauty—   187 *1849–65* if not I? But still   188 *1849* They were
dreams, so let them vanish; yet   *1863,1865* They were dreams, so let them
vanish, yet   *1868* They were, so let them vanish, yet in beauty,   189 *1849*
Stay—thus they pass in song! | *He sings.*)   *Berg* {rejected} Stay;— hear Aprile
sing!   193 *1849* (such   195 *1849* From summits where   197 *1849*
island-gain.)

187 *passing*: surpassing.
190 *Heap cassia*: in this lament for his past dreams Paracelsus imagines
himself building a 'pile' or funeral pyre heaped with aromatics. Many of their
names smack of Browning's reading. In Psalm 45:8 aloes and cassia are
mentioned, with myrrh. Sandalwood is used in Eastern cremations, and also
made into an ointment. Labdanum is an aromatic resin ('stripes', strips).
Johnson defines 'nard' as 'spikenard', quoting *Paradise Lost*, v. 292–3: 'through
groves of myrrh, / And flowering odours, cassia, nard, and balm'. 'Nard, and
cassia's balmy smells' also occur together in *Comus*, 990. 'Dull nard' may
possibly be due to a misreading of a passage in Barten Holyday's translation of
Persius (1673, p. 335), where we hear of a neglected funeral feast: '[One] with
neglect into thy Urn will throw / Thy bones without perfumes, careless to
know / Whether he buy dull-smelling Cinnamun, / Or Casia corrupt with
Cherry-gumme'. Balsam is a product of aromatic resin. DeVane believed that
the lines were much influenced by Christopher Smart: *Browning's Parleyings:
The Autobiography of a Mind* (1927), p. 115.
194 *Down sea-side mountain pedestals*: perhaps the remains of columns, or
ruined altars, as in a 'classical landscape' in the tradition of Claude and Poussin.
199 *worm-eaten shroud*: the wrappings of Egyptian mummies were valued for
medicinal purposes and for their aromatic properties.

Which breaks to dust when once
        unrolled;— —   200
    Or shredded perfume like a cloud
    From closet, long to quiet vowed
    With mothed & dropping arras hung,
    Mouldering her lute & books among
    As when a Queen, long dead, was young.   205

Mine, every word!—& on such pile shall die
My lovely fancies—with fair perished things,
Themselves fair & forgotten—yes, forgotten
Or why abjure them?—So I made this rhyme
That fitting dignity might be preserved: . . .   210
No little proud was I— —tho' the list of drugs
Smacks of my old vocation, & the verse
Halts like the best of Luther's psalms— —.
F/.   But, Aureole,
Talk not thus wildly & madly; I am here—
Did you know all!—but I have travelled far   215
To learn your wishes . . Be yourself again!
For in this mood I recognize you less
Than in the horrible despondency
I witnessed last: you may account this, joy, . . .
But rather let me gaze on your despair   220
Than hear your incoherent words, & see
That flushed cheek & intensely sparkling
        eye . . .
P/.   Why, man, I was lighthearted in my prime, —

1835 202 From closet long to quiet vow'd,   205 queen,   206 word;
and   207 fancies with   208 and forgotten; yes, forgotten,   211 was I;
though   214 madly.   216 wishes. Be yourself again;   219 I witness'd
last. You may account this joy;   222 flush'd cheek and intensely-sparkling
eye.

Which breaks to dust when once
    unrolled;   200
Or shredded perfume, like a cloud
From closet long to quiet vowed,
With mothed and dropping arras hung,
Mouldering her lute and books among,
As when a queen, long dead, was young.   205

Mine, every word! And on such pile shall die
My lovely fancies, with fair perished things,
Themselves fair and forgotten; yes, forgotten,
Or why abjure them? So, I made this rhyme
That fitting dignity might be preserved;   210
No little proud was I; though the list of drugs
Smacks of my old vocation, and the verse
Halts like the best of Luther's psalms.
    Festus.   But, Aureole,
Talk not thus wildly and madly. I am here—
Did you know all! I have travelled far, indeed,   215
To learn your wishes. Be yourself again!
For in this mood I recognize you less
Than in the horrible despondency
I witnessed last. You may account this, joy;
But rather let me gaze on that despair   220
Than hear these incoherent words and see
This flushed cheek and intensely-sparkling
    eye.
    Paracelsus. Why, man, I was light-hearted in
    my prime,

---

201 *1849* And shred dim perfume,   202 *1849* From chamber long   204–5
1849 Mouldering the lute and books among | Of queen, long dead, who lived
there young.   206 *1849* word!—   213 *1849* psalms!   215 *1849* Did you
know all, indeed! I have travelled far   222 *1849* eye!   *223 {Reading of
1849–68} *1888, 1889* prime

  203 *mothed*: OED has no other example of this word.
  206 *Mine, every word*: Paracelsus is a poet. Cf. 225, 546.
  213 *Luther's psalms*: writing on 'Luther's Psalm' in *Fraser's Magazine* for
January, 1831, Carlyle had emphasized the lack of music in Luther's Spiritual
Songs: translating one, he comments that it 'jars upon our ears' (*The Works*,
Centenary ed, xxvii. 161). Cf. Browning's nightmare about 'a complete ver-
sion of the Psalms by Donne': p. 111 above.

I am lighthearted now— —what would you
          have?
— —   Tis the very augury of success I want!   226
          Why should I not be joyous even as then?
F/.   Joyous? & how? & what remains for
                joy?
          You have declared the Ends (which I am sick
          Of naming) are impracticable . . .
P/.   Aye,   230
          Pursued as I pursued them . . the arch-fool!
—   Listen—my plan will please you not, 'tis like,
          But you are little versed in the world's ways:—
          This is my plan, (first drinking its good
                luck!)—
          I will accept *all* helps!—all I despised   235
          So rashly at the outset, equally
          With early impulses which lately seemed
          The mere persuasion of fantastic dreams . . . .
          All helps . . . no one sort shall exclude the
                rest:—
          I seek to KNOW & to ENJOY:—well then,—   240
          For all my cause should seem the cause of God
          Once more, as first I dreamed,—it shall not
                baulk me
          Of the meanest, earthliest, sensualest delight
          That may be realised;—for joy is gain,   245
          And gain is gain however small: nor, should

1835 224 now;   225 {No equivalent in *MS* or *1835*.}   228 Joyous!
and   229 ends   230 impracticable.   232 Listen: my . . . . like;   233
ways . . .   234   plan—(first . . . . luck)—   235 helps;   237
impulses,   238 dreams;   240 ENJOY. Well then—   241, 247 {No
equivalent in *MS* or *1835*.}

I am light-hearted now; what would you have?
Aprile was a poet, I make songs—   225
'T is the very augury of success I want!
Why should I not be joyous now as then?
   Festus. Joyous! and how? and what remains for
     joy?
You have declared the ends (which I am sick
Of naming) are impracticable.
   Paracelsus.   Ay,   230
Pursued as I pursued them—the arch-fool!
Listen: my plan will please you not, 't is like,
But you are little versed in the world's ways.
This is my plan—(first drinking its good
    luck)—
I will accept all helps; all I despised   235
So rashly at the outset, equally
With early impulses, late years have quenched:
I have tried each way singly: now for both!
All helps! no one sort shall exclude the
    rest.
I seek to know and to enjoy at once,   240
Not one without the other as before.
Suppose my labour should seem God's own
    cause
Once more, as first I dreamed,—it shall not
    baulk me
Of the meanest earthliest sensualest delight
That may be snatched; for every joy is gain,   245
And gain is gain, however small. My soul
Can die then, nor be taunted—"what was
    gained?"

---

232 *1849* like;   237 *Berg* impulses, ⟨which lately seem'd⟩ ⟨which⟩ [late years
have quenched;]   238 *1849* each way singly—   *Berg* {rejected} two ways,
singly—   239 *1849* helps—   240 *1849* to KNOW and to ENJOY   243 *1849*
dreamed, it shall not balk   246 *1849* And why spurn gain, however small?
My soul   247 *1849* taunted "what

---

237 *impulses*: impulses which: cf. textual notes.

On the other hand those honeyed pleasures
  follow
As tho' I had not spurned them hitherto,
Shall they o'ercloud my spirits rapt
  communion   250
With the tumultuous Past, the teeming Future
Glorious with visions of a full success . . . .

F/.   Success!
P/.   And wherefore not? why not
  prefer
The grand results obtained in my best state
Of being, to those derived from seasons dark   255
As the thoughts they bred? when I was
  best—my youth
Unwasted—seemed success not surest too?
Is it not Darkness' nature to obscure?
— — I am a wanderer: I remember well
One journey, how I feared the track was
  missed,—   260
So long the city I desired to reach
Lay hid—when suddenly its spires afar
Flashed thro' the circling clouds— —you may
  conceive
My transport:—soon the vapours closed again,
But I had seen the city, & one such glance   265
No darkness could obscure:— —nor shall sad
  days
Destroy the vivid memories of the
  Past:
I will fight the battle out!—a little spent
Perhaps—but still an able combatant: 270
You look at my grey hair & furrowed brow?
But I can turn even weakness to account— —
Of many tricks I know, 'tis not the least

1835 250 spirit's   251 past, the teeming future,   258 darkness'   262
hid,   263 Flash'd through . . . . clouds;   267 {No equivalent in *MS* or
1835.}   268 past: 270 combatant.   271 brow;   272 account:

Nor, on the other hand, should pleasure follow
As though I had not spurned her hitherto,
Shall she o'ercloud my spirit's rapt
    communion   250
With the tumultuous past, the teeming future,
Glorious with visions of a full success.
    Festus. Success!
    Paracelsus.   And wherefore not? Why not
        prefer
Results obtained in my best state of being,
To those derived alone from seasons dark   255
As the thoughts they bred? When I was best, my
    youth
Unwasted, seemed success not surest too?
It is the nature of darkness to obscure.
I am a wanderer: I remember well
One journey, how I feared the track was
    missed,   260
So long the city I desired to reach
Lay hid; when suddenly its spires afar
Flashed through the circling clouds; you may
    conceive
My transport. Soon the vapours closed again,
But I had seen the city, and one such glance   265
No darkness could obscure: nor shall the
    present—
A few dull hours, a passing shame or two,
Destroy the vivid memories of the past.
I will fight the battle out; a little spent
Perhaps, but still an able combatant.   270
You look at my grey hair and furrowed brow?
But I can turn even weakness to account:
Of many tricks I know,'t is not the least

248 *1849* hand, if pleasure meets me   251 *1863, 1865* Past, ...
Future,   252 *1849–65* success!   256 *1849* best—   257 *1849*
Unwasted—   263–4 *1849* clouds; conceive my joy! | Too soon the vapours
closed o'er it again,   266 *1849* present *1863, 1865* Present—   267 *Berg*
{rejected} A few desponding days, a little shame   268 *1863, 1865*
Past.   269 *1849* out!—a little tired, *1863, 1865* out!—a little spent   270
1849 Perhaps—

To push the ruins of my frame whereon
The fire of vigour trembles scarce alive   275
Into a heap, & send the flame aloft!
—   What should I do with Age?—so sickness lends
An aid;—it being, I fear, the source of all
We boast of: mind is nothing but disease
And natural health is ignorance:—
F/.   There is   280
But one good symptom in this notable scheme:
I feared your sudden project had in view
To wreak immediate vengeance on your
     foes,—
Tis not so: I am glad.
P/.   And if I please
To spit on them—to trample them,—what
     then?   285
Tis sorry warfare truly but the fools
Provoke it: I ne'er sought to domineer,—
The mere asserting my supremacy   287a
Has little mortified their self-conceit   b
—   I took my natural station & no more;   c
But if they *will* provoke me,—will not suffer
Forbearance on my part—if I can have
No quality in the shade, but must put forth   290
Power for power—my strength against
     theirs—
Must teach them their own game with their
     own arms . . .
Why be it so, & let them take their chance!
I am above them like a God—there's no
Hiding the fact—&, had I been but wise,   295
Had ne'er concerned myself with scruples, nor
Communicated aught to such a race,—
But been content to own myself a Man,   300

1835 277 What . . . . age? so   280 ignorance.   283 foes;   285 on them,
to trample them,   287 domineer;   287b self-conceit;   291 for
power;   297 race;   298, 299 {No equivalent in *MS* or *1835*.}   300
man,

To push the ruins of my frame, whereon
The fire of vigour trembles scarce alive,   275
Into a heap, and send the flame aloft.
What should I do with age? So, sickness lends
An aid; it being, I fear, the source of all
We boast of: mind is nothing but disease,
And natural health is ignorance.
    Festus.   I see   280
But one good symptom in this notable scheme.
I feared your sudden journey had in view
To wreak immediate vengeance on your
    foes;
'T is not so: I am glad.
    Paracelsus.   And if I please
To spit on them, to trample them, what
    then?   285
'T is sorry warfare truly, but the fools
Provoke it. I would spare their self-conceit
But if they must provoke me, cannot suffer
Forbearance on my part, if I may keep
No quality in the shade, must needs put forth   290
Power to match power, my strength against their
    strength,
And teach them their own game with their own
    arms—
Why, be it so and let them take their chance!
I am above them like a god, there 's no
Hiding the fact: what idle scruples, then,   295
Were those that ever bade me soften it,
Communicate it gently to the world,
Instead of proving my supremacy,
Taking my natural station o'er their head,
Then owning all the glory was a man's!   300

276 *1849–65* aloft!   277 *1849* so sickness   281 *1849* notable plan: *283
1849–68 foes; *1888, 1889* foes   284 *1849* And if I pleased   287 *1849* Pro-
voke it: I had spared   288 *1849* provoke me—   289 *1849* part—   294
1849 God—in vain *1863* God, there's no   295 *1849* To hide the
fact—   299 *1849–65* their heads,   300 *1849* man's,

And in my elevation Man's would be . . .   301
But live & learn, tho' life's so short: as
    'tis,—
— — Tho' no more than the wreck of my past
    self, . .
I fear, dear Pütter, that your lecture-room
Must wait awhile for its best ornament,—   305
The penitent Empiric who set up
For somebody, but soon was taught his place . .
Now, but too happy to be let confess
His error, snuff the candles, &
    illustrate
Your tenets' soundness in his person . . . wait,   311
Good Pütter!

F/.   He who sneers thus, is a God!
P/.   Ay, Ay, laugh at me! I am very glad
You are not gulled by all this swaggering
    ——you
Can see the root of the matter!—how I strive   315
To put a good face on the overthrow
I have experienced—& to hide & bury
My degradation in its length & breadth
—   And how the motives I would make you think
Just mingle as is due with nobler passions,—   320
The cursed lusts I modestly allow
May influence me as I am mortal still,—
Are goading me, & fast supplanting all
My youth's desires:— —you are no stupid
    dupe,

_1835_ 301 man's   302 short! as 't is—   306 empiric,   310 {No equival-
ent in _MS_ or _1835_.}   311 person.   314 swaggering;   317 experienced,
and   318 and breadth;   322 me—as I am mortal still—   324 desires:
you . . . . dupe;

—And in my elevation man's would be.
But live and learn, though life's short, learning,
    hard!
And therefore, though the wreck of my past
    self,
I fear, dear Pütter, that your lecture-room
Must wait awhile for its best ornament,   305
The penitent empiric, who set up
For somebody, but soon was taught his place;
Now, but too happy to be let confess
His error, snuff the candles, and illustrate
(*Fiat experientia corpore vili*)   310
Your medicine's soundness in his person. Wait,
Good Pütter!
    Festus.   He who sneers thus, is a god!
    Paracelsus. Ay, ay, laugh at me! I am very glad
You are not gulled by all this swaggering;
    you
Can see the root of the matter!—how I strive   315
To put a good face on the overthrow
I have experienced, and to bury and hide
My degradation in its length and breadth;
How the mean motives I would make you think
Just mingle as is due with nobler aims,   320
The appetites I modestly allow
May influence me as being mortal still—
Do goad me, drive me on, and fast supplant
My youth's desires. You are no stupid
    dupe:

301 *1849* And in . . . . would be!   302 *1849* short; learning, hard!   *Berg*
short, learning hard!   After 302: *1849* Still, one thing I have learned—not to
despair: 307 *1849* place—   311 *Berg* Your medecine's   312 *1849, 1863*
a God!   322 *1849* me—as I am mortal still—   323 *1849* drive me   *Berg*
⟨and⟩ drive me   324 *1849* desires: you . . . , dupe;

302 *life's short, learning, hard!*: an allusion to the first aphorism of Hippo-
crates, father of medicine, in its familiar Latin form: 'Ars longa, vita brevis'. Cf.
ii. 497.
306–7 *who set up* / *For somebody*: who claimed to be someone of importance.
310 *(Fiat experientia*: 'let the experiment be done on a useless body': prover-
bial. More often 'fiat experimentum in corpore vili'.

You find me out— —yes, I had sent for you   325
To palm these childish lies upon you, Festus!
Laugh,—*you* shall laugh at me!

F/·   —Dear Aureole, then
The Past is nothing? is our intercourse
Yet to begin— —have I to swear I mean
No flattery in this or that? Whatever   330
You be, this is no degradation . . these
Unworthy thoughts no inmates of your mind;
Or wherefore this disorder? you are troubled
As much by the intrusion of base views
Familiar to your adversaries, as they   335
Would be should your high qualities alight
Amid their murky souls: & even so
A stray wolf which the winter forces down
From the bleak hills suffices to affright
A village in the vales— —while foresters   340
Sleep sound tho' all night long the famished
     troops
Snuff round & scratch against their crazy
     huts:— — —
These evil things are monsters & will flee.

P/.   May you be happy, Festus, my own
                 friend!

F/.   Nay, further—the delights you fain would
                 think   345
Have superseded nobler aims,—the harmless
And ordinary stimulants, will never
Content you— — —

P/.   Ah, forbear!—I once
             despised— — —
But that soon passes: we are high at first

You find me out! Yes, I had sent for you   325
To palm these childish lies upon you, Festus!
Laugh—you shall laugh at me!
   Festus.   The past, then, Aureole,
Proves nothing? Is our interchange of love
Yet to begin? Have I to swear I mean
No flattery in this speech or that? For you,   330
Whate'er you say, there is no degradation;
These low thoughts are no inmates of your mind,
Or wherefore this disorder? You are vexed
As much by the intrusion of base views,
Familiar to your adversaries, as they   335
Were troubled should your qualities alight
Amid their murky souls; not otherwise,
A stray wolf which the winter forces down
From our bleak hills, suffices to affright
A village in the vales—while foresters   340
Sleep calm, though all night long the famished
   troops
Snuff round and scratch against their crazy
   huts.
These evil thoughts are monsters, and will flee.
   Paracelsus. May you be happy, Festus, my own
      friend!
   Festus. Nay, further; the delights you fain
      would think   345
The superseders of your nobler aims,
Though ordinary and harmless stimulants,
Will ne'er content you. . . .
   Paracelsus.   Hush! I once despised
      them,
But that soon passes. We are high at first

---

327 *1863, 1865* Past,   331 *1849* degradation,   332 *1849* mind; *341
{Reading of *1849–68*.}   *1888, 1889* famished troop   342 *1849* huts: 348
1849 despised them, *Berg* despised . . .   349 *1849* passes:

328 *interchange of love*: cf. *Richard III*, II. i. 26.
333 *disorder*: disturbance: cf. *King John*, III. iv. 102: 'such disorder in my wit'.

In our demands, nor will abate a jot   350
Of their strict value . . . but time passes o'er
And humbler spirits accept what we refuse—
In short when some such comfort is doled out
As these delights— —we cannot long retain
The bitter contempt which urges us at first   355
To hurl it back— —but hug it to our breast
And thankfully retire:—this life of mine
Must be lived out & a grave thoroughly
    earned:—
I am just fit for that & nought beside.
— — I told you once, I cannot now Enjoy   360
Unless I deem my Knowledge gains thereby,—
Nor can I Know without warm tears revealing
The need of linking some Delight to
    Knowledge,—
So on I drive . . . Enjoying all I can
And Knowing all I can:—I speak, of course,   365
Confusedly—*this* will better explain . . feel
    here!
Quick beating, is it not? a fire which must
Be worked off someway, this as well as any:
So Festus sees me fairly launched;—his calm
Compassionate look might have disturbed me
    once,   370
But now, far from rejecting, I invite it— —
I can lament with him, & lay myself
Open before him, & receive his pity,
And hope, if he command hope—& believe
What he would have me;—satiating myself   375
With his enduring love:—& he shall leave me
To give place to some credulous disciple
Who holds that God is wise, but Paracelsus
Has his peculiar merits— —I suck in

1835 351 value;   352 refuse;   357 retire.   361 knowledge gains
thereby;   363 delight to knowledge: 364 drive—enjoying   365
knowing all I can.   366 Confusedly; *this* . . . . explain—   371 it.   374
hope; and believe   375 me—   379 merits.

In our demand, nor will abate a jot   350
Of toil's strict value; but time passes o'er,
And humbler spirits accept what we refuse:
In short, when some such comfort is doled out
As these delights, we cannot long retain
Bitter contempt which urges us at first   355
To hurl it back, but hug it to our breast
And thankfully retire. This life of mine
Must be lived out and a grave thoroughly
    earned:
I am just fit for that and nought beside.
I told you once, I cannot now enjoy,   360
Unless I deem my knowledge gains through joy;
Nor can I know, but straight warm tears reveal
My need of linking also joy to
    knowledge:
So, on I drive, enjoying all I can,
And knowing all I can. I speak, of course,   365
Confusedly; this will better explain—feel
    here!
Quick beating, is it not?—a fire of the heart
To work off some way, this as well as any.
So, Festus sees me fairly launched; his calm
Compassionate look might have disturbed me
    once,   370
But now, far from rejecting, I invite
What bids me press the closer, lay myself
Open before him, and be soothed with pity;
I hope, if he command hope, and believe
As he directs me—satiating myself   375
With his enduring love. And Festus quits me
To give place to some credulous disciple
Who holds that God is wise, but Paracelsus
Has his peculiar merits: I suck in

350 *1849–65* In our demands,   355 *1849–65* The bitter contempt   360 *1849*
Enjoy,   362 *1849* Know,   364 *1849* So on I drive—   368 *1849* some-
way, this as well as any!   374 *1849* And hope, if he command hope: *1863*,
1865 I hope, if . . . hope;   376 *1849* love: 379 *1849* merits.

His homage—chuckle o'er his admiration   380
And then dismiss him in his turn:—night
   comes,
And I shall give myself to painful study
And patient searching after hidden lore,
—   Shall wring some bright truth from its prison;
   my frame
Shall tremble, & my thin lips swell—my hair   385
Tingle—& all for triumph! & the morn
Shall break on my pent room & dwindling
   lamp
And scattered papers & unfinished scrawls,
And with a failing heart & throbbing brow
I shall review my captured truth—&
   trace   390
Its end & consequence, its further bearings,
Its true affinities, the views it opens,
The length it goes in perfecting my Scheme,
And view it sternly circumscribed—cast down   395
From the high place my fond hopes yielded
   it,—
Proved worthless,—which in getting yet had
   cost
Another wrench to this fast-falling frame;—
And I shall quaff the cup that chases
   sorrow
And lapse back into youth again—& take   400
My fluttering pulse for evidence that God
Means good to me, & see my hopes come true,
And flee away from this remorseless care
Which clogs a spirit born to soar so free

1835 380 homage, chuckle .... admiration, 382 study; 383
lore 384 Shall wring 385 swell, 386 Tingle, 388 scatter'd
papers, and unfinish'd scrawls; 390 captur'd truth, and 391 {No
equivalent in *MS* or *1835*.} 394 scheme, 400 again, and

That homage, chuckle o'er that admiration,   380
And then dismiss the fool; for night is
    come,
And I betake myself to study again,
Till patient searchings after hidden lore
Half wring some bright truth from its prison; my
    frame
Trembles, my forehead's veins swell out, my hair 385
Tingles for triumph. Slow and sure the morn
Shall break on my pent room and dwindling
    lamp
And furnace dead, and scattered earths and ores;
When, with a failing heart and throbbing brow,
I must review my captured truth, sum up   390
Its value, trace what ends to what begins,
Its present power with its eventual bearings,
Latent affinities, the views it opens,
And its full length in perfecting my scheme.
I view it sternly circumscribed, cast down   395
From the high place my fond hopes yielded
    it,
Proved worthless—which, in getting, yet had
    cost
Another wrench to this fast-falling frame.
Then, quick, the cup to quaff, that chases
    sorrow!
I lapse back into youth, and take again   400
My fluttering pulse for evidence that God
Means good to me, will make my cause his own.
See! I have cast off this remorseless care
Which clogged a spirit born to soar so free,

*381 *1849, 1889* come, *1863–88* come. {corrected in DC}   386 *1849–65*
triumph!   388 *1849* ores,   394 *1849* scheme;   398 *1849* frame;
After 400: *1849* Mere hopes of bliss for proofs that bliss will be,   401 *1849*—
My fluttering pulse, *1863, 1865* My fluttering pulse,   402 *1849* own;

387 *pent*: narrow, confined.
404 *Which clogged a spirit*: cf. Donne, 'Of the Progresse of the Soule . . . The
Second Anniversary', lines 9–10 of 'The Harbinger': 'No soule (whiles with
the luggage of this clay / It clogged is) can follow thee halfe way'. At i. 761,
above, we hear of the soul 'clogged by sickness'. Cf. *Prometheus Unbound*, III. iv.
202: 'The clogs of that which else might oversoar . . .'

And my dim chamber shall become a tent,   405
And Festus shall sit by me, & sweet Michal
Shall make as tho' my ardent words should find
No echo in a maiden's quiet soul—   410
But her pure bosom shall heave, her eyes fill
    fast
With tears, her lips shall tremble, all the while!
Ha, ha!

F/.   —It seems then, you expect to reap
No unreal joy from this your present course;
That you expect . . .

P/.   To die! I owe that much   415
To what I *was*, at least— —I should be sad
To live contented after such a fall— —
To thrive & fatten after such reverse!
The whole plan is a makeshift, but will last
My time:

F/.   And you have never mused & said   420
"I had a noble purpose—& the strength
"To compass it; but I have stopped halfway
"And have bestowed the firstfruits of my toil
"On objects little worthy to receive them:
"Why linger round them still? why clench my
    fault?   425
"Why seek for consolation in defeat
"In vain endeavours to derive a beauty
"From ugliness? why seek to make the most
"Of what no power can change, in place of
    striving
"With mighty effort to redeem the past,   430
"To gather up the treasures I cast down,

1835 407, 408 {No equivalent in *MS* or *1835*.}   412 tremble   416 I *was* at
least.   420 My time . . . | . . . . mused and said,   421 purpose,
and   425 {*MS* may read 'clinch' in this line.}   426 defeat—

And my dim chamber has become a tent,   405
Festus is sitting by me, and his Michal . . .
Why do you start? I say, she listening here,
(For yonder—Würzburg through the orchard-
    bough!)
Motions as though such ardent words should
    find
No echo in a maiden's quiet soul,   410
But her pure bosom heaves, her eyes fill fast
With tears, her sweet lips tremble all the while!
Ha, ha!
  Festus. It seems, then, you expect to reap
No unreal joy from this your present course,
But rather . . .
  Paracelsus. Death! To die! I owe that much   415
To what, at least, I was. I should be sad
To live contented after such a fall,
To thrive and fatten after such reverse!
The whole plan is a makeshift, but will last
My time.
  Festus. And you have never mused and said,   420
"I had a noble purpose, and the strength
"To compass it; but I have stopped half-way,
"And wrongly given the first-fruits of my toil
"To objects little worthy of the gift.
"Why linger round them still? why clench my
    fault?   425
"Why seek for consolation in defeat,
"In vain endeavours to derive a beauty
"From ugliness? why seek to make the most
"Of what no power can change, nor strive
    instead
"With mighty effort to redeem the past   430
"And, gathering up the treasures thus cast down,

---

408 *1849–65* (For yonder's Würzburg through the orchard-boughs)   417
1849 fall—   421 *1849* and full strength   423 *1849* "And wrongly give the
first fruits *1863–68* "And wrongly given the firstfruits   424 *1849*
gift: 426 *1849* defeat—   430 *1849* past, *1863, 1865* Past

425 *clench*: clinch, confirm.

"And hold a steadfast course 'till I arrive
"At their fit destination & my own:"
You have ne'er pondered this?   434

"To hold a steadfast course till I arrive
"At their fit destination and my own?"
You have never pondered thus?
    Paracelsus.   Have I, you ask?
Often at midnight, when most fancies come,   435
Would some such airy project visit me:
But ever at the end . . . or will you hear
The same thing in a tale, a parable?
You and I, wandering over the world wide,
Chance to set foot upon a desert coast.   440
Just as we cry, "No human voice before
"Broke the inveterate silence of these rocks!"
—Their querulous echo startles us; we turn:
What ravaged structure still looks o'er the sea?
Some characters remain, too! While we read,   445
The sharp salt wind, impatient for the last
Of even this record, wistfully comes and goes,
Or sings what we recover, mocking it.
This is the record; and my voice, the wind's.
                               [*He sings.*

After 438: *1849* It cannot prove more tedious; listen then!   440 *1849*
coast: 445 *1849* Some characters *Berg* ⟨Those⟩ [Some] characters   446
1849 impatient for the last *Berg* impatient for ⟨its prey⟩ [the last]   447 *1849*
wistfully comes *Berg* ⟨sullen⟩ [wistfully] comes

P/.   (*sings*)   Over the sea our galleys went,—   450
    —Cleaving prows in order brave,
    With speeding wind & a bounding
      wave—
    —A gallant Armament:
    Each bark built out of a forest-tree
      Left leafy & rough as first it grew   455
    And nailed all over the gaping sides
    Within & without with black-bull
      hides
    Seethed in fat & suppled in flame,—

Over the sea our galleys went,   450
With cleaving prows in order brave
To a speeding wind and a bounding
    wave,
A gallant armament:
Each bark built out of a forest-tree
    Left leafy and rough as first it grew,   455
And nailed all over the gaping sides,
Within and without, with black
    bull-hides,
Seethed in fat and suppled in flame,

---

452 *1849* wave—   457 *1849* black-bull hides,

450 *Over the sea*: Festus has asked why Paracelsus has not tried to 'redeem the past' by 'gathering up the treasures' which he has 'cast down' and attempting 'to hold a steadfast course' until the 'fit destination' is reached. Paracelsus replies that he will explain 'in a tale, a parable', why he has never undertaken this 'airy project'. He describes himself and Festus as brave seamen embarked on a long voyage. Coming to an apparently desert coast, they are surprised to see there a 'ravaged structure' with 'characters' carved on it. The song he now sings is the story which the characters spell out, 'The sad rhyme of the men who proudly clung / To their first fault, and withered in their pride'. It describes how courageous voyagers make a landfall, in spite of the warning of their pilot. On the shore they build shrines for the statue which has been on the deck of each of their hundred ships. They seem to be approached by islanders who say that they have a fit resting-place for these 'majestic forms'; but then they awake from what has only been a 'deep dream' and find that the rock is bare and that there are no 'gentle islanders'. They depart, leaving behind their 'gifts', the 'precious freight' which they have no heart to take back.
    'There is no need to find significance in every detail', as L. R. M. Strachan wrote in *NQ*, vol. 176 (1939), p. 29. '. . . Paracelsus is aware that, though he has accomplished much, he has not yet "attained", nor has he even found the fittest recipients for his message . . .' Two friends commented on this lyric. Domett described it as 'An allegory showing how his first work though a mistake & a failure—had become so dear, he could not try to improve it / So he had attempted to gain his object with his unassisted natural powers alone'. Commenting on the revised text of 1849, Joseph Arnould wrote: 'I like all the alterations I have made out, except only those in "over the Sea our galleys went", which I had grown too fond of in its original beauty ever to like so well in any other form': Donald Smalley, 'Joseph Arnould and Robert Browning', *PMLA* lxxx (1965), p. 99.
    The verse is reminiscent in some respects of 'The Ancient Mariner' and 'Christabel'. Browning had also obviously read 'The Lotos-Eaters', published in Tennyson's *Poems* of '1833' (December 1832).
    453 *armament*: 'A force equipped for war: generally used of a naval force': Johnson.

So each good ship was rude to
    see, 460
Rude & bare to outward view,—
But each upbore a stately tent:—
Cedar-pales in scented row
Kept out the flakes of dancing brine;—
An awning drooped the mast below, 465
That neither noon-tide, nor star-shine,
Nor moonlight cold which maketh
    mad,
    Might pierce the regal tenement.
When the sun dawned, gay & glad 470
We set the sail & plied the oar;
But when the night-wind blew like
    breath,
For joy of one day's voyage more
We sang together on the wide sea
Like men at peace on a peaceful
    shore;— 475
Each sail was loosed to the wind so
    free,
Each helm made sure by the
    twilight-star,
And in a sleep as calm as death
We, the voyagers from afar,
    Lay stretched—each weary crew 480
In a circle round ⟨their⟩ [its] wondrous
    tent,
Whence gleamed soft light & curled
    rich scent
    And with light & perfume, music
    too . . .
At morn, ⟨they⟩ [we] started beside the
    mast, 485
And still each ship was sailing fast!

1835 459, 466 {No equivalent in *MS* or *1835*.}   473 more,   483
too: 484 {No equivalent in *MS* or *1835*.}

To bear the playful billows' game:
So, each good ship was rude to see,   460
Rude and bare to the outward view,
    But each upbore a stately tent
Where cedar pales in scented row
Kept out the flakes of the dancing brine,
And an awning drooped the mast below,   465
In fold on fold of the purple fine,
That neither noontide nor starshine
Nor moonlight cold which maketh mad,
    Might pierce the regal tenement.
When the sun dawned, oh, gay and glad   470
We set the sail and plied the oar;
But when the night-wind blew like
    breath,
For joy of one day's voyage more,
We sang together on the wide sea,
Like men at peace on a peaceful
    shore;   475
Each sail was loosed to the wind so
    free,
Each helm made sure by the twilight
    star,
And in a sleep as calm as death,
We, the voyagers from afar,
    Lay stretched along, each weary crew   480
In a circle round its wondrous
    tent
Whence gleamed soft light and curled rich
    scent,
    And with light and perfume, music too:
So the stars wheeled round, and the darkness
    past,
And at morn we started beside the mast,   485
And still each ship was sailing fast.

---

462 *1849* tent;   464 *1849* brine: 479 *1849* We, the strangers from afar,   486
1849–65 fast!

467–8 *starshine | Nor moonlight*: cf. Tennyson, 'The Ballad of Oriana', 24: 'By
starshine and by moonlight'. (*Poems, Chiefly Lyrical*, 1830).

Now one morn land appeared!— —a
    speck
    Dim trembling betwixt sea & sky:—
—Not so the Isles our voyage must find
    Should meet our longing eye: 490
But the heaving sea was black behind
Many a night & many a day,
And land, tho' but a rock, was nigh,
So we broke the cedar-pales away,
And let the purple flap in the wind,   495
    And a statue bright was on every
    deck!
We shouted, every man of us,
And steered right into the harbour
    thus,
With pomp & pæan glorious.

An hundred Shapes of lucid stone!   500
    All day we built its shrine for each—
—A shrine of rock for every one,—
    Nor paused 'till in the westering sun
    We sate together on the beach
To sing because our task was done . . .   505
When lo! what shouts & merry songs!
What laughter all the distance stirs!
A loaded raft & happy throngs
Of gentle Islanders!
"Our isles are just at hand," they cried,   510
    "Like cloudlets faint in even
    sleeping,

1835 488 and sky—   489 Not . . . . isles   493 nigh;   495 wind: 500
shapes   505 To sing, because our task was done;   509 islanders!   510
cried;

Now, one morn, land appeared—a
　　speck
Dim trembling betwixt sea and sky:
"Avoid it," cried our pilot, "check
　　"The shout, restrain the eager eye!"   490
But the heaving sea was black behind
For many a night and many a day,
And land, though but a rock, drew nigh;
So, we broke the cedar pales away,
Let the purple awning flap in the wind,   495
　　And a statue bright was on every
　　　　deck!
We shouted, every man of us,
And steered right into the harbour
　　thus,
With pomp and pæan glorious.

A hundred shapes of lucid stone!   500
　　All day we built its shrine for each,
A shrine of rock for every one,
Nor paused till in the westering sun
　　We sat together on the beach
To sing because our task was done.   505
When lo! what shouts and merry songs!
What laughter all the distance stirs!
A loaded raft with happy throngs
Of gentle islanders!
"Our isles are just at hand," they cried,   510
　　"Like cloudlets faint in even
　　　　sleeping;

487 *1849* One morn, the land appeared!— *1863, 1865* Now, one morn, land appeared!— 488 *1849* sky— 489, 490 *1849* Avoid it, cried our pilot, check | The shout, restrain the longing eye! 500 *1849* An hundred 501 *1849* built a shrine for each— 502 *1849* every one— 503 *1849–65* Nor paused we till 505 *1849* To sing, because our task was done; 508–9 *1849* What raft comes loaded with its throngs | Of gentle islanders? 510 *1849* "The isles . . . . cried; *511 {Reading of *1863–68*} *1849* faint at even sleeping, *1888, 89* faint in even sleeping · {raised full stop}

511 *cloudlets*: cf. Coleridge, 'First Advent of Love', 2: 'thro' fleecy cloudlet peeping', the earliest example in OED and probably Browning's source for the word.

"Our temple-gates are opened wide,
"Our olive groves thick shade are
    keeping
"For these majestic Forms," they cried:
Then we awoke with sudden start   515
From our deep dream, & knew too late
How bare the rock, how desolate,
Which had received our precious
    freight
—Yet we called out "Depart!
"Our gifts, once given, must here
    abide!   520
"Our work is done—we have no heart
"To mar our work;" we cried!

F/.   In truth? . .
P/.   Nay wait,—all this in tracings faint
On rugged stones,—strewn here & there—but
    piled
In order once: then follows—mark what
    follows;— — —   525
"The sad rhyme of the Men who proudly clung
"To their first fault, & withered in their pride!"
F/.   Come back then, Aureole; as you fear God,
    come!
This is foul sin—come back—renounce the
    past,
Forswear the future . . . look for joy no more,   530

1835 514 forms," they cried.   516 knew, too late,   518 freight:
520 abide: 521 done;   522 work," we cried.   523 In truth? | Nay,
wait: 524 stones, strewn . . . . there,   525 once; then . . . . what fol-
lows—   526 *men*   529 sin; come back: 530 future;

"Our temple-gates are opened wide,
  "Our olive-groves thick shade are
        keeping
"For these majestic forms"—they cried.
Oh, then we awoke with sudden start   515
From our deep dream, and knew, too late,
How bare the rock, how desolate,
Which had received our precious
        freight:
    Yet we called out—"Depart!
"Our gifts, once given, must here
        abide.   520
    "Our work is done; we have no heart
"To mar our work,"—we cried.

  Festus. In truth?
  Paracelsus. Nay, wait: all this in tracings faint
On rugged stones strewn here and there, but
        piled
In order once: then follows—mark what
        follows!   525
"The sad rhyme of the men who proudly clung
"To their first fault, and withered in their pride."
    Festus. Come back then, Aureole; as you fear
        God, come!
This is foul sin; come back! Renounce the
        past,
Forswear the future; look for joy no more,   530

---

514 *1849* "For the lucid shapes you bring"—they cried.   516 *1849* dream; we
knew,   518 *1849* To which we had flung our precious freight: 520 *1849*
abide: 522 *1849* "To mar our work, though vain"—we cried.   After
523; *1849–65* May still be read on that deserted rock,   525 *1849* once; . . . .
what follows—   *1863, 1865* once: . . . . what follows: 527 *1849–65*
pride!"   529 *1849* back: renounce the past,   *1863, 1865* back. Renounce the
Past,   530 *1849* future; look . . . . more,   *1863, 1865* Future; look . . . .
more   *1868* future; look . . . . more

---

526 '*The sad rhyme*: Hugo von Hofmannsthal used these two lines as the
epigraph to *Das Bergwerk von Falun.*

But wait for death amid all peaceful sights
And trust me for the event— —peace if not
    joy!—
Return with me to Einsiedeln, dear Aureole!

P/.   No way, no way!— —it would not turn to
    good— —
A spotless child sleeps on the flowering moss—   535
Tis well for him; & one deformed by sin,
Envying such slumber may desire to put
His guilt away . . . shall he return at once
To boyhood's carelessness? our sires knew well
(Spite of the grave discoveries of their sons)   540
The fitting course for such— —dark cells, dim
    lamps,
A stone-floor one may writhe on like a
    worm . . .
No mossy pillow, blue with violets!

F/.   I see no symptom of these overbearing
And tyrannous passions:—you are calmer
    now:—   545
This verse-making can purge you well enough
Without the terrible penance you describe;—
You love me still—the lusts you fear will never
Outrage your friend: to Einsiedeln, once more!
Say but the word!

P/.   No, no: those lusts forbid;   550
They crouch, I know,—cowering with
    half-shut eye
Beside you—'tis their nature. Thrust yourself
Between them & their prey . . . let some fool
    style me

1835 533 Aureole.   534 way: it . . . . good.   538 away: 542
worm;   543 violets.   545 passions. You are calmer now.   547
describe.   548 still: 549 friend.   552 you;   553 and their prey;

But wait death's summons amid holy sights,
And trust me for the event—peace, if not
   joy.
Return with me to Einsiedeln, dear Aureole!
   Paracelsus. No way, no way! it would not turn
     to good.
A spotless child sleeps on the flowering moss—   535
'T is well for him; but when a sinful man,
Envying such slumber, may desire to put
His guilt away, shall he return at once
To rest by lying there? Our sires knew well
(Spite of the grave discoveries of their sons)   540
The fitting course for such: dark cells, dim
   lamps,
A stone floor one may writhe on like a
   worm:
No mossy pillow blue with violets!
   Festus. I see no symptom of these absolute
And tyrannous passions. You are calmer
   now.   545
This verse-making can purge you well enough
Without the terrible penance you describe.
You love me still: the lusts you fear will never
Outrage your friend. To Einsiedeln, once more!
Say but the word!
   Paracelsus.   No, no; those lusts forbid: 550
They crouch, I know, cowering with half-shut
   eye
Beside you; 't is their nature. Thrust yourself
Between them and their prey; let some fool
   style me

---

532 *1849* joy!   533 *1849* Aureole.   534 *1849* way: it   539 *1849* To rest by lying there? Our   *Berg* {rejected} To boyhood's careless rest? Our { A revised reading is indicated, but is now illegible.}   548 *1849–68* fear,

536 *but when a sinful man*: Domett has a partly-illegible reference to Moore's 'Paradise and the Peri', in *Lalla Rookh*: near the end of this part of the poem a 'man of crime' envies the carefree innocence of a child.
550 *Paracelsus*: 'Paracelsus all through is an example of all who aim at mighty objects beyond their power—in the ambitousness of youth': Domett.

Or King or quack, it matters not,—& let
Your wisdom urge them to forego their treat!   555
No, no: learn better & look deeper, Festus:
If you knew how a devil sneers within me
While you are talking now of this, now that
As tho' we differed scarcely save in trifles!

F/.   I know what you would say:—all change
        proceeds,   560
Whether for good or ill; keep that from me!
Do not confide *those* secrets: I was born
To hope,—& you . . .

P/.   To trust:—you know the rest.

F/.   Listen: I do believe the trust you boast,
Was self-delusion at the best; so long   565
As God would kindly pioneer your path,—
Would undertake to screen you from the
        world,
Procure you full exemption from their lot
The common hopes & fears, on the mere
        pretext
Of your engagement in his service,—yield you   570
A limitless license . . . make you God in fact,
And turn your slave,—you were content to say
Most courtly praises: what is it at last
But selfishness without example?—None
Could trace God's will so plain as you, while
        yours   575
Remained implied in it—but *now*, you fail,
And we who prate about that will are fools;—
In short, God's service must be ordered here
As he determines fit, & not your way,

1835 554 king . . . not, and   556 No, no; learn . . . . Festus.   561
me;   565 best.   567 world—   571 license—make you God, in
fact,   576 Remain'd . . . . it; but *now*   577 fools.

Or king or quack, it matters not—then try
Your wisdom, urge them to forego their treat!   555
No, no; learn better and look deeper, Festus!
If you knew how a devil sneers within me
While you are talking now of this, now that,
As though we differed scarcely save in trifles!
    Festus. Do we so differ? True, change must
        proceed,   560
Whether for good or ill; keep from me, which!
Do not confide all secrets: I was born
To hope, and you . . .
    Paracelsus.   To trust: you know the fruits!
    Festus. Listen: I do believe, what you call trust
Was self-delusion at the best: for, see!   565
So long as God would kindly pioneer
A path for you, and screen you from the
    world,
Procure you full exemption from man's lot,
Man's common hopes and fears, on the mere
    pretext
Of your engagement in his service—yield you   570
A limitless licence, make you God, in fact,
And turn your slave—you were content to say
Most courtly praises! What is it, at last,
But selfishness without example? None
Could trace God's will so plain as you, while
    yours   575
Remained implied in it; but now you fail,
And we, who prate about that will, are fools!
In short, God's service is established here
As he determines fit, and not your way,

---

554 *1849–68* not, and try   555 *1849* Your wisdom then, at urging their
retreat!   After 561: *1849* God made you and knows what you may
become—   565 *1849* Was self-reliance at the best:

566 *pioneer*: clear, open up.
573 *at last*: like the French 'enfin', as Lee and Locock point out.
578 *God's service*: cf. Milton's sonnet on his blindness, 9–10: 'God doth not
need / Either man's work or his own gifts'.

And this you cannot brook: such discontent   580
Is weak:—renounce all creatureship—affirm
An absolute right to have & to dispose
Your energies— —as tho' the rivers should say
"We rush to the ocean—what have we to do
"With feeding streamlets, lingering in the vales   585
"Sleeping in lazy pools?" Set up that plea.
That will be bold at least.

P/.   Tis like enough:
The serviceable spirits are those, no doubt,
The East produces;—lo, the Master nods—
And they raise terraces & garden-grounds   590
In one night's space,—& this done, straight
     relapse
Into a century's sleep— — —to the great
     honour
Of him that framed them wise & beautiful;
Till a lamp's rubbing, or some chance akin
Release their limbs:— —I am of different
     mould.   595
I would have soothed my Lord & slaved for
     him
And done him service past my narrow bond,
And thus I get rewarded for my pains!
Beside 'tis vain to talk of forwarding
His glory otherwise—*this* is the sphere   600
Alone of its increase, as far as we
Can be concerned, or I am much
     deceived;— —
We are his glory, & if *we* be glorious
Is not the thing achieved?

1835 581 weak.   583 energies; as though . . . . say—   584 ocean;   586
plea,   589 The east produces. Lo, the master nods,   591 space;
and,   592 sleep,   593 and beautiful,   595 limbs.   600 other-
wise;   603 glory; and . . . . glorious,

And this you cannot brook. Such discontent   580
Is weak. Renounce all creatureship at once!
Affirm an absolute right to have and use
Your energies; as though the rivers should say—
"We rush to the ocean; what have we to do
"With feeding streamlets, lingering in the vales,   585
"Sleeping in lazy pools?" Set up that plea,
That will be bold at least!
    Paracelsus.   'T is like enough.
The serviceable spirits are those, no doubt,
The East produces: lo, the master bids,—
They wake, raise terraces and garden-grounds   590
In one night's space; and, this done, straight
   begin
Another century's sleep, to the great
   praise
Of him that framed them wise and beautiful,
Till a lamp's rubbing, or some chance akin,
Wake them again. I am of different
   mould.   595
I would have soothed my lord, and slaved for
   him
And done him service past my narrow bond,
And thus I get rewarded for my pains!
Beside, 't is vain to talk of forwarding
God's glory otherwise; this is alone   600
The sphere of its increase, as far as men
Increase it; why, then, look beyond this
   sphere?
We are his glory; and if we be glorious,
Is not the thing achieved?

580 *1849* brook!   585 *1849* in the marshes,   587 *Par. 1849* Perhaps,
perhaps! *1863* 'T is like enough! *1865* 'Tis like enough   588 *1849* Your
only serviceable spirits are those   589 *1849* The east produces:—lo, the
master nods, *1863–68* The East produces: lo, the master nods,   590 *1849*
And they raise terraces, spread garden-grounds *1863–68* And they raise ter-
races and garden-grounds

588 *The serviceable spirits*: such as the genii in the *Arabian Nights.*
590 *garden-grounds*: as at *Sordello*, iv. 460.
600 *this*: this mortal sphere.

F/.   Shall one like me
Judge hearts like your's?— —tho years have
   changed you much,   605
And you have left your first love, & retain
Its empty shade to gild your crooked ways,
Yet I still hold that you *have* honoured God—
And has your course been all without reward?
For wherefore this repining at defeat,   610
Had triumph ne'er inured you to high hopes?
— — I urge you to forsake the life you curse
And what success attends me?—simply talk
Of passion, weakness, & remorse— —in short
Anything but the naked truth—you choose   615
This so despised career & cheaply hold
My fullest happiness, or other Men's:— —
Once more return!
P/.   —And quickly—Oporinus
Has pilfered half my secrets by this time—
And we depart by day-break:—I am weary   620
I know not how— —not even the wine-cup
   soothes
My brain to-night— — —
Do you not thoroughly despise me, Festus?
. .   No flattery! . . one like you needs not be told
We live & breathe deceiving & deceived . . .   625
Do you not scorn me from your heart of
   hearts?
Me—& my cant—my petty subterfuges—

1835 608 God;   614 and remorse; in short,   615 Any thing . . . .
truth: 617 men's.   618 And quickly.   620 day-break. I am weary,
| I know not how;   625 and deceived.   627 Me and my cant—

Festus.   Shall one like me
Judge hearts like yours? Though years have
   changed you much,   605
And you have left your first love, and retain
Its empty shade to veil your crooked ways,
Yet I still hold that you have honoured God.
And who shall call your course without reward?
For, wherefore this repining at defeat   610
Had triumph ne'er inured you to high hopes?
I urge you to forsake the life you curse,
And what success attends me?—simply talk
Of passion, weakness and remorse; in short,
Anything but the naked truth—you choose   615
This so-despised career, and cheaply hold
My happiness, or rather other men's.
Once more, return!
     Paracelsus.   And quickly. John the thief
Has pilfered half my secrets by this time:
And we depart by daybreak. I am weary,   620
I know not how; not even the wine-cup
   soothes
My brain to-night . . .
Do you not thoroughly despise me, Festus?
No flattery! One like you needs not be told
We live and breathe deceiving and deceived.   625
Do you not scorn me from your heart of
   hearts,
Me and my cant, each petty subterfuge,

---

608 *1849* honoured God;   615 *1849* Any thing but the naked truth: 616
1849 and rather praise   617 *1849* Than take my happiness, or other
men's.   618 *1849* And soon. Oporinus *1863–68* And quickly. Oporinus
626 *1849* hearts?   627 *1849* Me and my cant—my petty subterfuges—
1863 Me and my cant, my petty subterfuges,

---

618 *John the thief*: Johannes Oporinus: see line 30 ff., above, and pp. 509 ff.
below.

620 *I am weary*: quoting at length from the remainder of Part IV, Leigh Hunt
commented: 'Few things we know in poetry surpass in beauty the manner in
which the affliction that had been sustained by Festus, concealed by his calm
and generous spirit till now, is here disclosed': op. cit., p. 408b.

These rhymes & all this frothy shower of
  words,
My glozing self-deceit, my outward crust
Of lies which wrap, as tetter morphew furfair   630
Wrap the sound flesh . . so see you flatter
  not!—
Even God flatters!—but my friend, at least,
Is true: I would depart secure henceforth
Against all further insult hate & wrong
From puny foes: my one friend's scorn shall
  brand me!   635
No fear of sinking deeper!—

F/.   No, dear Aureole!
No, no—I came to counsel faithfully:— —
There are old rules made long ere we were
  born
By which I judge you— —I, so fallible
So infinitely low beside your mighty   640
Majestic spirit: . . . even I can see
You own some higher law . . they make that
  out
Sin—which is no sin— —weakness—which is
  strength,
But I have only these, such as they are
To guide me,—& I blame you where they bid   645
As long as any chance remains of winning
Your troubled soul to peace . . the more that
  sorrow

1835 628 rhymes, and . . . . words—   629 self-deceit—   631 flesh?—so
. . . . not!   633 true. I would depart,   635 me—   636 deeper.   637
No, no; I . . . . faithfully: 639 you. I, so fallible,   641 spirit—   642
law.   643 Sin which is no sin—weakness which is strength;   645 me;
and . . . . bid,   647 peace;

My rhymes and all this frothy shower of
     words,
My glozing self-deceit, my outward crust
Of lies which wrap, as tetter, morphew, furfair   630
Wrap the sound flesh?—so, see you flatter
     not!
Even God flatters: but my friend, at least,
Is true. I would depart, secure henceforth
Against all further insult, hate and wrong
From puny foes; my one friend's scorn shall
     brand me: 635
No fear of sinking deeper!
     Festus.   No, dear Aureole!
No, no; I came to counsel faithfully.
There are old rules, made long ere we were
     born,
By which I judge you. I, so fallible,
So infinitely low beside your mighty   640
Majestic spirit!—even I can see
You own some higher law than ours which
     call
Sin, what is no sin—weakness, what is
     strength.
But I have only these, such as they are,
To guide me; and I blame you where they bid,   645
Only so long as blaming promises
To win peace for your soul: the more, that
     sorrow

628 *1849* rhymes, and . . . . words—   629 *1849* self-deceit—   630 *1849*
lies,   *631 {Reading of *1849–68*}   *1888, 89* Wrapt the sound   632 *1849*
Why, even God flatters!   *1863, 1865* Even God flatters!   635 *1849* foes: my
. . . . me—   637 *1849* faithfully: 640 *1849* your spirit   *1863, 1865* your
mighty,   641 *1849* Mighty, majestic!—even   642 *1849, 1868–89* which
call *1863, 1865* which calls   643 *1849* strength;   645 *1849* where they
blame,

629 *glozing*: specious.
630 *tetter*: a pustular eruption of the skin: cf. *Hamlet*, I. v. 71–3: 'And a most
instant tetter bark'd about, / Most lazar-like, with vile and loathsome crust, /
All my smooth body'. Johnson defines morphew as 'A scurf on the face' and
'furfur' as 'Husk or chaff, scurf or dandruff, that grows upon the skin'.

Has fallen on me of late, and they have helped
    me
So that I faint not under my distress:
But wherefore should I scruple to confess   650
That spite of all, as brother judging brother,
Your fate is most inexplicable to me:
And should you perish yet without reward

—   Some great reward—I have too hastily
Relied on love's effect . . you may have sinned 655
But you have loved: as a mere human matter,

—   As I would have God deal with fragile Men
In the end . . I say that you will triumph yet!

Pl.   You have felt sorrow, Festus? 'tis
    because
You love me— —sorrow, & sweet Michal
    your's?   660
Well thought on . . never let her know this last
Dull winding up of all—these miscreants dared
Insult me—me she loved;—so grieve her not!

Fl.   Your ill success can little grieve her
    now— — —

Pl.   Michal is dead!—pray Christ we do not
    craze!   665

Fl.   Aureole— —dear Aureole—look not on me
    thus!— —
Fool,—fool! this is the heart grown
    sorrow-proof!.
I cannot bear those eyes;— —

Pl.   Nay, really dead?

Fl.   Tis scarce a year— —

Pl.   Stone-dead? then you have laid
    her
Among the flowers ere this— —now, do you
    know,   670

1835 649 distress.   655 effect.   656 loved. As . . . . matter—   657 As
. . . . men   660 You love me. Sorrow, and . . . . yours! | Well thought
on;   662 all: 663 loved; so . . . . not.   664 now.   666 Aureole,
dear Aureole, look . . . . thus!   667 Fool, fool! this . . . . sorrow-
proof—   668 eyes.   669 Stone dead!

Has fallen on me of late, and they have helped
   me
So that I faint not under my distress.
But wherefore should I scruple to avow   650
In spite of all, as brother judging brother,
Your fate is most inexplicable to me?
And should you perish without recompense
And satisfaction yet—too hastily
I have relied on love: you may have sinned,   655
But you have loved. As a mere human matter—
As I would have God deal with fragile men
In the end—I say that you will triumph yet!
   Paracelsus. Have you felt sorrow, Festus?—'t is
     because
You love me. Sorrow, and sweet Michal
   yours!   660
Well thought on: never let her know this last
Dull winding-up of all: these miscreants dared
Insult me—me she loved:—so, grieve her not!
   Festus. Your ill success can little grieve her
     now.
   Paracelsus. Michal is dead! pray Christ we do
     not craze!   665
   Festus. Aureole, dear Aureole, look not on me
     thus!
Fool, fool! this is the heart grown
   sorrow-proof—
I cannot bear those eyes.
   Paracelsus.   Nay, really dead?
   Festus. 'T is scarce a month.
   Paracelsus.   Stone dead!—then you have laid
     her
Among the flowers ere this. Now, do you
   know,   670

652 *1849* Your fate to me is most inexplicable: *1863–68* Your fate to me is
most inexplicable?   663 *1849* loved; so grieve her not. *1863* loved: so,
grieve her not. *1865* loved:—so, grieve her not.   664 *1865* Your suc-
cess   669 *1849* month . . .

---

661 *Well thought on*: as in *King Lear*, v iii. 250.
665 *Michal is dead!*: his tardy understanding of this is evidence of the self-
centred character of Paracelsus.

I can reveal a secret which shall comfort
Even you . . I have no julep as they think
To cheat the grave—but a far better
   secret;— —
Know then, you did not ill to trust your Love
To the cold earth— —I have thought much of
   it—   675
For I believe we do not wholly die:—

F/.   Aureole . . .

P/.   Nay, do not laugh—there is a reason
For what I say—I think the soul can never
Taste death— —I am just now, as you may see
Very unfit to put so strange a thought   680
In an intelligible dress of words— — —
But take it as my trust, she is not dead!

F/.   But not on this account alone?— —you
   surely . .

. . .   Aureole, you have believed this all along?

P/. — —And Michal sleeps among the roots &
   dews,   685
While I am moved at Basil, & wondering
With Nuremburg, & hoping & despairing
As tho' it mattered how the farce plays out
So it be quickly played— —Away, Away!
Have your will, rabble! while we fight the prize   690
Troop you in safety to the snug back-seats,
And leave a clear arena for the Brave
About to perish for your sport:—Behold!

1835 672, 673 you. I have no julep, as they think, | To cheat the grave; but . . . .
secret.   674 love   675 earth: 676 die.   677 laugh;   678
say: 679 death. I am, just . . . . see,   681 words;   682 dead.   683
alone? you surely,   687 Nuremberg, and   689 play'd.   692 brave
693 sport . . .

I can reveal a secret which shall comfort
Even you. I have no julep, as men think,
To cheat the grave; but a far better
   secret.
Know, then, you did not ill to trust your love
To the cold earth: I have thought much of
   it: 675
For I believe we do not wholly die.
   Festus. Aureole!
   Paracelsus. Nay, do not laugh; there is a reason
For what I say: I think the soul can never
Taste death. I am, just now, as you may see,
Very unfit to put so strange a thought   680
In an intelligible dress of words;
But take it as my trust, she is not dead.
   Festus. But not on this account alone? you
      surely,
—Aureole, you have believed this all along?
   Paracelsus. And Michal sleeps among the roots
      and dews,   685
While I am moved at Basil, and full of schemes
For Nuremberg, and hoping and despairing,
As though it mattered how the farce plays out,
So it be quickly played. Away, away!
Have your will, rabble! while we fight the prize,   690
Troop you in safety to the snug back-seats
And leave a clear arena for the brave
About to perish for your sport!—Behold!

---

677 *1849* Aureole . . .   686 *1849* moved at Basil,   *Berg* {rejected} moved in
Basil,

---

672 *julep*: a medicated drink.
681 *an intelligible dress of words*: cf. Pope, *An Essay on Criticism,* 318: 'Expres-
sion is the dress of thought'.
690 *fight the prize*: contend for the prize, as in Scott, *Woodstock,* xiv: 'I . . .
have fought prizes'.
693 *About to perish for your sport*: like gladiators: cf. *King Lear,* IV. i. 37: 'As flies
to wanton boys are we to th' gods— / They kill us for their sport'. Cf. iii. 766 ff.

5.   PARACELSUS ATTAINS.

Scene, *A cell in the Hospital of S. Sebastian at Salzburg. 1541.*
        Festus, Paracelsus.

F/.   No change!—the weary night is well nigh
              spent,
           The lamp burns low, & thro the casement-
              bars
           The grey morn glimmers feebly— —yet no
              change!
           Another night, & still no sigh has stirred
           That fall'n discoloured mouth, no pang relit   5
           Those fixed eyes, quenched by the decaying
              body
           Like torch-flame choaked in dust;—while all
              beside
           Was breaking, to the last they held out bright
           As a strong-hold where life intrenched
              itself . . .
           But they are dead now— —very blind &
              dead:— —   10
— — He will drowse into death without a groan!

1835 9 intrench'd itself;   10 and dead.

PART V.

PARACELSUS ATTAINS.

SCENE.—*Salzburg; a cell in the Hospital of St. Sebastian.* 1541.

FESTUS, PARACELSUS.

Festus. No change! The weary night is well-
    nigh spent,
The lamp burns low, and through the casement-
    bars
Grey morning glimmers feebly: yet no
    change!
Another night, and still no sigh has stirred
That fallen discoloured mouth, no pang relit   5
Those fixed eyes, quenched by the decaying
    body,
Like torch-flame choked in dust. While all
    beside
Was breaking, to the last they held out bright,
As a stronghold where life intrenched
    itself;
But they are dead now—very blind and
    dead: 10
He will drowse into death without a groan.

1849 SCENE.—*A cell in the hospital of St. Sebastian, at Salzburg.* 1541
3 *1849* feebly—   7 *1849* dust: 10 *1849* and dead.   11 *1849–65* groan!

SCENE.—*Salzburg*: cf. the passage from the *Biographie Universelle* on pp. 504–5
below. Thirteen years have elapsed.

My Aureole, my forgotten, ruined Aureole!
The days are gone, are gone! how grand thou
    wert,— —
And now not one of those who struck thee
    down
Poor, glorious Spirit! concerns him even to stay   15
And satisfy himself his little hand
Could turn God's image to a livid thing!

Another night, & yet no change!—'tis much
That I should ⟨look on⟩ [sit by him] & bathe his
    brow
And chafe his hands . . 'tis much—but he will
    sure   20
Know me, & look on me & speak to me
Once more—but only once!—⟨h⟩ His hollow
    cheek
Looked, all night long as tho' a creeping laugh
At his own state were just about to break
From the dying man . . . my brain swam & my
    throat   25
Swelled ⟨thick, &⟩ yet [for all] I could not turn
    away!
In truth they told me how he seemed at
    first
Resolved to live—to let no power forsake
    him;—
Thus striving to keep up his shattered strength
Until they brought him to this stifling cell   30
— — At once his features fell— —an hour made
    white
The flushed face, & relaxed the quivering
    limb—
Only the eye remained intense awhile
As tho' it recognized the tomb-like place,

1835 12 My Aureole; my forgotten, ruin'd Aureole!   13 wert: 14
down—   15 spirit—   20 hands—'t is much;   25 man: 26
Swell'd, yet for all I . . . . away.   30 cell: 32 The flush'd face and relax'd
. . . . limb;   34 though . . . . place;

My Aureole—my forgotten, ruined Aureole!
The days are gone, are gone! How grand thou
    wast!
And now not one of those who struck thee
    down—
Poor glorious spirit—concerns him even to stay   15
And satisfy himself his little hand
Could turn God's image to a livid thing.

Another night, and yet no change! 'T is much
That I should sit by him, and bathe his
    brow,
And chafe his hands; 't is much: but he will
    sure   20
Know me, and look on me, and speak to me
Once more—but only once! His hollow
    cheek
Looked all night long as though a creeping laugh
At his own state were just about to break
From the dying man: my brain swam, my throat
    swelled,   25
And yet I could not turn away. In
    truth,
They told me how, when first brought here, he
    seemed
Resolved to live, to lose no
    faculty;
Thus striving to keep up his shattered strength,
Until they bore him to this stifling cell: 30
When straight his features fell, an hour made
    white
The flushed face, and relaxed the quivering
    limb,
Only the eye remained intense awhile
As though it recognized the tomb-like place,

13 *1849* thou wert: 20 *1849* hands—'tis much;   28 *1849* to live—   31
1849 fell—32 *1849* face and . . . . limb;   *1863* face and . . . . limb,   1865 face
and . . . . limb   34 *1849* recognised . . . . place;

And then he lay, as here he lies:—
                    Ay, here!   35
Here is earth's noblest, nobly garlanded!
Her bravest champion with his well-won meed!
Her best production—all that makes amends
For countless generations fleeting fast
And followed by no trace—the all-surpassing   40
Creature she cites when Angels would dispute
The title of her brood to rank with them . .
Angels, this is our Angel! those bright
    forms
Are ⟨h⟩ Human— —but not his,—those are
    but ⟨m⟩ Men   45
Whom the rest press around & kneel before—
Those palaces are dwelt in by ⟨m⟩ Mankind—
— — Other provision is for him you seek . .
Behold earth's paragon!—now, raise thee,
    Clay!   50

God! Thou art Love! I build my faith on that:
Even as I watch beside thy tortured child
Unconscious whose hot tears fall fast by him,
So doth thy right-hand guide us thro' the
    world
Wherein we stumble:—God! what shall we
    say?   55
— — How has he sinned—how else should he have
    done?
Surely he sought thy praise—thy praise, for all
He might be wedded to the task so well
As to forget awhile its proper end— —
Dost thou well, Lord? . . . Thou canst not but
    prefer   60
That I should range myself upon his side . . .

1835 35 lay as here he lies . . . | Ay, here: 36 noblest nobly gar-
landed—   37 champion, with . . . . meed—   39 generations,   41
angels   43 angel!— those   44 {No equivalent in *MS* or *1835*.}   45
Are human, but not his: those are but men   47 mankind;   48 Other. . . .
seek.   49 {No equivalent in *MS* or *1835*.}   50 paragon! Now, raise thee,
clay!   55 stumble.

And then he lay as here he lies.
                                  Ay, here!   35
Here is earth's noblest, nobly garlanded—
Her bravest champion with his well-won prize—
Her best achievement, her sublime amends
For countless generations fleeting fast
And followed by no trace;—the creature-god   40
She instances when angels would dispute
The title of her brood to rank with them.
Angels, this is our angel! Those bright forms
We clothe with purple, crown and call to thrones,
Are human, but not his; those are but
     men   45
Whom other men press round and kneel before;
Those palaces are dwelt in by mankind;
Higher provision is for him you seek
Amid our pomps and glories: see it here!
Behold earth's paragon! Now, raise thee, clay!   50

God! Thou art love! I build my faith on that.
Even as I watch beside thy tortured child
Unconscious whose hot tears fall fast by him,
So doth thy right hand guide us through the
     world
Wherein we stumble. God! what shall we
     say?   55
How has he sinned? How else should he have
     done?
Surely he sought thy praise—thy praise, for all
He might be busied by the task so much
As half forget awhile its proper end.
Dost thou well, Lord? Thou canst not but
     prefer   60
That I should range myself upon his side—

How could he stop at every step to set
Thy glory forth?—hadst thou but granted him
Success, thy honour would have crowned his
    triumph—
A halo round a star!— —or say he erred,   65
Save him, dear God—it will be like
    thee—bathe him
In light & life!. Thou art not made like us—
We should be wrath in such a case—but
    ⟨t⟩ Thou
Wilt smile on him! . . . forgive these passionate
    thoughts
Which come unsought & will not pass away!   70
I know thee—who hast kept my path & made
Light for me in the darkness— —tempering
    sorrow
So that it reached me like a solemn joy— —
It were too strange that *I* should doubt thy
    love . . .
But what am *I*? Thou madest him & knowest   75
How he was fashioned; *I* could never err
That way—the quiet place beside thy feet
Reserved for me was ever in my thoughts;—
But He—Thou shouldst have favoured him as
    well!

Ah! he wakens—Aureole, I am here,—'tis
    Festus!   80
— — I cast away all wishes save one wish— —
Let him but know me,—only speak to me! . .
He mutters— —louder & louder:— —Any
    other
Than I—with brain less laden—would collect

1835 63 forth? Hadst Thou   65 star . . . Or say he err'd: 66 God; it will
be like thee: 67 us: 68 case; but Thou   69 him. Forgive . . . .
thoughts,   70 unsought, and . . . . away.   71 thee, who . . . . path,
and   73 reach'd . . . . joy;   74 love: 76 fashion'd.   77 way: 79
But he—Thou . . . . favour'd   80 wakens! Aureole, I am here—   84 I,
with brain less laden,

How could he stop at every step to set
Thy glory forth? Hadst thou but granted him
Success, thy honour would have crowned
    success,
A halo round a star. Or, say he erred,—   65
Save him, dear God; it will be like thee: bathe
    him
In light and life! Thou are not made like us;
We should be wroth in such a case; but
    thou
Forgivest—so, forgive these passionate
    thoughts
Which come unsought and will not pass away!   70
I know thee, who hast kept my path, and made
Light for me in the darkness, tempering
    sorrow
So that it reached me like a solemn joy;
It were too strange that I should doubt thy
    love.
But what am I? Thou madest him and knowest   75
How he was fashioned. I could never err
That way: the quiet place beside thy feet,
Reserved for me, was ever in my thoughts:
But he—thou shouldst have favoured him as
    well!

Ah! he wakens! Aureole, I am here! 't is
    Festus!   80
I cast away all wishes save one wish—
Let him but know me, only speak to me!
He mutters; louder and louder; any
    other
Than I, with brain less laden, could collect

---

66 *1865* be ke Thee: 72 *1849* darkness—tempering sorrow,   74 *1849*
love: 79 *1849, 1863* Thou . . . . well!   *1865* Thou . . . . well   80 *1849*
Ah! he wakes! Aureole, I am here—'tis Festus!   *1863, 1865* Ah! he wakes!
Aureole, I am here! 't is Festus!   82 *1849* me—only   83 *1849* mutters—

What he pours forth;—dear Aureole do but
   look!   85
Is it talking or singing this he utters fast?
Misery! that he should fix me with his eye,
Quick talking— —to some other all the while!
If he would husband this wild vehemence
Which frustrates its intent:—I heard . . . I know   90
I heard my name amid those rapid words:—
O he will know me yet! could I divert
This current— —lead it somehow gently back
Into the channels of the past . . his eye
Brighter than ever—it must recognize me!   95

I am Erasmus,—I am here to pray
That Eremita use his wondrous skill . . . .
The schools of Paris & of Padua send
These questions for your learning to
   resolve . . .
We are your students, noble Master:—leave   100
This wretched cell,—what business have you
   here?
Our class awaits you— —come to us once
   more!
(O Agony!—the utmost I can do
Touches him not . . . how else arrest his ear?)
I am commissioned . . . . (I shall craze like
   him—   105
I will be mute & see what God shall send.
P/.   Stay—stay with me! . . .
F/.   —I will—I am come here
To stay with you . . . . Festus you loved of
   old—

1835 85 forth. Dear Aureole,   87 Misery, that . . . . eye—   88 talking
to   90 intent . . . I heard,   94 His eye,   95 ever,   96 Eras-
mus: 97 skill: 99 resolve.   100 master.   101 cell;   102 you;
come to us once more.   104 not;   105 commission'd . . . I shall   107
Stay, stay with me! | I will;   108 you—Festus . . . . old;

What he pours forth. Dear Aureole, do but
   look!   85
Is it talking or singing, this he utters fast?
Misery that he should fix me with his eye,
Quick talking to some other all the while!
If he would husband this wild vehemence
Which frustrates its intent!—I heard, I know   90
I heard my name amid those rapid words.
Oh, he will know me yet! Could I divert
This current, lead it somehow gently back
Into the channels of the past!—His eye
Brighter than ever! It must recognize me!   95

I am Erasmus: I am here to pray
That Paracelsus use his skill for me.
The schools of Paris and of Padua send
These questions for your learning to
   resolve.
We are your students, noble master: leave   100
This wretched cell, what business have you
   here?
Our class awaits you; come to us once
   more!
(O agony! the utmost I can do
Touches him not; how else arrest his ear?)
I am commissioned . . . I shall craze like
   him.   105
Better be mute and see what God shall send.
   Paracelsus. Stay, stay with me!
   Festus.   I will; I am come here
To stay with you—Festus, you loved of
   old;

---

87 *1849* Misery, that . . . . eye— *1863–68* Misery, that . . . . eye,   91 *1849* words: 92 *1849* O he will   93 *1849* current—   94 *1863*, *1865* Past!—   95 *1849* It must recognise!   *After 95: 1849–65* Let me speak to him in another's name. *Omitted 1868–89.*   101 *1849* cell;   102 *1849* more.   105 *1849* like him— *1863*, *1865* like him!

96 *I am Erasmus:* cf. textual notes, above.

Festus—you know—you must know . .

P/.   Festus . . . where's

Aprile then? has he not chaunted softly   110
The melodies I heard all night— —I could not
Get to him for a cold hand on my breast,
But I made out his music well enough—
O well enough . . . . if they have filled him full
With magical music as they freight a star   115
With light, & have remitted all his sin,
They will forgive me too— —I shall Know
   too! . .

F/.   Festus—Festus! . .

P/.   — —I would have asked if he
Knows as he Loves . . . if I shall Love as well
As Know— —but that cold hand, like lead—
   so cold— — —.   120

F/.   Dear Aureole— —

P/.   Ah the curse, Aprile, Aprile!
We get so near— —so very, very near!

—   Tis an old tale—Jove strikes the Titans down
Not when they set about their mountain-piling
But when another rock would crown their
   work!—   125

— —   And Phaeton . . . doubtless his first radiant
   plunge
Astonished Mortals—but the Gods were calm
And Jove prepared his thunder—all old tales!

1835 109 Festus, you know, you must know. | Festus! Where's   111 night?
113 enough,   114 enough. If they have fill'd   117 too, I shall know too . . .
118 Festus, Festus! | I would have ask'd   119 KNOWS as he LOVES—if I shall
LOVE as well   120 As KNOW; but that cold hand, like lead—so cold.   122
very near.   123 'T is an old tale: 127 Astonish'd mortals; but the gods
were calm,   128 thunder: all old tales.

Festus, you know, you must know!
    Paracelsus.   Festus! Where 's
Aprile, then? Has he not chanted softly   110
The melodies I heard all night? I could not
Get to him for a cold hand on my breast,
But I made out his music well enough,
O well enough! If they have filled him full
With magical music, as they freight a star   115
With light, and have remitted all his sin,
They will forgive me too, I too shall
    know!
    Festus. Festus, your Festus!
    Paracelsus.   Ask him if Aprile
Knows as he Loves—if I shall Love and Know?
I try; but that cold hand, like lead—so
    cold!   120
    Festus. My hand, see!
    Paracelsus.   Ah, the curse, Aprile, Aprile!
We get so near—so very, very near!
'T is an old tale: Jove strikes the Titans down,
Not when they set about their mountain-piling
But when another rock would crown the
    work.   125
And Phaeton—doubtless his first radiant
    plunge
Astonished mortals, though the gods were calm,
And Jove prepared his thunder: all old tales!

---

117 *1849* me too, I too shall know! *Berg* {rejected} me too, and I shall
know!   125 *1849–65* crown their work!   127 *1849–65* mortals;

123 *Jove strikes the Titans down*: cf. Virgil, *Georgics*, i. 281 ff., lines 375 ff. in
Dryden's translation: 'With Mountains pil'd on Mountains, thrice they strove /
To scale the steepy Battlements of *Jove*: / And thrice his Lightning and red
Thunder play'd, / And their demolish'd Works in Ruin laid'. Cf. Ovid,
Metamorphoses i. 151 ff.
126 *Phaeton*: Phaet(h)on begged his father Phoebus to allow him to drive his
chariot for one day, but forgot his father's instructions: 'The flying horses
became sensible of the confusion of their driver, and immediately departed
from the usual track. Phaeton repented too late of his rashness, and already
heaven and earth were threatened with an universal conflagration, when
Jupiter . . . struck the rider with one of his thunderbolts, and hurled him
headlong from heaven into the river Po': Lemprière.

F/.   And what are these to you?

P/.   Ay, they must laugh
So cruelly, so well— — —most like I never   130
Could tread a single pleasure underfoot
But they were grinning by my side . . were
    chuckling
To see me toil & drop away by flakes:—
Hell-spawn! I am glad— —most glad that thus
    I fail!
—   Your cunning has o'ershot its aim;—one year   135
One month perhaps & I had served your turn!
—   You should have curbed your spite
    awhile:— —but now
Who will believe 'twas You that held me back?
Listen: there's shame & hissing &
    contempt— —
And none but laughs who names me— —none
    but spits   140
Measureless scorn upon me . . . 'tis on *me*
The quack, the liar, the arch-cheat—all on *me*!
And thus your famous plan to sink Mankind
In uttermost despair by teaching them
One of their race had probed the inmost truth   145
Had done all Man could do, yet failed in all . .
— —   Your plan has proved abortive— —*They*
    despair?
Ha ha, why they are hooting the empiric
The ignorant & incapable fool who thrust
Himself upon a work beyond his wits,   150
Nor doubt[ing] but ⟨the⟩ the simplest of
    themselves
Could bring the matter to triumphant issue!

1835 130 well;   132 side,   133 toil, and . . . . flakes.   134 glad, most glad,   135 aim. One year, | One month, perhaps, and . . . . turn: 137 You . . . . curb'd your spite awhile. But now,   138 't was you   139 shame, and hissing, and contempt,   141 me; 't is on *me*,   142 *me*.   143 mankind   146 man . . . . fail'd in all—   147 Your . . . . abortive.   148 Ha, ha! why . . . . empiric,

Festus. And what are these to you?
Paracelsus.   Ay, fiends must laugh
So cruelly, so well! most like I never   130
Could tread a single pleasure underfoot,
But they were grinning by my side, were
    chuckling
To see me toil and drop away by flakes!
Hell-spawn! I am glad, most glad, that thus I
    fail!
Your cunning has o'ershot its aim. One year,   135
One month, perhaps, and I had served your turn!
You should have curbed your spite awhile. But
    now,
Who will believe 't was you that held me back?
Listen: there's shame and hissing and
    contempt,
And none but laughs who names me, none but
    spits   140
Measureless scorn upon me, me alone,
The quack, the cheat, the liar,—all on me!
And thus your famous plan to sink mankind
In silence and despair, by teaching them
One of their race had probed the inmost truth,   145
Had done all man could do, yet failed no less—
Your wise plan proves abortive. Men
    despair?
Ha, ha! why, they are hooting the empiric,
The ignorant and incapable fool who rushed
Madly upon a work beyond his wits;   150
Nor doubt they but the simplest of
    themselves
Could bring the matter to triumphant issue.

---

130 *1849–68* well;   After 134: *1849* You that hate men and all who wish their good—   140 *1849* me—   141 *1849* upon me—   150 *1849* Madly upon *Berg* ⟨Himself⟩ ⟨Rashly⟩ [Madly] upon   152 *1849* issue!

148 *empiric*: 'such persons as have no true education in, or knowledge of, physical practice, but venture upon hearsay and observation only': Johnson (quoting John Quincy).

So pick & choose among them all, Accursed!
Try now,—persuade some other to slave for
 you
To ruin body & soul to work your ends!   155
No—no! I am the first & last, I think!
F/. Sweet friend— —who are accursed? who has
    done— — —
P/. What have I done? you dare ask that? or
    You
Brave Ones— —Oh, *you* can chime in boldly,
 backed
By them— —& what had *you* to do, wise
 Peers?   160
—Only observe— —why fiends may learn
 ⟨of⟩ [from] them!
How they talk calmly of my throes—my fierce
Aspirings—terrible watchings each one
 claiming   168
Its price of blood & brain—how they dissect
And sneeringly disparage the few truths   170
Got at a life's cost— —they too hanging the
 while
About my neck— —their lies misleading me
Their dead names browbeating me!—Damned
 Crew
Is there a reason for your hate?— —my truths   175
Have shaken a little the palm about each brow?

1835 153 accursed! 155 ends: 156 No, no; I . . . . think. 159 Brave
ones? Oh, *you* . . . . back'd 160 By them; and . . . . peers? 161–165
{No equivalent in *MS* or *1835*.} 166 Only observe: why . . . . from
them! 168 Aspirings, terrible watchings— 169 and brain; 171
cost; 172 neck, their . . . . me, 173 brow-beating me. Wretched
crew! 174 {No equivalent in *MS* or *1835*.}

So, pick and choose among them all, accursed!
Try now, persuade some other to slave for
    you,
To ruin body and soul to work your ends!   155
No, no; I am the first and last, I think.
    Festus. Dear friend, who are accursed? who has
        done . . .
    Paracelsus. What have I done? Fiends dare ask
        that? or you,
Brave men? Oh, you can chime in boldly,
    backed
By the others! What had you to do, sage
    peers?   160
Here stand my rivals; Latin, Arab, Jew,
Greek, join dead hands against me: all I ask
Is, that the world enrol my name with theirs,
And even this poor privilege, it seems,
They range themselves, prepared to disallow.   165
Only observe! why, fiends may learn from them!
How they talk calmly of my throes, my fierce
Aspirings, terrible watchings, each one claiming
Its price of blood and brain; how they dissect
And sneeringly disparage the few truths   170
Got at a life's cost; they too hanging the while
About my neck, their lies misleading me
And their dead names browbeating me! Grey
    crew,
Yet steeped in fresh malevolence from hell,
Is there a reason for your hate? My truths   175
Have shaken a little the palm about each prince?

---

153 *1849* So pick and choose among them all, Accursed!   *1863, 1865* So pick and
choose, among them all, accursed!   155 *1849* ends: 156 *1849*
think!   157 *1849* friend;   161 *1849* rivals, truly—Arab, Jew,   164 *Berg*
poor ⟨recompense⟩ [privilege],   165 *1849* disallow!   166 *1849* observe:
why *1863–68* observe: why,   167 *1849* throes—   168 *1849* watch-
ings—   174 *Berg* {rejected} Steeped in the fresh malevolence of {?}
hell,   176 *1849* each head?

---

176 *the palm*: the symbol of his fame.

Just think, Aprile— —all these leering dotards
Were bent on nothing less than to be Kings
As we! that yellow blear-eyed wretch, in chief,
To whom the rest cringe low with feigned
　　respect—   180
Galen—of Pergamus & Hell——nay speak
The tale, old man—how we met face to
　　face . . .*
F/.   Peace, peace— —ah see!   186
P/.   —In truth my delicate witch,
My serpent-queen, you did but well to hide   193
The juggles I had else detected— — —fire

{Sidenote:}*He did in effect affirm that he had disputed with Galen in the
vestibule of Hell.

1835 177 Aprile,   178 kings   179 wretch   181 Galen, of Pergamos and
hell;   183, 4 {No equivalent in *MS* or *1835*.}   186 Peace, peace; ah, see!
In truth   185, 187–92 {No equivalent in *MS* or *1835*.}   194 detected.

Just think, Aprile, all these leering dotards
Were bent on nothing less than to be crowned
As we! That yellow blear-eyed wretch in chief
To whom the rest cringe low with feigned
    respect,   180
Galen of Pergamos and hell—nay speak
The tale, old man! We met there face to face:
I said the crown should fall from thee. Once
    more
We meet as in that ghastly vestibule:
Look to my brow! Have I redeemed my pledge?   185
    Festus. Peace, peace; ah, see!
    Paracelsus.   Oh, emptiness of fame!
Oh Persic Zoroaster, lord of stars!
—Who said these old renowns, dead long ago,
Could make me overlook the living world
To gaze through gloom at where they stood,
    indeed,   190
But stand no longer? What a warm light life
After the shade! In truth, my delicate witch,
My serpent-queen, you did but well to hide
The juggles I had else detected. Fire

---

178 *1849* than being crowned   180 *1849* respect—   181 *1849* Galen, of
Pergamos and hell;   183 *1849* thee: 186 *1865* fame

---

181 *Galen*: see iii. 945 n. Paracelsus constantly attacked Galen, regarding
him, with Aristotle and Avicenna, as one of the great misleaders of medical
research.
   184 *that ghastly vestibule*: of Hell: cf. 174, 181.
   185 *Look to my brow!*: it is I who am crowned!
   187 *Oh Persic Zoroaster*: the *Biographie Universelle* has an exceptionally long
and ambitious article on this 'reformer and sacred writer of Persian magic' and
astrology, 'who appears before us in the midst of the obscurity of Oriental
antiquity with the numerous attributes and characters of legislator, prophet,
pontiff, high priest, and philosopher'. Shelley wrote of 'The Magus Zoroaster'
in one of the most eloquent passages in *Prometheus Unbound* (I i. 191 ff.)
Browning refers to 'Zoroaster on his terrace' in 'One Word More', 163.
   192 *my delicate witch*: in his delirium he imagines that he sees again a beautiful
woman whose blandishments he has been strong enough to resist in the past.
The words 'My serpent-queen' suggest that she is a lamia. In *The Anatomy of
Melancholy*, Part III, sect.2, mem.1, subsect. 1, Burton describes how a 'young
man, a philosopher', met and married 'such a phantasm in the habit of a fair
gentlewoman', and how at the wedding Apollonius 'found her out to be a
serpent, a lamia', whereupon she disappeared. This is the source of Keats's
Lamia, which influenced these lines. Burton mentions, in the same place, that
Erastus wrote '*de lamiis*', and that Paracelsus was 'a great champion' of the
belief in such creatures.
   194 *juggles*: cheats, as at ii. 9, ii. 178.

May well run harmless o'er a breast like yours!   195
The cave was not [so] darkened by the smoke
But that your white limbs dazzled me— —O
          white,
And panting as they twinkled, wildly dancing!
I cared not for your passionate gestures then,—
But now, I have forgotten the Charm of
          Charms   200
While I remember that quaint dance;—& thus
I am come back, not for those mummeries,
But to love you, & to kiss your little feet
Soft as an ermine's winter-coat!

F/.   —A light   205
Will struggle thro these thronging words at
          last,
As in the angry & tumultuous West
A soft star trembles thro' the drifting
          clouds— —
— —These [are] the strivings of a spirit which
          hates
So sad a vault should coop it, & calls up   210
The past to stand between it & its fate:
Were he at Einsiedeln— —Or Michal
          here . . . .

P/.   Cruel . . I seek her now—I kneel—I
          shriek—
I clasp her vesture— —but she fades—still
          fades
—   And she is gone—sweet Human Love is gone!   215
Tis only when they spring to heaven that
          Angels
Reveal themselves to you— —they sit all day
Beside you & lie down at night by you

May well run harmless o'er a breast like yours!   195
The cave was not so darkened by the smoke
But that your white limbs dazzled me: oh,
    white,
And panting as they twinkled, wildly dancing!
I cared not for your passionate gestures then,
But now I have forgotten the charm of charms,   200
The foolish knowledge which I came to seek,
While I remember that quaint dance; and thus
I am come back, not for those mummeries,
But to love you, and to kiss your little feet
Soft as an ermine's winter coat!
    Festus.   A light   205
Will struggle through these thronging words at
    last,
As in the angry and tumultuous West
A soft star trembles through the drifting
    clouds.
These are the strivings of a spirit which
    hates
So sad a vault should coop it, and calls up   210
The past to stand between it and its fate.
Were he at Einsiedeln—or Michal
    here!
    Paracelsus. Cruel! I seek her now—I kneel—I
    shriek—
I clasp her vesture— but she fades, still
    fades;
And she is gone; sweet human love is gone!   215
'T is only when they spring to heaven that
    angels
Reveal themselves to you; they sit all day
Beside you, and lie down at night by you

205, 6 *1849* A sense | Will struggle   *206 {Reading of *1849–68*}   *1888, 1889*
last.   211 *1849* past . . . . fate: *1863, 1865* Past . . . . fate.

202 *quaint*: strange, charming, with a strong suggestion of the erotic.
206 *these thronging words*: cf. 2 *Henry IV*, II. i. 107.
215 *sweet human love*: cf. *Alastor*, 203, an important influence here.

Who care not for their presence—muse or
    sleep—
And all at once they leave you & you know
    them!   220
We are so fooled—so cheated!—even now
I am not too secure against foul play—
The shadows deepen—& the walls contract—
No doubt some treachery is going on!
Tis very dusk— —where are we put, Aprile?   225
Have they left us in the lurch? this murky
    loathsome
Death-trap—this slaughter-house . . is not the
    hall
In the golden City! . . keep by me, Aprile
— — There is a hand groping amid the blackness
To catch us . . have the spider-fingers got you   230
Dearest?—hold on me for your life— —if once
They pull you . . Hold— —
                    Tis but a dream!—no more.
I have you still— —the sun comes out again
Let us be happy— —all will yet go well!
Let us confer—is it not like, Aprile,   235
That spite of gone-by trouble, this ordeal
    passed,
The value of my labours ascertained,
Just as some stream foams long among the
    rocks
But after glideth glassy to the sea
So, full content shall henceforth be my lot?   240

1835 221 fool'd, so cheated! Even now   222 play: 223 deepen,
and   225 dusk Where   228 city! Keep by me, Aprile,   230 us. Have
. . . . you,   231 Dearest? Hold . . . . life;   232 Hold . . . | 'T is but a
dream—   233 again;   235 confer:

Who care not for their presence, muse or
    sleep,
And all at once they leave you, and you know
    them!   220
We are so fooled, so cheated! Why, even now
I am not too secure against foul play;
The shadows deepen and the walls contract:
No doubt some treachery is going on.
'T is very dusk. Where are we put, Aprile?   225
Have they left us in the lurch? This murky
    loathsome
Death-trap, this slaughter-house, is not the
    hall
In the golden city! Keep by me, Aprile!
There is a hand groping amid the blackness
To catch us. Have the spider-fingers got you,   230
Poet? Hold on me for your life! If once
They pull you!—Hold!
                                'Tis but a dream—no more!
I have you still; the sun comes out again;
Let us be happy: all will yet go well!
Let us confer: is it not like, Aprile,   235
That spite of trouble, this ordeal
    passed,
The value of my labours ascertained,
Just as some stream foams long among the
    rocks
But after glideth glassy to the sea,
So, full content shall henceforth be my lot?   240

---

219 *1849* presence—muse or sleep—   223 *1849* deepen, and the walls con-
tract—   *1863, 1865* deepen and the walls contract—   224 *1849–65* going
on!   227 *1849* Death-trap—this slaughter-house—   231 *1849* life;
232 *1849* more.   233 *1849* still—   234 *1849* happy—   240 *Berg* {re-
jected} A full content

228 *the golden city*: the ideal to which he had aspired: cf. *The Revolt of Islam*,
1005–6: 'When myriads at thy call shall throng around / The Golden City'. Cf.
i. 590, above, and *Sordello*, v. 11.
230 *spider-fingers*: cf. Massinger, *The Maid of Honour*, I. ii. 47–8.

What think you, Poet?—Louder! your clear
     voice
Vibrates too like a harp-string: . . is it so?
"How couldst thou still remain on earth,
     should God
"Grant thee the great approval thou dost seek?
"I, thou & God, can comprehend each other,   245
"But Men would murmur & with cause
     enough;—
"For when they saw thee stainless of all sin,
"Preserved & sanctified by inward light,
"They would complain 'a comfort shut from
     us
"'He drinketh unespied— —for we live on   250
"'Nor taste the quiet of a constant joy
"'For ache, & care & doubt & weariness,—
"'While He is calm! Help is vouchsafed to Him
"'And hid from us!'"—twere best consider
     that
—You reason well, Aprile,—but at least   255
Let me know this, & die!—is that too much?
I will learn this, if God so please, & die!

If thou shalt please, dear God, if thou shalt
     please!
.... We are so weak we know our motives least
In their confused beginning: . . . if at first   260
I sought . . but wherefore bare my heart to
     thee?
I know thy mercy—& already thoughts
Flock fast about my soul to comfort it,
To intimate I cannot wholly fail,—
That love & praise would clasp me willingly   265

1835 241 poet? Louder! Your   242 harp-string.   246 men would mur-
mur, and . . . . enough;   250 unespied;   253 he . . . . him,   254 us!'"
'T were . . . . that: 255 You . . . . Aprile;   262 mercy; and

What think you, poet? Louder! Your clear
   voice
Vibrates too like a harp-string. Do you ask
How could I still remain on earth, should
   God
Grant me the great approval which I seek?
I, you, and God can comprehend each other,   245
But men would murmur, and with cause
   enough;
For when they saw me, stainless of all sin,
Preserved and sanctified by inward light,
They would complain that comfort, shut from
   them,
I drank thus unespied; that they live on,   250
Nor taste the quiet of a constant joy,
For ache and care and doubt and weariness,
While I am calm; help being vouchsafed to me,
And hid from them.—'T were best consider
   that!
You reason well, Aprile; but at least   255
Let me know this, and die! Is this too much?
I will learn this, if God so please, and die!

If thou shalt please, dear God, if thou shalt
   please!
We are so weak, we know our motives least
In their confused beginning. If at first   260
I sought . . . but wherefore bare my heart to
   thee?
I know thy mercy; and already thoughts
Flock fast about my soul to comfort it,
And intimate I cannot wholly fail,
For love and praise would clasp me willingly   265

---

252 *1849* ache, and care, and doubt,   254 *1849–65* them!—   260 *1849*
beginning: 261 *1863* bear my heart to Thee?   *1865* bare my heart to
Thee?   263 *1863* soul to comfort it   *1865* soul and comfort it,

---

261 *bare my heart to thee*: cf. *Pauline*, 124: 'Still I can lay my soul bare in its fall'.

Could I resolve to seek them:—Thou art good
And I should be content, yet,— —yet first
    show
I have done wrong in daring!—rather give
The supernatural consciousness of strength
That fed my youth . . one only hour of that   270
With Thee to help— —O what should bar me
    then! . . .

Lost, lost!—thus things are ordered here! God's
    creatures,
And yet he takes no pride in us! . none! none!
Truly there needs another life to come!
If this be all—(I must tell Festus that)—   275
And other life await us not . . . for one
I say 'tis a poor cheat—a stupid bungle
A wretched failure . . I, for one, protest
Against it— —& I hurl it back with scorn! . . .

Well—onward tho' alone: small time remains,   280
And much to do:—I must have fruit—must
    reap
Some profit from my toils . . I doubt my body
Will hardly serve me through— —while I have
    laboured
It has decayed— —& now that I demand
Its best assistance it will crumble fast— —   285
A sad thought—a sad fate!—how very full

1835 266 them . . . Thou art good,   267 content; yet— yet   272 Lost,
lost! thus . . . order'd here! God's creatures!   277 cheat, a stupid
bungle,   278 failure.   280 Well, onward though   281 do: I must have
fruit,   282 toils.   283 through: while I have labour'd   284 decay'd;
and   285 assistance, it . . . . fast:

Could I resolve to seek them. Thou art good,
And I should be content. Yet—yet first
    show
I have done wrong in daring! Rather give
The supernatural consciousness of strength
Which fed my youth! Only one hour of that   270
With thee to help—O what should bar me
    then!

Lost, lost! Thus things are ordered here! God's
    creatures,
And yet he takes no pride in us!—none, none!
Truly there needs another life to come!
If this be all—(I must tell Festus that)   275
And other life await us not—for one,
I say 't is a poor cheat, a stupid bungle,
A wretched failure. I, for one, protest
Against it, and I hurl it back with scorn.

Well, onward though alone! Small time remains,   280
And much to do: I must have fruit, must
    reap
Some profit from my toils. I doubt my body
Will hardly serve me through; while I have
    laboured
It has decayed; and now that I demand
Its best assistance, it will crumble fast: 285
A sad thought, a sad fate! How very full

---

266 *1849* them: 267 *1849* content;   270 *1849* That fed my youth—one
only hour of that   *1863* That fed my youth! One only hour of that   279 *1849*
Against it—and . . . . scorn!   *1863*, *1865* Against it, and . . . . scorn!   280
1849–65 alone: 286 *1849* thought—

274 *another life to come!*: Lee and Locock cite 1 Corinthians 15:32 and mention
that 'Browning often employs St. Paul's argument for immortality—*i.e.*, the
futility and irrationality of human life, with its limitless desires and transcen-
dent aspirations, on any other hypothesis than that of personal and conscious
survival after death'. They rightly refer to 'Cleon'.
275 *(I must tell Festus that)*: Paracelsus still thinks he is speaking to Aprile.
286 *a sad fate!*: 'Paracelsus' lament . . . is closely paralleled by Cleon's (ll.
309–27)': Lee and Locock.

Of wormwood 'tis, that just at Altar-service,
The rapt hymn rising with the rolling smoke,
When glory dawns, & all is at the best,—
The sacred fire may flicker & grow faint   290
And die———for want of a wood-piler's
    help!
Thus fades the flagging body, & the soul
Is pulled down in the overthrow:—well—
    well—
Let Men catch every word—let them lose
    nothing
Of what I say . . something may yet be
    done:— — —   295

They are ruins! trust me who am one of you!
All ruins— —glorious once but lonely
    now— —
It makes my heart sick to behold you crouching
Beside your desolate fane— —its arches dim
Its crumbling columns grand against the
    moon— —   300
Could I but rear them up once more— —but
    that
May never be—so leave them! Trust me
    Friends!
Why should you linger here when I have built
A far resplendent Temple, all your own
Trust me—they are but ruins! . . . see—Aprile   305
They will not heed! yet were I not prepared
With better refuge for them, never should
    tongue
Of mine reveal how blank their dwelling
    is— — —
I would sit down in silence with the rest!

1835 291 And die,   294 men   295 say; something . . . . done.   297
once, but lonely now: 299 fane; its arches dim,   300 moon: 302 be,
so . . . . Trust me friends,   304 temple, all your own?   305 Trust me,
they are but ruins! see Aprile,   308 is;   309 rest.

Of wormwood 't is, that just at altar-service,
The rapt hymn rising with the rolling smoke,
When glory dawns and all is at the best,
The sacred fire may flicker and grow faint   290
And die for want of a wood-piler's help!
Thus fades the flagging body, and the soul
Is pulled down in the overthrow. Well,
    well—
Let men catch every word, let them lose
    nought
Of what I say; something may yet be
    done.   295

They are ruins! Trust me who am one of you!
All ruins, glorious once, but lonely
    now.
It makes my heart sick to behold you crouch
Beside your desolate fane: the arches dim,
The crumbling columns grand against the
    moon,   300
Could I but rear them up once more—but
    that
May never be, so leave them! Trust me,
    friends,
Why should you linger here when I have built
A far resplendent temple, all your own?
Trust me, they are but ruins! See, Aprile,   305
Men will not heed! Yet were I not prepared
With better refuge for them, tongue of
    mine
Should ne'er reveal how blank their dwelling
    is:
I would sit down in silence with the rest.

---

289 *1849* dawns, and . . . . best—   *1863, 1865* dawns and . . . . best—   293
1849 overthrow: 294 *1849* word—   297 *1849* ruins—glorious   300
1849 moon: *1863, 1865* moon—   308 *Berg* {rejected} Should not reveal

Ha— —what? spit at me— —& grin & shriek   310
Contempt into my ear—my ear which drank
God's accents once—& curse me?—why Men,
    Men,
I am not formed for it— —those hideous eyes
Will be before me sleeping, waking, praying
— — They will not let me even die— —Spare, spare
    me   315
—   Sinning or no, forget that,—only spare me
That horrible scorn— —you thought I could
    support it
But now you see what silly fragile creature
I am— —I am not good nor bad enough . .
Not Christ— —nor Cain— —yet even Cain
    was saved   320
From hate like this— —let me but totter
    back— —
Perhaps I shall forget those jeers which creep
Into my very brain, & shut these scorched
Eyelids & keep those mocking faces
    out— — —

Listen Aprile! I am very calm—   325
—   Be not deceived—there is no passion here
Where the blood leaps like an imprisoned
    thing— — —
I am calm: I will exterminate the race!
Enough of that: 'tis said & it shall be:
And now be merry— —safe and sound am I,   330

1835 310 Ha, what? spit at me, and   312 once, and curse me? Why men,
men,   313 form'd for it;   314 praying;   315 die: spare, spare
me,   317 scorn; you . . . . it,   319 I am. I am not . . . . enough,   320
Christ, nor Cain,   321 this: let . . . . back,   324 Eyelids, and . . . .
out.   325 calm: 326 Be not deceived, there . . . . here,   327
imprison'd thing.   329 be . . .

Ha, what? you spit at me, you grin and shriek   310
Contempt into my ear—my ear which drank
God's accents once? you curse me? Why men,
      men,
I am not formed for it! Those hideous eyes
Will be before me sleeping, waking, praying,
They will not let me even die. Spare, spare
      me,   315
Sinning or no, forget that, only spare me
The horrible scorn! You thought I could support
      it,
But now you see what silly fragile creature
Cowers thus. I am not good nor bad enough,
Not Christ nor Cain, yet even Cain was
      saved   320
From Hate like this. Let me but totter
      back!
Perhaps I shall elude those jeers which creep
Into my very brain, and shut these scorched
Eyelids and keep those mocking faces
      out.

Listen, Aprile! I am very calm: 325
Be not deceived, there is no passion here
Where the blood leaps like an imprisoned
      thing:
I am calm: I will exterminate the race!
Enough of that: 't is said and it shall be.
And now be merry: safe and sound am I   330

---

314 *1849* Follow me sleeping, waking, praying God,   315 *1849* And will not
let me even die: 317 *1849* That horrible scorn; *1863* That horrible
scorn!   *317 *1849–68* support it, *1888, 1889* support it.   320 *Berg* {de-
letes but then restores this line.}   321 *Berg* {rejected} For hate *1849* From
hate like this: let . . . . back, *1863–68* From hate like this. Let . . . .
back!   327 *1849* thing.   330 *1849* merry—safe and sound am I,

---

320 *Not Christ nor Cain*: cf. *Adonais*, 305–6: 'his branded and ensanguined
brow, / Which was like Cain's or Christ's' (Pottle).

Who broke thro' their best ranks to get at
  you,
And such a havoc, such a rout Aprile!— — —
F/.   Have you no thought, no memory for
  me
Aureole?—I am so wretched . . . my pure
  Michal
Is gone— —& you alone are left to me,   335
And even you forget me— —take my hand
Lean on me thus . . do you not know me
  Aureole?
P/.   Festus,—my own friend—you are come at
  last?— — —
As you say, 'tis an awful enterprise— — —
But you believe I shall go thro' with it:—   340
Tis like you, & I thank you;— —thank him for
  me
Dear Michal!— —see how bright S! Saviour's
  spire
Flames in the sunset—all its figures quaint
Gay in the glancing light—you might conceive
  them
A troop of yellow-vested, white-haired
  Jews   345
F/.   Not that blessed time—not our youth's time,
  dear God!
P/.   Ha— —stay—true I forget— —all is done
  since!
And he is come to judge me:—how he
  speaks,—

1835 335 gone, and   336 hand—   337 thus.   338 Festus, my own
friend, you . . . . last?   343 sunset;   344 light: 346 {No equivalent in
MS or *1835*.}   348 Ha—stay! true,

Who broke through their best ranks to get at
      you.
And such a havoc, such a rout, Aprile!
      Festus. Have you no thought, no memory for
            me,
Aureole? I am so wretched—my pure
      Michal
Is gone, and you alone are left me now,   335
And even you forget me. Take my hand—
Lean on me thus. Do you not know me,
      Aureole?
      Paracelsus. Festus, my own friend, you are come
            at last?
As you say, 't is an awful enterprise;
But you believe I shall go through with it: 340
'T is like you, and I thank you. Thank him for
      me,
Dear Michal! See how bright St. Saviour's
      spire
Flames in the sunset; all its figures quaint
Gay in the glancing light: you might conceive
      them
A troop of yellow-vested white-haired
      Jews   345
Bound for their own land where redemption
      dawns.
      Festus. Not that blest time—not our youth's
            time, dear God!
      Paracelsus. Ha—stay! true, I forget—all is done
            since,
And he is come to judge me. How he speaks,

---

331 *1849* you;   335 *1849–65* left to me,   336 *1849* me: 337 *1849–65* on
me,   339 *1849* enterprise—   341 *1849* I thank you;   346 *1849–65* land
where redemption dawns! *Berg* land, where redemption dawns!   348
1849–65 since!   349 *1849* me:

342 *St. Saviour's spire*: cf. i. 59–60.
345 *yellow-vested . . . Jews*: Jews were sometimes required to wear yellow, a
colour associated with betrayal and treason. Tritheim or Trithemius (on
whom see Browning's note, p. 505 below) defended Jews against the accusa-
tion of the Inquisition that they profaned the host and indulged in ritual
murder, and he was one of Paracelsus's teachers.

How calm—how well! yes, it is true—all true: 350
All quackery—all deceit! myself can laugh
The first at it, if you desire— —but still
You know the obstacles which taught me tricks
So foreign to my nature— —envy & hate,—
Blind opposition,—brutal prejudice—   355
Bald ignorance— —what wonder if I sunk
To humour them the way they most approved?
My cheats were never palmed on such as you
Dear Festus . . . I will kneel if you require me,
Impart the meagre knowledge I possess,   360
Explain its bounded nature, & avow
My insufficiency—what e'er you will:—
I give the fight up!—let there be an end,—
A privacy—, an obscure nook for me— —
I want to be forgotten even by God!   365
But if that cannot be,— —dear Festus, lay me
When I shall die, within some narrow grave
—   Not by itself— —for that would be too
        proud:— —
But where such graves are thickest; see it look
Nowise distinguished from the hillocks round   370
So that the peasant at his brother's bed
Shall tread upon my own & know it not;
So we shall all be equal at the last,
Or classed according to life's natural ranks,
Fathers, sons, brothers, friends— —not rich
        nor wise   375
Nor gifted: lay me thus,—then say "He lived
"Too much advanced before his brother
        Men:—
"They kept him still in Front— —'twas for
        their good,
"But still a dangerous station— —strange it
        were

1835 350 calm, how . . . . true, all true; 351 quackery; 352
desire: 359 Festus. 364 A privacy, an . . . . me. 368 Not by
itself—for . . . . proud— 377 men: 378 front; 379 station.

How calm, how well! yes, it is true, all true;   350
All quackery; all deceit; myself can laugh
The first at it, if you desire: but still
You know the obstacles which taught me tricks
So foreign to my nature—envy and hate,
Blind opposition, brutal prejudice,   355
Bald ignorance—what wonder if I sunk
To humour men the way they most approved?
My cheats were never palmed on such as you,
Dear Festus! I will kneel if you require me,
Impart the meagre knowledge I possess,   360
Explain its bounded nature, and avow
My insufficiency—whate'er you will:
I give the fight up: let there be an end,
A privacy, an obscure nook for me.
I want to be forgotten even by God.   365
But if that cannot be, dear Festus, lay me,
When I shall die, within some narrow grave,
Not by itself—for that would be too
     proud—
But where such graves are thickest; let it look
Nowise distinguished from the hillocks round,   370
So that the peasant at his brother's bed
May tread upon my own and know it not;
And we shall all be equal at the last,
Or classed according to life's natural ranks,
Fathers, sons, brothers, friends—not rich, nor
     wise,
Nor gifted: lay me thus, then say, "He lived   375
"Too much advanced before his brother
     men;
"They kept him still in front: 't was for their
     good
"But yet a dangerous station. It were
     strange

---

351 *1849–65* deceit!   354 *1849* envy, and hate—   355 *1849* opposi-
tion—brutal prejudice—   363 *1849–65* fight up!   365 *1849–65* God!

---

364 *A privacy*: 'Retirement; retreat; place intended to be secret': Johnson.

"That he should tell God he had never ranked   380
"With Men:—so here at least he is a Man!"

P/.   That God shall take thee to his breast, dear
Spirit,

— —   Unto his breast, be sure!— —& here on earth
Shall splendour sit upon thy name forever!

—   Sun!—all the heaven is glad for thee! . . what
care   385
If lower mountains light their snowy phares
At thine effulgence yet acknowledge not
The source of day?— —their theft shall be
their bale,—
For after-ages shall retrack the beams,
And put aside the crowd of busy ones   390
And worship thee alone— —the Master mind
The Thinker, the Explorer, the Creator—
And who should sneer at the convulsive throes
With which thy deeds were born,—would
scorn as well
The winding sheet of subterraneous fire   395
Which, pent & writhing, sends no less at last,
Huge islands up amid the simmering sea!

—   Behold thy might in me! thou hast infused
Thy soul in mine— —& I am grand as thou
Seeing I comprehend thee— —I so simple   400
Thou so august! I recognize thee, first!
I saw thee rise & I have watched thee well
And tho' no glance reveal that thou acceptest
My homage— —thus no less I proffer it
And bid thee enter gloriously thy Rest!   405

P/.   —Festus!— —

F/.   — —I am for noble Aureole, God!

1835 381 "With men: so . . . . man!"   385 Sun! all . . . . thee: 389 after
ages   391–2 alone—the master-mind, | The thinker, the explorer, the
creator;   394 born   399 mine; and   401 thee first;   405 rest!

"That he should tell God he had never ranked   380
"With men: so, here at least he is a man."
    Festus. That God shall take thee to his breast,
      dear spirit,
Unto his breast, be sure! and here on earth
Shall splendour sit upon thy name for ever.
Sun! all the heaven is glad for thee: what
    care   385
If lower mountains light their snowy phares
At thine effulgence, yet acknowledge not
The source of day? Their theft shall be their
    bale:
For after-ages shall retrack thy beams,
And put aside the crowd of busy ones   390
And worship thee alone—the master-mind,
The thinker, the explorer, the creator!
Then, who should sneer at the convulsive throes
With which thy deeds were born, would scorn as
    well
The sheet of winding subterraneous fire   395
Which, pent and writhing, sends no less at last
Huge islands up amid the simmering sea.
Behold thy might in me! thou hast infused
Thy soul in mine; and I am grand as thou,
Seeing I comprehend thee—I so simple,   400
Thou so august. I recognize thee first;
I saw thee rise, I watched thee early and late,
And though no glance reveal thou dost accept
My homage—thus no less I proffer it,
And bid thee enter gloriously thy rest.   405
    Paracelsus. Festus!
    Festus.   I am for noble Aureole, God!

---

381 *1849–65* man!"   382 *1849* his breast, dear Spirit,   *1863,1865* His breast,
dear spirit,   384 *1849–65* ever!   388 *1849* The source of day? Men look up
to the sun: 395 *1849–65* The winding sheet of subterraneous fire   *1868* The
winding-sheet of subterraneous fire   397 *1849–65* sca!   401 *1849* august! I
recognise   *1863,65* august! I recognize   405 *1849–65* rest!

386 *phares*: lighthouses, beacons.
388 *their bale*: their destruction, their disadvantage.
389 *Retrack*: 'track or trace again', OED, which has no earlier example.
391 *the master-mind*: the first example in OED is Pope, *Iliad*, xviii. 557.
397 *Huge islands*: volcanic islands.

I am upon his side, come weal or woe!
His portion shall be mine!—He has done well!
—   I would have sinned, had I been strong enough,
As he has sinned! Reward him or I waive   410
Reward!—if thou canst find no place for him,
He shall be King elsewhere, & I will be
His slave for ever! . . . . . there are two of us!—
P/.   Dear Festus!
F/.   —Here, dear Aureole! ever by you!
P/.   Nay speak on, or I dream again— —Speak
on!   415
—   Some story—anything . . only your voice—
I shall dream else—speak on
F/.   Thus the Mayne glideth
Where my Love abideth.
Sleep's no softer: it proceeds   420
On thro' lawns, on thro' meads
On & on whate'er befall,
Meandering & musical
Tho' the niggard pasturage
Bears not on its shaven edge   425
Aught but weeds & waving grasses
To behold it as it passes,
Save here & there a scanty patch
Of primroses too faint to catch
A weary bee— —   430
P/.   More,—more—say on!
F/.   And scarce it pushes
Its gentle way thro' strangling rushes

1835 412 king elsewhere, and   415–16 Nay, speak on, or I dream again.
Speak on! | Some story, any thing—only your voice.   417 else. Speak
on!   419 love abideth;   431 More, more;

I am upon his side, come weal or woe.
His portion shall be mine. He has done well.
I would have sinned, had I been strong enough,
As he has sinned. Reward him or I waive　　　　410
Reward! If thou canst find no place for him,
He shall be king elsewhere, and I will be
His slave for ever. There are two of us.
　　Paracelsus. Dear Festus!
　　Festus. 　　　　　Here, dear Aureole! ever by you!
　　Paracelsus. Nay, speak on, or I dream again.
　　Speak on!　　　　　　　　　　　　　　　415
Some story, anything—only your voice.
I shall dream else. Speak on! ay, leaning so!
　　Festus. Thus the Mayne glideth
　　　　Where my Love abideth.
　　　　Sleep 's no softer: it proceeds　　　　420
　　　　On through lawns, on through meads,
　　　　On and on, whate'er befall,
　　　　Meandering and musical,
　　　　Though the niggard pasturage
　　　　Bears not on its shaven ledge　　　　425
　　　　Aught but weeds and waving grasses
　　　　To view the river as it passes,
　　　　Save here and there a scanty patch
　　　　Of primroses too faint to catch
　　　　A weary bee.　　　　　　　　　430
　　Paracelsus. More, more; say on!
　　Festus. 　　　　　And scarce it pushes
　　　　Its gentle way through strangling rushes

---

407 *1849–65* woe!　　408 *1849–65* mine! He has done well!　　410 *1849–65*
sinned! Reward　　413 *1849–65* ever! There are two of us!　　418–19 *1849*
Softly the Mayne river glideth | Close by where my love abideth;　　424 *1849*
niggard pasture's edge　　430 *1849* bee . . .　　431 *1849* The river pushes

　418 *Thus the Mayne glideth*: Festus sings softly, to remind his friend of their
early days in Würzburg, 'which the Mayne / Forsakes her course to fold as with
an arm' (ii. 127–8). W. J. Fox particularly praised 'the touching allusiveness,
towards the close of the poem, to the scenery and circumstances of the early life
of Paracelsus, as indicated at the commencement': *The Monthly Repository*,
November 1835: Litzinger and Smalley, p. 42. Domett comments that Brown-
ing 'has stolen a spell' from Milton.

Where the glossy king-fisher
Flutters when noon-heats are near
Glad the shelving banks to shun   435
Red & steaming in the sun
Where the shrew-mouse with pale throat
Burrows—& the speckled stoat—
Where the quick sand-pipers flit
In & out the soft & wet   440
Clay that breeds them, brown as they:
— —   Nought disturbs its quiet way
Save some lazy stork that springs
Trailing it with legs & wings
Whom the shy fox from the hill   445
Arouses— —
P/.   My heart—they loose my heart those simple
        words—
Its darkness passes which nought else could
        touch—
Like some dark snake that force may not expel
Which glideth out to music sweet & low:—   450
What were you doing when your voice broke
        thro'
A chaos of ugly images? . . . . It is you indeed!
—   Are you alone here?
F/.   All alone:—you know me?
—   This cell?
P/.   An unexceptionable vault—
Good brick & stone—the bats kept out, the rats   455
Kept in— —a snug nook:—how should I
        mistake it?
F/.   But wherefore am I here?
P/.   —   Ah!— —well remembered:—
Why, for a purpose— —for a purpose, Festus!

1835 438 Burrows, and . . . . stoat,   441 they.   447 My heart! they . . . .
heart, those simple words;   448 passes, which . . . . touch;   450 low.

Where the glossy kingfisher
Flutters when noon-heats are near,
Glad the shelving banks to shun,   435
Red and steaming in the sun,
Where the shrew-mouse with pale throat
Burrows, and the speckled stoat;
Where the quick sandpipers flit
In and out the marl and grit   440
That seems to breed them, brown as they:
Nought disturbs its quiet way,
Save some lazy stork that springs,
Trailing it with legs and wings,
Whom the shy fox from the hill   445
Rouses, creep he ne'er so still.
Paracelsus. My heart! they loose my heart,
    those simple words;
Its darkness passes, which nought else could
    touch:
Like some dark snake that force may not expel,
Which glideth out to music sweet and low.   450
What were you doing when your voice broke
    through
A chaos of ugly images? You, indeed!
Are you alone here?
   Festus.   All alone: you know me?
This cell?
   Paracelsus. An unexceptionable vault:
Good brick and stone: the bats kept out, the rats   455
Kept in: a snug nook: how should I mistake
    it?
   Festus. But wherefore am I here?
   Paracelsus.   Ah, well remembered!
Why, for a purpose—for a purpose, Festus!

---

438 *1849* stoat,   441 *1849* they.   442 *1849* Nought disturbs the river's
way,   446 *Berg* {rejected} Rouses, couch he ne'er so still.   454 *1849*
vault—   455 *1849* stone—   456 *1849* Kept in—   457 *1849* Ah! well
remembered:

---

444 *Trailing it*: following the course of the river.

Tis like me . . . here I trifle while time fleets,
And this occasion, lost, will ne'er return!   460
You are here to be instructed . . I will tell
Their message— —but I have so much to say
I fear to leave half out—all is confused
Within—but doubtless you will learn in time
— — They would not have despatched me else — —
       no doubt   465
I shall see clearer soon:— —

F/.   Tell me but this,—
You are not in despair?

P/.   —   — I?—and for what?

F/.   Alas, alas,—he knows not as I feared— — —

P/.   What is it you would ask me with that
       earnest
Dear, searching face?

F/.   How feel you, Aureole?

P/.   —   —   Well;   470
Well:—'tis a strange thing;—I am dying,
     Festus,
And now the storm of life is fast subsiding
I first perceive how swift the whirl has been:
I was calm then, who am so dizzy now,—
Calm in the thick of the tempest, but no less   475
A partner of its motion & mixed up
With its career: the hurricane is spent,
And the good boat speeds thro' the brightening
     weather
But is it earth or sea that heaves below?
The gulf rolls like a meadow-swell
     —o'erstrewn   480
With ravaged boughs & remnants of the shore
— — And now some islet loosened from the land,

1835 459 'Tis like me: 461 instructed.   462 message; but . . . .
say,   463 out: 464 Within; but . . . . time.   465 They . . . . dis-
patch'd me else: 466 soon. | Tell . . . . this—   468 alas! he knows
not,   471 Well: 'tis a strange thing.   477 career.   478 through the
bright'ning weather;   480 meadow-swell,

'T is like me: here I trifle while time fleets,
And this occasion, lost, will ne'er return.   460
You are here to be instructed. I will tell
God's message; but I have so much to say,
I fear to leave half out. All is confused
No doubt; but doubtless you will learn in time.
He would not else have brought you here: no
      doubt   465
I shall see clearer soon.
      Festus.   Tell me but this—
You are not in despair?
      Paracelsus.   I? and for what?
      Festus. Alas, alas! he knows not, as I feared!
      Paracelsus. What is it you would ask me with
      that earnest
Dear searching face?
      Festus.   How feel you, Aureole?
      Paracelsus.   Well: 470
Well. 'T is a strange thing: I am dying,
      Festus,
And now that fast the storm of life subsides,
I first perceive how great the whirl has been.
I was calm then, who am so dizzy now—
Calm in the thick of the tempest, but no less   475
A partner of its motion and mixed up
With its career. The hurricane is spent,
And the good boat speeds through the brightening
      weather;
But is it earth or sea that heaves below?
The gulf rolls like a meadow-swell, o'erstrewn   480
With ravaged boughs and remnants of the shore;
And now some islet, loosened from the land,

---

460 *1849,1863* return!   463 *1849* out: 465 *Berg* {rejected} He would not
else have left me time: no doubt   470 *1849–1865* Dear, searching . . . .
Well!   471 *1849–65* Well: 'tis a strange thing.   473 *1849* been: 480
1849 For the gulf rolls like a meadow, overstrewn   *482 *1849–68, 1889*
islet,   1888 slet, {corrected in DC.}

Swims past with all its trees, sailing to ocean,
— — And now the air is full of uptorn canes
Light strippings from the fan-trees—
  —tamarisks   485
Unrooted with their birds still clinging to
  them,— —
All high in the wind:—even so my varied life
Drifts by me— —I am young, old, happy, sad
Hoping, desponding, acting, taking rest
And all at once!—that is,—those past
  conditions   490
Flock back upon me . . . if I choose to single
Some certain epoch from the crowd,—'tis but
To will,—& straight the rest dissolve away
And that particular state is present only,
With all its circumstance forgotten long   495
But now distinct & vivid as at first,—
I being a careless looker-on—nought more!
Indifferent & amused— —but nothing more!
And this is Death;—I understand it all:
There is new Being waiting me,—& new   500
Perceptions must be born in me before
I plunge therein,—this last is Deaths affair,
And he is filling me, minute by minute,
With Power,—& while my foot is on the
  threshold
Of boundless Life—the portals yet unopened— 505
All preparations not complete within—
I turn new Knowledge upon old Events
And the effect is— — —but I must not tell
— It is not fair— —your own turn will arrive
Some day— —dear Festus you will die like
  me,—   510
Your turn will come so that you do but
  wait!— —   510a

1835 483 ocean.   485 Like strippings from the fan-trees;   486 Unrooted,
with . . . . them,   487 wind.   488 me. I . . . . sad,   490 once: that
is,   491 me.   497 looker-on,   498 and amused,   499 death: I . . . .
all.   500 being waiting me, and new   502 therein; this . . . .
Death's   504 power, and   505 life—the   507 knowledge upon old
events,   508 is . . . But I must not tell;   509 It . . . . fair.   510 day.
Dear . . . . me—

Swims past with all its trees, sailing to ocean;
And now the air is full of uptorn canes,
Light strippings from the fan-trees,
    tamarisks   485
Unrooted, with their birds still clinging to
    them,
All high in the wind. Even so my varied life
Drifts by me; I am young, old, happy, sad,
Hoping, desponding, acting, taking rest,
And all at once: that is, those past
    conditions   490
Float back at once on me. If I select
Some special epoch from the crowd, 't is but
To will, and straight the rest dissolve away,
And only that particular state is present
With all its long-forgotten circumstance   495
Distinct and vivid as at first—myself
A careless looker-on and nothing more,
Indifferent and amused, but nothing more.
And this is death: I understand it all.
New being waits me; new perceptions must   500
Be born in me before I plunge therein;
Which last is Death's affair; and while I speak,
Minute by minute he is filling me
With power; and while my foot is on the
    threshold
Of boundless life—the doors unopened yet,   505
All preparations not complete within—
I turn new knowledge upon old events,
And the effect is . . . but I must not tell;
It is not lawful. Your own turn will come
One day. Wait, Festus! You will die like
    me.   510

488 *1849* me.   493 *1863* away   *1865* away;   495 *1849* circumstance,
497 *1849* looker-on, and nothing more!   *1863, 1865* looker-on and nothing
more!   498 *1849* amused, ... more!   *1863, 1865* amused . . . . more!
1868 amused . . . . more.   510 *1849–65* like me!

485 *fan-trees*: fan-palms.
492–3 *'t is but / To will*: all I have to do is to wish, and . . .

F/.   Tis of that past life that I burn to hear . . . .
P/.   You wonder it engages me just
            now?
         In truth, I wonder too—what's life to me?
         Where'er I look is fire—where'er I listen
         Music, & where I tend bliss evermore.   515
         Yet I can not refrain:— —'tis a refined
         Delight to view those chances once again;—
         I am so near the perils I escape
         That I must play with them & turn them over
         To feel how fully they are past & gone:—   520
         Still, it is like, some further cause exists
         For this peculiar mood— —some hidden
            purpose— —
         Did I not tell you something of it, Festus?
         I had it fast— —but it has somehow slipt
         Away from me— —it will return anon.— —   525
F/.   (Indeed his cheek seems young again—his
            voice
         Complete with its old tones!—that little laugh
         Concluding every phrase—with upturned eye
         As though one stooped above his head to
            whom
         He looked for confirmation & approval— —   530
         Where was it gone so long, so well
            preserved? . .
         And the forefinger pointing as he speaks
         Like one who traces in an open book
         The matter he declares— —'tis many a year
         Since I remarked it last:—& this in him   535
         But now a ghastly wreck!—)
                              —And can it be
         Dear Aureole? you have then found out at last
         The utter vanity of worldly things?

1835 513 too.   514 fire,   517 again.   520 and gone.   521 Still it is
like   522 purpose;   524 fast,   525 me; it will return anon.   526
again,   527 tones—   528 phrase; with up-turn'd eye,   530 and
approval: 534 declares;   535 last: and this in him . . .   537 Aureole,

Festus. 'T is of that past life that I burn to hear.
Paracelsus. You wonder it engages me just
    now?
In truth, I wonder too. What 's life to me?
Where'er I look is fire, where'er I listen
Music, and where I tend bliss evermore.   515
Yet how can I refrain? 'T is a refined
Delight to view those chances,—one last view.
I am so near the perils I escape,
That I must play with them and turn them over,
To feel how fully they are past and gone.   520
Still, it is like, some further cause exists
For this peculiar mood—some hidden
    purpose;
Did I not tell you something of it, Festus?
I had it fast, but it has somehow slipt
Away from me; it will return anon.   525
    Festus. (Indeed his cheek seems young again, his
    voice
Complete with its old tones: that little laugh
Concluding every phrase, with upturned eye,
As though one stooped above his head to
    whom
He looked for confirmation and approval,   530
Where was it gone so long, so well
    preserved?
Then, the fore-finger pointing as he speaks,
Like one who traces in an open book
The matter he declares; 't is many a year
Since I remarked it last: and this in him,   535
But now a ghastly wreck!)
                   And can it be,
Dear Aureole, you have then found out at last
That worldly things are utter vanity?

---

511 *1849–65* 'Tis of that past . . . . hear! *Berg* 'T is of ⟨that⟩ [your] past . . . .
hear ⟨. . .⟩ [!]   521 *1849–65* Still it is like   530 *1849* confirmation and
applause,—   531 *1849* so long, being kept so well?

514 *Where'er I look is fire*: cf. *Paradise Lost*, i. 180 ff.

That Man is made for weakness, & should wait
In patient ignorance till God appoint   540

P/.   Ha, the purpose! the true purpose! that is
          it!

— —   How could I fail to apprehend!— —you here,
I thus!—but no more trifling;—I see all—
I know all;—my last mission shall be done
If strength suffice:—no trifling!—stay —this
          posture   545
Hardly befits one thus about to speak—
I will arise.—

F/.   Dear Aureole— —are you wild? . .
You cannot leave your couch— —

P/.   —No help! No help!
Not even your hand!— —so!— —there, I
          stand once more!
Speak from a couch?—why I ne'er lectured
          thus!—   550
My gown— —the scarlet lined with
          fur:— —now put
The chain about my neck—my signet-ring
Is still upon my hand, I think— —even so.

— —   Last my good sword,—ha trusty Azoth? leapest
Beneath thy masters grasp for the last time?   555
This couch shall be my throne: I bid this cell
Be consecrate . . this wretched bed become
A shrine— —for here God speaks to Men thro'
          me!
Now, Festus, I am ready to begin.

F/.   I am blind with wonder!

P/.   Listen, therefore, Festus!   560
There will be time enough, but none to spare . .
I must content myself with telling only
The most important points: you doubtless feel

1835 539 man   541 purpose; the true purpose: that   543, 544 I thus! But
. . . . trifling; I see all, | I know all: 545 suffice. No trifling! Stay;   546
speak: 547 I will arise. | Dear Aureole,   548 couch. | No help; no
help;   549 hand. So!   550 couch? why . . . . thus.   552 neck;   553
even so;   554 Last, my good sword; ha, trusty Azoth,   557 conse-
crate;   558 A shrine; for . . . . men through me!   560 wonder.   561
spare.   563 points.

That man is made for weakness, and should wait
In patient ignorance, till God appoint . . .   540
    Paracelsus. Ha, the purpose: the true purpose:
      that is it!
How could I fail to apprehend! You here,
I thus! But no more trifling: I see all,
I know all: my last mission shall be done
If strength suffice. No trifling! Stay; this
    posture   545
Hardly befits one thus about to speak:
I will arise.
    Festus.   Nay, Aureole, are you wild?
You cannot leave your couch.
    Paracelsus.   No help; no help;
Not even your hand. So! there, I stand once
    more!
Speak from a couch? I never lectured
    thus.   550
My gown—the scarlet lined with fur; now
    put
The chain about my neck; my signet-ring
Is still upon my hand, I think—even so;
Last, my good sword; ah, trusty Azoth, leapest
Beneath thy master's grasp for the last time?   555
This couch shall be my throne: I bid these walls
Be consecrate, this wretched cell become
A shrine, for here God speaks to men through
    me.
Now, Festus, I am ready to begin.
    Festus. I am dumb with wonder.
    Paracelsus.   Listen, therefore, Festus!   560
There will be time enough, but none to spare.
I must content myself with telling only
The most important points. You doubtless feel

---

541 *1849* the purpose; the . . . . it! *1863* the purpose, the . . . . it *1865*, *1868* the purpose, the . . . . it!   554 *1849*, *1863* ha, trusty Azoth,   557 *1849* consecrate;   558 *1849* shrine; for . . . . me! *1863*, *1865* shrine, for . . . . me!   563 *1868* doubtlsss

554 *trusty Azoth*: see Browning's note, p. 509 below.

That I am happy, Festus?—very happy?

F/.   Tis no delusion which uplifts him
      thus!—   565
    Then you [are] pardoned, Aureole, all your sin?

P/.   Pardon?— —& wherefore pardon?— —

F/.   Tis God's praise
    That Man is bound to seek,—& you . . .

P/.   . . Have lived!
    We have to live, alone, to set forth well
    God's praise: 'tis true, I sinned much, as I
      thought—   570
    And, in effect, need mercy— —for I strove
    To do that very thing . . but, do your best
    Or worst—praise rises & will rise for ever!
    Pardon from ⟨h⟩ Him?— —who calls me to
      ⟨h⟩ Himself
    To teach me better, & exalt me higher?   575
    He might laugh, as I laugh!

F/.   But all this comes
    To the same thing— —'tis fruitless for
      Mankind
    To fret themselves with what concerns them
      not:
    They are no use that way— —they should lie
      down
    Content as God has made them, nor go mad   580
    In thriveless cares to better their condition;—

P/.   No, No! mistake me not . . let me not
      work
    More harm than I have done!—this is my
      case:— —
    If I go joyous back to God, yet bring
    No offering—if I render up my soul   585
    Without the fruits it was ordained to bear,—

1835 564 Festus; very happy.   565 thus . . .   568 man . . . . seek,
and   569 live alone   570 praise. 'T is . . . . thought,   571 And in effect
need mercy,   572 thing;   573 Or worst, praise rises, ... ever.   574
Him, who   575 better and . . . . higher!   576 laugh as I laugh.   577
thing. 'T is . . . . mankind   579 way: 581 condition.   582 No, no;
mistake me not;   583 done. This is my case: 585 offering;   586 bear;

That I am happy, Festus; very happy.
   Festus. 'T is no delusion which uplifts him
     thus!   565
Then you are pardoned, Aureole, all your sin?
   Paracelsus. Ay, pardoned: yet why pardoned?
   Festus.   'T is God's praise
That man is bound to seek, and you . . .
   Paracelsus.   Have lived!
We have to live alone to set forth well
God's praise. 'T is true, I sinned much, as I
     thought,   570
And in effect need mercy, for I strove
To do that very thing; but, do your best
Or worst, praise rises, and will rise for ever.
Pardon from him, because of praise
     denied—
Who calls me to himself to exalt himself?   575
He might laugh as I laugh!
   Festus.   But all comes
To the same thing. 'T is fruitless for
     mankind
To fret themselves with what concerns them
     not;
They are no use that way: they should lie
     down
Content as God has made them, nor go mad   580
In thriveless cares to better what is ill.
   Paracelsus. No, no; mistake me not; let me not
     work
More harm than I have worked! This is my
     case:
If I go joyous back to God, yet bring
No offering, if I render up my soul   585
Without the fruits it was ordained to bear,

---

567 *1849–65* Ay, pardoned!   *573 {Reading of *1849–68, 1889*}   *1888* ever
{corrected in DC}   576 *1849* Then all comes *Berg* ⟨But⟩ [Then] all this
comes   583 *1849–65* I have done! This

---

569 *We have to live alone*: we have only to live.

If I appear to love God better for
My sins— —as one who has no claim on
    him,—
Be not deceived;—it may be only thus
With me— —or higher prizes may await   590
The mortal persevering to the end:—
Beside I am not all so valueless
—   I have been something, tho' too soon I left
Following the instincts of that happy time . . . .
F/.   What happy time?— —for God's sake — —
    for Man's sake   595
What time was happy? all I hope to know
That answer will decide . . . what happy time?
P/.   When but the time I vowed myself to
    Man?
F/.   Great God, thy judgments are
    inscrutable!
P/.   Yes— —it was in me— —I was born for
    it:—   600
I . . . Paracelsus:—it was mine by right:—
Doubtless a searching & impetuous spirit
Might learn from its own motions that some
    task
Like this awaited it about the world— — —
Might seek somewhere in this blank life of ours   605
For fit delights to stay its longings vast,
And, grappling strenuously with Fate, compel
    her
To fill the creature full, whom she dared frame
Hungry for joy:—&—bravely tyrannous—
Grow in demand—still craving more &
    more— — —   610

1835 588 sins, as . . . . him,   590 me;   591 end.   592 Beside, I . . . .
valueless;   595 time? For God's sake, for man's sake,   597
decide.   598 When, but . . . . vow'd myself to man.   600 Yes, it was in
me; I was born for it—   601 I, Paracelsus: it . . . . right.   604
world;   606 vast;   609 joy; and, bravely tyrannous,   610 demand,
still . . . . and more,

If I appear the better to love God
For sin, as one who has no claim on
   him,—
Be not deceived! It may be surely thus
With me, while higher prizes still await   590
The mortal persevering to the end.
Beside I am not all so valueless:
I have been something, though too soon I left
Following the instincts of that happy time.
    Festus. What happy time? For God's sake, for
      man's sake,   595
What time was happy? All I hope to know
That answer will decide. What happy time?
    Paracelsus. When but the time I vowed myself
      to man?
    Festus. Great God, thy judgments are
      inscrutable!
    Paracelsus. Yes, it was in me; I was born for
      it—   600
I, Paracelsus: it was mine by right.
Doubtless a searching and impetuous soul
Might learn from its own motions that some
   task
Like this awaited it about the world;
Might seek somewhere in this blank life of ours   605
For fit delights to stay its longings vast;
And, grappling Nature, so prevail on
   her
To fill the creature full she dared thus frame
Hungry for joy; and, bravely tyrannous,
Grow in demand, still craving more and
   more,   610

---

589 *1849* deceived: 590 *Berg* {rejected} while higher prizes doubtless
wait   592 {Omitted from *1849*}   593–4 *1849* For I too have been some-
thing, though too soon | I left the instincts of that happy time!   594 *1849–65*
time!   598 *1849* When, but the time I vowed my help to man?   608
1849–65 she dared to frame

---

601 *I, Paracelsus*: perhaps a play on the meaning of his name (beyond Celsus),
as Lee and Locock suggest.
609 *Hungry for joy*: cf. 'Cleon', 323 ff., particularly 328: 'the joy-hunger'.

And make the joy conceded prove a pledge
Of further joy to follow— —bating nothing
Of its desires, but seizing all pretence
To turn the knowledge & the rapture wrung
From Destiny as an extreme, last boon,   615
Into occasion for new covetings,
New strifes, new triumphs: doubtless a strong
    spirit
Might do all this unaided & alone,
So glorious is our nature— —so august
Man's inborn uninstructed impulses— — —   620
His naked Spirit so majestical!
— — But it was born in me! I was made so:
Thus much time saved—the feverish
    appetites—
The tumult of unproved desire—the aimless
Uncertain yearnings—near-sighted ambition,   625
Distrust, mistake—& all that ends in tears
⟨Was⟩ [Were] saved me, tho' the lion-heart
    repines not
At working thro' such lets its purpose out: 627a
. . . . You may be sure I was not all exempt
From human trouble,—just so much of doubt
As bade me plant a surer foot upon   630
The sun-road— —kept my eye unruined 'mid
The fierce & flashing splendour—set my heart
Trembling so much as warned me I stood there
On sufferance . . not to idly gaze, but have
Remembrance of a darkling Race— — save
    that,   635
I stood at first where all aspire at last
To reach: the secret of the world was mine.
I knew, I felt . . not as one knows or feels
Aught else— —a vast perception unexpressed,   638a

1835 617 triumphs.   619 nature,   621 spirit   622 But . . . . me: I was
made so.   623 saved: the feverish appetites,   624 desire,   625 yearn-
ings, near-sighted ambition,   626 mistake,   627a out.   629 trou-
ble: 635 race;   637 reach—   638 felt,   638a else; a . . . . un-
express'd,

And make each joy conceded prove a pledge
Of other joy to follow—bating nought
Of its desires, still seizing fresh pretence
To turn the knowledge and the rapture wrung
As an extreme, last boon, from destiny,   615
Into occasion for new covetings,
New strifes, new triumphs:—doubtless a strong
     soul,
Alone, unaided might attain to this,
So glorious is our nature, so august
Man's inborn uninstructed impulses,   620
His naked spirit so majestical!
But this was born in me; I was made so;
Thus much time saved: the feverish
     appetites,
The tumult of unproved desire, the unaimed
Uncertain yearnings, aspirations blind,   625
Distrust, mistake, and all that ends in tears
Were saved me; thus I entered on my course.
You may be sure I was not all exempt
From human trouble; just so much of doubt
As bade me plant a surer foot upon   630
The sun-road, kept my eye unruined 'mid
The fierce and flashing splendour, set my heart
Trembling so much as warned me I stood there
On sufferance—not to idly gaze, but cast
Light on a darkling race; save for that doubt,   635
I stood at first where all aspire at last
To stand: the secret of the world was mine.
I knew, I felt, (perception unexpressed,

---

613 *Berg* {rejected} Of all desire,   614 *Berg* {rejected} and its rapture,
{comma not deleted}   615 *1849* Destiny,   618 *Berg* Alone, unaided,
might ⟨conceive of⟩ [attain to] this,   627 *1849–65* course!   631 *1849* sun-
road—kept . . . . mid   632 *1849* splendour—

---

624 *unproved*: 'Not put to proof or trial; untried. *Obs.*' OED.
631 *sun-road*: not in OED.
635 *darkling*: obscure, mysterious. Cf. Isaiah 9:2: 'The people that walked in
darkness have seen a great light'. Paracelsus believes that he has a Messianic
mission.

Uncomprehended by our narrow thought,
But somehow felt & known in every shift   640
And change in the spirit I bear— —nay, dare I
     say
In every pore of this fast-fading frame   641a
I felt, I knew what God is, what We are,*
What Life is . . . how God tastes an infinite joy
In infinite ways . . one everlasting Bliss
From whom all Being emanates, all Power   645
Proceeds— —in whom is Life for evermore,
Yet whom Existence in its lowest form
Includes— —where dwells Enjoyment there is
     He!
With still a flying point of bliss remote—
A happiness in store afar—a sphere   650
Of distant glory in full view . . thus climbs
Pleasure its heights forever & forever!
The centre-fire heaves underneath the earth,
And the earth changes like a human face;
The molten ore bursts up among the rocks   655
Winds into the stone's heart . . outbranches
     bright
In hidden mines . . spots barren river-beds . .
Crumbles into fine sand where sunbeams
     bask— — —
God joys therein!—the wroth sea's waves are
     edged
With foam white as the bitten lip of hate   660
When in the solitary waste strange groups
Of young volcanos come up, cyclops-like
Staring together with their eyes on
     flame — — —
God tastes a pleasure in their uncouth pride!

{Sidenote:} *"Paracelse faisait profession du Pantheisme le plus grossier."
     Renauldin.

1835 642 we are, *{Footnote: as *MS* except "Panthéisme".}   643 life
is—   644 ways—one everlasting bliss,   645 being . . . . power   646
Proceeds; in . . . . life   647 existence   648 Includes; where dwells
enjoyment   651 view;   655 rocks—   660 foam, white . . . .
Hate: 663 flame,

Uncomprehended by our narrow thought,
But somehow felt and known in every shift   640
And change in the spirit,—nay, in every
    pore
Of the body, even,)—what God is, what we
    are,
What life is—how God tastes an infinite joy
In infinite ways—one everlasting bliss,
From whom all being emanates, all power   645
Proceeds; in whom is life for evermore,
Yet whom existence in its lowest form
Includes; where dwells enjoyment there is
    he:
With still a flying point of bliss remote,
A happiness in store afar, a sphere   650
Of distant glory in full view; thus climbs
Pleasure its heights for ever and for ever.
The centre-fire heaves underneath the earth,
And the earth changes like a human face;
The molten ore bursts up among the rocks,   655
Winds into the stone's heart, outbranches
    bright
In hidden mines, spots barren river-beds,
Crumbles into fine sand where sunbeams
    bask—
God joys therein. The wroth sea's waves are
    edged
With foam, white as the bitten lip of hate,   660
When, in the solitary waste, strange groups
Of young volcanos come up, cyclops-like,
Staring together with their eyes on
    flame—
God tastes a pleasure in their uncouth pride.

---

648 *1849–65* is He!   652 *1849–65* and for ever!   659 *1849–65*
therein!   660 *1849* Hate,   663 *1849* flame;—   664 *1849–65* pride!

651–2 *thus climbs | Pleasure its heights*: very Elizabethan in suggestion, though
no close parallel has been found. Cf. *Tamburlaine the Great*, Part I, II. vii. 24: 'Still
climbing after knowledge infinite'.
653 *The centre-fire*: cf. *Sordello*, ii. 805.
662 *cyclops-like*: because the Cyclops had one eye.

Then all is still: earth is a wintry clod,   665
But spring-wind, like a dancing psaltress, passes
Over its breast to waken it— —rare verdure
Buds here & there upon rough banks, between
The withered tree-roots & the cracks of frost
Like a smile striving with a wrinkled face,   670
The grass grows bright, the boughs are swollen with blooms
Like chrysalids impatient for the air:
The shining dorrs are busy— —beetles run
Along the furrows . . ants make their ado . .
Above birds fly in merry flocks— —the lark   675
Soars up & up, shivering for very joy;
Afar the ocean sleeps . . . white fishing gulls
Flit where the strand is purple with its tribe
Of nested limpets: savage creatures seek
Their loves in wood & plain: . . . & God renews   680
His ancient rapture! Thus He dwells in all,

1835 665 clod;   667 it;   670 face;   673 busy;   674 furrows, ants
. . . . ado;   677 sleeps; white fishing-gulls

Then all is still; earth is a wintry clod: 665
But spring-wind, like a dancing psaltress,
    passes
Over its breast to waken it, rare verdure
Buds tenderly upon rough banks, between
The withered tree-roots and the cracks of frost,
Like a smile striving with a wrinkled face;   670
The grass grows bright, the boughs are swoln
    with blooms
Like chrysalids impatient for the air,
The shining dorrs are busy, beetles run
Along the furrows, ants make their ado;
Above, birds fly in merry flocks, the lark   675
Soars up and up, shivering for very joy;
Afar the ocean sleeps; white fishing-gulls
Flit where the strand is purple with its tribe
Of nested limpets; savage creatures seek
Their loves in wood and plain—and God
    renews   680
His ancient rapture. Thus he dwells in all,

---

666 *Berg* psaltress, passes. {'passes' underlined, and the word 'leaps' written in
the margin in pencil, possibly not by Browning.}   667 *1849* waken
it;   672 *1849* air;   673 *1849* busy;   675 *1849* flocks—   680 *1849* plain;
681 *1849–65* rapture!

---

673 *dorrs*: Johnson defines 'dorr' as 'A kind of flying insect, remarkable for
flying with a loud noise'.
679 *limpets*: 'Was Browning quite hazy about the limpet?', asked 'G. G. L.' in
NQ 187 (July–Dec. 1944), p. 194, suggesting that he may have been thinking of
mussels. On p. 237 L. R. M. Strachan urged that Browning should be given the
benefit of the doubt.
681 *Thus he dwells in all*: 'The passage reveals a marked and persistent trend
of finalism which combines the nisus of the Platonic–Aristotelian tradition
with nineteenth-century biological concepts of "Progression"': Roppen, p.
116.

From Life's minute beginnings, up at last
To Man—the consummation of this Scheme
Of Being—the completion of this Sphere
Of Life: whose attributes had here & there   685
Been scattered o'er the visible world before,
Asking to be combined . . . dim fragments
     meant
To be united in some wondrous Whole,—
Imperfect qualities throughout Creation
Suggesting some one Creature yet to make . . .   690
— (So would a Spirit deem, intent on watching   690a
The purpose of the world from its faint rise   b
To its mature development)—some point   691
Whereto those wandering rays should all
     converge—
Might: neither put forth blindly, nor controlled
Calmly by perfect knowledge—to be used
At risk—inspired or checked by hope & fear:—   695
Knowledge:—not intuition, but the slow
Uncertain fruit of an inhancing toil
Strengthened by love: Love:—not serenely
     pure,
But power from weakness, like a chance-sown
     plant
Which cast on stubborn soil puts forth changed
     buds   700
And softer stains unknown in happier
     climes . . .
Love which endures, & doubts, & is oppressed
And cherished—suffering much & much
     sustained,—

1835 682–690a life's {etc.— lower case} 689 creation,   691 devolope-
ment)—   695 inspir'd or check'd . . . . and fear—   698 Strengthen'd by
love—love: 701 stains, unknown . . . . climes:

From life's minute beginnings, up at last
To man—the consummation of this scheme
Of being, the completion of this sphere
Of life: whose attributes had here and there   685
Been scattered o'er the visible world before,
Asking to be combined, dim fragments
     meant
To be united in some wondrous whole,
Imperfect qualities throughout creation,
Suggesting some one creature yet to make,   690
Some point where all those scattered rays should
     meet
Convergent in the faculties of man.
Power—neither put forth blindly, nor controlled
Calmly by perfect knowledge; to be used
At risk, inspired or checked by hope and fear: 695
Knowledge—not intuition, but the slow
Uncertain fruit of an enhancing toil,
Strengthened by love: love—not serenely pure,
But strong from weakness, like a chance-sown
     plant
Which, cast on stubborn soil, puts forth changed
     buds   700
And softer stains, unknown in happier climes;
Love which endures and doubts and is oppressed
And cherished, suffering much and much
     sustained,

---

687 *1849* combined—   688 *1849* whole—   690 *1849* make—   693
1849 Power;   696 *1849* Knowledge;   698 *1849* love: love;

690 *Suggesting some one creature*: 'see Aids to Reflection—Coleridge':
Domett. The reference is to 'Aphorism xxxvi' or rather to the longish com-
ment on it (from which Domett quotes with reference to 742–3 below). The
passage occurs on pp. 111–12 of the ed. of 1825.
     699 *a chance-sown plant*: cf. Scott, *The Lady of the Lake*, II. xix. 11: 'Ours is no
sapling, chance-sown by the fountain'.

A blind, unfailing & devoted Love:—
And half-enlightened, often-checquered
     Trust:— —   705
Anticipations, hints of these & more
Are strewn confusedly everywhere—all seek
An object to possess & stamp their own;
All shape out dimly the forthcoming Race,
The heir of hopes too fair to turn out false,   710
And Man appears at last: so far the seal
Is put on Life: one stage of Being complete,
One Scheme wound up: & from the grand
     result
A supplementary reflux of light
Illustrates all the inferior grades, explains   715
Each back step in the circle:—not alone
The clear dawn of those qualities shines out,
But the new glory mixes with the heaven
And earth—Man, once descried, imprints for
     ever
His presence on all lifeless things—the winds   720
Are henceforth voices—wailing or a shout,
A querulous mutter or a quick gay laugh,—

And blind, oft-failing, yet believing love,
A half-enlightened, often-chequered
    trust:—   705
Hints and previsions of which faculties,
Are strewn confusedly everywhere about
The inferior natures, and all lead up higher,
All shape out dimly the superior race,
The heir of hopes too fair to turn out false,   710
And man appears at last. So far the seal
Is put on life; one stage of being complete,
One scheme wound up: and from the grand
    result
A supplementary reflux of light
Illustrates all the inferior grades, explains   715
Each back step in the circle. Not alone
For their possessor dawn those qualities,
But the new glory mixes with the heaven
And earth; man, once descried, imprints for
    ever
His presence on all lifeless things: the winds   720
Are henceforth voices, wailing or a shout,
A querulous mutter or a quick gay laugh,

704 *1849–65* A blind, 708 *1849* natures;   711 *1849* And Man appears at
last: *714 *MS* light *1835–89* light,   719 *1849* earth: Man,   721
1849–65 voices, in a wail or shout,   722 *1849* mutter, or . . . . laugh— *1863*,
1865 mutter, or . . . . laugh,

711 *And man appears at last*: cf. Introduction, p. 118, above. DeVane refers to
Paradise Lost 'V, 403–505' and 'Pope's *Essay on Man* (VII)': p. 55. The Milton
reference should read 'V, 469–505', and that to *An Essay on Man* 'I, 207ff.'
   714 *A supplementary reflux of light*: cf. Lyell, *Principles of Geology*, i. 117 (1830):
'The heat and cold which surround the globe are in a state of constant and
universal flux and reflux'.
   715 *Illustrates*: lends lustre to. Stressed on the second syllable, as in Johnson,
and in 'Soliloquy of the Spanish Cloister', 37. The comma at the end of 714
seems uncalled for, but occurs in all eds. (though not in the MS).
   720 *the winds / Are henceforth voices*: Browning may be remembering the
account of the origin of mythology in *The Excursion*, iv. 631 ff.

Never a senseless gust now Man is born:
The herded pines commune, & have deep
   thoughts,
A secret they assemble to discuss   725
When the sun drops behind their trunks which
   glare
Like grates of hell: the peerless cup afloat
Of the lake-lily is an urn some nymph
Swims bearing high above her head: no bird
Whistles unseen, but thro' the gaps above   730
That let light in upon the gloomy woods
A Shape peeps from the breezy forest-top,
Arch with small puckered mouth & mocking
   eye:
The morn has enterprise—deep quiet droops
With evening;— —triumph when the sun takes
   rest,—   735
Voluptuous transport when the cornfields ripen
Beneath a warm moon like a happy
   face:— — —
And this to fill us with regard for Man,
Deep apprehension of his passing worth,
Desire to work his proper nature out,   740
To ascertain his rank & final place—

Never a senseless gust now man is born.
The herded pines commune and have deep
    thoughts,
A secret they assemble to discuss   725
When the sun drops behind their trunks which
    glare
Like grates of hell: the peerless cup afloat
Of the lake-lily is an urn, some nymph
Swims bearing high above her head: no bird
Whistles unseen, but through the gaps above   730
That let light in upon the gloomy woods,
A shape peeps from the breezy forest-top,
Arch with small puckered mouth and mocking
    eye.
The morn has enterprise, deep quiet droops
With evening, triumph takes the sunset
    hour,   735
Voluptuous transport ripens with the corn
Beneath a warm moon like a happy
    face:
—And this to fill us with regard for man,
With apprehension of his passing worth,
Desire to work his proper nature out,   740
And ascertain his rank and final place,

723 *1849–65* born!   724 *1849* commune,   *724 {Reading of *1849–68*,
1889} *1888* thoughts {comma added in DC}   733 *1849–65* eye: 734
1849 enterprise,—   735 *1849* evening; triumph .... sunset   *738
{Reading of *1849–65*} *1868–89* man.   741 *1849* place;

For all these things tend upward—progress is
The law of Life—Man is not Man as yet:
Nor shall I deem his object served, his end
Attained, his genuine strength put fairly out,   745
While only here & there a star dispels
The darkness—here & there a towering Mind
O'erlooks its crawling fellows:—when the
  ⟨h⟩ Host
Is out at once to the despair of night,—
When all Mankind is perfected alike,   750
Equal in full-blown powers—then—not till
  then
Begins the general infancy of Man;
For wherefore make account of feverish starts
Of restless members of a dormant Whole
Impatient nerves which quiver while the Body   755
Slumbers as in a grave? O long ago
The brow was twitched—the tremulous lids
  astir—

For these things tend still upward, progress is
The law of life, man is not Man as yet.
Nor shall I deem his object served, his end
Attained, his genuine strength put fairly forth,   745
While only here and there a star dispels
The darkness, here and there a towering mind
O'erlooks its prostrate fellows: when the
   host
Is out at once to the despair of night,
When all mankind alike is perfected,   750
Equal in full-blown powers—then, not till
   then,
I say, begins man's general infancy.
For wherefore make account of feverish starts
Of restless members of a dormant whole,
Impatient nerves which quiver while the body   755
Slumbers as in a grave? Oh long ago
The brow was twitched, the tremulous lids
   astir,

742 *1849* upward—   743 *1849* The law of life—man's self is not yet
Man! *1863, 1865* The law of life, man's self is not yet Man!   752 *1849–65*
infancy!   754 *1849* whole—

742 *progress*: 'Last, about my being "strongly against Darwin, rejecting the
truths of science and regretting its advance"—you only do as I should hope and
expect in disbelieving *that* . . . In reality, all that seems *proved* in Darwin's
scheme was a conception familiar to me from the beginning: see in Paracelsus
the progressive development from senseless matter to organized, until man's
appearance (*Part* V.). Also in *Cleon*, see the order of "life's mechanics,"—and I
daresay in many passages of my poetry: for how can one look at Nature as a
whole and doubt that, wherever there is a gap, a "link" must be "mis-
sing"—through the limited power and opportunity of the looker?': *Trumpeter*,
p. 34. The whole letter, written in 1881, should be consulted. Cf. Introduction,
above, and the books there cited.
   Domett notes in the margin: '"All things strive to ascend, and ascend in their
striving. And shall man alone stoop?" &c Coleridge', quoting the Comment
on Aphorism xxxvi from *Aids to Reflection* (cf. 690 n., above). The previous
sentence of the Comment, the whole of which seems to have made a deep
impression on Browning, is this: 'Thus all lower Natures find their highest
Good in semblances and seekings of that which is higher and better.'
   750 *perfected*: cf. Shelley, 'The Daemon of the World', 517: 'Thus human
things are perfected'.
   754 *members of a dormant whole*: cf. Romans 12:5: 'So we, being many, are one
body in Christ, and every one members one of another'.
   755 *Impatient nerves*: 'The greater part of our body, of our humanity itself, yet
sleeps a deep sleep: Novalis by Carlyle': Domett, quoting a Fragment given in
Carlyle's essay on Novalis in the *Foreign Review* in 1829 (repr. in his *Collected
Works*, Centenary ed., xxvii. 39).

The peaceful mouth disturbed—half uttered
    speech
Ruffled the lip . . . sometimes the teeth set hard
The breath drawn sharp, the strong right hand
    clenched stronger,   760
As it would pluck a lion by the maw . . .
The glorious creature laughed out even in sleep!
But when aroused—each giant-limb awake—
Each sinew strung—the great heart pulsing
    fast—
He shall start up, & stand on his own earth   765
Then shall his long triumphant march begin—
Thence shall his being date—what thus
    collected
He shall achieve, shall be set down to him!
When all the race is perfected alike
As ⟨m⟩ *Man*, that is:—all tended to Mankind   770
And, Man produced, [all has its end] thus far;
But in completed Man begins anew
A tendency to God: prognostics told
Man's near approach; so in Man's self arise
August anticipations, symbols, types   775
Of a dim splendour ever on before
In the eternal circle Life pursues:
For men begin to pass their nature's bound
To have new hopes & cares which fast
    supplant

1835 759 Ruffled the lip; sometimes the teeth were set,   760 clench'd
stronger—   761 maw: 763 awake,   764 strung,   765 earth—
767 date;   772–790 man {etc: lower case}   773 God.   776 before,

The peaceful mouth disturbed; half-uttered
  speech
Ruffled the lip, and then the teeth were set,
The breath drawn sharp, the strong right-hand
  clenched stronger,   760
As it would pluck a lion by the jaw;
The glorious creature laughed out even in sleep!
But when full roused, each giant-limb awake,
Each sinew strung, the great heart pulsing
  fast,
He shall start up and stand on his own earth,   765
Then shall his long triumphant march begin,
Thence shall his being date,—thus wholly
  roused,
What he achieves shall be set down to him.
When all the race is perfected alike
As man, that is; all tended to mankind,   770
And, man produced, all has its end thus far:
But in completed man begins anew
A tendency to God. Prognostics told
Man's near approach; so in man's self arise
August anticipations, symbols, types   775
Of a dim splendour ever on before
In that eternal circle life pursues.
For men begin to pass their nature's bound,
And find new hopes and cares which fast
  supplant

766, 7 *1849* And so begin his long triumphant march, | And date his being
thence,—thus wholly roused,   *1863, 1865* Thence shall his long triumphant
march begin, | Thence shall his being date,—thus wholly roused,   768
1849–65 him!   770 *1849* As Man, that is: *1863* As Man, that is;   776 *1849*
before,   777 *1849* circle run by life: *1863, 1865* circle run by life.

---

761 *pluck a lion by the jaw*: cf. *King John*, ii. i. 138: 'plucks dead lions by the
beard'.

773 *A tendency to God*: 'Man is the higher sense of our planet & the thing
which connects it with the upper world—the eye which it turns towards
heaven—Novalis do.': Domett, quoting from the same page ('thing' should be
'star').

Their proper joys & griefs—they grow too
 great   780
For narrow creeds of right & wrong which
 fade
Before unmeasured thirst for good, while
 peace
Rises within them ever more & more
— Such men are even now upon the earth,
Serene amid the half-formed creatures round   785
Whom they should save & join with them at
 last;
Such was my Task, & I was born to it
Free, as I said but now, from much that chains
Spirits high-dowered but limited & vexed
By a divided & delusive Aim,   790
A shadow mocking a reality
Whose truth avails not wholly to disperse
The flitting mimic which itself has bred,
And so remains perplexed & nigh put out
By its fantastic fellow's wavering gleam . . .   795
But, from the first the cheat could lure me not:
I never fashioned out a fancied good
Distinct from Man's—a service to be done
— A glory to be ministered unto
With powers put forth at Man's expence,
 withdrawn   800
From labouring in his behalf, a strength
Reserved that might avail him: I ne'er cared
Lest his success ran counter to success
Elsewhere—for God is glorified in Man,
And thereto I devoted soul & limb.   805
Yet, constituted thus, & thus endowed,
I failed: I gazed on Power till I grew blind

1835 780 and griefs; 781 and wrong, 782 good; 783–4 more. / Such
. . . . earth— 787 task, and . . . . it— 789 high-dower'd, 790
aim— 795 gleam; 798 man's; a . . . . done— {lower case,
798–822} 801 behalf; 804 Elsewhere: for . . . . man, 805 And to
man's glory vow'd I soul and limb. 807 power . . . . blind.

Their proper joys and griefs; they grow too
    great   780
For narrow creeds of right and wrong, which
    fade
Before the unmeasured thirst for good: while
    peace
Rises within them ever more and more.
Such men are even now upon the earth,
Serene amid the half-formed creatures round   785
Who should be saved by them and joined with
    them.
Such was my task, and I was born to it—
Free, as I said but now, from much that chains
Spirits, high-dowered but limited and vexed
By a divided and delusive aim,   790
A shadow mocking a reality
Whose truth avails not wholly to disperse
The flitting mimic called up by itself,
And so remains perplexed and nigh put out
By its fantastic fellow's wavering gleam.   795
I, from the first, was never cheated thus;
I never fashioned out a fancied good
Distinct from man's; a service to be done,
A glory to be ministered unto
With powers put forth at man's expense,
    withdrawn   800
From labouring in his behalf; a strength
Denied that might avail him. I cared not
Lest his success ran counter to success
Elsewhere: for God is glorified in man,
And to man's glory vowed I soul and limb.   805
Yet, constituted thus, and thus endowed,
I failed: I gazed on power till I grew blind.

780 *1849* griefs; and outgrow all   *1863, 1865* griefs; they outgrow all   781
1849–65 The narrow   789 *1849* high-dowered,   796 *1849* cheated
so;   799 *1849–65* unto,   *1868* unto.   802 *1849* avail him!   807 *1849*
blind—

    780 *proper*: appropriate (at this stage of man's development).
    782 *the unmeasured thirst for good*: cf. *Paradise Lost*, v. 398–9: 'our nourisher,
from whom / All perfect good unmeasured out, descends'.

Power: I could not take my eyes from that
— That only was to be preserved—
   increased
At any risk, displayed, struck out at once   810
The sign & note & character of Man.
I saw no use in the Past— —only a scene
Of degradation, ugliness & tears
— The record of disgraces best forgotten;
A sullen page in human chronicles   815
To be erased: I saw no cause why Man
Should not be all-sufficient even now,
Or why his annals should be forced to tell
That once the tide of light about to break
Upon the world was sealed within its spring,   820
Although my own name led the brightness in: 820a
I would have [had] one ⟨night {?}-⟩ [day-], one
   moments space
Change Mans' condition—push each
   slumbering claim
To mastery oer the elemental world
At once to full maturity,—then roll
Oblivion o'er its work & hide from Man   825
What night had ushered morn—not so, dear
   Child
Of after-days, wilt thou reject the Past
Big with deep warnings of the proper tenure
By which thou hast the earth . . for thee the
   Present
Shall have distinct & trembling beauty, seen   830
Beside its shadow whence in strong relief
Its features shall stand out—nor yet on thee

1835 808 that—   809 preserved,   810 risk; display'd, struck . . . .
once—   811 sign, and note, and character of man.   812 past: 813
ugliness, and tears;   817 now;   821 had one day, one moment's
space,   822 man's condition,   824 maturity: 825 work, and . . . .
man   826 usher'd morn. Not so, dear child   829 earth: 831
shadow—whence, in strong relief,   832 out:

Power; I could not take my eyes from that:
That only, I thought, should be preserved, increased
At any risk, displayed, struck out at once—   810
The sign and note and character of man.
I saw no use in the past: only a scene
Of degradation, ugliness and tears,
The record of disgraces best forgotten,
A sullen page in human chronicles   815
Fit to erase. I saw no cause why man
Should not stand all-sufficient even now,
Or why his annals should be forced to tell
That once the tide of light, about to break
Upon the world, was sealed within its spring: 820
I would have had one day, one moment's space,
Change man's condition, push each slumbering claim
Of mastery o'er the elemental world
At once to full maturity, then roll
Oblivion o'er the work, and hide from man   825
What night had ushered morn. Not so, dear child
Of after-days, wilt thou reject the past
Big with deep warnings of the proper tenure
By which thou hast the earth: for thee the present
Shall have distinct and trembling beauty, seen   830
Beside that past's own shade whence, in relief,
Its brightness shall stand out: nor yet on thee

808 *1849* On power; I could . . . . that—   *1863, 1865* On power; I could . . . .
that: *810 {Reading of *1849–68, 1889*} *1888* once- {corrected in DC} 812
1863, 1865 Past: 813 *1849* Of degradation, imbecility—   *1863, 1865* Of
degradation, imbecility,   816 *1849* erase.   817 *1849–65* Should not be
all-sufficient even now;   823 *1849* To mastery   825 *1849–68* Oblivion
o'er the tools, and   827 *1849–65* Past,   829 *1849–1865* earth: the Present
for thee *1868* earth: the present for thee   *831 *1849* Past's own shade,
whence, *1863,* Past's own shade whence, *1865* Past's own shade
when, *1868–89* past's own shade when,   832 *1849–68* nor on thee yet

Shall burst the Future as successive zones
Of several wonder open on some Spirit
Flying secure & glad from heaven to heaven,   835
But Hope & Fear & Love shall keep thee
   Man!   837
All this was hid from me: as one by one
My dreams grew dim, my wide aims
   circumscribed,
The actual good within my reach decreased   840
While obstacles sprung up this way & that
To keep me from effecting half the sum
Small as it proved: as objects, mean within
The primal aggregate, remained alone
Of all the company, &, even the least,   844a
More than a match for my concentred
   strength   845
What wonder if I saw no way to shun
Despair?—for Power seemed shut from Man
   forever.
In this conjuncture, as I prayed to die,
A strange adventure made me know one sin
Had spotted my career from its uprise   850
And as the poor melodious wretch
   disburthened
His heart & moaned his weakness in my ear
I learned my own deep error: Love's undoing
Taught me the worth of Love in Man's estate   855
And what proportion Love should hold with
   Power
In his right constitution . . . . Love preceding
Power— —with much Power always much
   more Love
Love still too straitened in its present means
And earnest for new Power to set it free.   860

1835 834 spirit   835 heaven;   836 {No equivalent in *MS* or
1835.}   837 But hope, and fear, and love, shall keep thee man!   839
circumscribed—   840 As actual good . . . . decreased,   847 Despair? for
power seem'd shut from man for ever.   849 One Sin   850
uprise;   851 {No equivalent in *MS* or *1835*.}   854–874 love's {etc: lower
case}   857 constitution: love   858 Power—with much power . . . .
love;   859 means,

Shall burst the future, as successive zones
Of several wonder open on some spirit
Flying secure and glad from heaven to heaven: 835
But thou shalt painfully attain to joy,
While hope and fear and love shall keep thee man!
All this was hid from me: as one by one
My dreams grew dim, my wide aims
     circumscribed,
As actual good within my reach decreased,   840
While obstacles sprung up this way and that
To keep me from effecting half the sum,
Small as it proved; as objects, mean within
The primal aggregate, seemed, even the
     least,
Itself a match for my concentred
     strength—   845
What wonder if I saw no way to shun
Despair? The power I sought for man, seemed
     God's.
In this conjuncture, as I prayed to die,
A strange adventure made me know, one sin
Had spotted my career from its uprise;   850
I saw Aprile—my Aprile there!
And as the poor melodious wretch disburthened
His heart, and moaned his weakness in my ear,
I learned my own deep error; love's undoing
Taught me the worth of love in man's estate,   855
And what proportion love should hold with
     power
In his right constitution; love preceding
Power, and with much power, always much more
     love;
Love still too straitened in his present means,
And earnest for new power to set love free.   860

---

833 *1849–65* Future,   837 *1849* hope, and fear, and love, ... man!   *1865*
hope and fear and love . . . . man   847 *1849* God's!   849 *1849* One
Sin   859 *1849, 1863* in its present means,   860 *1849–68* to set it free.

I learned this, & supposed the whole was
    learned:
And thus when Men received with stupid
    wonder
My first revealings & would worship me
—   And I despised & loathed their proffered
    praise—
—   When, with awakened eyes, they took revenge   865
For past credulity in casting shame
On my real knowledge—& I hated them . . . .
It was not strange I saw no good in Man
To overbalance all the wear & waste
Of faculties, displayed in vain, but born   870
To prosper in some better sphere: & why?
In my own heart Love had not been made wise
To trace Love's faint beginnings in Mankind;
To know even Hate is but a mask of Love's;
To see a good in evil, & a hope   875
In ill success— —to sympathize—be proud
Of their half-reasons, faint aspirings, struggles
Dimly for truth, their poorest fallacies,
And prejudice, & fears & cares & doubts—
All with a touch of nobleness for all   880
Their error, all ambitious, upward tending
Like plants in mines which never saw the sun
But dream of him, & guess where he may be,
And do their best to climb & get to him.
All this I knew not & I failed:—let Men   885
Regard me, & the Poet dead long ago
Who loved too rashly— —& shape forth a
    Third

1835 863 My first revealings—would have worshipp'd me—   864 And
. . . . proffer'd praise;   873 love's . . . . mankind—   876 In ill-
success.   878 truth—   879 and fears, and cares, and doubts;   884 and
get to him: 885 not, and I fail'd; let men   886 and the poet   887
rashly; and . . . . third,

I learned this, and supposed the whole was
    learned:
And thus, when men received with stupid
    wonder
My first revealings, would have worshipped me,
And I despised and loathed their proffered
    praise—
When, with awakened eyes, they took revenge   865
For past credulity in casting shame
On my real knowledge, and I hated them—
It was not strange I saw no good in man,
To overbalance all the wear and waste
Of faculties, displayed in vain, but born   870
To prosper in some better sphere: and why?
In my own heart love had not been made wise
To trace love's faint beginnings in mankind,
To know even hate is but a mask of love's,
To see a good in evil, and a hope   875
In ill-success; to sympathize, be proud
Of their half-reasons, faint aspirings, dim
Struggles for truth, their poorest fallacies,
Their prejudice and fears and cares and doubts;
All with a touch of nobleness, despite   880
Their error, upward tending all though weak,
Like plants in mines which never saw the sun,
But dream of him, and guess where he may be,
And do their best to climb and get to him.
All this I knew not, and I failed. Let men   885
Regard me, and the poet dead long ago
Who loved too rashly; and shape forth a
    third

---

879 *1849* prejudice, and fears, and cares,   880–1 *1849–65* Which all touch
upon nobleness, despite | Their error, all tend upwardly though weak,   887
1849 Who once loved rashly; and shape forth a third,

---

   871 *in some better sphere*: cf. *Pauline*, 634, *Sordello*, i. 561 ff., and many other
passages in Browning.
   882 *Like plants in mines*: an image highly appropriate to Paracelsus.
   886–7 *the poet . . . Who loved too rashly*: Aprile. Cf. *Othello*, v. ii. 347: 'one that
lov'd not wisely, but too well'.

And better tempered spirit warned by both,
As from the over-radiant star too mad
To drink the light-springs, beamless thence
    itself—   890
And the dark orb which borders the abyss
Ingulphed in icy night,—might have its course
A temperate & equidistant World:
Meanwhile I have done well, tho' not all
    well:—
As yet Men cannot do without contempt   895
—   'Tis for their good, ⟨—'tis⟩ [&] therefore fit
    awhile
That they reject me & speak scorn of me,   897
But after, they will know me well: I stoop   899
Into a dark tremendous sea of cloud   900
But tis but for a time; I press God's lamp
Close to my breast,—its splendour soon or late
Will pierce the gloom . . I shall emerge one
    day.
You understand me?—I have said enough?
F/.   Now die, dear Aureole!
P/.   Festus—let my hand—   905
This hand—lie in your own— —my own true
    friend!
Aprile! hand in hand with you, Aprile!
F/.

And this was Paracelsus!

―――――――――――――――――――――――――――――――

1835 888 spirit, warn'd by both;   893 world: 894 though not all
well.   895 men . . . . contempt—   897 me, and . . . . me;   898 {No
equivalent in *MS* or *1835*.}   902 breast—its splendour, soon or late,   903
gloom:

And better-tempered spirit, warned by both:
As from the over-radiant star too mad
To drink the light-springs, beamless thence
    itself—   890
And the dark orb which borders the abyss,
Ingulfed in icy night,—might have its course
A temperate and equidistant world.
Meanwhile, I have done well, though not all
    well.
As yet men cannot do without contempt;   895
'T is for their good, and therefore fit
    awhile
That they reject the weak, and scorn the false,
Rather than praise the strong and true, in me:
But after, they will know me. If I stoop
Into a dark tremendous sea of cloud,   900
It is but for a time; I press God's lamp
Close to my breast; its splendour, soon or late,
Will pierce the gloom: I shall emerge one day.
You understand me? I have said enough?
    Festus. Now die, dear Aureole!
    Paracelsus.   Festus, let my hand—   905
This hand, lie in your own, my own true friend!
Aprile! Hand in hand with you, Aprile!

    Festus. And this was Paracelsus!

---

*890 {Reading of *1849–65*} *1868–89* the life-springs,   894 *Berg* I have (done)
[lived] well,   895 *1849* contempt—   898 *1849* true, in me.   *Berg* true in
me,   899 *1849* know me!   902 *1849* breast—   903 *1849* day!   906
1849 your own—

    889 *As from the over-radiant star*: the 'temperate' world is contrasted with a star
which is too eager 'To drink the light-springs', and with 'the dark orb'. The
former (as Dr. Sidney Kenderdine points out to us) must be either Mercury or
Venus, the two planets closer to the sun than the earth. The 'dark orb' is
probably Uranus, the discovery of which in 1781 caused a considerable stir,
partly because it upset mystical notions based on the number of the planets. It
was the outermost planet then known. The reference to Uranus could of
course be regarded as an anachronism.
    899 *If I stoop*: heavenly bodies are sometimes said to 'stoop': OED 3b. Cf.,
also, i. 347 ff, above.
    907 *Aprile!*: a comparison with iii. 387 shows the spiritual distance which
Paracelsus has travelled.

NOTE.

THE liberties I have taken with my subject are very trifling; and
the reader may slip the foregoing scenes between the leaves of
any memoir of Paracelsus he pleases, by way of commentary.
To prove this, I subjoin a popular account, translated from the
"Biographie Universelle, Paris," 1822, which I select, not as   5
the best, certainly, but as being at hand, and sufficiently concise
for my purpose. I also append a few notes, in order to correct
those parts which do not bear out my own view of the charac-
ter of Paracelsus; and have incorporated with them a notice or
two, illustrative of the poem itself.   10

"PARACELSUS (Philippus Aureolus Theophrastus Bombastus
ab Hohenheim) was born in 1493 at Einsiedeln, ([1]) a little town
in the canton of Schwyz, some leagues distant from Zurich.
His father, who exercised the profession of medicine at Villach
in Carinthia, was nearly related to George Bombast de   15
Hohenheim, who became afterward Grand Prior of the Order
of Malta: consequently Paracelsus could not spring from the
dregs of the people, as Thomas Erastus, his sworn enemy,
pretends.* It appears that his elementary education was much

* I shall disguise M. Renauldin's next sentence a little. "Hic(Erastus sc.)   20
Paracelsum trimum a milite quodam, alii a sue exectum ferunt: constat imber-

A few minor variants between the versions of this Note are not recorded
here. The text is that of *1888*.

16 *MS,1835* became in the event Grand Prior

1 *very trifling*: this is misleading: see Introduction.

5 *1822*: the date of vol. xxxii, which includes the article on Paracelsus. The
first volume of the *Biographie* appeared in 1811, the 52nd and last in 1828.

6 *as being at hand*: Griffin and Minchin emphasize the influence of this huge
collection: 'he used it for *Sordello*, he took from it the subject of his proposed
tragedy of *Narses*, it helped him to *King Victor and King Charles*, and it sug-
gested the idea of *The Return of the Druses*': p. 25.

11 PARACELSUS: Browning translates closely the passages which he gives:
omissions and minor errors or variations are noted below.

12 *(Hohenheim)*: 'fameux alchimiste et enthousiaste du seizième siècle,'
omitted.

17 *could not spring*: 'n'est point sorti'. *Thomas Erastus*: Thomas Liebler, called
Erastus (1523–83), of whom Pagel gives an excellent account on pp. 311 ff. of
his classic study. Erastus wrote *Disputationes de Medicina Nova Paracelsi* in four
parts, Basle 1572 (i–iii), 1573 (iv).

20 *M. Renauldin*: Léopold Joseph Renauldin was the author of the article in
the *Biographie*. The omitted passage is as follows: 'Celui-ci raconte aussi

neglected, and that he spent part of his youth in pursuing the
life common to the travelling *literati* of the age; that is to say, in
wandering from country to country, predicting the future by
astrology and cheiromancy, evoking apparitions, and practis-
ing the different operations of magic and alchemy, in which he   5
had been initiated whether by his father or by various ecclesias-
tics, among the number of whom he particularizes the Abbot
Tritheim, (²) and many German bishops.

bem illum, mulierumque osorem fuisse." A standing High-Dutch joke in
those days at the expense of a number of learned men, as may be seen by   10
referring to such rubbish as Melander's "Jocoseria," etc. In the prints from his
portrait by Tintoretto, painted a year before his death, Paracelsus is *barbatulus*,·
at all events. But Erastus was never without a good reason for his faith—*e.g.*
"Helvetium fuisse (Paracelsum) vix credo, vix enim ea regio tale monstrum
ediderit." (De Medicina Nova.)   15

3–5 *MS, 1835* the future from the inspection of the stars and the lines of the
hand, evoking apparitions, and repeating the different operations
   9 *MS* illum et ⟨i.w.⟩ [μισογύναιον] fuisse."
   1835 illum et μισογυνον fuisse."
   1849 illum fuisse."
   9, 10 *MS* joke of those
   10 *MS,1835* of a vast number
   *11 *1888,1889* rubbish at

(*Disput. de medic. novâ Paracelsi*, pars 1, pag. 237) que Paracelse subit la castra-
tion à l'âge de trois ans. D'autres disent qu'il perdit sa virilité par suite de la
morsure d'un cochon. Ce qu'il y a de certain, c'est qu'il n'avait point de barbe,
et qu'il détestait les femmes'. Browning seems to have translated this into
Latin, guided by Erastus, who had written, in his *Disputationum de Medicina
Nova Philippi Paracelsi Pars Prima*: 'Hoc in loco, narratum mihi est exectos ei
testes fuisse a milite, dum anseres pasceret . . . Eunuchum fuisse cum alia
multa, tum facies indicant: & quod, Oporino teste, feminas prorsus despexit':
p. 238. 'In this place I was told that his testicles had been cut off by a soldier,
while he was feeding geese . . . That he was a eunuch his face and many
other signs indicate; and the fact, to which Oporinus bears witness, that he
utterly despised women': p. 238. Bitiskius relates the tradition that he had been
castrated by a boar at the age of three: *Opera*, i. [¶6]v. cf. p. 506 n.
   8 *many German bishops*: 'plusieurs évêques allemands', a common rendering
of 'plusieurs' by Browning.
   11 *Melander's 'Jocoseria'*: a book of anecdotes and jokes published c. 1597 and
several times reprinted. Browning used the title of this 'little old rare book' for
a late collection of short poems, *Jocoseria*, 1883. 'My edition is in three vol-
umes', he told Furnivall, '—of which I only possess the latter two—bound in
one: a gift from my Father when I was young': *Trumpeter*, p. 65. By coinci-
dence, an article on this old book appeared in *Blackwood's* for February 1883,
while Browning was proof-reading his own *Jocoseria*. It mentions that the
story of the Pied Piper appears in it, under the title 'De Diabolo horrenda
historia' (p. 269).
   11–12 *his portrait by Tintoretto*: the frontispiece to Vol. i of the edition by
Bitiskius states that it is based on a portrait from the life by Tintoretto,
although this ascription is no longer accepted. 'Barbatulus', with a light beard.
   14 *"Helvetium fuisse*: 'I scarcely believe (Paracelsus) to have been Swiss,
for this part of the world could scarcely have produced such a monster': *de
Medicina Nova, Pars Prima*, p. 237.

"As Paracelsus displays everywhere an ignorance of the
rudiments of the most ordinary knowledge, it is not probable
that he ever studied seriously in the schools: he contented
himself with visiting the Universities of Germany, France and
Italy; and in spite of his boasting himself to have been the   5
ornament of those institutions, there is no proof of his having
legally acquired the title of Doctor, which he assumes. It is only
known that he applied himself long, under the direction of the
wealthy Sigismond Fugger of Schwatz, to the discovery of the
Magnum Opus.   10
"Paracelsus travelled among the mountains of Bohemia, in
the East, and in Sweden, in order to inspect the labours of the
miners, to be initiated in the mysteries of the oriental adepts,
and to observe the secrets of nature and the famous mountain
of loadstone.(^{3}) He professes also to have visited Spain, Por-   15
tugal, Prussia, Poland, and Transylvania; everywhere com-
municating freely, not merely with the physicians, but the old
women, charlatans and conjurers of these several lands. It is
even believed that he extended his journeyings as far as Egypt
and Tartary, and that he accompanied the son of the Khan of   20
the Tartars to Constantinople, for the purpose of obtaining the
secret of the tincture of Trismegistus from a Greek who inhab-
ited that capital.
"The period of his return to Germany is unknown: it is only
certain that, at about the age of thirty-three, many astonishing   25
cures which he wrought on eminent personages procured him
such a celebrity, that he was called in 1526, on the recommen-
dation of Œcolampadius, (^{4}) to fill a chair of physic and surgery
at the University of Basil. There Paracelsus began by burning
publicly in the amphitheatre the works of Avicenna and Galen,   30
assuring his auditors that the latchets of his shoes were more
instructed than those two physicians; that all Universities, all
writers put together, were less gifted than the hairs of his beard
and of the crown of his head; and that, in a word, he was to be

3 *MS,1835* he should have ever studied
16 *MS, 1835* where he communicated freely,
17 *MS,1835* but with the old
34 *MS,1835* that, finally, he was

9–10 *the Magnum Opus*: the ultimate goal of the alchemists.
11 "*Paracelsus travelled*: 'According to the habit of the alchemists': *Biographie*.
23 *that capital*: Renauldin's next passage is given by Browning as a footnote:
see p. 504 n. below.
25 *many*: for 'plusieurs', again.

regarded as the legitimate monarch of medicine. 'You shall
follow me,' cried he, 'you, Avicenna, Galen, Rhasis, Montag-
nana, Mesues, you, gentlemen of Paris, Montpellier, Germany,
Cologne, Vienna,* and whomsoever the Rhine and Danube
nourish; you who inhabit the isles of the sea; you, likewise, 5
Dalmatians, Athenians; thou, Arab; thou, Greek; thou, Jew: all
shall follow me, and the monarchy shall be mine.'†

"But at Basil it was speedily perceived that the new Profes-
sor was no better than an egregious quack. Scarcely a year
elapsed before his lectures had fairly driven away an audience 10
incapable of comprehending their emphatic jargon. That
which above all contributed to sully his reputation was the
debauched life he led. According to the testimony of

---

* Erastus, who relates this, here oddly remarks, "mirum quod non et
Garamantes, Indos et *Anglos* adjunxit." Not so wonderful neither, if we believe 15
what another adversary "had heard somewhere,"—that all Paracelsus' system
came of his pillaging "Anglum quendam, Rogerium Bacchonem."
† See his works *passim*. I must give one specimen:—Somebody had been
styling him "Luther alter." "And why not?" (he asks, as he well might).
"Luther is abundantly learned, therefore you hate him and me; but we are at 20
least a match for you.—Nam et contra vos et vestros universos principes
Avicennam, Galenum, Aristotelem, etc. me satis superque munitum esse novi.
Et vertex iste meus calvus ac depilis multo plura et sublimiora novit quam
vester vel Avicenna vel universæ academiæ. Prodite, et signum date, qui viri
sitis, quid roboris habeatis? quid autem sitis? Doctores et magistri, pediculos 25
pectentes et fricantes podicem." (Frag. Med.)

---

3 *MS* Mesue,—*1835* Mesue;
4 *MS,1835* and all soever
4 *MS,1835* whom the Rhine and the Danube
1849 whomsoever the Rhine and the Danube
11 *MS* ⟨his⟩ [their] emphatic
* 15 Garamantes, { Editors' emendation} *MS,1835–1889* Garamantos,
15–17 {*MS, 1835* lack the second sentence of this footnote.}

---

15 *Garamantes*: 'Garamantes, Indos, Anglos, Suecos & Danos': op. cit., p.
240.

16 *another adversary*: Browning may be remembering a passage in the intro-
ductory matter to Leo Suavius's *Paracelsi . . . Compendium* (see note to p. 512, l.
15, below): 'nisi fortè pauca inseram ex Rogerio Bachone Anglo, à quo
Paracelsus videtur hausisse quamplurima': 'unless perhaps I shall insert a few
passages from Roger Bacon, an Englishman from whom Paracelsus seems to
have appropriated a great deal'.

21 *Nam et contra vos*: 'For I know that I am more than sufficiently armed
against both you and all your leaders, Avicenna, Galen, Aristotle, etc. And this
bald and hairless head of mine knows far more and loftier things than either
your Avicenna or all the Academies. Bring forward the evidence and give a
sign what sort of men you are, what strength you possess, what stuff you are
made of, Doctors and Masters of Arts, scratching your lice and rubbing your
arses': *AVR. PHILIP. THEOPH. PARACELSI . . . Opera Omnia* (ed. F.
Bitiskius, 3 vols., Geneva, 1658), i. 346b.

Oporinus, who lived two years in his intimacy, Paracelsus
scarcely ever ascended the lecture-desk unless half drunk, and
only dictated to his secretaries when in a state of intoxication: if
summoned to attend the sick, he rarely proceeded thither
without previously drenching himself with wine. He was   5
accustomed to retire to bed without changing his clothes;
sometimes he spent the night in pot-houses with peasants, and
in the morning knew no longer what he was about; and,
nevertheless, up to the age of twenty-five his only drink had
been water.([5])   10

"At length, fearful of being punished for a serious outrage on
a magistrate, ([6]) he fled from Basil towards the end of the year
1527, and took refuge in Alsatia, whither he caused Oporinus
to follow with his chemical apparatus.

"He then entered once more upon the career of ambulatory 15
theosophist.* Accordingly we find him at Colmar in 1528; at
Nuremberg in 1529; at St. Gall in 1531; at Pfeffers in 1535; and
at Augsburg in 1536: he next made some stay in Moravia,
where he still further compromised his reputation by the loss
of many distinguished patients, which compelled him to 20
betake himself to Vienna; from thence he passed into Hungary;
and in 1538 was at Villach, where he dedicated his 'Chronicle'
to the States of Carinthia, in gratitude for the many kindnesses
with which they had honoured his father. Finally, from Min-
delheim, which he visited in 1540, Paracelsus proceeded to Salz- 25
burg, where he died in the Hospital of St. Stephen (*Sebastian* is

* "So migratory a life could afford Paracelsus but little leisure for applica-
tion to books, and accordingly he informs us that for the space of ten years he
never opened a single volume, and that his whole medical library was not
composed of six sheets: in effect, the inventory drawn up after his death states 30
that the only books which he left were the Bible, the New Testament, the
Commentaries of St. Jerome on the Gospels, a printed volume on Medicine,
and seven manuscripts."

24–25 *MS,1835* Mindelheim, where he was in 1540,
26 *MS,1835* (*Sebastian*, he means),
1849–68 (*Sebastian*, is meant),
33 *MS* manuscripts." *Renauldin*.
1835 manuscripts.—*Renauldin*.

23 *the many kindnesses*: 'toutes les bontés'.
25–26 *proceeded to Salzburg*; 'alla mourir à Saltzbourg'.
26 *Sebastian*: Browning is right. The *Biographie* has 'Saint-Etienne', Paracel-
sus's Will 'apud S. Sebastianum'.
27 "*So migratory*: in the *Biographie* this sentence comes before the passage
beginning 'The period' given above (p. 502). Browning omits one further
book mentioned by Renauldin, no doubt by a slip: it is the Concordance to the
Bible.

meant), Sept. 24, 1541.''—(Here follows a criticism on his writings, which I omit.)

(1) *Paracelsus* would seem to be a fantastic version of *Von Hohenheim*; Einsiedeln is the Latinized Eremus, whence Paracelsus is sometimes called, as in the correspondence of Erasmus, Eremita; Bombast, his proper name, probably acquired, from the characteristic phraseology of his lectures, that unlucky signification which it has ever since retained.

(2) Then Bishop of Spanheim, and residing at Würzburg in Franconia; a town situated in a grassy fertile country, whence its name, Herbipolis. He was much visited there by learned men, as may be seen by his "Epistolæ Familiares," Hag. 1536: among others, by his staunch friend Cornelius Agrippa, to

4 *MS* Hohenheim, Einsiedeln and the latin Eremus, (whence Paracelsus is sometimes called, as in the correspondence of Erasmus, Eremita,) are I suppose one and the same town.   *1835* {as *MS* except for slight differences in punctuation. This sentence is used as a footnote to 'Einsiedeln' on the first page of the notes in *MS* and *1835*.}
1849 {as *1888* except 'is the Latin Eremus' and 'his proper name, originally acquired'.}
1863, 65 {as *1888* except 'is the Latin Eremus,'}   11 *MS* its latin name *1835* its Latin name

1–2 *a criticism on his writings*: this comprises more than half of the article, and presents Paracelsus in a very different light from that of Browning. Renauldin clearly wishes to be fair, and warns his readers against Erastus, on the one hand, 'who pursued him relentlessly', and T. de Murr, on the other, 'who has often misrepresented the facts in order to present the scientific knowledge and character of Paracelsus in a favourable light'. He sums up thus: 'the employment of a vernacular language, writing rather for the people than for men of learning, introducing the cabalistic art into medicine (because it dispenses with the necessity of the learning which derives from study), using a host of mystical and barbarous terms which make the more impression on the multitude the more unintelligible they are—such are the means which served our bold reformer in good stead. His philosophical and medical system is curious by its very absurdity'.
3 (1) Pagel concludes that 'None of the interpretations of the meaning of this name [Paracelsus] has been satisfactory': p. 5. The word 'bombast' does not in fact derive from 'Bombastes'.
9 (2) Ambiguous. The letter which Browning quotes is the preliminary epistle from Cornelius Agrippa to Trithemius in the former's *De Occulta Philosophia libri tres* (1533, p. [aa iij] r), not the reply from Trithemius to Cornelius Agrippa. The opening of the address 'Ad Lectorem', which occurs immediately before the epistle here quoted, had already served (in an adapted version) for the epigraph to *Pauline*. 'Hag.', Haga Comitum (The Hague). 'R. P.' is Browning's abbreviation of 'Reverende Pater'. The original punctuation, which is preferable, has no comma after 'cabalisticis' or 'delitescunt'. In English: 'When recently, reverend father, I conversed with you for some time in your cloister in Würzburg, we discussed together many matters relating to chemistry, many relating to magic, many relating to the Cabbalistic mysteries, and all the rest which still lies hidden with secret lores and arts'.

whom he dates thence, in 1510, a letter in answer to the
dedicatory epistle prefixed to the treatise De Occult.
Philosoph., which last contains the following ominous allusion
to Agrippa's sojourn: "Quum nuper tecum, R. P. in cœnobio
tuo apud Herbipolim aliquamdiu conversatus, multa de 5
chymicis, multa de magicis, multa de cabalisticis, cæterisque
quæ adhuc in occulto delitescunt, arcanis scientiis atque artibus
una contulissemus," etc.

(3) "Inexplebilis illa aviditas naturæ perscrutandi secreta et
reconditarum supellectile scientiarum animum locupletandi, 10
uno eodemque loco diu persistere non patiebatur, sed Mercurii
instar, omnes terras, nationes et urbes perlustrandi igniculos
supponebat, ut cum viris naturæ scrutatoribus, chymicis
præsertim, ore tenus conferret, et quæ diuturnis laboribus noc-
turnisque vigiliis invenerant una vel altera communicatione 15
obtineret." (Bitiskius in Præfat.) "Patris auxilio primum,
deinde propria industria doctissimos viros in Germania, Italia,
Gallia, Hispania, aliisque Europæ regionibus, nactus est
præceptores; quorum liberali doctrina, et potissimum propria
inquisitione ut qui esset ingenio acutissimo ac fere divino, 20
tantum profecit, ut multi testati sint, in universa philosophia,
tam ardua, tam arcana et abdita eruisse mortalium neminem."
(Melch. Adam. in Vit. Germ. Medic.) "Paracelsus qui in intima
naturæ viscera sic penitus introierit, metallorum stirpiumque

4 *MS,1835* to his sojourn:
13 *MS-1863* supponebat et cum

9 (3) 'That insatiable desire to examine thoroughly the secrets of nature and
to enrich his mind with the wealth of the recondite sciences would not suffer
him to remain long in one and the same place but inflamed him (like Mercury)
with the ardour to travel through all lands, nations and cities, so that he might
converse personally with men who had studied the natural sciences, above all
with chemists, and might learn in one exchange or at most two whatever they
had obtained by their daily labours or their nocturnal vigils': Bitiskius, i.
[¶6]v.

16 *"Patris*: 'First with the help of his father, and then by his own industry, he
obtained as his teachers the most learned men in Germany, Italy, France, Spain
and the other parts of Europe; by means of the liberal teaching of whom, and
especially by his own enquiry (he being a man of most acute and almost
godlike mind), he made such progress as many have borne witness, that no
man in all of philosophical study has brought to the light of day matters so
arduous, so secret, and so well concealed'. Melchior Adamus, *Vitae Ger-
manorum Medicorum* (Heidelberg, 1620), p. 28.

23 *"Paracelsus*: 'Paracelsus had delved so deeply into the bowels of nature,
and with such incredible intellectual acuteness examined and discovered the
powers and properties of minerals and plants for the curing of all dis-
eases—even those commonly despaired of and deemed incurable—that it
appeared that medicine was both born and perfected with him': Petrus Ramus
as quoted in Adamus, p. 29.

vires et facultates tam incredibili ingenii acumine exploraverit
ac perviderit, ad morbos omnes vel desperatos et opinione
hominum insanabiles percurandum; ut cum Theophrasto nata
primum medicina perfectaque videtur." (Petri Rami Orat. de
Basilea.) His passion for wandering is best described in his own   5
words: "Ecce amatorem adolescentem difficillimi itineris haud
piget, ut venustam saltem puellam vel fœminam aspiciat:
quanto minus nobilissimarum artium amore laboris ac cujus-
libet tædii pigebit?" etc. ("Defensiones Septem adversus
æmulos suos." 1573. Def. 4ta. "De peregrinationibus et   10
exilio.")

(4) The reader may remember that it was in conjunction
with Œcolampadius, then Divinity Professor at Basil, that
Zuinglius published in 1528 an answer to Luther's Confession
of Faith; and that both proceeded in company to the subse-   15
quent conference with Luther and Melanchthon at Marpurg.
Their letters fill a large volume.—"D.D. Johannis Œcolam-
padii et Huldrichi Zuinglii Epistolarum lib. quatuor." Bas.
1536. It must be also observed that Zuinglius began to preach
in 1516, and at Zurich in 1519, and that in 1525 the Mass was   20
abolished in the cantons. The tenets of Œcolampadius were
supposed to be more evangelical than those up to that period
maintained by the glorious German, and our brave Bishop
Fisher attacked them as the fouler heresy:—"About this time
arose out of Luther's school one Œcolampadius, like a mighty   25
and fierce giant; who, as his master had gone beyond the
Church, went beyond his master (or else it had been impossible
he could have been reputed the better scholar), who denied the
real presence; him, this worthy champion (the Bishop) sets
upon, and with five books (like so many smooth stones taken   30
out of the river that doth always run with living water) slays

2 *MS,1835* disperatos
6–7 *1835* hand piget,
12 *MS,1835* The reader will remember
15 *MS,1835* and that he accompanied him to
22 *MS,1835* those at that period

6 "*Ecce amatorem*: 'Behold a young lover is not irked by a most difficult
journey, if (at least) it is undertaken to enable him to gaze at a beautiful girl or
woman: how much less will he be irked by toil, however tedious, if he is in love
with the most noble arts?' Paracelsus made similar statements in various places:
see, e.g., Bitiskius i. 257b, and the preface to *Paragranum* (quoted in Hartmann,
p. 18).
    14 *Zuinglius*: cf. note to iii. 955, above.

the Philistine; which five books were written in the year of our
Lord 1526, at which time he had governed the see of Rochester
twenty years." (Life of Bishop Fisher, 1655). Now, there is no
doubt of the Protestantism of Paracelsus, Erasmus, Agrippa,
etc., but the nonconformity of Paracelsus was always scandal-   5
ous. L. Crasso ("Elogj d'Huomini Letterati," Ven. 1666)
informs us that his books were excommunicated by the
Church. Quenstedt (de Patr. Doct.) affirms "nec tantum novæ
medicinæ, verum etiam novæ theologiæ autor est." Delrio, in
his Disquisit. Magicar., classes him among those "partim   10
atheos, partim hæreticos" (lib. i. cap. 3). "Omnino tamen
multa theologica in ejusdem scriptis plane atheismum olent, ac
duriuscule sonant in auribus vere Christiani." (D. Gabrielis
Clauderi Schediasma de Tinct. Univ. Norimb. 1736.) I shall
only add one more authority:—"Oporinus dicit se (Paracel-   15
sum) aliquando Lutherum et Papam, non minus quam nunc
Galenum et Hippocratem redacturum in ordinem minabatur,
neque enim eorum qui hactenus in scripturam sacram scripsis-
sent, sive veteres, sive recentiores, quenquam scripturæ nuc-
leum recte eruisse, sed circa corticem et quasi membranam   20
tantum hærere." (Th. Erastus, Disputat. de Med. Nova.) These
and similar notions had their due effect on Oporinus, who, says
Zuingerus, in his "Theatrum," "longum vale dixit ei (Para-

---

8 *MS–1868* Quensledt

3 *Life of Bishop Fisher: The Life & Death of that renowned John Fisher Bishop of Rochester*, by Thomas Baily (1655), p. 42.
6 *L. Crasso*: Lorenzo Crasso, *Elogii d'huomini letterati*, 2 vols. (Venice, 1666), ii. 47.
8 *Quenstedt: Dialogus, de Patriis illustrium doctrinâ et scriptis Virorum omnium ordinum ac facultatum*, by Johannes Andreas Quenstedt (Wittenberg, 1654), pp. 132–3. 'He is not only the author of a new Medicine, but also of a new Theology'.
9 *Delrio: Disquisitionum Magicarum Libri Sex Authore Martino del Rio* (3 vols., 1606), p. 21.
11 *"Omnino*: 'Generally speaking, however, many of the theological observations in his writings smell plainly of atheism, and sound somewhat harsh to the ears of a true Christian'. The passage may be found in *Jo. Jacobi Mangeti . . . Bibliotheca Chemica Curiosa* (Geneva, 1702), i. 142a.
15 *"Oporinus dicit*: 'Oporinus states that he (Paracelsus) used sometimes to threaten that Luther and the Pope would be cut down to size by him one day, just as Galen and Hippocrates were now, since none of those who had so far written on sacred scripture, whether in the past or more recently, had plucked out any part of its true kernel: they got stuck, so to speak, on the rind or skin': Erastus, loc. cit., p. 239.
23 *Zuingerus: Theatrum Humanae Vitae*, by Theodorus Zuingerus (29 vols. in 4 Basle, 1586–7). Oporinus is mentioned in relation to Paracelsus on pp. 2583, 3176 and 3204 of this enormous work, but the index provides no reference to

celso), ne ob præceptoris, alioqui amicissimi, horrendas blas-
phemias ipse quoque aliquando pœnas Deo Opt. Max. lueret."

(5) His defenders allow the drunkenness. Take a sample of
their excuses: "Gentis hoc, non viri vitiolum est, a Taciti seculo
ad nostrum usque non interrupto filo devolutum, sinceritati   5
forte Germanæ coævum, et nescio an aliquo consanguinitatis
vinculo junctum." (Bitiskius.) The other charges were chiefly
trumped up by Oporinus: "Domi, quod Oporinus amanuensis
ejus sæpe narravit, nunquam nisi potus ad explicanda sua acces-
sit, atque in medio conclavi ad columnam τετυφωμένος adsis-   10
tens, apprehenso manibus capulo ensis, cujus κοίλωμα hos-
pitium præbuit, ut aiunt, spiritui familiari, imaginationes aut
concepta sua protulit:—alii illud quod in capulo habuit, ab ipso
Azoth appellatum, medicinam fuisse præstantissimam aut
lapidem Philosophicum putant." (Melch. Adam.) This famous   15
sword was no laughing-matter in those days, and it is now a
material feature in the popular idea of Paracelsus. I recollect a
couple of allusions to it in our own literature, at the moment.

> Ne had been known the Danish Gonswart,
> Or Paracelsus with his long sword.   20
>   'Volpone, act ii. scene 2.
>
> Bumbastus kept a devil's bird
> Shut in the pummel of his sword,
> That taught him all the cunning pranks
> Of past and future mountebanks.
>   'Hudibras,' part ii. cant. 3.

This Azoth was simply *"laudanum suum."* But in his time he   25
was commonly believed to possess the double tincture—the
power of curing diseases and transmuting metals. Oporinus

---

3 *MS* ⟨this⟩ [the] drunkenness:—
8 *MS* by Oporinus: ⟨who afterwards repented of his treachery" Dedic:⟩

the passage here quoted: 'bade farewell to him for a long time, lest he too might
some day have to pay the penalty to Almighty God for the horrifying blas-
phemies of his teacher, who had been so good a friend to him in other respects'.

4 "*Gentis hoc*: 'This is a venial sin not of the man but of the race, descended in
an unbroken line from the age of Tacitus to our own day, and perhaps as old as
Germanic integrity, and joined with it by some bond of blood relationship':
Bitiskius, i (Praefatio), p. [¶ 6]v.

8 "*Domi*: 'At home, as his secretary Oporinus has often narrated, he never
addressed himself to his expositions without being drunk, and in the middle of
the gathering he would lean against a column, dead drunk, producing his
imaginings or conceptions, holding in his hand the hilt of his own sword—that
sword whose cavity concealed (as they say) his familiar spirit: others think that
what he had in the hilt (and which he himself called 'Azoth') was a most
remarkable drug or the Philosopher's Stone': Melchior Adamus, op. cit., pp.
35–6. Cf. Erastus, *De Medicina Nova*, i. 236.

often witnessed, as he declares, both these effects, as did also
Franciscus, the servant of Paracelsus, who describes, in a letter
to Neander, a successful projection at which he was present,
and the results of which, good golden ingots, were confided to
his keeping. For the other quality, let the following notice   5
vouch among many others:—"Degebat Theophrastus
Norimbergæ procitus a medentibus illius urbis, et vaniloquus
deceptorque proclamatus, qui, ut laboranti famæ subveniat,
viros quosdam authoritatis summæ in Republica illa adit, et
infamiæ amoliendæ, artique suæ asserendæ, specimen ejus pol-   10
licetur editurum, nullo stipendio vel accepto pretio, horum
faciles præbentium aures jussu elephantiacos aliquot, a com-
munione hominum cæterorum segregatos, et in val-
etudinarium detrusos, alieno arbitrio eliguntur, quos virtute
singulari remediorum suorum Theophrastus a fœda   15
Græcorum lepra mundat, pristinæque sanitati restituit; conser-
vat illustre harum curationum urbs in archivis suis tes-
timonium." (Bitiskius.)* It is to be remarked that Oporinus

---

* The premature death of Paracelsus casts no manner of doubt on the fact of
his having possessed the Elixir Vitæ: the alchemists have abundant reasons to   20
adduce, from which I select the following, as explanatory of a property of the
Tincture not calculated on by its votaries:—"Objectionem illam, quod Para-
celsus non fuerit longævus, nonnulli quoque solvunt per rationes physicas:
vitæ nimirum abbreviationem fortasse talibus accidere posse, ob Tincturam
frequentiore ac largiore dosi sumtam, dum a summe efficaci et penetrabili   25
hujus virtute calor innatus quasi suffocatur." (Gabrielis Clauderi Schediasma.)

---

5 MS his trust: for   1835 his trust. For
7 1863–88 procitus MS—1849 prociscus

2–3 in a letter to Neander: as Griffin and Minchin point out (p. 71), Browning
owes this information to the Praefatio of Bitiskius.
  6 "Degebat Theophrastus: 'Paracelsus lived at Nuremberg where he was
challenged by the native doctors and proclaimed a mountebank. So in order to
succour his failing reputation he approached some of the most powerful men in
the republic and, in a bid to lessen his notoriety and assert his skill, promised to
give them an example of it entirely without reward or fee. On the orders of
these willing listeners a group of lepers, chosen entirely against their own will,
were segregated from human contact, and thrust into a hospital. These Theop-
hrastus cleansed of their foul Grecian leprosy and restored to their former
health through the singular efficacy of his medications. The city preserves the
noble account of their cure in its archives' (vol. i, p. ¶¶ r.). Bitiskius has
'stipulato' not 'stipendio'.
  22 "Objectionem illam: 'That objection that Paracelsus was not long-lived is
answered by some in medical terms to the effect that the lives of such people
may possibly be very much abridged through taking the Tincture too often
and in overlarge quantities until the native heat [of the body] is, so to speak,
suffocated by its extremely potent, penetrative force'. This passage occurs on
the same page of the Bibliotheca Chemica Curiosa of Mangetus as that quoted
above, on p. 508, 11 n. Browning has very slightly adapted the passage.

afterwards repented of his treachery: "Sed resipuit tandem, et quem vivum convitiis insectatus fuerat defunctum veneratione prosequutus, infames famæ præceptoris morsus in remorsus conscientiæ conversi pœnitentia, heu nimis tarda, vulnera clausere exanimi quæ spiranti inflixerant." For these "bites" of 5 Oporinus, see Disputat. Erasti, and Andreæ Jocisci "Oratio de Vit. ob. Opor¹;" for the "remorse," Mic. Toxita in pref. Testamenti, and Conringius (otherwise an enemy of Paracelsus), who says it was contained in a letter from Oporinus to Doctor Vegerus.* 10

Whatever the moderns may think of these marvellous attributes, the title of Paracelsus to be considered the father of modern chemistry is indisputable. Gerardus Vossius, "De Philos³ et Philosᵘᵐ sectis," thus prefaces the ninth section of cap. 9, "De Chymia"—"Nobilem hanc medicinæ partem, diu 15 sepultam, avorum ætate quasi ab orco revocavit Th. Paracel-

---

* For a good defence of Paracelsus I refer the reader to Olaus Borrichius' treatise—"Hermetis etc. Sapientia vindicata," 1674. Or, if he is no more learned than myself in such matters, I mention simply that Paracelsus introduced the use of Mercury and Laudanum. 20

---

1 *MS–1865* afterward
4 *MS,1835* pænitentiâ, heu nimis tardâ vulnera
6 *MS–1863* Andreas Jociscus . . . . *vit et ob.*   *1865,68* Andreae Jocisci . . . . vit. ob
7 *MS,1835* Mic. Toxites
11,12 *MS,1835* attributes, they have confirmed P.'s title to be considered the father of modern chymistry. Gerardus
*16 *MS* diu sepultam, avorum ætate   *1835–1868* diu sepultam avorum ætate   *1888–89* diu sepultam avorum ætate,
17, 18 {This footnote ends with '1674.' in *MS, 1835.*}   *1849* as *1888* except 'I had better mention'

---

1 "*Sed resipuit*: 'Finally, however, he came to his senses and pursued the dead man with veneration whom alive he had pursued with opprobrium. His infamous gnawings at his teacher's fame were turned into gnawings of conscience through penitence—too late, alas, to staunch on the corpse the wounds inflicted on the living man': Bitiskius, Praefatio, i. p. [¶6]r.
6 *Disputat. Erasti*: cf. p. 500, 17 n. above.
6 *Andreae Jocisci: Oratio de ortu, vita, et obitu Ioannis Oporini Basiliensis, Typographicorum Germaniae principis* (Strassburg, 1569).
7 *Mic. Toxita*: at the end of vol. iii of Bitiskius's ed., separately paginated, we find the 'Testamentum' of Paracelsus, preceded by 'Michaelis Toxitis Praefatio'.
8 *Conringius*: Bitiskius refers to the letter from Oporinus to Vegerus in his Praefatio.
15 "*Nobilem hanc medicinæ partem*: 'This noble part of medicine, long since buried, was in the time of our ancestors recalled, as if from the abode of the dead': *De Philosophia et Philosophorum Sectis* (The Hague, 1658), p. 70.
17 *Olaus Borrichius: Hermetis, Aegyptiorum, et Chemicorum Sapientia ab Hermanni Conringii animadversionibus vindicata per Olaum Borrichium* (Copenhagen, 1674), particularly pp. 279–88, 295–9, and 417–40.

sus." I suppose many hints lie scattered in his neglected books, which clever appropriators have since developed with applause. Thus, it appears from his treatise "De Phlebotomia," and elsewhere, that he had discovered the circulation of the blood and the sanguification of the heart; as did after him   5 Realdo Colombo, and still more perfectly Andrea Cesalpino of Arezzo, as Bayle and Bartoli observe. Even Lavater quotes a passage from his work "De Natura Rerum," on practical Physiognomy, in which the definitions and axioms are precise enough: he adds, "though an astrological enthusiast, a man of 10 prodigious genius." See Holcroft's translation, vol. iii. p. 179—"The Eyes." While on the subject of the writings of Paracelsus, I may explain a passage in the third part of the Poem. He was, as I have said, unwilling to publish his works, but in effect did publish a vast number. Valentius (in Præfat. in 15 Paramyr.) declares "quod ad librorum Paracelsi copiam attinet, audio a Germanis prope trecentos recenseri." "O fœcunditas ingenii!" adds he, appositely. Many of these, were, however, spurious; and Fred. Bitiskius gives his good edition (3 vols. fol. Gen. 1658) "rejectis suppositis solo ipsius nomine 20

6,7 *MS,1835* after him Andreas Cæsalpinus of Arezzo, who died 1603, aged 84, as Bayle observes.
  9 *MS,1835* in which his definitions
* 17 *MS—1849* audio *1863—89* audio,
  17 *MS* resenseri—"   *1835* resenseri."
  20 *1849* suppositas

4—5 *the circulation of the blood*: an exaggeration. As Pachter comments, 'The circulation of the blood could be discovered only in an age which had invented pumps' (p. 39). As Griffin and Minchin point out (p. 71), Browning will have seen the words 'Paracels. nouit circulationem sanguinis—et sanguificationem cordis' in the margin of p. †3v of Bitiskius's second volume.
  7 *Bayle and Bartoli*: Pierre Bayle's *Dictionnaire Historique et Critique* was first published at Rotterdam in 2 vols. in 1697, and later enlarged and supplemented more than once. It was translated into English in 1710 (4 vols.), and in 1734—41 (10 vols.) Bartoli discusses the circulation of the blood on pp. 205ff of his *De' Simboli trasportati al morale*, ed. Angelo Cerutti (London, n.d.); cf. Introduction to *Sordello*. He mentions the importance of both Realdo Colombo and Andrea Cesalpino.
  11 *Holcroft's translation*: *Essays on Physiognomy*, by J. C. Lavater, trans. Thomas Holcroft, 3 vols., 1793.
  13 *a passage*: iii. 912 ff.
  15 *Valentius*: see Jacques Gohory ('Leo Suavius'), *Theophrasti Paracelsi Philosophiae et Medicinae utriusque universae, Compendium* (Basle, 1568), p. 5: 'so far as the great number of the works of Paracelsus is concerned, I hear that almost three hundred are mustered by the Germans'.
  20 *"rejectis suppositis*: 'only those having been rejected which are suppositious and notable only by reason of his name, of which a great number are in circulation': Bitiskius, i. p. [¶ 5]r.

superbientibus quorum ingens circumfertur numerus." The
rest were "charissimum et pretiosissimum authoris pignus,
extorsum potius ab illo quam obtentum." "Jam minime eo
volente atque jubente hæc ipsius scripta in lucem prodisse
videntur; quippe quæ muro inclusa ipso absente, servi cujus-   5
dam indicio, furto surrepta atque sublata sunt," says Valentius.
These have been the study of a host of commentators, amongst
whose labours are most notable, Petri Severini, "Idea Medi-
cinæ Philosophiæ. Bas. 1571;" Mic. Toxetis, "Onomastica.
Arg. 1574;" Dornei, "Dict. Parac. Franc. 1584;" and "P¹   10
Philos^æ Compendium cum scholiis auctore Leone Suavio.
Paris." (This last, a good book.)

(6) A disgraceful affair. One Liechtenfels, a canon, having
been rescued *in extremis* by the *"laudanum"* of Paracelsus,
refused the stipulated fee, and was supported in his meanness   15
by the authorities, whose interference Paracelsus would not
brook. His own liberality was allowed by his bitterest foes,
who found a ready solution of his indifference to profit in the
aforesaid sword-handle and its guest. His freedom from the
besetting sin of a profession he abhorred—(as he curiously says   20
somewhere, "Quis quæso deinceps honorem deferat profes-

---

1 *1835* ingeus
2 *1835* piguus,
5,6 *1849,1863* cuiusdem
7,8 *MS–1868* among whose
15 *MS,1835* refused to come down with the stipulated fee,

2 *"charissimum*: 'a very dear and precious pledge of the author, extorted
rather than obtained from him': ibid.
3 *"Jam minime*: 'These writings scarcely seem to have been brought to the
light of day with his consent or under his instructions, inasmuch as being
concealed in a wall they were, according to a servant's account, stolen and
spirited away during his absence'. The passage occurs on p. 16 of the work of
'Leo Suavius' mentioned above, in the 'Valentii Antrapassi Silerani Praefatio in
opus Paramyricum', a brief eulogy by the pseudonymous Valentius (some-
times known as 'Valentius Retius') printed as a proem to various treatises by
such Paracelsists as Adam v. Bodenstein. Browning has substituted 'Jam' for
'tamen' at the beginning.
9 *Mic. Toxetis*: Mich. Toxites, *Onomasticum medicum et explicatio verborum
Paracelsi*, is mentioned in the article in the *Biographie Universelle*, as are the
books by Severini and Gerhard Dorn.
11 *auctore Leone Suavio*: see p. 512, 15 n, above.
13 *One Liechtenfels*: Cornelius von Liechtenfels: Adamus tells the story on p.
30 of his *Vitae*.
21 *"Quis quæso*: 'Who, I ask, will now honour a profession which is practised
and administered by such nefarious scoundrels?' This particular jibe, similar to
hundreds in his writings, has not been found.

sione tali, quæ a tam facinorosis nebulonibus obitur et adminis-
tratur?")—is recorded in his epitaph, which affirms—"Bona
sua in pauperes distribuenda collocandaque erogavit," *hon-
oravit*, or *ordinavit*—for accounts differ.

2 *his epitaph*: as Griffin and Minchin point out (p. 72 n), Adam 'prints in full
the epitaph . . . to which Browning . . . refers. . . Did Browning then carefully
compare even the versions of an epitaph? Melchior Adam supplies the answer;
to the word "erogavit" he adds a marginal note, *Alii, honoravit vel ordinavit*'.
(*Vitae*, p. 31).

APPENDIX A

Browning's prefaces to the editions of 1868 and 1888

THE poems that follow are printed in the order of their publication.[1] The first piece in the series, I acknowledge and retain with extreme repugnance, indeed purely of necessity; for not long ago I inspected one, and am certified of the existence of other transcripts, intended sooner or later to be published abroad: by forestalling these, I can at least correct some misprints (no syllable is changed) and introduce a boyish work by an exculpatory word.[2] The thing was my earliest attempt at 'poetry always dramatic in principle, and so many utterances of so many imaginary persons, not mine,'[3] which I have since written according to a scheme less extravagant and scale less impracticable than were ventured upon in this crude preliminary sketch—a sketch that, on reviewal, appears not altogether wide of some hint of the characteristic features of that particular *dramatis persona* it would fain have reproduced: good draughtsmanship, however, and right handling were far beyond the artist at that time.

R.B.

London, December 25, 1867.

I PRESERVE, in order to supplement it, the foregoing preface. I had thought, when compelled to include in my collected works the poem to which it refers, that the honest course would be to reprint, and leave mere literary errors unaltered. Twenty years' endurance of an eyesore seems more than sufficient: my faults remain duly recorded against me, and I claim permission to somewhat diminish these, so far as style is concerned, in the present and final edition where 'Pauline' must needs, first of my performances, confront the reader. I

---

[1] From 1863 onwards, however, 'the pieces first published in 1842, 1845, and 1855, respectively, under the titles of "Dramatic Lyrics," "Dramatic Romances," and "Men and Women"' had been 'collected and redistributed', as Browning had pointed out in a note facing the first page of the text of Vol. i (1863). The redistribution continued. Details may be found in Appendix D of the Oxford Standard Authors edition, *Browning: Poetical Works 1833–1864*, ed. Ian Jack (1970, repr. 1975): they will be repeated in Vol. iii of the present edition.

[2] Cf. Introduction to *Pauline*, above.

[3] Quoted (but for the word 'poetry') from the Advertisement to *Bells and Pomegranates*, No. III, 'Dramatic Lyrics'.

have simply removed solecisms, mended the metre a little, and endeavoured to strengthen the phraseology—experience helping, in some degree, the helplessness of juvenile haste and heat in their untried adventure long ago.

The poems that follow are again, as before, printed in chronological order; but only so far as proves compatible with the prescribed size of each volume, which necessitates an occasional change in the distribution of its contents.[1] Every date is subjoined as before.[2]

R.B.

London: *February* 27, 1888.

---

[1] *Sordello* now followed *Pauline* in Vol. i, for example, *Paracelsus* being printed in Vol. ii.

[2] The dates are omitted in the present edition, as they are unnecessary and might cause confusion.

APPENDIX B

Browning's alterations in the 'Mill' and Rylands copies of *Pauline*

1. The 'Mill' copy. (For a description see pp. 3 and 15 above.) Note: the alterations are made in ink. Changes which leave the original mark uncancelled are given in that form, though Browning probably intended replacement of, not addition to, the original.

Line	1833	Mill
5	fear,	fear;
12	veins,—	veins;—
15	star.	star!
17	me; {point very faint}	me; {a correction of imperfect type}
23	God.	God:—
31	truth.	truth:
36	But	But,
36	thee,	thee
40	us—	us:—
58	wood;	wood, {or;}
61	eyes—	eyes:—
64	mute;	mute,—
68	sleep—	sleep:—
81	theirs—	theirs;—
85	life—	life;—
92	that	yet
104	wings.	wings:
123		{Inked line below l. 123.}
132	valueless,	valueless;
139	them—	them!—
140	years!	years.
151	ever;	ever!
154	not—	not:—
155	thee—	thee:—
171	Scarce	Not
171	men—	men:—
174	droopingly,	droopingly;

Line	1833	Mill
178	air,	air;
185	change	change:
187	course	course—
189	country—	country;—
202	bid	bid:
217	up,	up;
222	melody,	melody
224	less,	less
227	watcher,	watcher
228	him,	him
243	if, indeed,	if indeed
250	Power,	Power
251	world,	world.
257	trust.	trust:
272	tracked	tracked,
284	me—	me,—
284	imagination	Imagination
291	itself,	itself;
306	myself,	myself,—
313	myself—	*myself*—
315	For	And
315	them—	them
320	own,	own;
335	Proserpine's	Prosérpine's
336	An'	And
338	painful,	painful,—
361	Was	Is
361	shone	shines
362	clime,	clime
365	heaven,	Heaven,
377	seen,	seen
387	exemplified,	exemplified,—
388	And	at
392	so	so,
405	one,	One,
405	offend,	offend;
407	Pauline,	Pauline;
418	there!	there
425	liberty,	liberty;
427	be,	be.
452	gardens,	gardens
459	them—	them;—

Line	1833	Mill
467	this"—	this—
467	think;	think;"
484	thee—	thee
484	life	life,—
497	be as a wreck	be a mere wreck
516	seclusion—	seclusion:—
521		{Inked line below l. 521.}
536	his.	his:
539	smiles,	smiles
541	name—	name;—
544	would	should
546	perish—	perish;—
548	extend them,	extend to them,
550	there—	there:—
567	king	King
571	doom,	doom;
572	him	Him
573	boy,	Boy,
587	near me—	near me,—
592	me—	me;—
594	prison;	prison, {or 'prison': a deletion may be intended}
594	sphere—	sphere:—
601	not,	not;
607	mean—	mean;—
610	fill—	fill;—
614	dwellings.	dwellings:
637	love	Love
637	reason—	Reason—
639	reason	Reason
641	All love	All Love
641	that love	that Love
645	love	Love
652	prey.	prey—
661	red-beam,	red beam,
669	soul,	soul,—
670	sympathy,	sympathy,—
672	fears,	fears;—
673	energies;	energies;—
686	And . . . . sophistries.	{Whole line deleted, after 'sophistries.' had been changed to 'sophistries . . . .'}

Line	1833	Mill
692	too	too—
699	fever—	fever;—
700	prepared—	prepared;—
711	angel—	angel;—
711	flower;	flower {or 'flower,'}
730	world;	world,
730	thought—	thought:—
745	spray.	spray,
782	arch,	arch;—
783	root	roots
805	wanders.	wanders. . . . .
811 *fn.*	que'ébaucher.—	que d'ébaucher.—
fn.	intelligible	inintelligible
818	point that I	point I
879	indistinct. Ere	indistinct: ere
882	fixed—	fixed:—
885	first stage;—	First Stage;—
892	"E'en	E'en
		{Inverted commas deleted in following lines also.}
899	looks,	looks
900	love-breath,	love-breath;
903	Pauline,	Pauline,—
906	side,	side;
910	me.	me:
939	intuition.	intuition—
944	fixed,	fixed;
963	she,	She,
964	sister,	Sister,
987	gone	gone,
989	sin,	sin
993	pride,	pride;
996	me.	me:
999	definite—	definite;—
1000	lost,	lost;
1007	joy,	joy;
1027	giant—	giant:—

2. A copy of the first edition of *Pauline* in the John Rylands Library of the University of Manchester contains a number of revisions, most of them inserted after careful erasure of the original reading in a way similar to that used in the Lowell

copy at Harvard. All but 6 out of approximately 150 revisions are of punctuation. In addition certain passages are marked off by short diagonal strokes in the margin; these include the 13 lines beginning 'I am made up of an intensest life,' (l.268) and 18 lines beginning 'They came to me in my first dawn of life,' (l.318). The revisions may well be Browning's: about two thirds of them anticipate the changes made in *1868*, and the rest, though peculiar to this copy, are in a similar style, producing a coherent pattern of revision throughout the poem. On the other hand, *1868* is much more thoroughly revised: it has about four times as many new readings, adds a line and a half at l.403, and omits a half line after l.457. *Rylands* therefore shows a different state of revision from that in *Lowell*, which has most of the changes made in *1868* and includes directions such as 'Run on' where two sections are to be printed together, though, curiously, it omits the necessary correction 'Extend to them,' (l.548) which does appear in *Rylands*—and in the *Mill* copy. There is, however, no very significant relationship between the *Rylands* and *Mill* revisions—they have only 15 variants in common—though there are signs in *Rylands* that Browning had read Mill's critical commentary: he is evidently self-conscious about his use of 'so', and inserts a comma after the word in 18 of the lines where it occurs. The revisions in general produce a smoother, more formal style of punctuation than that of *1833*; superfluous commas are removed, but many dashes are replaced by more specific pointing—usually commas or colons. The following are the revised readings in the Rylands copy which do not appear in *1868*: 25 faithful! {as in *1888*} 57 hills: 64 mute 81 sad, 121 throne; 121 sank 137 life, {in *1868* but not *Lowell*} 143 within— 155 thee! They 178 air;— 185 change: 250 Power 253 book; 258 come— 262 exist 263 rule them,— 324 chief 383 so, 419 But, there, 443 so, 450 so, 456 fruit-flushed, 484 life, 487 So, {in *1868* but not *Lowell*} 517 sing; 546 perish: 557 beauty: 564 Sweet, 607 mean: so, my still-baffled 685–6 now; And, ...sophistries— 692 too. 747 rocks: 768 gleams: 769 one, {?} 782 arch; 797 (Float. . . .Pauline) 811 {footnote} soi-même,—et 835 him—*Now*? 891 forebodings,— 956 deformed

We are indebted to the authorities of the John Rylands Library for permission to print the above readings, and to Mr Philip Kelley for drawing our attention to the copy.

APPENDIX C

Browning's preface to the first edition of *Paracelsus*

The following preface is found only in the first edition:

I am anxious that the reader should not, at the very outset—mistaking my performance for one of a class with which it has nothing in common—judge it by principles on which it was never moulded, and subject it to a standard to which it was never meant to conform. I therefore anticipate his discovery, that it is an attempt, probably more novel than happy, to reverse the method usually adopted by writers whose aim it is to set forth any phenomenon of the mind or the passions, by the operation of persons and events; and that, instead of having recourse to an external machinery of incidents to create and evolve the crisis I desire to produce, I have ventured to display somewhat minutely the mood itself in its rise and progress, and have suffered the agency by which it is influenced and determined, to be generally discernible in its effects alone, and subordinate throughout, if not altogether excluded: and this for a reason. I have endeavoured to write a poem, not a drama: the canons of the drama are well known, and I cannot but think that, inasmuch as they have immediate regard to stage representation, the peculiar advantages they hold out are really such only so long as the purpose for which they were at first instituted is kept in view. I do not very well understand what is called a Dramatic Poem, wherein all those restrictions only submitted to on account of compensating good in the original scheme are scrupulously retained, as though for some special fitness in themselves—and all new facilities placed at an author's disposal by the vehicle he selects, as pertinaciously rejected. It is certain, however, that a work like mine depends more immediately

20 *what is called a Dramatic Poem*: Byron's *Manfred* and Hayward's translation of *Faust* are among works with 'A Dramatic Poem' as sub-title. Browning here agrees with the *Edinburgh* reviewer of Sir Henry Taylor's *Philip Van Artevelde*, a 'Dramatic Romance' with which *Paracelsus* was more than once to be compared: 'A Dramatic Poem is a literary hybrid, combining in one both play and poem, without possessing the completeness, or fulfilling the purposes of either. Unlike the play, it cannot be represented on the stage—unlike the poem, it excludes all description and sentiment, except such as may be conveniently placed in the mouth of some of the *dramatis personæ* . . . in the dramatic form, with its exclusion of all save dialogue and soliloquy, and its division into acts and scenes, we see no advantage, independent of its applicability to dramatic representation': *Edinburgh Review*, no. cxxi (Oct. 1834), p. 7.

24 *the vehicle he selects*: cf. *Sordello*, ii. 484 n.

on the intelligence and sympathy of the reader for its success—indeed were my scenes stars it must be his co-operating fancy which, supplying all chasms, shall connect the scattered lights into one constellation—a Lyre or a Crown. I trust for his indulgence towards a poem which had not been imagined six months ago; and that even should he think slightingly of the present (an experiment I am in no case likely to repeat) he will not be prejudiced against other productions which may follow in a more popular, and perhaps less difficult form.

15th March, 1835.

---

6 *an experiment*: a word used in the Advertisement to *Lyrical Ballads* (1798) and in the preface to *The Revolt of Islam*.

APPENDIX D

The annotated copy of *Paracelsus* at Yale

For a description, see the textual introduction to *Paracelsus*, pp. 124–5. The following list indicates where the annotations produce a reading which is significantly different from that of 1849. Some variants arise from the copyist's failure to alter the text of the 1835 edition. Positive variants, i.e., those forming part of the copyist's insertion, are marked with an asterisk.

Part	Line	Yale	1849
I	92	appetite for	appetites for
	105	(old Trithem	(Old Tritheim
	*108	here at hand unbosom	here at home unbosom
	*112	Will ride {?} between us	Will rise between us:—
	137,137a	I forbode, this weighty talk| Has . . . . revive . . .	I forbode!
	*153	Destiny	destiny:
	155	And taught me	Taught me
	162	When you shall deign	When you deign
	164	this Evening's conference will produce.	this evening's conference!
	*167	Of our belief in what is man's best scheme of life	Of our best scheme of life, what is man's end,
	168	faiths ever	faiths e'er agreed
	*190	lusts of the World { written faintly in the margin.}	Lusts of the world,
	*198	power satiates them; or lust, or gold;	Power satiates these, or lust, or gold;
	202	his own sake,	his sake,
	212	that! that you abide	that! Prove you abide
	233	where I had been born {'where' written faintly in the margin.}	Where I was born
	*242	lore—and not the least {?best}	lore: and not the best
	*247	Now this new . . . . old:	And this new . . . . old,
	261	fierce and brief,	fierce as brief,
	322,3	than a security | of its existence; or whether	than security|Of its exist-ence; whether
	*357	learn—the Black arts they so teach. {'Black Arts' also written faintly above the line.}	learn and teach; Black Arts,
	360	God! A sullen friend	God! A sullen fiend
	*366	To teach to gratify her Master	Teach, gratify, her master
	369	I, who am singled	I, singled

Part	Line	Yale	1849
I	400	writes the Sea	writes the sea
		{Lines 400–14 are written on an inserted slip in the copyist's hand; lines 400–402, written in a different hand similar to Browning's, are also visible, followed by the words '& 16 {?} more lines'.}	
	*469	with man so much	with men so much
	486	I touch on it: these	I touch on that; these
	*519A	around thee. What their sense	around thee—what their sense
	*541,542	strength: wilt thou|with them Adventure for my sake and man's, {'wilt thou' may be deleted: there are faint signs of a line through the words.}	strength:|"Wilt thou adventure for my sake and man's,
	*558	exploring things {?}	exploring thus
	590	clouds!	clouds?
	*606	I have my belief . . . . no—	Than my belief, . . . no.
	608	I will put away	I put away
	614	*here* is a plague-spot, here	here is a plague-spot, here,
	*633	love—would raise	love, and raise
	*676	truth—that there will be	truth, that there will be
	742	*chance*—for hitherto,	chance—for hitherto,
	751	has oft given vent	have oft given vent
	775	Therefor to set	Therefore, set
	*781	to put forth first our strength,	To put forth just our strength,
	*814	schistose ore.	schistous ore.
II	*17	which I{?} should . . . . fulfil.	which should . . . . fulfil
	*21	attainments in	attainment, in
	*24	records {?} of such	recordings of such
	*25	—Scroll'd{?} in like	—Scrawled in like
	*34	which he had gained	which he gained:
	52	*now* he *knows*	now he knows
	*100	Knowing a charm	—Knowing a charm
	*144	I ran over the seven little fields,	I ran o'er the seven little grassy fields,
	155	Throughout a career	Through a career
	*174	widens; Lost	widens; last
	178	*Now*— . . . .juggle bends	Now— . . . . juggler bends
	*248	my toils or {?} wanderings,	my toil and wanderings,
	288	fatal clear—	fatal-clear—
	*304	come, thou last.—	come! thou last
	*311	'And we trusted	And yet we trusted
	*314	'Our ⟨faith⟩ [fault]!—such trust, & all a dream!	Our fault: such trust, and all, a dream!
	319–22	{These lines, headed 'Insert p. 56', are written in a hand similar to Browning's, with no over-writing, on the verso of the insertion slip for p. 57 (lines 347–51).}	
	*331	come, once more therefore come!	Once more, therefore, come, O come!
	*339	& men {?} they	and man they
	339A	Aprile A spirit better armed	A spirit better armed,

Part	Line	Yale	1849
II	*341	Poet that shalt	Poet who shall
	*358	The syren's.	The siren's!
	*368	the sober teacher, cautious striver	the sober searcher, cautious striver,
	*411	it as if they were akin.	it, as if they were akin:
	*417	& learns the cause	and learned the cause?)
	434	clothe in	clothe it in
	*444	"God's spirits being made	"God's sprites being made
	445	"God grants . . . . be its world,	"He grants . . . . be its world,
	484	He would grant	And He would grant
	*501–2	fade, leave our task undone {?}|Rather {?Neither} grow wise	fade, and leave our task undone.|Rather, grow wise
	*649	Who in His great love {?altered from 'creation'} acts	Who in creation acts
	657	no little word, Aprile.	no little word, Aprile!
	660	at least, Aprile. Let *me* love too!	at least! Let me love, too!
III	2	fit that all time, and chance,	fit that all, time, chance,
	13	in a certain sense, I waive.	in a sense, I waive:
	*60	and the hopes rose, &	And then the hopes rose and
	73	voice that said	voice which said,
	*133,4	itching to know|vary, and view	itching to turn,|Vary, and view
	136	demonstrate to it	demonstrate to itself
	251	proving *me*	proving me
	268	Sorrowing then only, when	Sorrowing alone when
	*283	luxury—Festus:—	luxury, my Festus—
	*296	then, I may {'I {?} say' added after 'may'}	then, I say,
	*302	In . . . . seek, {deleted}	In . . . . seek,
	357	main; and accordingly	main; accordingly
		{From line 378 (i.e. from the beginning of the inserted slip on p. 91 in the 1835 edition) only the copyist's hand is visible in the alterations; there are no signs of other notes below them.}	
	*385	Recieves {sic} not into its beatitude	Receives not into its beatitudes
	*386	More martyrs . . . . sake. Heaven	Mere martyrs . . . . sake; heaven
	*490	with favour even fantastic	with favour e'en fantastic
	544	words well your words, I seize,	well what words I seize,
	618	amazement brings	amazement draws,
	625	A teacher that	The teacher that
	*697	tho' twisted	And twisted
	698	from this sad drudgery,	from drudgery,
	*722	life once left	life thus left,
	*769	we still may slacken	we straight may slacken
	821	measure *Your* mind's	Measure your mind's
	900	then and would withhold	then, and withhold
IV	139	poisoning blains,	poisonous blains,
	*143	to you those human	to you these human
	164	her wit assigns me,	her wits assign me,
	254	The grand results obtain'd	Results obtained
	*302A	Still . . . . learnt,	Still . . . . learned—
	*311	medicine's soundness	medicine's soundness

Part	Line	Yale	1849
IV	323	on, and fast supplant all	on, and fast supplant
	332	thoughts no inmates	thoughts are no inmates
	363	The need of	My need of
	486	{After 'fast!' there is an omission mark, and the words '(a space here left)' in the margin.}	{Space between ll. 486 and 487.}
	*509	Of happy islanders?	Of gentle islanders?
	565	Was self-delusion at the best: for see!	Was self-reliance at the best: for, see!
	603	*We* are His	We are His
	653	perish yet without re-compense	perish without recompense
V	147	plan has proves	plan proves
	*183,4	from thee|We meet	from thee: once more|We meet
	182	*{footnote not deleted.}	{No footnote.}
	249	that a comfort	that comfort
	480	The gulf rolls	For the gulf rolls
	*590	or . . . . prizes still, await	while . . . . prizes still await
	612	bating nothing	bating nought
	*743	not yet man!	not yet Man!
	777	circle life pursues:	circle run by life:
	782	Before unmeasured	Before the unmeasured
	802	Reserved that might	Denied that might

The following is a list of lines which were altered for the 1849 edition, but which remain unemended in the Yale copy. (Only substantive alterations are included.)

Part I: lines 28, 29, 32, 33, 57, 73–5, 131, 152, 169, 169b, 181, 212, 238, 272, 305a, 415–17, 422, 436, 446, 514, 538, 543, 581, 593, 599a, 626, 628, 693, 736.

Part II: lines 4 (not in Yale), 26, 27, 56, 90, 96, 114 (deleted, but revised version not given), 141, 177, 223 (not in Yale), 271, 342, 353, 390, 482, 527, 580, 618, 631, 658.

Part III: lines 33, 46, 67, 91, 114, 135, 158, 171, 176, 196, 209, 233, 281, 288, 390, 399a, 571, 579, 718, 854, 863, 883, 889, 898, 899, 931, 1014, 1026, 1034.

Part IV: lines 11, 44, 129, 140, 339, 343, 423, 450, 526, 527, 582, 603, 650, 659.

Part V: lines 30, 31, 74, 75, 76, 80, 106, 127, 174 (not in Yale), 205, 221, 322, 369, 372, 379, 510a, 622, 803.

Browning's notes at the end of the poem are not altered in the Yale copy.

APPENDIX E

Poems published but not collected by 1840

Between October 1834 and May 1836 Browning published five poems in the *Monthly Repository* (then edited by W. J. Fox), under the signature 'Z.' The first of them, a love sonnet, he never republished. Two appeared in *Dramatic Lyrics* (*Bells and Pomegranates*, no. III) in November 1842. Each of the other two was later incorporated in a longer poem.

SONNET.[1]

Eyes, calm beside thee, (Lady could'st thou know!)
  May turn away thick with fast-gathering tears:
I glance not where all gaze: thrilling and low
  Their passionate praises reach thee—my cheek
    wears
Alone no wonder when thou passest by;
Thy tremulous lids bent and suffused reply
To the irrepressible homage which doth glow
  On every lip but mine: if in thine ears
Their accents linger—and thou dost recall
  Me as I stood, still, guarded, very pale,
Beside each votarist whose lighted brow
Wore worship like an aureole, 'O'er them all
  'My beauty,' thou wilt murmur, 'did prevail
'Save that one only:'—Lady could'st thou know!

August 17, 1834.

1 *Monthly Repository*, October 1834 (NS, vol. viii, p. 712). Reprinted in *Robert Browning: Personalia* (1890), where Gosse wrote: 'I owe the identification of this sonnet, which Mr. Browning had forgotten, to Mrs. Bridell-Fox' (p. 34 n.). It may have been addressed to Eliza Flower, but that is pure conjecture based on chronology.

THE KING.[1]

A KING lived long ago,
In the morning of the world,
When earth was nigher heaven than now:
And the King's locks curled
Disparting o'er a forehead full
As the milk-white space 'twixt horn and horn
Of some sacrificial bull—
Only calm as a babe new-born.
For he was got to a sleepy mood,
So safe from all decrepitude,
Age with its pine so sure gone by,
(As though gods loved him while he dreamed,)
That, having lived thus long, there seemed
No need that he should ever die.

Among the rocks his city was:
Before his palace, in the sun,
He sate to see his people pass,
And judge them every one
From its threshold of smooth stone.
They haled him many a valley-thief
Caught in the sheep-pens—robber-chief,
Swarthy and shameless—beggar-cheat—
Spy-prowler—or some pirate found
On the sea-sand left aground;
Sometimes from out the prison-house
The angry priests a pale wretch brought,
Who through some nook had pushed and pressed,
Knees and elbows, belly and breast,
Worm-like into the temple,—caught
He was by the very god,
Who ever in the darkness strode
Backward and forward, keeping watch
O'er his brazen bowls, such rogues to catch:
These, all and every one,
The King judged, sitting in the sun.

---

1 *Monthly Repository*, November 1835 (NS, vol. ix, pp. 707–8). Revised
and used in *Pippa Passes* as a song sung by Pippa in Part III: Luigi overhears
it. There is a discussion of the poem by John Grube in UTQ xxxvii (1967–8),
pp. 69–73.

Old councillors, on left and right,
Look'd anxious up—but no surprise
Disturbed the old King's smiling eyes,
Where the very blue had turned to white.
A python swept the streets one day—
The silent streets—until he came,
With forky tongue and eyes on flame,
Where the old King judged alway;
But when he saw the silver hair,
Girt with a crown of berries rare
That the god will hardly give to wear
To the maiden who singeth, dancing bare,
In the altar-smoke by the pine-torch lights,
At his wondrous forest rites,—
But which the god's self granted him
For setting free each felon limb
Faded because of murder done;—
Seeing this, he did not dare
Assault the old King smiling there.

PORPHYRIA and JOHANNES AGRICOLA

These two poems were published together in the *Monthly Repository* for January 1836 (NS, vol. x, pp. 43–5). They were reprinted (with the general title 'Madhouse Cells') in *Dramatic Lyrics* in November 1842, and included in every collected edition of Browning's poems. The slight verbal variants between their first printing and subsequent printings will be recorded in vol. iii of the present edition. The epigraph to 'Johannes Agricola' from the *Dictionary of All Religions*, 1704, occurs only in the *Monthly Repository* printing.

LINES[1]

Still ailing, wind? wilt be appeased or no?
    Which needs the other's office, thou or I?
Dost want to be disburdened of a woe,
    And can in truth my voice untie
Its links, and let it go?

Art thou a dumb wrong'd thing that would be
    righted,
    Entrusting thus thy cause to me? forbear:
No tongue can mend thy pleadings; faith requited
    With falsehood,—love at last aware
Of scorn,—hopes early blighted,—

We have them—but I know not any tone
    So fit as thine to falter forth a sorrow:
Dost think men would go mad without a moan
    If they knew any way to borrow
A pathos like thine own?

Which sigh would'st mock of all the sighs? that one
    So long escaping from lips starv'd and blue,
Which lasts while on her pallet-bed the nun
    Stretches her length—her foot comes through
The straw she shivers on,

You had not thought she was so tall,—and spent,
    Her shrunk lids ope, and her lean fingers shut
So close, their sharp and livid nails indent
    The clammy palm: then all is mute—
That way the spirit went.

Or would'st thou rather that I understand
    Thy will to help me—like the dog I found
Once pacing sad the solitary strand,
    That would not take my food, poor hound,
But whined, and licked my hand?

1 *Monthly Repository*, May 1836 (NS, vol. x, pp. 270–1). In 1864 the lines
appeared in *Dramatis Personæ*, as the first part of section vi of 'James Lee',
with slight textual differences. The stanzas which follow in 1864 constitute an
interesting comment on the above poem: 'All this, and more, comes from
some young man's pride / Of power to see,—in failure and mistake, /
Relinquishment, disgrace, on every side,— / Merely examples for his sake, /
Helps to his path untried . . .'

APPENDIX F

Poems never published by Browning

Note: While it would be inappropriate to include in this edition all Browning's 'Fugitives', from the schoolboy couplets in Griffin and Minchin (pp. 29–30) to the snatches written in ladies' albums when he was old and famous, it would be wrong to omit the following poems, all included in *New Poems by Robert Browning and Elizabeth Barrett Browning*, ed. Sir Frederic G. Kenyon, 1914. For a useful collection of minor pieces see Park Honan, 'The Texts of Fifteen Fugitives by Robert Browning' in *Victorian Poetry*, vol. 5, no. 3 (pp. 157–69).

Several scholars have assumed that these first two poems were included in 'Incondita', a juvenile collection which failed to find a publisher and was subsequently destroyed. It seems more likely, as Maynard argues (pp. 172, 427 n. 40), that they were 'among the latest of his childhood efforts, works written at fourteen after the entire "Incondita" had been put behind him'.

THE FIRST-BORN OF EGYPT[1]

That night came on in Egypt with a step
So calmly stealing in the gorgeous train
Of sunset glories flooding the pale clouds
With liquid gold, until at length the glow
Sank to its shadowy impulse and soft sleep   5
Bent o'er the world to curtain it from life—
Vitality was hushed beneath her wing—
Pomp sought his couch of purple—care-worn grief
Flung slumber's mantle o'er him. At that hour
He in whose brain the burning fever fiend   10
Held revelry—his hot cheek turn'd awhile
Upon the cooler pillow. In his cell
The captive wrapped him in his squalid rags,
And sank amid his straw. Circean sleep!

1 First printed by Bertram Dobell in 'The Earliest Poems of Robert Browning', *Cornhill Magazine*, January 1914 (NS, vol. xxxvi), pp. 4–6. He gives as his source a letter from Sarah Flower to W. J. Fox dated '*May* 31st (1827)', and quotes her comment: 'They are "the boy" Robert Browning's *æt*. 14'. This means that the lines were written early in 1827 at the latest. In the same year Kenyon reprinted this and the following poem in *New Poems*, pp. 3 ff. There are no textual differences except that Dobell ends the poem with a dash, Kenyon with a period. The source of the poem is Exodus 11–12.

2 *gorgeous train*: cf. Coleridge, 'Religious Musings', 256: 'With all his gorgeous company of clouds'.

6 *to curtain it from life*: cf. *Queen Mab*, iv. 8: 'To curtain her sleeping world'.

Bathed in thine opiate dew false hope vacates   15
Her seat in the sick soul, leaving awhile
Her dreamy fond imaginings—pale fear
His wild misgivings, and the warm life-springs
Flow in their wonted channels—and the train—
The harpy train of care forsakes the heart.   20

Was it the passing sigh of the night wind
Or some lorn spirit's wail—that moaning cry
That struck the ear? 'tis hushed—no! it swells on
On—as the thunder peal when it essays
To wreck the summer sky—that fearful shriek   25
Still it increases—'tis the dolorous plaint,
The death cry of a nation—

It was a fearful thing—that hour of night.
I have seen many climes, but that dread hour
Hath left its burning impress on my soul   30
Never to be erased. Not the loud crash
When the shuddering forest swings to the red bolt
Or march of the fell earthquake when it whelms
A city in its yawning gulf, could quell
That deep voice of despair. Pharaoh arose   35
Startled from slumber, and in anger sought
The reason of the mighty rushing throng
At that dark hour around the palace gates,
—And then he dashed his golden crown away
And tore his hair in frenzy when he knew   40
That Egypt's heir was dead—From every home,
The marbled mansion of regality
To the damp dungeon's walls—gay pleasure's seat
And poverty's lone hut, that cry was heard
As guided by the Seraph's vengeful arm   45
The hand of death held on its withering course,
Blighting the hopes of thousands.—

I sought the street to gaze upon the grief
Of congregated Egypt—there the slave
Stood by him late his master, for that hour   50

25 *that fearful shriek*: cf. Coleridge, 'Kosciusko', 1: 'O what a loud and
fearful shriek was there'.
33 *the fell earthquake*: cf. *The Revolt of Islam*, 4496: 'An earthquake trampl-
ing on some populous town'; and 'Liberty', 8, 12.

Made vain the world's distinctions—for could
    wealth
Or power arrest the woe?—Some were there
As sculptured marble from the quarry late
Of whom the foot first in the floating dance,
The glowing cheek hued with the deep'ning flush   55
In the night revel—told the young and gay.
No kindly moisture dewed their stony eye,
Or damp'd their ghastly glare—for they felt not.
The chain of torpor bound around the heart
Had stifled it for ever. Tears stole down   60
The furrow'd channels of those withered cheeks
Whose fount had long been chill'd, but that night's
    term
Had loosed the springs—for 'twas a fearful thing
To see a nation's hope so blasted. One
Press'd his dead child unto his heart—no spot   65
Of livid plague was nigh—no purple cloud
Of scathing fever—and he struck his brow
To rouse himself from that wild phantasy
Deeming it but a vision of the night.
I marked one old man with his only son   70
Lifeless within his arms—his withered hand
Wandering o'er the features of his child
Bidding him [wake] from that long dreary sleep,
And lead his old blind father from the crowd
To the green meadows—but he answer'd not;   75
And then the terrible truth flash'd on his brain,
And when the throng roll'd on some bade him rise
And cling not so unto the dead one there,
Nor voice nor look made answer—he was gone.
But one thought chain'd the powers of each mind   80
Amid that night's felt horror—each one owned
In silence the dread majesty—the might
Of Israel's God, whose red hand had avenged
His servants' cause so fearfully—

    53 *As sculptured marble*: cf. *The Eve of St. Agnes*, 14: 'The sculptured dead',
and 297: 'smooth-sculptured stone'.
    61 *The furrow'd channels*: cf. 'Kosciusko', 12: 'a Patriot's furrow'd cheek'.
    70–5 *I marked . . . green meadows*: 'It is to be presumed that these lines
were thus italicised [no doubt underlined] by Miss Flower because she
wished to draw Mr. Fox's attention to them as being particularly good':
Dobell.
    83 *had avenged*: 'Vengeance is mine; I will repay, saith the Lord': Romans
12:19.

THE DANCE OF DEATH[1]

And as they footed it around,
They sang their triumphs o'er mankind!

de Stael.

FEVER

Bow to me, bow to me;
Follow me in my burning breath,
Which brings as the simoom destruction and death.
My spirit lives in the hectic glow
When I bid the life streams tainted flow   5
In the fervid sun's deep brooding beam
When seething vapours in volumes steam,
And they fall—the young, the gay—as the flower
'Neath the fiery wind's destructive power.
This day I have gotten a noble prize—   10
There was one who saw the morning rise,
And watch'd fair Cynthia's golden streak
Kiss the misty mountain peak,
But I was there, and my pois'nous flood
Envenom'd the gush of the youth's warm blood.   15
They hastily bore him to his bed,
But o'er him death his swart pennons spread:
The skilléd leech's art was vain,
Delirium revelled in each vein.
I mark'd each deathly change in him;   20
I watch'd his lustrous eye grow dim,
The purple cloud on his deep swol'n brow,
The gathering death sweat's chilly flow,

---

1 From the same source as the previous poem, and similarly reprinted in
New Poems, (where an incorrect period at the end of line 79 is omitted).
DeVane states that the poem 'reveals the influence of Coleridge's *Fire,
Famine and Slaughter*', but the dialogue between Falsehood and Vice in Shel-
ley's note to *Queen Mab*, iv. 178, 179 may be more relevant. Cf., too, *The
Revolt of Islam*, 379 ff. ('The Fiend, whose name was Legion; Death, Decay,
/ Earthquake and Blight, and Want, and Madness pale, / Wingèd and wan
diseases . . .'), 2767 ff. ('My name is Pestilence . . .') and 4180 ff. Motto:
untraced.
3 *simoom*: 'A hot, dry, suffocating sand-wind which sweeps across the
African and Asiatic deserts . . .': OED. The word occurs in Coleridge's
'Religious Musings', 269, as well as in Byron.
9 *the fiery wind's destructive power*: cf. 'Religious Musings', 391–2.
17 *death his swart pennons*: cf. *Queen Mab*, ix. 138: 'Time his dusky pen-
nons'.
21 *his lustrous eye*: cf. 'Julian and Maddalo', 285: 'eyes lustrous and glazed'.

The dull dense film obscure the eye,
Heard the last quick gasp and saw him die.   25

PESTILENCE

My spirit has past on the lightning's wing
O'er city and land with its withering;
In the crowded street, in the flashing hall
My tramp has been heard: they are lonely all.
A nation has swept at my summons away   30
As mists before the glare of day.
See how proudly reigns my hand
In the black'ning heaps on the surf-beat strand
[Where]* the rank grass grows in deserted streets
[Where] the terrified stranger no passer meets   35
[And all] around the putrid air
[Gleams] lurid and red in Erinnys stare
Where silence reigns, where late swell'd the lute,
Thrilling lyre, mellifluous flute.
There if my prowess ye would know   40
Seek ye—and bow to your rival low.

AGUE

Bow to me, bow to me;
My influence is in the freezing deeps
Where the icy power of torpor sleeps,
Where the frigid waters flow   45
My marble chair is more cold below;
When the Grecian brav'd the Hellespont's flood
How did I curdle his fever'd blood,
And sent his love in tumescent wave
To meet with her lover an early grave.   50
When Hellas' victor sought the rush

*Paper removed where sealed. [Dobell's note]
24 *the dull dense film*: cf. 'Religious Musings', 143, and *The Revolt of Islam*, 1821–2: 'A film then overcast / My sense with dimness'.
37 *Erinnys*: not in OED. Gk. 'Ερινύς (or 'Ερινύς), the Erinys, an avenging deity.
47 *the Grecian*: Leander.
49 *tumescent*: OED has no example before 1882. Browning may take it from *Georgics*, ii. 479: 'maria alta tumescant' (deep seas swell).
51 *Hellas' victor*: Alexander the Great.

Of the river to lave in its cooling gush,
Did he not feel my iron clutch
When he fainted and sank at my algid touch?
These are the least of the trophies I claim—   55
Bow to me then, and own my fame.

MADNESS

Hear ye not the gloomy yelling
Or the tide of anguish swelling,
Hear ye the clank of fetter and chain,
Hear ye the wild cry of grief and pain,   60
Followed by the shuddering laugh
As when fiends the life blood quaff?
See! see that band,
See how their bursting eyeballs gleam,
As the tiger's when crouched in the jungle's lair,   65
In India's sultry land.
Now they are seized in the rabies fell,
Hark! 'tis a shriek as from fiends of hell;
Now there is a plaining moan,
As the flow of the sullen river—   70
List! there is a hollow groan.
Doth it not make e'en *you* to shiver—
These are they struck of the barbs of my quiver.
Slaves before my haughty throne,
Bow then, bow to me alone.   75

CONSUMPTION

'Tis for me, 'tis for me;
Mine the prize of Death must be;
My spirit is o'er the young and gay
As on snowy wreaths in the bright noonday
They wear a melting and vermeille flush   80
E'en while I bid their pulses hush,
Hueing o'er their dying brow
With the spring (?) of health's best roseate glow

54 *algid*: L. algidus, cold. Johnson gives the word, without an example.
69 *plaining moan*: cf. Coleridge, 'The Destiny of Nations', 308.
83 Dobell's query.

When the lover watches the full dark eye
Robed in tints of ianthine dye,   85
Beaming eloquent as to declare
The passions that deepen the glories there.
The frost in its tide of dazzling whiteness,
As Juno's brow of chrystal brightness,
Such as the Grecian's hand could give   90
When he bade the sculptured marble 'live,'
The ruby suffusing the Hebe cheek,
The pulses that love and pleasure speak
Can his fond heart claim but another day,
And the loathsome worm on her form shall prey.   95
She is scathed as the tender flower,
When mildews o'er its chalice lour.
Tell me not of her balmy breath,
Its tide shall be shut in the fold of death;
Tell me not of her honied lip,   100
The reptile's fangs shall its fragrance sip.
Then will I say triumphantly
Bow to the deadliest—bow to me!

85 *ianthine*: violet-coloured. The only earlier example in OED is from the Douay Bible (Exodus 25:5). Browning may have had it direct from Latin (or Greek). By coincidence, Ianthe is the heroine of *Queen Mab*.
90 *the Grecian's hand*: Pygmalion's.
92 *Hebe*: the Roman goddess of youth and spring.
95 *loathsome worm*: as in *The Revolt of Islam*, 399.
97 *lour*: cf. Shelley, 'Falsehood and Vice' (cf. first note, above), 91: 'The pestilence expectant lowers'.
98 *balmy breath*: *Othello*, v. ii. 16.

LINES TO THE MEMORY OF JAMES DOW[1]

Words we might else have been compelled to say
In silence to our hearts, great love, great praise
Of thee, our father! have been freely said
By those whom none shall blame; and while thy life
Endures, a beauteous thing, in their record,   5
We may desist; but thou art not alone;
A part of those thou lovedst here so well
Repose beside thee, and the Eyes that saw
Thy daily course of good, could never see
The light their presence cast upon thy path;   10
Soft Sanctuary-tapers of thy house
Close-curtained when the Priest came forth; on
    these
Let peace be, Peace on thee, our Mother, too!
Serenest Spirit; do we vainly dream
Some portion of the constant joy you spread   15
Around you, living, comforts even yet
The Child that never knew you, and the Girl
In whom your gentle soul seemed born again
To bless us longer? Peace like yours be ours
Till the same quiet home receive us all!   20

1 These lines are engraved on a tombstone in the additional burial ground
belonging to St Mary's Church, Barnsley, Yorkshire, and have been trans-
cribed for us by Mr Edward G. Tasker. The condition of the stone makes
one or two details of punctuation uncertain.
    The following shorter version of the lines was printed in the *Cornhill
Magazine* for February 1914 (p. 145), with this introductory note: 'This
Sonnet by Robert Browning, addressed to the memory of his par-
ents—from a MS. in the handwriting of Miss Browning—was among the
papers disposed of at the Browning Sale in May 1913.—EDITOR.'
    Words I might else have been compelled to say
    In silence to my heart,—great love, great praise
    Of thee, my Father—have been freely said
    By those whom none shall blame; and while thy life
    Endures, a beauteous thing, in their record
    I may desist; but thou art not alone:
    They lie beside thee whom thou lovest most;
    Soft sanctuary-tapers of thy house,
    Close-curtained when the Priest came forth,—on these
    Let peace be, peace on thee, my Mother too!
    The child that never knew you, and the Girl
    In whom your gentle souls seemed born again
    To bless us longer. Peace like yours be mine
    Till the same quiet home receive us all.
Later the same year Kenyon reprinted the lines in *New Poems*, with the
heading 'Lines to the Memory of his Parents (1866)' and the following note:
'These lines by Robert Browning, addressed apparently to the memory of
his parents—from a MS. in the handwriting of Miss Browning—were
among the papers disposed of at the Browning Sale in May 1913. They

A FOREST THOUGHT[1]

In far Esthonian solitudes
The parent-firs of future woods
Gracefully, airily spire at first
Up to the sky, by the soft sand nurst:
Self-sufficient are they, and strong   5
With outspread arms, broad level and long;
But soon in the sunshine and the storm
They darken, changing fast their form—

---

were probably written in 1866, the year of his father's death. They were
first printed in the *Cornhill Magazine*, February 1914'.
   The inscription on the tombstone was first printed by E. G. Bayford in
Notes and Queries for 12 June 1948. Bayford gives the full heading, which
records the burial of James Dow, MD (29 April 1776—9 October 1832), his
wife Sarah, their infant son Edward James, and their daughter Sarah Helen
and states that the stone had been 'placed by the surviving Children William
Alexander and Margaret'. In l. 11 Bayford has 'Sanctuary-papers' for
'Sanctuary-tapers', as well as several insignificant variants in accidentals. He
asserts that the inscription 'first appeared in 1832', obviously assuming that
it had been written and engraved soon after the death of Dr Dow. As John
Maynard pointed out in *Victorian Poetry* (vol. 14, 1976, 67–9: cf. *Browning's
Youth*, 403 n. 30), however, it is probable that Browning first met Dow in
1836. Dow was a lawyer whose name appears frequently in Macready's
Diaries. On 20 March 1837 Macready wrote: 'Forster and Browning
arrived—cheerful evening—though more of the conversation turned on
Dow than I could have wished. Browning related an amusing story of his
application to him for an epitaph on his father—to which, when Browning
had promised it, he added his mother, her [his] sister, and an infant two
years old; and subsequently, on receiving the report of the marble-mason of
Barnsley, wished two more lines to be added to the complete epitaph as the
stone would hold two more!': *Diaries*, i. 380. (According to the stone the
infant son lived less than one year). It is clear that the poem must be dated
1836 or early 1837.

---

1 First printed in *Country Life* for 10 June 1905 (p. 797), with the following
note: '[This hitherto unpublished poem by Robert Browning was written in
circumstances which lend special interest to the fac-simile of the MS. of
which the first page is here reproduced. The lines were addressed to friends
on the occasion of the christening of their eldest son, to whom the poet
stood godfather. On returning to the house after the christening, Browning
went into a room by himself and there wrote the poem and handed it to the
parents. The MS. written thus impromptu is that now published, having
been carefully preserved in the pages of an album of the period, recently
bequeathed to the writer of this note. . . . The dedication runs: "Written and
inscribed to W. A. and A. D. by their Sincere Friend, Robert Browning, 13
Nelson Sq., November 4, 1837."—ED.]' The facsimile is of the first four-
teen lines only. We retain the colon at the end of line 4, changed to a semi-
colon in the reprintings in *Browning and Domett* (p. xi), Griffin and Minchin
(p. 307), The Centenary Edition (iii. 418) and *New Poems* (p. 23). In the
last-named Kenyon guesses that 'The opening lines are a reminiscence of
Browning's visit to Russia'.
   3 *spire*: cf. Coleridge, 'The Picture', 113–14: 'the crowded firs / Spire
from thy shores'.

Low boughs fall off, and in the bole
Each tree spends all its strenuous soul—   10
Till the builder gazes wistfully
Such noble ship-mast wood to see,
And cares not for its soberer hue,
Its rougher bark and leaves more few.

But just when beauty passes away   15
And you half regret it could not stay,
For all their sap and vigorous life,—
Under the shade, secured from strife
A seedling springs—the forest-tree
In miniature, and again we see   20
The delicate leaves that will fade one day,
The fan-like shoots that will drop away,
The taper stem a breath could strain—
Which shall foil one day the hurricane:
We turn from this infant of the copse   25
To the parent-firs,—in their waving tops
To find some trace of the light green tuft
A breath could stir,—in the bole aloft
Column-like set against the sky,
The spire that flourished airily   30
And the marten bent as she rustled by.

So shall it be, dear Friends, when days
Pass, and in this fair child we trace
Goodness, full-formed in you, tho' dim
Faint-budding, just astir in him: 35
When rudiments of generous worth
And frankest love in him have birth,
We'll turn to love and worth full-grown,
And learn their fortune from your own.
Nor shall we vainly search to see   40
His gentleness—simplicity—
Not lost in your maturer grace—
Perfected, but not changing place.

9 *bole*: the first occurrence of a word which, with its compounds, occurs some 27 times in Browning. Cf. l. 28.
12 *ship-mast wood*: cf. Keats, *Isabella*, 133: 'ship-mast forests'.
22 *fan-like shoots*: cf. Southey, *The Poet's Pilgrimage to Waterloo*, II. iv., st. 46: 'loftiest trees . . . their fan-like foliage rear'.
29 *Column-like*: cf. Southey, 'English Eclogues', vi. 6: 'Peers taller, lifting, column-like, a stem'.

May this grove be a charmed retreat . . .
May northern winds and savage sleet 45
Leave the good trees untouched, unshorn
A crowning pride of woods unborn:
And gracefully beneath their shield
May the seedling grow! All pleasures yield 50
Peace below and peace above,
The glancing squirrels' summer love,
And the brood-song of the cushat-dove!

53 *the cushat-dove*: cf. Scott, *Lay of the Last Minstrel*, II. xxxiv. 9.